To my darling b
on your birtud

C000253071

The Last Great
Cavalryman

The Last Great Cavalryman

The Life of General Sir Richard McCreery

Commander Eighth Army

Richard Mead

Pen & Sword
MILITARY

First published in Great Britain in 2012 by
Pen & Sword Military
an imprint of
Pen & Sword Books Ltd
47 Church Street
Barnsley
South Yorkshire
S70 2AS

ISBN: 978 1 84884 465 0

Typeset in 11pt Ehrhardt by
Mac Style, Beverley, E. Yorkshire

Printed and bound in the UK by CPI Group (UK) Ltd, Croydon, CRO 4YY

Pen & Sword Books Ltd incorporates the Imprints of Pen & Sword Aviation,
Pen & Sword Family History, Pen & Sword Maritime, Pen & Sword Military,
Pen & Sword Discovery, Wharncliffe Local History, Wharncliffe True Crime,
Wharncliffe Transport, Pen & Sword Select, Pen & Sword Military Classics,
Leo Cooper, The Praetorian Press, Remember When, Seaforth Publishing
and Frontline Publishing.

For a complete list of Pen & Sword titles please contact
PEN & SWORD BOOKS LIMITED
47 Church Street, Barnsley, South Yorkshire, S70 2AS, England
E-mail: enquiries@pen-and-sword.co.uk
Website: www.pen-and-sword.co.uk

Contents

List of Maps

Introduction

Arguably the most famous of Great Britain's armies in the Second World War was the Eighth, but to the layman it is frequently associated exclusively with the Battle of El Alamein in October 1942 and the subsequent advance to Tunis. It is often forgotten that the army was formed twelve months before El Alamein and that it remained in the field until the end of the War in Europe, by which time it had also slogged its way across Sicily and up Italy from the toe to the Alps. The final seven months of its existence were among the most successful, whilst its last battle was even more decisive than El Alamein. During this period it was commanded by one of the outstanding British generals of the War, Sir Richard McCreery.

Dick McCreery is much less well known to history than some of Eighth Army's other commanders, most notably Field Marshal Montgomery. He does of course feature in many military histories and in the published diaries, memoirs and biographies of those who were around him at the time, but it was his lot to achieve high command in a campaign which was seen at the time as a sideshow. Whereas from July 1943 until June 1944 Italy was the only place on land where the British and Americans were fighting the Germans, after the liberation of Rome it became of secondary importance as the campaign in north-west Europe gained pace. Although Churchill himself strove to promote its potential, he was unable to counter the view of the Americans, strongly supported by Stalin, that the focus of their energy should be on the direct route into Germany, whilst the campaign in the 'soft underbelly of Europe' should be left to atrophy.

McCreery's contribution to the War was not limited to the Italian campaign, in which he fought from the landings at Salerno to the capitulation of the German armies. He also served in France in 1940 in the period immediately after Dunkirk when the British were attempting to shore up their French allies, raised one of the new armoured divisions in the UK, acted as adviser on armoured vehicles to General Auchinleck, the C-in-C Middle East, and was then appointed Chief of Staff to General Alexander, Auchinleck's successor. In the last role he was believed by many to have suggested the solution to victory at the Battle of El Alamein. His immediate post-war career was equally distinguished, as C-in-C and High

Commissioner in Austria, followed by command of the British Army of the Rhine and then appointment as British Representative on the Military Staff Committee of the United Nations. At the end of 1949 however, at the age of only 51, McCreery resigned his commission and retired from public life, to the dismay of many of his friends and admirers.

As one of the most important British army officers during the War and its immediate aftermath, I had thought for some time that Dick McCreery deserved a closer look. My initial soundings aroused the same response: why had no one thought of doing this before? In fact someone had. In 1973 *General Sir Richard McCreery: A Portrait* was privately published, written by Major General John Strawson, an experienced historian who had himself served under McCreery in Italy. General Strawson's book is impossible to get hold of through normal commercial channels and, although I had long known of it, I had not read it before embarking on my research. It was commissioned by McCreery's widow, Lettice, for the benefit of his children and grandchildren and, in Strawson's words, 'does not pretend to be a survey of Dick McCreery's life, but rather a portrait of his character, illustrated by incidents from his life.' Strawson accepted at the time that a proper biography remained to be written. When I approached the McCreery family they readily agreed with me that one was long overdue.

I was delighted to find that the family had retained a considerable amount of relevant material. I was hopeful that there would be some letters and other documents. I was not expecting to find that McCreery had kept a pocket diary, recording what he did on nearly every day from the beginning of 1921 to two days before his untimely death in 1967. The diary was for the most part a chronicle of events rather than an expression of opinions, but it provided a wonderful framework to his story. It was complemented from time to time by letters, as McCreery was a tireless correspondent, writing to his mother and maternal grandmother during the Great War and, following his marriage, to Lettice several times a week whenever he was away, although inevitably the wartime letters were very circumspect due to censorship and offered relatively little of value on the military side. I was also delighted to discover that John Strawson had handed over to Lettice a large file of both letters and completed questionnaires from those whose help he had sought nearly forty years ago. As none of his respondents were still available for interview, this was like finding buried treasure.

I then learnt that McCreery had begun to write his military memoirs, with a view to having them published. He completed drafts of three chapters and submitted these to an authors' agent in 1966, only to receive a most discouraging response, but he resumed working on it shortly before his death in the following year. He also wrote a contemporary account of his part in the forlorn attempt to stem the German advance south of the Somme in

1940 and, very much later in 1959, a long article for his regiment's magazine entitled 'Reflections of a Chief of Staff', which covered his wartime service in North Africa.

There was thus a wealth of material available and an opportunity not only to consider the man himself, but also to revisit through his own eyes some of the important events with which he had been associated.

There was more to Dick McCreery than his military career. Apart from his family he had two passions. One was gardening. He left behind new lawns, flower beds and shrubberies wherever he was posted for more than a few months and improved the already fine garden which his mother had created at Stowell Hill. From 1939 onwards his choice of diary was that of the Royal Horticultural Society and I like to think that, when things were not going well, he took some comfort from the RHS's suggestions for each week. At the height of the crisis at Salerno, for instance, the advice in the diary to 'Sow an early maturing Cauliflower in a cold frame' may have provided a momentary reminder of a gentler world whilst he was writing just below it, 'We are in for a very tough fight before our reinforcements arrive.'

McCreery's other passion was for equestrian sport. He learned to ride at a very early age and, following the Great War, became one of the finest horsemen of his generation, competing at the highest level at polo, steeplechasing and skill-at-arms competitions and taking every opportunity to hunt. His membership of a cavalry regiment, where such activities were expected of the officers, facilitated this enormously, and it was as a cavalryman that his contemporaries thought of him during the 1920s and 30s. The six years of the Second World War were to prove that he was much more than that, but somehow the cavalry spirit imbued whatever he did and he would often use equestrian analogies to demonstrate a point. He was, nevertheless, level-headed rather than impetuous, more of an Oliver Cromwell than a Prince Rupert.

The cavalry arm had a lean time on the Western Front during the Great War, although it was to act for a few weeks in its traditional role at both the beginning and the end of the long campaign. Between the wars there was much debate about its function, but mechanization became inevitable and Dick's regiment, the 12th Lancers, was one of the first two to give up its horses. Dick embraced the new order and became an expert in armoured warfare, but his own use of tanks and armoured cars reflected to some extent his cavalry background. In the fighting to destroy the Germans in the Po Valley in 1945, the release of his main armoured formation through the gap created by his infantry and into the open spaces beyond was a textbook cavalry manoeuvre.

There were other members of cavalry regiments who went on to great heights in the Army after the War, but they all had been commissioned after

1918 and had thus seen mechanization come relatively early in their military careers, whereas Dick McCreery's generation was the last actually to fight on horseback in the traditional role. He himself, regardless of his high appointments and the breadth of his military experience, remained at heart always a 12th Lancer. He was the only member of the cavalry arm after 1918 to lead a British army in wartime and, for this reason at least, does indeed deserve to be called the last great cavalryman.

Prologue

The flat plain spread out 5,000 feet below the Auster, which flew alone along the front. There was little danger from enemy aircraft as Allied air superiority was nearly complete and friendly fighters would not be far away. If it slipped much further to the north, on the other hand, the plane would attract heavy anti-aircraft fire, so the pilot was flying as circumspect a course as possible.

Sitting next to him the general looked out of the window of the 'whizzer'. In the clear winter sunshine he could see the problem very clearly. There was one road leading directly to the great river which represented the last barrier to victory, but it ran down the middle of a narrow strip of dry land little more than two miles wide, with the huge lake and a flooded area on its right and another large flooded area on its left. For the enemy it was a highly defensible position and for him an immense problem.

The key was the lake and its adjacent floods. Not for the first time he thought of the strange amphibious vehicles which he had recently seen in training. If he possessed a springboard for a brigade of infantry mounted in these, he would be able to attack behind the enemy's line and turn his left flank. Speaking through the intercom over the noise of the plane he asked the pilot to fly towards the coast. Within a few minutes he could see what he wanted, a small wedge of land on the southern shore of the lake. If he could put his troops across the intervening river and onto that strip, he would have his springboard.

Turning to his pilot, the general signalled to him to return to base. His mind was now absolutely clear on the plan. Success would secure control of the final battlefield and bring an end to a very long and arduous campaign. Failure was not an option.

Chapter 1

The McCreerys and the McAdams

The origins of the McCreerys almost certainly lie in Scotland, the name being a corruption of the Gaelic *Mac Ruaidhri*, meaning the son of a powerful ruler. The branch of the clan from which Dick McCreery was descended had left its original domicile for Ireland many generations before he was born, possibly even arriving there as part of the seventeenth-century 'Plantation of Ulster', the colonization of the six counties of Northern Ireland by Protestants from England and Scotland. The family's history in its new location is obscure, but Dick's paternal great-grandfather, Samuel McCreery, was born in about 1791 and he married his wife, Mary, in 1819. He farmed at Killyclogher Farm, near Omagh in County Tyrone, where the couple produced three sons and a daughter, the youngest son being Dick's grandfather, Andrew Buchanan McCreery, who was born in 1831.

Ireland in the 1840s was a deeply unhappy country. The economy was very largely agricultural, the staple crop being the potato – introduced in the seventeenth century, it had proved to be notoriously unreliable, a situation which was exacerbated when the potato blight arrived in the country. Long before 1845, when the Great Famine caused by the blight began, the choice for much of the population was to starve or to leave and an enormous percentage took the latter option. By the early 1840s the flow of emigrants had become a flood and the favoured destination was the United States. In the New World they found themselves popular, largely because of their willingness to work hard in occupations which the increasingly affluent Americans disdained, the men in the construction of new roads, canals and later railways, the women in service in private households.

The circumstances of the Protestant farmers of Ulster were generally more favourable than those of the native Catholic Irish, but Killyclogher Farm could not sustain all the sons of the McCreery family. Like so many of their countrymen, Andrew and his brother James, some five years older, probably saw little future in a country which offered for the landless a very hard and unrewarding life in contrast to the prospects presented by the United States, and thus it was to America that they sailed in 1846, when Andrew was only 14 or 15. Like most of their compatriots they began their new life in the north-east, working initially as shop assistants in Hamilton

Easter & Co's department store in Baltimore,[1] but the discovery of gold in California in 1848 drew Andrew westwards in the following year with tens of thousands of others. There are different accounts of how he travelled, one saying that he worked his passage as a teamster, driving supplies for the miners, another suggesting that he sailed around Cape Horn. As one of the 'Forty-niners', he was always proud of his membership of the Society of California Pioneers, open only to those who had who arrived and settled in the Golden State before 1850.

Andrew certainly embodied the pioneer spirit. At first he took on menial jobs, such as sweeping out saloons at night, and saving most of the money he earned. Showing the first signs of commercial acumen, once he had accumulated enough he decided not to pan or dig for gold himself, but instead to provide goods and services at a profit to those who did. This appears to have included at one point cornering the market for candles. By the time the Gold Rush ended he had amassed enough capital to make some real-estate investments in San Francisco, which would become the foundations of a considerable fortune. Andrew specialized in waterfront lots on which he would build houses and commercial properties to rent or sell and which, as the bay was reclaimed, became steadily more valuable. One of his early acquisitions was 211 Sansome Street in the centre of the city, which was to become his principal town residence, whilst 114 Sansome Street would later serve as the headquarters of the McCreery Estate Company. Other major properties were Central Park at Eighth and Market Streets, which he offered to the City – only to be refused – and the Western Union Building at Pine and Montgomery Streets. Considered by those who knew him to be very clever but mildly eccentric, even as a much older man he used to collect all the rents himself with horse and buggy.

Andrew's growing prominence in the business community resulted in him being amongst the twenty-two leading businessmen invited to become founding shareholders of the Bank of California in 1864. The bank's financing of silver mining operations on the Comstock led to it generating huge profits in its early years – through this and his real-estate activities Andrew became a very wealthy man. He also moved in the upper echelons of San Francisco society, becoming a life member of the San Francisco Art Association, a member of the Burlingame Club in San Mateo and of the Bohemian Club. As a philanthropist he founded one of the first libraries in the city and endowed a bed at Lane Hospital, later to become part of Stanford University.

In 1864 Andrew married Isabelle De Milt Swearingen. Belle was born in Virginia in 1844, into a long established family of Dutch origin. Her parents had migrated west during the Gold Rush and were thus themselves pioneers. The family was extremely well connected, her sister Sue being the wife of the lawyer Stephen J. Field, a 'Forty-niner' who was already Chief Justice of California and was later appointed to the Supreme Court in Washington D.C. The wedding took place at Grace Church in San Francisco, but no guests were invited and the subsequent announcement took the city's society by surprise.

Andrew's wealth allowed the couple to travel to Europe regularly and Belle was greatly attracted to the Old World. Andrew bought for her Castello di Urio, a villa on Lake Como, as well as a house in Paris, and she increasingly spent her time at one of these and later also in substantial rented properties in England, collecting a large number of fine paintings and tapestries. She entered British society at a high level and was even considered to be one of the Prince of Wales's set, whilst Andrew, for the most part, preferred to remain in California. If Andrew and Belle were not estranged, they certainly led very separate lives.

In addition to his main home in San Francisco Andrew bought a country property north-west of the city, though this was later sold. In 1895 he paid $98,000 for the Rancho Real de los Aguilas. This ranch of more than 30,000 acres lay in San Benito County in the country east of the Gabilans, the range of hills inland from Monterey. The initial land grant had been made by the Mexican Government in 1844, prior to the acquisition of California by the United States. Andrew spent much time there in his later years and acquired other parcels of nearby land, including the Langtry Farms owned by Lily Langtry, the actress and former lover of the Prince of Wales. The whole property was usually referred to as the McCreery Ranch. Andrew also owned a farm near Baltimore, where he had worked immediately after his arrival in the United States, although he appears to have spent little time there.

Notwithstanding their frequent travelling and several homes, the McCreerys found time to have three sons – Richard, born in 1866, Lawrence, born in 1869, and Walter, born in Zurich on 13 August 1871. The brothers were brought up in an atmosphere of gracious living, and Walter Adolph McCreery became in due course as cosmopolitan as his parents, sharing his mother's affection for Europe. He was privately educated in the United States and then followed his brother Lawrence to Magdalene College, Cambridge in 1891, graduating with a 2nd Class law degree in 1894. He had no need to earn his living, so enjoyed the life of an English country gentleman, with a strong focus on equestrian sports. Having learnt to ride at an early age, he became a highly accomplished polo player and in his twenties developed a great enthusiasm for foxhunting. Through social contacts he became a member of the Blackmore Vale Hunt, whose country lay in north Dorset and south-west Somerset. He would stay for the season at Compton Castle, a Victorian Gothic pile at Compton Pauncefoot, rented for about five years in the mid to late 1890s by his mother Belle, and during one such visit he met Emilia Jane ('Minnie') McAdam.

The fortunes of the McAdam family had been established by Minnie's great, great grandfather, John Loudon McAdam. Born in Ayr, in 1756, financial difficulties in his family in 1770 forced him to go to New York to work for his uncle as a merchant and prize agent, selling ships captured by the Royal Navy. The outbreak of the War of Independence in 1775 caused problems for Loyalists and McAdam's uncle decided to retire, but he himself continued with the business and married the daughter of a wealthy lawyer. By the time of American independence in 1783 he was able to sell the business and return to Scotland with more than enough to buy a house and country estate and, among other activities, to become a trustee of the Ayrshire Turnpike. However, renewed financial problems caused him to go south to Bristol and it was while he was there that he proposed to a parliamentary committee a new method of road-building, involving cambering for better drainage and the application of compressed stone and gravel on a firm surface, replacing the muddy tracks that had been used since the Romans left. Known as 'macadamization', it was universally adopted in Britain and later spread throughout the world.

John Loudon McAdam declined the offer of a baronetcy, but one was later accepted by his son and Minnie's great grandfather, James Nicoll McAdam, who became surveyor to a large number of turnpike trusts and was popularly known as the 'Colossus of Roads'.[2] James Nicoll McAdam's grandson, James John Loudon McAdam, joined the 10th Hussars from Sandhurst at the very young age of 17, served in the Indian Mutiny and then transferred to the 7th Dragoon Guards. In 1871 he married Frances Elizabeth Monck, the daughter of John Bligh Monck of Coley Park in Berkshire, and Minnie was born in 1874.

When Walter and Minnie met, she was living with her parents at Greenhill House in Sherborne, built in 1607 and regarded as the best house of its era in the town. Her father had retired from the Army with the rank of major and, having sold the McAdam's Tindon End Estate in Essex for nearly £50,000, had moved to Dorset in order to hunt with the Blackmore Vale. He was a man of some substance locally, becoming a Justice of the Peace and a Governor of Sherborne School. After a brief courtship Walter and Minnie were married in Sherborne Abbey on 6 April 1897. They may have visited the United States that year, but seem to have spent more time in England and it was at Kibworth Harcourt in Leicestershire that their eldest son, Richard Loudon McCreery, was born on 1 February 1898.

Chapter 2

Childhood and Schooldays

In spite of his Scottish and Irish roots and the American background of his father,[1] Dick McCreery was brought up and educated as then befitted an upper middle-class Englishman. Not long after he was born the family moved into a large house called The Coplow, at Billesdon in Leicestershire, where Minnie produced two more boys in quick succession, Robert Bruce ('Bob') in January 1899 and Walter Selby ('Selby') in April 1900. It was not until 1906 that the last of Walter and Minnie's children, John Buchanan ('Jack'), was born. The first three brothers grew up together and became very close.

Walter had probably located the family in Leicestershire for the excellent hunting (The Coplow used to host a meet annually for the Quorn), but he was looking for a permanent home and in 1902 he found one in the shape of Bilton Park, just outside Rugby. Bilton Park boasted a substantial house of eleven bedrooms, together with two cottages and extensive farm buildings and stabling, all situated in more than 90 acres of grounds – but best of all it had a full-sized polo ground and training gallops. This appealed immensely to Walter, who had by this time become a serious polo player, competing successfully in the sport at the 1900 Olympic Games in Paris. Under the rules of the day, team events could comprise members of different nationalities. Walter's was led by the French Comte Jean de Madre, whilst the other two members, Frederick Freake and Walter Buckmaster, were both Englishmen. Competing under the title of BLO Polo Club, Rugby, they took the silver medal. In the same year both Walter and his brother Lawrence represented the United States in a match against an English team in which both Freake and Buckmaster played, but more frequently Walter, and occasionally Lawrence, played alongside the two Englishmen in a team of Cambridge graduates called the Old Cantabs which was unbeaten for two years, winning the Champion Cup at Hurlingham in 1900.

Unsurprisingly the boys were taught to ride almost as soon as they could walk and Dick, Bob and Selby all became excellent horsemen. Walter in the meantime turned Bilton Park into a venue for polo, hosting a regular tournament there, and also owned and ran a number of racehorses. Equestrian sport was not his only enthusiasm, however, as he also had a passion for modern methods of transport, notably the car and the aeroplane.

He bought increasingly larger and faster cars – one of his great pleasures was racing the train to Rugby all the way from London – and took every opportunity to go aloft in the primitive flying machines of the day. One of the earliest of these to be seen in the Midlands was actually assembled in a shed on the Bilton estate.

In 1903 Dick and Bob travelled for the first time with their parents to the United States. They sailed for New York on the White Star liner *Cedric*, a voyage on which Dick realized for the first time that he was prone to travel sickness. Their brief stay in New York included a visit to the zoo, after which they travelled to California by train. Both children much preferred the train to the boat and loved going through the Rockies, which were still covered in snow. In San Francisco they stayed in the Palace Hotel before visiting their grandparents at their ranch.

At about this time a new and important person entered Dick's life in the person of Miss Catherine Stay, who had been employed as the boys' governess. Always called 'Da', she became a firm favourite with all of them, very much a part of the family, and right up to her death well into her nineties Dick would visit her frequently at her home in Sherborne and write to her when he was away. She taught the children not only when they were at Bilton but also on their travels, accompanying them across the Atlantic.

The first proper school which Dick attended was the nearby Bilton Grange. However, as with all those of his social group, a more rigorous education beckoned and in 1906 he was sent away to board at St Michael's School, Westgate-on-Sea. St Michael's had been founded in 1869 by the Reverend John Hawtrey, who had been a boy at Eton and, after becoming a master there, had decided with the permission of the college to remove the lowest forms of the school for their preparatory education. Situated initially in some buildings in Slough, it was removed to Westgate, on the north coast of Kent near Margate, by Hawtrey's son Edward, in 1883. The close relationship with Eton was maintained and a high percentage of the boys went on there at the age of 13 for their secondary education.

There is virtually no information about Dick's career at St Michael's, as all the school records have disappeared. He certainly made satisfactory academic progress, as he was second in the school trials[2] in the first term of his final year and was awarded the First Division prize in July 1911 at the conclusion of his prep school career. He played cricket, writing to his grandmother in his first summer term that he was practising every day and that he had made 18, 21 and 40 runs, but whether he ever represented the school or what other activities he undertook remain unknown.

Whilst Dick was at St Michael's, his parents' marriage started to fall apart. The fault lay with Walter, who had begun to behave erratically. At the end of January 1909 he returned from San Francisco to Bilton Park, where he became violent and abusive – indeed it was subsequently alleged that he tried to kill Minnie.[3] Minnie, a woman of strong character, summoned a doctor who ordered Walter to be put under the control of two male nurses. Lunacy proceedings were instituted against him and in April a court order was obtained, appointing a receiver of his property. Proceedings were also begun to give Minnie custody of the children. Walter managed to escape to Belgium and thence to San Francisco, where he filed in the California Superior Court a petition for divorce against Minnie on the grounds of her cruelty in having him confined and a receiver appointed. Minnie, supported by her powerful mother, responded by filing for alimony for herself and maintenance for the children.

Walter then applied to the Court of Appeal in the United Kingdom for the receiver's appointment to be discharged and this was done provisionally in February 1910. Although subsequent proceedings were brought by Minnie to have the receiver re-appointed, the terms of a settlement were agreed and on 10 March a memorandum of agreement was executed between them under California law, giving her custody of the children and providing for her support and for their education and maintenance, following which the receiver was finally discharged and the divorce proceedings dropped. Walter and Minnie lived separate lives from this time, Walter in California and at Bilton Park, Minnie with her mother and the children at Greenhill House. She had legal custody, while he had the right to visit the children at any time and the obligation to pay for their visits to him. There was also provision for access by Andrew and Belle to their grandchildren. Walter retained Bilton Park, although Minnie took much of the furniture. The final provision was that if she remarried the payment would be reduced to cover only the children's education.

Walter's settlement with Minnie was not the end of the matter. His family in the United States was also deeply concerned by his behaviour and in 1912 he was put under restraint there and declared to be an incompetent person by the California Superior Court, which appointed a Mr McPike as the guardian of his person and estate. Somehow Walter managed to escape back to England where he found that Bilton Park had been stripped of its furniture and let to a tenant and that his beloved motor cars had also disappeared, under the instructions of McPike. He took McPike and various other parties to the High Court in London, which in due course found in his favour and ordered his property to be restored to him, largely on the strength of an opinion from two eminent doctors that he was sane and capable of managing his affairs. The ban of incompetency in the United States, however, remained until February 1914, when Walter succeeded in having it lifted.

In March 1913 Andrew McCreery died, leaving $100,000 in trust for Minnie for the support and education of her children, with interests in the remainder for each of them on their 21st birthdays. A year after his death, a new modifying memorandum was entered into by Walter and Minnie, the main provisions of which were to transfer Walter's one-sixth share of Andrew's estate to a trust. There was a first charge on the trust's income, of which two-thirds was for the support, education and maintenance of the children. The income would be paid directly to the boys after their 21st birthdays. The new memorandum also referred to the setting up of the McCreery Estate Company by Andrew's heirs to hold all his real property assets, including the McCreery Ranch, and Walter's trust receiving stock in the new corporation which on his death would pass to his children. The effect of all these agreements was to provide a degree of financial security for Dick and his brothers for the rest of their lives, although there were a number of occasions when Dick's lack of cash management resulted in his running an overdraft.

It is difficult to assess the precise impact on his children of Walter's behaviour and the subsequent separation, but Da was later to say that Dick had had a difficult boyhood. Certainly it was one of the elements which forged his character, including almost certainly his own attitude to marriage, but perhaps also other traits such as his approach to alcohol, which he rarely consumed and then only in moderation, unlike his father who was a considerable tippler. It does seem, however, that the strong bonds with his mother, grandmother and brothers provided a significant measure of stability.

It was against this backdrop that Dick went to Eton, where he was placed in Hugh de Havilland's House in the Michaelmas Half of 1911.[4] Although he had not been admitted as a scholar, he began immediately to distinguish himself academically, graduating from the Fourth Form to the Removes after his first term. From the outset he was recognized as a *'bona fide* Army Class candidate', so it seems that his choice of future career was made at a young age, doubtless fostered by his maternal grandfather[5] and even by Walter, whose activities on the polo field brought him into frequent contact with British Army officers.

The Army Class was a feature of Eton and certain other public schools with a tradition of providing officers for the Army. Its aim was to prepare boys for the entrance examination to either the Royal Military College at Sandhurst or the Royal Military Academy at Woolwich, rather than for the Higher School Certificate. Admission to the Army Class was by performance in the school trials and could be achieved either from the Removes – the class between the Fourth and Fifth Forms – or from the Fifth Form itself. A high standard was demanded, both overall and specifically in maths. The curriculum was focused on science, maths, history and English, with French for the top division of the class. This was at the expense of the classical subjects, Latin and Greek, studied in the rest of the school.

Dick entered the Army Class at the earliest possible opportunity, after a year in the Removes, and made rapid progress thereafter, moving up a class in every one of the next four halves and arriving in the top Army Class IA in his penultimate half. His exceptionally rapid progress meant that he was as much as two years ahead of some of his contemporaries. A. S. C. Brown, who was in his class and later a fellow officer in his regiment, recalled: 'He was much cleverer than most of us and to us older ones he was very quiet and shy.'[6] Notwithstanding the age difference, Dick performed at the top of each of his classes, winning the Trials Prize three times out of his six terms in the Army Class and the Divinity Prize on one occasion as well. The prizes were always books and the first was a handsome red leather bound copy of *Jorrocks' Jaunts and Jollities* by R. S. Surtees, a very appropriate choice in the light of Dick's enthusiasm for hunting.

Dick never made it into the record books for sporting achievement. This may be partly because he grew slowly at first, before shooting up and possibly outgrowing his strength, remaining for the rest of his life very slightly built for his height, and partly because he left the school at a very early age. He certainly played cricket and in the summer of 1914 he coxed de Havilland's second boat in the Junior House Fours bumping races, but he never represented the school in any sport. Bob and Selby joined Dick at de Havilland's, the former in the Michaelmas Half of 1912 and the latter in the Lent Half of 1914, but unlike Dick both remained in the school for a full four years and were thus old enough to play for the house cricket XI.

One activity which Dick did pursue was membership of the Officers' Training Corps, which he joined in the Lent Half of 1913. The OTC was an entirely voluntary organization, remaining so even after the outbreak of the Great War in 1914, but membership was probably considered highly desirable for those anticipating a full-time army career. He left before he could gain promotion beyond the rank of private.

His early departure also meant that Dick was too young to be invited to join the largely social societies which exercised a profound impact on life at Eton. He never became a member of his house debating society or house library, let alone of 'Pop',[7] all of which admitted members only by election and which provided the nearest equivalent of house and school prefects. This, his innate shyness and the loss of a large percentage of his generation to the Great War may have meant that he inherited less of a network than some, but the mere fact that he had been at the school bound him to other Old Etonians. Dick's near contemporaries included a future prime minister, Anthony Eden, and two men who would play a significant part in his military career, Oliver Leese and Herbert Lumsden, but there is no evidence that he knew any of them at the time.

Holidays from Eton, as latterly from St Michael's, were spent largely at Greenhill House, although there were visits to the seaside and, during the Christmas holiday of 1913/14, a trip to Switzerland. Minnie kept to her agreement and the boys were allowed to spend time with Walter at Bilton Park and on one occasion accompanied him to the family villa in Italy, although Walter used to complain bitterly that he was never allowed to have Christmas with them. For all his faults, he remained devoted to his children, wrote to them regularly in the most affectionate terms and encouraged them to see him as often as they could. Whilst at Bilton they were able to ride every day, hunting and playing polo as soon as they were old enough, and to be driven by their father very fast in one of his many cars, the favourite in the immediate pre-war years being a Lozier, one of the most expensive American models, which Walter decided to have armoured at even greater cost as war approached in 1914. Dick inherited both his father's interest in cars and his love of speed. He learnt to drive before he left school, taking out his grandmother's Singer, but never really enjoyed being a passenger, partly due to being prone to car sickness.

Dick sat the Sandhurst entrance exam in February 1915, the earliest possible opportunity after his seventeenth birthday. He wrote to his father that he believed he had done well and so it turned out. He was placed third in the list of those destined for the cavalry, the arm which he had already chosen, and 22nd overall out of 212 successful candidates, with many more having failed. De Havilland wrote to Minnie:

> Here is a last report that rightly ends a set in which I do not call to mind a single bad one. It isn't that they have been merely dull and proper, they are reports to be proud of, I really mean it. He has brains and uses them and in addition of late he has developed very considerably in himself. I think he was sorry to leave or so the boys tell me and I know we were sorry to lose him. His size prevented him doing much good at games but I am certain that he will make not only a keen but highly intelligent cavalry officer. You may be well satisfied with his time at Eton.

Chapter 3

The Western Front

Dick received the results of the Sandhurst entrance exam on 8 April 1915 and shortly afterwards was ordered to report to the College. With enormous officer losses on the Western Front, especially at the First Battle of Ypres in October and November 1914, the overall intake had been substantially increased by dint of doubling up in rooms and taking over the nearby Staff College, which was closed for the duration, whilst the course had been reduced from a year to barely four months. This scarcely allowed enough time for the cadets to learn drill and musketry, let alone the rather more practical skills required for survival on the Western Front.

Most of the officers commissioned during the Great War came from the Reserve of Officers, the Special Reserve, the Territorial Force and the ranks, although more than 20,000 were accepted on the strength of their experience in the OTC alone. In the circumstances it seems surprising that Sandhurst, together with the Royal Military College at Woolwich for those destined for the Royal Artillery and Royal Engineers, remained open to gentlemen cadets – indeed, as the war progressed the courses became longer again, eventually reverting to one year. The rationale may have been to retain the concept of the regular commission for those intending to make a career in the Army, while most of the other officers would be expected to return to civilian life as soon as hostilities were over. In practice, shells and bullets did not distinguish between the regular officers and the others, and many who had volunteered or been conscripted subsequently applied for and were granted regular commissions. In the Second World War, by contrast, both institutions were closed immediately war was declared, to become only two of many Officer Cadet Training Units, turning out officers with emergency commissions only.

Of Dick's intake at Sandhurst, a significant percentage would not survive the war. Of those who did, only two featured strongly in his later life, Gordon MacMillan of the Argyll & Sutherland Highlanders, who would in due course be a fellow student and close friend at the Staff College and would himself go on to become a senior general, and Christopher Peto of the 9th Lancers, whom he got to know well as a fellow cavalryman and who would serve under him in 1940.

On 11 August 1915 Dick was commissioned into the 12th (The Prince of Wales's Royal) Lancers as a Second Lieutenant. Why he chose this regiment or, indeed, why it accepted him, is a mystery. Given the strong family connections found in British regiments, and particularly cavalry regiments, one might have expected him to follow his grandfather into the 7th Dragoon Guards, although the death of John McAdam in 1910 meant that no specific influence could be exercised from that direction. It was certainly known that Dick was going to the cavalry before he took the Sandhurst entrance exam, so the choice must have been made during his last years at school. It is possible that there were members or former members of the regiment in Dorset or Somerset who could offer an introduction and recommendation, but another likely source was one of Walter's polo playing friends.

The 12th Lancers had an illustrious history. Raised as Bowles's Regiment of Dragoons in 1715 the regiment served on the Irish Establishment for much of the eighteenth century, recruiting locally during that time. The great Duke of Wellington joined the regiment, by then the 12th Light Dragoons, for two years prior to purchasing a captaincy in an infantry regiment and, following excursions to Corsica, Italy, Egypt and the Netherlands, it fought under him in the Peninsula, distinguishing itself at Salamanca and Waterloo. Of all his cavalry commanders the Honourable Frederick Ponsonby, who was wounded leading the regiment in a great charge at Waterloo, was one of those whom Wellington rated the highest. Employed thereafter against the Kaffirs in South Africa, in the closing stages of the Crimean campaign, during the Indian Mutiny and in the Boer War, by 1914 the regiment's reputation was as high as any.

Dick, however, was not to go to the 12th Lancers immediately, but was instead posted to the 6th Reserve Regiment of Cavalry, which was based in Dublin. Seventeen reserve regiments of cavalry were formed in 1914, although these were later reduced in number. Other than those for the Household Cavalry, each of these units had several regular or yeomanry regiments affiliated to it and in the case of the 6th these were the 5th and 12th Lancers and the 1st County of London Yeomanry (the Middlesex Hussars). Their primary purpose was to accept all new recruits, both officers and other ranks, and provide them with basic training. This included instruction in equitation, but by this time Dick was already an excellent horseman. There were a number of other skills to absorb, including the use of the cavalryman's basic weapons, the lance, the sword and the rifle and, for officers, the pistol – to gain some proficiency in the last two Dick attended the school of musketry at Dollymount. There was also an introduction to field operations and tactics, including mounted attacks by troops, squadrons and regiments, dismounted attacks and defence, reconnaissance and movement by day and night. The instructors were largely officers and NCOs who had been brought back from the reserves but were considered too old for active service, although as the war continued there were a number who had been wounded and were posted there during their recuperation.

Much of the specialist cavalry training received at the reserve regiments was to prove of little value. By the time Dick reported to his regiment in France on the penultimate day of 1915, the war of motion had long since passed and the opposing armies had settled into trench warfare in which the opportunities for the cavalry to engage in its traditional role were few and far between. It had not always been thus, indeed for the opening months of the war the 12th Lancers had operated exactly as it had been trained to do. The regiment had arrived in France just thirteen days after the United Kingdom's declaration of war and moved up immediately to join the British Expeditionary Force as part of 5 Cavalry Brigade in which, together with the 2nd Dragoons (Royal Scots Greys) and the 20th Hussars, it would serve for the duration.

The brigade was at Binche, east of Mons, when the Germans launched their major offensive and it acted as a rearguard to the BEF during the ensuing retreat. On 28 August 1914, near the village of Moy, the 12th Lancers fought one of the few successful cavalry actions of the time, when its HQ and C Squadrons surprised and almost annihilated the HQ and a squadron of the 2nd Prussian Dragoons in a textbook charge. It went on to inflict serious damage on the remainder of that regiment and rendered a whole enemy brigade ineffective for some days,[1] although it could do little to stop the overall enemy advance. The retreat from Mons was eventually halted south of the Marne and followed first by a strong Allied counter-attack which pushed the Germans away from Paris, and then by the 'race for the sea' as each side attempted to outflank the other before reaching stalemate with their flanks on the English Channel. By mid-October the 12th Lancers were positioned south-west of Ypres, where they were engaged in a number of skirmishes before being withdrawn from the line in late November.

Throughout 1915 the 12th Lancers, and indeed the cavalry as a whole, experienced the frustration which was to last for much of the war. One after another, attacks or more major offensives were planned, but in every case they were either cancelled or, if put into action, did not meet with enough success for the cavalry to be able to pass through the infantry into the open spaces beyond. The lack of employment for thousands of cavalrymen at a time when the BEF was taking serious casualties exercised the high command as well and, a few days before Dick arrived in France, a reorganization took place which enabled them to operate in an infantry role, whilst keeping them available for possible mounted operations. Each cavalry brigade provided a dismounted infantry battalion, with each regiment in the brigade providing a company, one of which at any one time would include the HQ. On 2 January 1916 the Dismounted Company of the 12th Lancers, comprising 15 officers and 372 other ranks and including the initial elements of the Dismounted Battalion's HQ, proceeded to the front for the first time to take over a section of the trenches at Vermelles from the infantry.

When Dick arrived a few days earlier at the regiment's winter quarters at Campagne les Boulonnais, about 20 miles from Boulogne and thus well behind the front line, he was posted to B Squadron, in which he would remain for the whole of his active service during the war. It was commanded during the period by two officers, the first being Captain (later Major) Willy Styles, the second a man with whom he would be long associated and who would be one of his mentors, Harold Charrington, usually known as 'Rollie'. Charrington had joined the regiment in 1905 and, other than an attachment to the Egyptian Army, had served with it ever since. Like Dick he was a very keen rider and an excellent polo player and the two men, despite the disparity in their age and seniority, had a great deal in common.

Dick was initially christened 'Nosey', a nickname which happily for him did not survive long. It was coined for his prominent nose, rather than any personality trait, indeed Charrington described him very many years later as shy and modest, going on to write that 'even in those early days, enthusiasm, ability and devotion to the interests of his men and the regiment were the outstanding elements of his character.'[2] It was not long before Dick had some experience of the trenches, going up in the last week of January with two more officers and 38 other ranks to join the Dismounted Company in the trenches as replacements for casualties and those who were sick. Activity on the front was muted at the time – only 4 men had been killed and 11 wounded by the time that the Dismounted Company returned to the regiment on 15 February, a modest tally by the standards of the war.

Conditions in the trenches were unpleasant, but the billets in Campagne were not a great deal better and were not improved by the bitter winter weather: if it was not freezing, the camp was a sea of mud. Dick's life was significantly improved by food parcels sent directly from Harrods by his mother and grandmother, usually including cakes of all varieties, but also items such as chicken and pork pies, which enabled him to vary his diet. Perhaps surprisingly, however, he reported that the food in the officers' mess was good. He also asked for and was sent some warm clothing, including a woolly waistcoat and a strong pair of boots.

Although the weather improved and by late April Dick was writing that it was as hot as summer, there was little real activity, and he was able to take leave in early May. Back with the regiment boredom was the main enemy, and it was vital to keep the men occupied and the horses exercised in the absence of any action. Numerous training schemes were organized, whilst 2

Cavalry Division, 5 Cavalry Brigade's parent formation, held a horse show. There were also boxing tournaments and athletic events, but any form of hunting or shooting was strictly forbidden by the high command, although there was at least one occasion on which a boar was illicitly pursued and riders also chased hares from time to time. An attempt by the Royal Horse Guards to hold a race meeting was stopped at the last moment by the killjoys at divisional headquarters. In early April the regiment moved to a new billeting area about 15 miles north, with B Squadron at Zouafques, where its officers' mess was located in 'a nice little chateau'. The Battle of the Somme began in July, but there was no employment at first for the 12th Lancers, although the Dismounted Company was in the line again further north.

At last, on 6 September, 5 Cavalry Brigade was ordered to move south and the regiment marched to Bray-sur-Somme, arriving there eight days later. A working party was immediately formed to build cavalry routes up to the front and on 16 September the brigade was put on half an hour's notice to move. The plan was for 2 Cavalry Division to operate on the right flank of the Fourth Army, with its objective being Bapaume and the higher ground to the north. At last it seemed that the regiment would see some action. Nothing happened, but the division was kept at one hour's notice for the whole of the following day, before being stood down on 17 September and ordered back to the Bonnay area. There were two other flurries of activity, first with C Squadron, sent to Mametz under the orders of XIV Corps on 19 September, and then A Squadron, sent up to Carnoy under the orders of 5 Division – in each case nothing came of it and on 2 October the 12th Lancers moved to a new camp north of Combles.

The autumn of 1916 passed without any action. Some attempt was made to keep the men amused, including a sports day in competition with the neighbouring 125th French Infantry Regiment, and once the regiment had moved to its winter quarters at Auchy-les-Hesdin it had access to a cinema and a gymnasium in an old tobacco factory. One real problem was the increasing difficulty of keeping the horses fit, as unrestricted U-boat warfare was having a marked effect on supplies of oats and the ration was reduced to 7lb per day, not enough to keep them in peak condition and exacerbating the impact of the weather, which was particularly wet in the autumn and then very cold. On the other hand, the lack of military activity meant that most officers were able to take home leave, Dick himself going on 10 December, although he was back by Christmas.

By the end of his first year in the 12th Lancers, Dick was almost an old hand. His troop commander, Victor Cartwright, had thought he looked far too young when he joined the regiment, but soon appreciated his qualities. 'He was an outstanding character in every way... popular with everyone, with a great sense of humour. I can never think of him without some sort of laughter coming from him.'[3] Underneath this cheerful exterior, however, Dick was by now extremely frustrated. His military activity consisted of incessant training schemes, duty as the orderly officer and, on one occasion, going mounted with two other subalterns and 136 other ranks to work on cable-laying. Possibly because of his riding skills he was detailed as a galloper to 2 Cavalry Division, but was only likely to be called for when the division was on the move and it remained resolutely stuck in winter quarters. Desperate to see some action, he approached his commanding officer, Lieutenant Colonel Fane, who had recently returned from convalescence after being injured at the First Battle of Ypres, to request a transfer to the infantry. In spite of pleading his case passionately, he was told that no transfers from the cavalry would be permitted for the foreseeable future.[4] He comforted himself with frequent food parcels and was asked, 'by popular demand', to request his grandmother to send a white tablecloth for the mess, 'dining room size just right'.

Chapter 4

Disaster and Triumph

1917 opened to bitterly cold weather, with heavy snow from mid-January into the second week of February. The horses continued to deteriorate and many of the men, including Dick, went sick. He had left his 'British Warm'[1] behind in England during his December leave and missed it greatly. As February progressed he felt increasingly unwell, experiencing headaches at first, then developing full-scale bronchitis. He was admitted to a military hospital in Boulogne, which he found very cold. The nurses, he thought, were good, but the matrons 'seemed to have very "cushy" jobs with nothing to do except walk round and call everyone by the wrong name.'[2] After a short time he was sent to Michelham House for Convalescent British Officers at Cap Martin, near Menton on the French Riviera, where the weather was much more benign and he was able to admire the orange trees.

Between 23 February and 5 April, the Germans conducted a planned and skilful withdrawal from their trenches on the Somme between Arras and Soissons to a strongly fortified line further east, known to them as the *Siegfried-Stellung* and to the Allies as the Hindenburg Line. This eliminated a dangerous bulge for the Germans and preempted a plan by the new French Commander-in-Chief, General Nivelle, to mount diversionary attacks from the west, including one by the BEF, before sending in the principal thrust from the River Aisne to the south. Undeterred by the new and much stronger German dispositions, Nivelle decided to go ahead with a similar plan. Douglas Haig of the BEF was deeply unhappy about this, preferring to attack in Flanders, but as Nivelle's subordinate he had no option but to concur.

The main British thrust would come from Edmund Allenby's Third Army just to the east of Arras, whilst Julian Byng's Canadian Corps would assault Vimy Ridge to the north of the town. On 5 April the 12th Lancers, with the rest of 5 Cavalry Brigade, marched from Auchy to Remaisnil and four days later to Grincourt, just behind the line, proceeding up the newly constructed cavalry track and joining 2 Cavalry Division on Telegraph Hill, about 2 miles south-east of Arras itself. However, although the Canadians had captured Vimy Ridge, the infantry attack around Feuchy stalled and the cavalry retired to Wailly, the 12th Lancers arriving there at 0330 hrs in the morning of 10 April. The march back took seven and a half hours in the dark over muddy tracks, and not until it was over could the officers and men, not to mention the horses, eat and drink for the first time since 0900 hrs on the previous morning. There was no shelter for humans or animals; some of the horses died of exposure and a few of the men were badly frost-bitten. The regiment remained at Wailly until 1230 hrs that afternoon, when it was turned out at short notice to return to Telegraph Hill and, after a short halt, to proceed on through Tilloy to Wancourt. There it came under German artillery fire, but a heavy snowstorm hid the regiment's movement from observation and there were few casualties. 5 Cavalry Brigade then formed up in an exposed position just in front of the old German third line, which the infantry had captured that morning, but the enemy was still holding beyond that, stalling any further advance by the cavalry.

At 1800 hrs the snow cleared and the 12th Lancers were spotted by the Germans, who laid down an artillery barrage for about fifteen minutes, killing 2 men, wounding 13 and causing about 30 casualties among the horses. With no further movement possible, the two brigades were ordered to be in the same position by 0500 hrs the next morning, but it was left to the discretion of their commanders whether or not to withdraw in the meantime. In the event 3 Cavalry Brigade withdrew, whilst 5 Cavalry Brigade, doubtless remembering the extremely difficult conditions of the previous night and also believing that the withdrawal of the cavalry might dishearten the sorely pressed infantry, stayed fast in position.

No sleep was possible in the bitterly cold weather, with snow on the ground, so each man stood to beside his horse for the whole night. Directly daylight broke on 11 April the Germans resumed their shelling, this time with far greater accuracy, continuing for two hours until the brigade was ordered to withdraw. The 12th Lancers were particularly badly hit, especially when one shell landed in the regimental HQ, and the situation was compounded by accurate machine-gun fire. The conduct of the troops was magnificent, with no flinching under fire, later attracting considerable praise from the divisional commander, but their presence on the battlefield was futile and the damage to the regiment considerable. In all 6 officers, some 50 other ranks and over 100 horses were killed or wounded. Among the officer casualties was Dick.

Dick was hit in the right thigh by a bullet, which severed the femoral artery. By an extraordinary piece of good luck it lodged there, otherwise he would have bled to death in a matter of minutes. The artery was tied off as soon as he reached the field hospital, but the subsequent loss of blood to the foot meant that gangrene set in. The surgeon told him that there was a considerable risk of the gangrene spreading and poisoning his whole system and that the only certain way of avoiding death would be to have the leg off. Dick replied that if he had the leg off he wouldn't be able to ride and that if he couldn't ride he wouldn't want to live, so refused permission to operate. The two smallest toes on his right foot were lost, however, together with the terminal joints on the other three, leaving him apparently seriously incapacitated. In addition there was severe damage to the muscles in his right thigh which had been torn by the entry of the bullet. After the operation he was taken to No. 20 General Hospital at Camiers, near Étaples, for the first stage of his recovery.

Reassuring messages were sent to all the family and by 15 April Dick was, according to a letter to his father, no longer in great pain – though as it was only four days after incurring his injury, it is more likely that he was either being stoical or taking a heavy dose of painkiller. In any event, it was not until 6 May that he was evacuated to England, the delay possibly partly due to the temporary suspension of journeys by hospital ships because of the submarine menace. He was taken to Princess Henry of Battenberg's Hospital for Officers at 30 Hill Street in Mayfair,[3] where his mother went at once to visit him. She was followed in due course by the rest of the family, including Bob, who was now at Sandhurst and who badgered Dick about which cavalry regiment to join, having decided that it would not be right for both of them to serve in the 12th Lancers. Dick's foot improved and the highly capable chief surgeon, Colonel Rigby,[4] was pleased with his patient's progress, although he doubted how easily he would be able to walk, let alone ride. He did not reckon with Dick's determination.

After a month Hill Street was shut and Dick was moved to the Astley Hospital for Officers at Dorchester House on Park Lane.[5] He was rather sad, as he had enjoyed Hill Street and found the new establishment much less congenial. One consolation was that, though he remained an in-patient, required to sleep in the hospital every night and to receive continuing medical attention, he was allowed to spend his days at the family's London flat, going there at about 11.30 am and returning to the hospital at 7.00 in the evening. By late June he was being fitted with crutches and was able to accompany his mother and other family members to the Hippodrome Theatre to see the famous comedian George Robey – although he made very slow progress down to the front stalls.

With less need for specialized medical attention, he was allowed to move down to Sherborne in late July, where his grandmother and mother had turned Greenhill House into a hospital for the duration of the war, with Mrs McAdam as the matron, Minnie as a sister and Da as one of the nurses.[6] Dr Rice-Oxley, the medical director of the Astley, continued to supervise his progress and was able to report to the president of the Medical Board in September that Dick's wounds had practically all healed, although he was continuing to experience difficulty in walking. By November, Dick was fit enough to travel to Bilton Park, which he enjoyed and which gave his father great pleasure. During Dick's stay in hospital in London Walter had visited him every week, but he was lonely at Bilton and very much welcomed the company of any of his sons.

By the end of the year Dick was fit to return to duty but not to active service. He was posted to the 1st Reserve Regiment of Cavalry based in Ireland, at The Curragh, the very large camp in County Kildare which was the main centre for the British Army in the country. Ireland had experienced considerable unrest since Dick had last been there in 1915, climaxing with the Easter Rising in 1916 and the trial and execution of Sir Roger Casement later that year, but was now relatively quiet again. In early 1917 the reserve regiments had been reorganized into nine regiments from the original seventeen. The 1st Reserve Regiment now took on recruits for all six lancer regiments, together with five of the yeomanry regiments.

Dick arrived on 2 January 1918. Like many others who had been wounded seriously enough to have been evacuated from France, but had reached the end of their convalescence, he was expected to pass his knowledge of conditions on the Western Front on to the new recruits. Wilfred Lyde, who was at The Curragh at the same time, remembered him as a most popular subaltern with natural charm and a winning smile, sensing even at that early stage that he was destined for command. To Dick's great pleasure his fellow officers included his brother Bob, who had joined the 17th Lancers and was in Ireland to master the essentials of the cavalryman's role in warfare before proceeding to the front. Bob was now, as Dick had been at the same age, an excellent horseman and was foremost among his contemporaries in organizing equestrian activities, including a point-to-point.

Dick, on the other hand, had to learn to ride again. The loss of his toes impeded him seriously in walking, although he learnt to do so very effectively, with a pronounced limp which would give rise to a number of mostly affectionate nicknames among the other ranks, such as 'Hopalong' and 'Rickety Dick'. The wound in his thigh contributed to the limp but was more serious for riding, as it had damaged the muscle which gripped the saddle.[7] Somehow he learnt not only to compensate for this but even, through what must have been sheer willpower, to ride again to the same high standard that he had enjoyed previously.

His skills may have been further improved by being required to attend a course at the Cavalry School when he eventually arrived back in France, having at last convinced a medical board that he was fit for active service. He took some leave in England on the way, during which he fitted in another visit to his father at Bilton and managed to see his grandmother Belle in Paris.[8] It was not until 11 September that he actually reported to the 12th Lancers for duty, having spent a frustrating week en route at the British Cavalry Base Depot at Rouen, which he described as the dirtiest camp imaginable. He rejoined B Squadron as a troop commander, having been promoted to lieutenant on 1 July 1917.

The active service of the 12th Lancers in the seventeen months since Dick had been wounded was characterized yet again by frequent disappointment. The Nivelle Offensive, which included the Battle of Arras, had been a disaster for the Allies and particularly for the French, who later experienced a rash of mutinies. Much was expected of the Battle of Cambrai in November 1917, when the use of tanks in great numbers promised the desired breakthrough. They did indeed help to take the front line forward by many miles before the advance once again came to a standstill, after which a vigorous German counter-offensive recovered much of the ground. The regiment had actually been in the saddle for much of the battle, but was frustrated in its advance by the failure to secure two key bridges. In the end it was reduced once again to sending into action the Dismounted Company, which acquitted itself well. The Dismounted Company saw yet more action during the Ludendorff Offensive in the last week of March 1918, when the Germans very nearly succeeded in reaching Amiens and threatened to break through to the sea. In the confusion of the Allied retreat the war became for a short time one of movement and the 12th Lancers had for once, but only briefly, operated on horseback, providing flank protection and reconnaissance to a number of formations as they fell back. The actions of one squadron, moving forward mounted but then fighting on foot in the Bois de Hangard in support of an Australian infantry brigade, led to the feature becoming known as Lancer Wood.

By the time Dick arrived back with the regiment, the overall picture had changed dramatically and, for the Allies, entirely favourably. The new Allied Commander-in-Chief, General Foch, had shown a masterly grasp of his now unified command, which was bolstered by the arrival of the first American troops. His counterstroke in July against the German salient south of the Marne, and the successful attack on the Somme on 8 August which removed any threat to Amiens – Ludendorff's 'Black Day of the German Army' – had made a serious impact on enemy morale. In the last week of September Foch launched a series of coordinated offensives along the whole front between the English Channel and Verdun, which met with rapid success.

The 12th Lancers now formed part of Henry Rawlinson's Fourth Army. Although still notionally in 5 Cavalry Brigade, in practice the regiment was attached to whichever formation was likely to need it, initially 5 Australian Division. Although considerable progress was made by the infantry, the opportunity to exploit gaps with the cavalry still eluded the Allies at first and on 23 October the regiment was withdrawn to Maretz, south-east of Le Cateau. On 4 November it was ordered to move forward again and cross the Sambre-Oise Canal at Landrecies. Over the next few days troops from the regiment were attached to 25, 50 and 66 Divisions, with patrols operating for the first time entirely successfully in conjunction with the infantry.

On 9 November the regiment's commanding officer, still Lieutenant Colonel Fane, took two troops of A Squadron up to the HQ of 50 Division, where he received the news that Dick's No 3 Troop of B Squadron, which had been attached to 198 and 199 Brigades, had cleared up a machine-gun post in Les Fontaines, thereby opening the road to Solre le Château, down which Dick had pushed patrols. The two troops from A Squadron were immediately sent by Fane to exploit this gap, taking Sars Poteries and entering Solre le Château itself, capturing a field gun, a machine gun and an immense amount of rolling stock on the railway, including a loaded ammunition train. On the following day patrols were pushed out towards the Belgian border, but the enemy were found to be holding a very strong position on the River Thure. The 12th Lancers concentrated in Solre le Château, where that evening the ammunition train was hit by German artillery fire, causing an immense explosion and the regiment's last fatality of the war. At 1100 hrs on the next day, 11 November, the 'war to end all wars' came to an end.

Henry Jackson, who was commanding 50 Division and had personally given Dick his orders that day, considered that he had carried out his task so well and so quickly that he deserved a special award, recommending him for the Military Cross.[9] On 18 December the news arrived at the regiment that he had been awarded the decoration. The citation in the *London Gazette* read as follows:

> On 9th November, 1918, east of the Avesnes–Maubeuge road, for valuable and dashing work when in command of a mounted patrol sent forward to get in touch with the retiring enemy. He pushed boldly forward skilfully clearing up an enemy machine-gun post which threatened to hold up the advance from the outset, capturing ten prisoners and one machine gun. He then cleared three villages and sent back a most accurate and clear report.

For Dick the war ended on a high note. His actions in the closing days had served to increase the regard in which he was held by his fellow officers in the regiment. Victor Cartwright, for instance, who was close to him for most of his active service in France, wrote much later that he had no superior as a troop commander. He had come close to death at Arras, a stroke of good fortune allowing him to survive a conflict in which a significant percentage of his generation had been swept away. Like most of his contemporaries who had served for some time on the Western Front, he could not fail to have been profoundly affected by the experience, but he probably believed that what they had achieved would make the world a better place. Few thought it possible that it could happen all over again.

Chapter 5

Peace and Tragedy

'It seems hard to realise, doesn't it,' wrote Dick to his maternal grandmother on the fourth day of peace, 'that the war is over at last, especially as we shall probably be out here for some time.'[1] 'Some time' turned out to be ten months. In the immediate aftermath of the Armistice the regiment stayed exactly where it had been when the guns fell silent, further progress frustrated by the need to clear the mines which had been skilfully laid by the retreating Germans. The only excitement came with the order to move to Philippeville, some 20 miles away in Belgium, ostensibly to restore order among the Germans, who were apparently no longer under the control of their officers, to protect the inhabitants and to rescue Allied prisoners. In the event, the lancers found that there were no disturbances of any sort, but rather an enormous party at which they were the guests of honour, with Rollie Charrington, temporarily in command, presented with an address by the mayor and council.

A fortnight later the 12th Lancers crossed the border into Germany near St Vith, but remained there for only a few days before returning to Belgium, where the regiment moved into what the war diary described as 'very suitable' billets at Ensival, close to the frontier south of Aachen. Many of the men were sent off on leave, and gradually those who had joined for the duration were discharged, to be replaced by new recruits. Dick was a regular officer and thus secure in his position, but he appears to have had no thoughts about leaving the regiment. In any event, opportunities were opening up for what he enjoyed most, equestrian sport. He showed how completely he had recovered his riding skills when he won the race open to subalterns of the 12th Lancers on a horse called Old Hat in the 5 Cavalry Brigade steeplechase near Verviers on 11 January 1919, following this with another victory on the same horse a week later at a Scots Greys point-to-point meeting, in a race open to all comers from 2 Cavalry Division – 'a very popular win' according to the war diary.

On 15 March Dick rode competitively for the first time on a horse which was to be a great and longstanding favourite, his official charger, Fox-Trot. He was to have the horse for many years, buying him from the government in 1925 for the princely sum of £12.[2] The horse proved to be particularly good at showjumping and was a steady and reliable hunter. Riding Fox-Trot,

Dick was placed 12th out of 80 at the French Army Horse Show at Wiesbaden that May, although by that time he was more often seen competing on his other charger, Kilbay, on which he did very well, including coming first in a dead heat in the Grand International Steeplechase at the Cologne Races in August.

Polo also restarted during the summer of 1919. Dick was able to take leave to coincide with the Bilton Park polo tournament in May and represented the 12th Lancers in the subalterns' team at the Rhine Army polo tournament in August, at the start of a regimental career in the sport which was to continue for another nineteen years. The facilities for polo in Belgium were rather primitive, so for this reason at least the officers were pleased to return to the British Isles in September 1919, but it was not to England that they were posted. Instead they were sent to The Curragh.

The relative peace which had followed the Easter Rising in 1916 came to an end when two members of the Royal Irish Constabulary were shot dead in January 1919, the first incident in what was later termed the Irish War of Independence. Sinn Féin, the main republican party, had gained 73 of the 105 Irish seats in the Parliament at Westminster in the General Election of the previous month, but those elected chose not to take up their seats but instead to form their own parliament, the Dáil Éirann, in Dublin. In the following September the Dáil was declared illegal and violence broke out, small scale at first and largely directed at the RIC. In early 1920 the Government began recruiting unemployed British ex-servicemen as temporary constables to assist the RIC. They became known as 'Black and Tans' from their uniforms and took the offensive, causing casualties not only within the Irish Republican Army but also among the civilian population. Violence escalated amid increasing bitterness on both sides.

It was in this context that the 12th Lancers began their service in Ireland, in which they were to act for the most part in support of the civil authority, escorting convoys, mounting patrols and from time to time carrying out organized 'drives' through the countryside to round up suspected IRA activists. Within the confines of The Curragh sport continued as before, with steeplechasing in the winter and polo in the summer. Dick was in the teams which won the Irish Inter-Regimental Cup in July 1920 and just failed to win the Irish Subalterns' Cup that August. Foxhunting in the Kildare countryside remained possible during the season, and there was ample 'hunting leave', during which Dick spent most of his time at Sherborne, hunting with the Blackmore Vale.

By this time the three oldest McCreery brothers were all based in Ireland, while Jack was still at Eton. Bob had joined the 17th Lancers in France in time to see out the last months of the war and was with his regiment at Gort, where he was the captain of the regimental subalterns' polo team. Selby had passed through Sandhurst and, unlike Bob, had elected to join Dick in the 12th Lancers, where he was proving to be every bit as good a polo player as his two older brothers. During Dick's leave in Sherborne, in January 1921, Bob came to stay for a few days on his way to attend a six-month course at the Cavalry School in Netheravon.

On 1 May 1921 the 12th Lancers began a long drive to round up wanted IRA men, starting at Killeigh, and moving in a circular route so as to arrive back at The Curragh twelve days later. Success was only modest, just a handful of wanted men captured. On 16 May, shortly after their return, Dick received the worst possible news. Bob, who had been recalled from the cavalry course to his regiment due to increasing industrial unrest in Ireland, had been killed by IRA gunmen.

On the previous day Bob had been playing tennis at Ballyturin House, the home of a local justice of the peace, Mr J. C. Bagot. He and his fellow guests, Captain Fiennes Cornwallis of his own regiment, Captain Blake, the District Inspector of the RIC, his wife and a Mrs Gregory, left the party and approached the main road along the drive. Seeing that the gate was partially closed, they pulled up and Captain Cornwallis got out to open it. As he did so he came under fire from a keeper's lodge on the other side of the road and was hit almost immediately. The rest of the party left the car and crouched on the ground. Bob was killed even before he could draw his pistol and although Captain Blake attempted to return fire he was shot down, as was his wife. Only Mrs Gregory, who had taken cover on the other side of the car, was unharmed and allowed to leave by the gunmen, running off to give the alarm. One of the Bagot daughters rode for help, but when the police arrived they were themselves ambushed and a constable was killed.

On the following afternoon Dick and Selby drove in a Rolls Royce armoured car from The Curragh to Galway. They were able to see Bob's body the next morning and to attend a memorial service at Galway Cathedral, before their brother's coffin and that of Captain Cornwallis were taken to the station, through streets lined with detachments from those regiments based locally, and from the Royal Navy and the RIC. The 17th Lancers were on parade at the station and the commanding officer and a guard of honour accompanied the coffins, with Dick and Selby, to Kingstown Harbour, where they were put aboard a ship for England. The two brothers arrived at Sherborne with Bob's coffin at noon on 19 May, to be met by Minnie and their grandmother, and the funeral was held in the packed Abbey an hour later. After the service the coffin was borne to its final resting place through streets in which the shops were closed and curtains drawn as a mark of respect.

On the same day a memorial service was held at the parish church at Bilton. Walter was too distressed to attend, let alone to travel to Sherborne.

He had not long returned from a visit to Algiers which had worn him out and he had taken Bob's death very badly. Dick and Selby had both received cables from the regiment requiring them to return, but saw him two days later en route to Ireland. They discovered to their embarrassment that Walter had done everything in his power to prevent their going back, sending a rambling telegram to both the War Office and their commanding officer. The War Office responded by granting them two weeks' leave, but Dick told his father that it would be impossible for them to take it at that time, as they were required for a new anti–IRA drive which was due to begin the following week. In the event they managed two more days with their father before returning to duty.

The brothers had been exceptionally close, with a little over two years separating the three of them. They had grown up together, played together, ridden together and gone to school together. They had all chosen the same profession and enjoyed the same interests. They had survived the trauma of their parents' separation and the most devastating war ever known. It was thus inevitable that Bob's death would be felt very deeply by the other two, but it almost certainly drew them together. Dick and Selby, though separated in due course by geography, remained closely attached for the rest of their lives and invariably looked out for each other's interests. Selby did question, not long after Bob's death, whether it was a mistake for the brothers to be in the same regiment and contemplated transferring to the 15th Hussars. Dick was strongly against the move, as was Minnie, and after initially putting off any decision for six months Selby eventually decided to stay put.[3]

In the meantime life went on as before, which meant the brothers' immediate participation in another 'drive', this time covering a huge amount of ground which might have been useful in terms of showing the flag, but did not result in any captures. Immediately it was over they left for England to take the rest of their compassionate leave, with Dick in particular physically and emotionally exhausted. Afterwards he and Selby were both back in England again, for the second most important Army polo competition, the Subaltern's Cup, which they lost narrowly in the final to the 1st Life Guards. Polo dominated that summer, as indeed it did every summer in peacetime, with success by the Subalterns at the Curragh tournament when they beat their own regiment's Seniors in the final.

Dick and Selby were also at Bilton for the polo tournament there, but it ended badly, with them falling out with their father – at the end of September 1921 he wrote, saying that he had finished with them. This was the precursor of some very strange behaviour by Walter which caused great concern in the family over the next year. In March 1922 Dick was called up to London to see his father, who was staying in Dukes' Hotel. Dick wrote in his diary that his father was 'certainly mad at present. He wouldn't come to Bilton with me, he is selling pictures and going to live in Hills' cottage.' Walter's physical health was not much better than his mental, but he relented about returning to Bilton Park, so Dick went down to stay there later in the month, finding him in a very poor state. The servants were all threatening to leave and Walter had banned his longstanding housekeeper, Emma Jakeman, from sleeping in the house, forcing her to lodge in the village.

A month later Walter left England, initially for Pau in France, going on subsequently to Algiers, where he was joined by Jakeman, leaving Dick to pay the large bill incurred for nursing him at Bilton. Walter then sent Jakeman back to let the house. Dick was drafted in after receiving a letter from her saying that his father was penniless in Algiers and he had to drop what he was doing and arrange funds for him. Walter arrived back in early July, somewhat improved mentally and physically and on much better terms with his sons, but by October he was distinctly poorly again and left for Algiers with Jakeman and all his dogs, intending to settle there permanently and, indeed, to become a French citizen.

On 3 November, while Dick was on a course at the Cavalry School at Weedon, Jakeman cabled him to say that Walter was very unwell with 'congestion of the brain'. Three days later he received another telegram, this time from a Doctor Attaix in Clermont Ferrand, to the effect that his father was now in a nursing home there and dangerously ill. Dick set off immediately for London, obtaining a passport there through the good offices of a friend at the Foreign Office, and was on the mailboat that night. By the afternoon of the next day he was in Clermont Ferrand, where his father recognized him, but was unable to speak. On the following day, 8 November, he became progressively weaker and died that evening. With Jakeman's help, Dick arranged for the body to be taken back to England. He then returned there himself via Paris, where he met Selby and his Uncle Richard, who had declined to come down to help him and whom he described as 'an impossible man'. The funeral was held at Bilton on 13 November.

In his will Walter left everything to his sons, after providing for an annuity for Jakeman. His assets were considerable, amounting to over $700,000 in the United States alone, the majority of the amount being the appraised value of his shares in the McCreery Estate Company. Bilton Park was sold some years later.[4] Extraordinarily, it transpired that Minnie was owed no less than $42,500, due to non-payment of her alimony of $500 per month: she subsequently received payments amounting to $19,250 from Walter's executors and the trustees of his residual estate, but under the terms of the 1914 memorandum she had no right to the balance.[5] Fortunately Minnie was in any event very comfortably off, while Dick was now able to receive directly his share of the income from the McCreery Estate Company and Walter's other assets.

In the winter of 1921/22, three events happened, one personal, one sporting and one professional, each of which were to make a marked impression on Dick's life. The first was a decision by his maternal grandmother to sell Greenhill House and to build a new house out in the country. A number of sites were inspected and the one preferred by his grandmother and mother and by Dick himself was in the Somerset countryside at Stowell Hill, near Templecombe, a favourite place for a family picnic. Construction took a long time and cost much more than expected, but at last in October 1923 the two women moved into what was a very fine Arts and Crafts-style house, built of stone and with stunning views to the south, a large garden and a small attached farm. This would be a much loved family home for the rest of Dick's life, occupied by his mother alone after his grandmother's death and then by Dick and his family following his retirement.

The second event was the purchase by Selby on Dick's behalf, at a horse sale at Mullacash, of a 6-year-old bay mare, barely 15.3 hands high, called Annie Darling. She was to be Dick's favourite horse of the very many he owned in his life, going on to become a brood mare after a successful racing career and producing a number of excellent foals. Ridden by Selby, she won the lightweight race in the Blackmore Vale Hunt point-to-point in the spring of 1922 and raced with success at other relatively minor meetings, but she seemed to be capable of much greater things. Dick decided to enter her for the Grand Military Gold Cup at Sandown Park, to be held on 16 March 1923.

There were seven runners in the 3-mile race, of whom the favourite was Clashing Arms, a very strong horse but with a reputation as a hard puller, ridden by Captain R. G. C. Vivian of the Life Guards. By the beginning of the second circuit, Clashing Arms and Annie Darling were a long way ahead of the field and galloping neck and neck, but Vivian was clearly experiencing great difficulty in keeping control of his mount. He himself was tiring rapidly and the horse was not jumping well, eventually swerving violently four fences from the finish and unseating his rider. The only other contender was now Broken Wand, ridden by Colonel Paynter, which made up some ground coming up the hill towards the last fence – but having jumped it successfully Paynter fell off on the flat, leaving Dick the clear winner.

It is impossible to overstate the cachet attaching to the winner of the Grand Military Gold Cup in military circles and especially amongst cavalry regiments – if Dick was not well known before his success, he was now recognized as one of the best riders of his generation in the country. The post-race celebrations involved a lot of champagne, as did the arrival of the cup itself two weeks later at the regiment.

By that time the regiment had returned to England, but before it did Dick had had news of the third important event, which was to shape his professional life for the next few years. In September 1921 Lieutenant Colonel Fane, after a long period in command, had been succeeded by Bill Truman, who was greatly admired by Dick. Truman was a man ahead of his time. With the cavalry finding it difficult to participate in any of the battles on the Western Front, he had managed to get himself posted first to a battalion of the Black Watch and then to the newly formed Royal Tank Corps, in which he commanded a battalion with great distinction. He was not only committed to new ideas about mobile warfare, but thought that every commanding officer should have his own light aeroplane for reconnaissance, so that he could 'see over the hill'. These quite revolutionary notions were to be a considerable influence on Dick's own thinking, although it would be many years before he could put them into practice.

The regard was mutual. Dick himself wrote later: 'One day I was riding over the open heath when [Truman] came up to me and told me that he had selected me to be the next adjutant; I could have been knocked off my horse with a feather, I had never thought of such an appointment for a moment, and I had done none of the courses which were necessary before one could be appointed.'6 Unfortunately, Truman had been severely wounded in the Great War and his health never really recovered, so he was forced to retire soon after the 12th Lancers moved to Tidworth to join 2 Cavalry Brigade in March 1922. With no officers of sufficient seniority in the regiment, he was succeeded by Lieutenant Colonel O. W. Brinton from the 21st Lancers, who nevertheless honoured Truman's decision.

Chapter 6

The Adjutant

Dick's appointment as adjutant took effect formally on 12 December 1921, but it was very nearly a year before he actually took up his duties. In the meantime he had to attend the courses which adjutants were supposed to have passed. The first of these was at the Small Arms School at Hythe, which ran for six weeks in February and March 1922. Formerly the School of Musketry, the purpose of the institution was to teach officers and senior NCOs how to use and maintain a large variety of personal weapons, from pistols to hand grenades.[1] Dick was not expecting to enjoy it, but he found it much more agreeable than he had feared. It was in a decidedly inconvenient place on the Kent coast, at least for Dick, who wanted to get in as much hunting as possible at the end of the season as well as to ride at both Cheltenham and Sandown. To enable these activities and to respond to the occasional crisis in his father's health, there was a great deal of train travel at unsociable hours.

The course at the Cavalry School took much longer, from May to the end of November, shortly after his father had died. For the most part it was at Netheravon House, which included an indoor riding school. This was much more convenient than Hythe, as the 12th Lancers were nearby at Tidworth and Dick could play polo for the regiment to his heart's content through the summer. However, the School moved later in the year from Netheravon to Weedon in Northamptonshire, where it was amalgamated with the Royal Artillery Riding Establishment to become the Army School of Equitation, and Dick spent the last two months of the course there, eventually passing out third of the twenty students. Strictly speaking he should also have passed a course at the School of Signals, but he was excused as Brinton wanted him back.

Dick took up his new duties on 4 December 1922. The one officer in a cavalry regiment in the 1920s who had to work hard was the adjutant and for this he received more pay than others of his rank. As the right-hand man of the commanding officer, he had to run the organization and administration of the regiment other than its logistical requirements, which were handled by the quartermaster. He was particularly concerned with discipline, both in general and as it related to individuals, and for the appearance of the regiment at parades and inspections, any deficiency being ascribed almost entirely to him. There was a great deal of office work on the regimental books and papers, and he was in charge of the drills and instruction of the young officers and recruits and the operation of the regimental riding school. He also had to accompany the commanding officer on a number of formal visits.

It might be thought so many duties would rule out significant leisure activities, but Dick was to demonstrate this need not be the case. While there were fewer occasions on which he was able to go hunting, he was too valuable to be excluded from the regimental polo team, becoming its captain at the end of the 1923 season, during which a team including Dick and Selby won the Subaltern's Cup. He also still found time to ride at race meetings – indeed, he won so frequently in 1924 that he was required by the National Hunt Committee to apply for a permit to ride as an amateur against professional jockeys. Although he had to decline an invitation to train for the 1924 Paris Olympics, he was able to showjump on Fox-Trot, coming second in the King's Cup at Olympia on the same day in 1924 that he won the sword, lance and revolver championship and winning the charger class at the International Horse Show.

It was perhaps small wonder then that, when a new commanding officer was appointed to the 12th Lancers in September 1923, he was advised by the commander of 2 Cavalry Brigade, Bertie Fisher, to change his adjutant quickly as 'he thinks too much about polo and hunting.'[2] Luckily for Dick the new CO, a man of strong character, could be counted on to make up his own mind on such an issue and he and Dick got on exceptionally well from the moment they met. John Blakiston-Houston, known to his friends as Mike and to many others as 'Bloody' Mike due to his frequent use of the epithet when roused, was the second commanding officer in succession to join from another regiment, in his case the 11th Hussars, but even more than his predecessor he identified completely with the 12th Lancers. After Rollie Charrington, he was to be the second mentor in Dick's life and the two men made a formidable team which transformed the regiment into one of the finest of its day.

Houston had no doubts about the professionalism of his subordinate, writing many years later that 'for Dick, his soldiering came first, and he considered it his duty to set an example of thoroughness and tireless devotion to his profession.'[3] This period seems in many ways to have been the making of Dick as a soldier, when he changed from an essentially lighthearted subaltern, more interested in sport than in parades and training schemes, into a consummate military professional. He was still a lieutenant when he began his period of appointment as adjutant and was not promoted to captain until September 1923, but even before then he managed to stamp his authority on those around him. His character fitted well with his new duties. Whilst he had a well developed sense of humour and a wonderful smile, he did not suffer fools gladly and was especially hard on those who had failed to do their homework or could not justify a decision. He had an explosive temper when things did not turn out as he wished and in such circumstances his language could be very ripe, but such outbursts subsided very quickly and he never held a grudge. This aspect of his character was not confined to his professional life. His great friend Willoughby Norrie of the 11th Hussars rode against him frequently and recalled one instance when he beat him by a head in a point-to-point: 'Dick was not exactly polite! This episode was soon forgotten and we were good friends half an hour after the race and discussed it all amicably.'[4]

Houston set out to ensure that his soldiers were occupied every minute of the day. There would be no lounging around in barracks as long as he was in command. Within three weeks of taking over, he had them building a regimental football pitch at Tidworth, he and his adjutant setting an example by taking up spades themselves, and when that was ready he volunteered them to Fisher for the construction of a brigade polo ground. This was followed by the institution of a much more imaginative idea, the 'Bongo Beaker'. After his death at Cambrai in 1917, it was discovered that Lieutenant G. Miller-Brown had left money for a trophy for some kind of regimental competition. His nickname had been Bongo, but the trophy probably owed its full name to its alliterative resonance, as it took the form not of a beaker but of a silver statuette of a mounted lancer. It was awarded every year to the troop which was the best overall in every aspect of military life, from cleanliness and tidiness of the barrack rooms to personal turnout, care of horses and skill at jumping and musketry. Snap inspections took place at frequent opportunities and the effect was to instil a level of keenness and enthusiasm which had hitherto been lacking.

Just one month after his arrival Houston had so galvanized the regiment that Dick was writing in his diary, after seeing his commanding officer's plans for individual training, 'Everyone will be busy here this winter.' Houston read his officers lectures about too much leave and not enough soldiering, followed this up by making it clear that any deficiencies identified by him would have to be addressed immediately and, to the horror of his subordinates, even stopped their prized 'hunting leave' when they failed to make his desired grade. By the middle of May 1924, eight months into Houston's appointment, the Inspector General of Cavalry wrote in his report that the 12th Lancers were the best horsed cavalry regiment that he had ever seen and in September the Earl of Cavan, the Chief of the Imperial General Staff, sent for Houston after an inspection of 2 Cavalry Brigade to compliment him on the regiment's turnout.

Houston's enthusiasm extended to the practical application of military skills, insisting that the regiment should perform to the highest standard on training schemes and on bigger manoeuvres involving other units and formations during their collective training. He never allowed himself a moment's rest and was apt to get very tired after two or three days on horseback. On one occasion he had a bad fall down a rabbit hole and became very confused, Dick noting in his diary that he had been 'an awful nuisance'. Dick told one story about him which also reflected the parsimonious attitude of the War Office at the time.

> Of course the '20s, when I was Mike Houston's adjutant, were very lean years. The total Army Estimates were only about £45,000,000. After every war there is always a long period of retrenchment. This far more than any reactionary attitude by the Cavalry was responsible for the almost total failure to develop tanks between the two world wars. The only sign of mechanization we had in those days was a troop of Austin scout cars, completely unarmoured baby Austins! We not only still had the pre-historic horse, we were also very short of men. On one exercise from Tidworth Mike Houston suddenly got very excited when he thought he saw a whole enemy division deployed on Chute Causeway, a high down a few miles north of Tidworth. Actually the 'division' was a flock of scattered sheep, at this time the infantry was so short of men that many platoons were represented by white flags![5]

As well as being short of men the 12th Lancers was also deficient in officers, as two successive commanding officers posted in from outside had demonstrated. These years were to see the admission of a number of new subalterns from Sandhurst, who would become the regimental and brigade commanders of the next war, but there was still a shortage of troop and squadron commanders and a number transferred into the regiment from elsewhere. They included Herbert Lumsden and Hugh Russell, both captains of about Dick's age who joined from the Royal Horse Artillery in 1925 and became, especially Lumsden, his close friends.

At about this time evidence began to emerge of a new passion in Dick's life. He took a great interest in the garden at Stowell, which had been transformed from an open field by his grandmother and mother and to which he made a significant contribution even before he lived there permanently. It was at Tidworth, however, and at all the subsequent barracks in which he was stationed during peacetime, that Dick turned the area occupied by the 12th Lancers into a symphony of lawns, shrubberies and especially flower beds. Although he could order fatigue parties to do some of the work, he himself loved to put in bulbs in the autumn and plant out annuals in the summer and, according to his friend and brother officer, Frank Spicer, woe betide anyone who interrupted him whilst he was watering the roses! The regiment won the Garrison Garden Cup two years running and there were many who said that Dick had achieved this feat single-handed.

The pressure under which Dick was now working required him to maintain a very high level of physical fitness. This was not always easy, not just for the lack of available time, but also because he was subject to a number of minor setbacks in his health, notably with his teeth which, typically of a time when diet was less well controlled and water not fluoridized, kept requiring treatment, and with blocked sinuses, which required an operation. His solution was walking. For a man who only had three toes on one of his feet, each missing a joint, and whose doctors had once thought he would never be able to walk properly again, he managed to cover great distances in a very short time, often accompanied by his dog Jeannie, given to him before the regiment left Ireland. On one occasion he walked to Amesbury and back, some 16 miles, after tea early one February, and only a week later walked the 12 miles to Netheravon and back to see a friend at the Machine Gun School.

Another longstanding enthusiasm of Dick's was for cars and in the mid-1920s he owned an American model, a Buick. Not unusually for the time, the vehicle was not completely reliable, punctures and a tendency to boil over being the most frequent problems. Often accompanied by his soldier servant Eldred,[6] who was able to develop some skill with the internal combustion engine as well as with horses, Dick was a good but very fast driver. In order to get to all his engagements he very often had to cover significant distances in a short period of time. An extreme example of this came in early January 1925, while he was staying at Yelvertoft in Northamptonshire to hunt with the Pytchley, but considered it his duty to attend the sergeants' mess dinner at Tidworth. Having hunted for much of the day he set out at 4.35 in the afternoon, encountering floods on the way but arriving at the dinner at 7.40. He eventually took his leave at 1.30 the following morning, arriving back at Yelvertoft at 4.15 am in time for another full day's hunting, a journey which demonstrated his commitment both to his regiment, earning the approval of the commanding officer and the sergeants, and to his sport. He did have his share of minor accidents and was absolutely mortified when he hit a young girl who ran out in front of the car in Ludgershall, but she proved to be only suffering from cuts and bruises and he was relieved to hear of her full recovery in due course.

In September 1924, Dick's three-year appointment was extended for a further year, emphasizing the regard in which he was held by Houston. In spite of his duties remaining undiminished, he was able to continue with his sport and in the summer of 1925 he was chosen, with Selby, for the British Army polo team to meet the visiting American Army team. Unlike Dick, Selby had focused on polo to the exclusion of other equestrian activities and was the better player, with a handicap of 6 against Dick's 5. He had been the fifth man in the British Army team which had visited the United States in the summer of 1923 and which had unexpectedly lost both its matches.

Although the British were keen to avenge this defeat, the same thing now happened again, the home side first losing 8–4 in a game in which Dick felt that he and Selby had both played badly, and then 6–4 in a very good and close game. The general opinion was that the Americans were better players overall and had also been better mounted.

The period of Dick's appointment as adjutant drew to a close in the autumn of 1925, Dick receiving a letter from the colonel of the regiment, Field Marshal Lord Birdwood, at that time Commander-in-Chief in India, thanking him for his excellent work. He had something else to look forward to, as the regiment had been warned that it was to go to Egypt in the New Year to relieve the 16th Lancers. Dick was very keen to accompany it, even turning down the offer of a good job at Sandhurst to begin in a year's time, as he preferred to be abroad for a longer period. Houston decided that he should now command the HQ Squadron, to which end he was sent on a two-month course at the Machine Gun School at Netheravon, as his squadron would include the regiment's machine gunners. In early December, to Dick's great disappointment, Houston told him that the 12th Lancers were now unlikely to go to Egypt, but would instead move rather more prosaically to Hounslow.

Though Dick had been a good soldier before his appointment as adjutant, he had blossomed under Houston and learnt a great deal from him. Houston had been a brilliant logistics officer in one of the cavalry divisions in the Great War and was also a master of minor tactics, although Dick felt that he was not measured enough to rise to high command in the field. Houston, for his part, had been immensely impressed with Dick's work and, very unusually for someone of his rank and position, put him in for an OBE. This was thought by the relevant authority to be too high an honour for so junior an officer, so Houston resubmitted a recommendation for an MBE, which was duly gazetted on 2 July 1926. It was the recommendation for the OBE, however, which expressed Houston's opinion most clearly:

This officer has just completed his period as Adjutant, and in my opinion has rendered very valuable service to the Army as a whole by his magnificent example in his zeal for work and his devotion to duty in every way.

He has ably demonstrated how sport of the right and healthy sort can be combined with work. He played in the Army Polo Team against America last year and in no way allowed this to interfere with his duties.

He has just completed a Machine Gun Course at Netheravon where he got a 'distinguished' and Colonel Jackson, Commanding M. G. School, writes:- 'This is the best course I have had since I have been at the School and is largely due to McCreery's very fine example.'

Chapter 7

Lettice

The 12th Lancers left Tidworth for Hounslow on a very wet day in February 1926, Dick having just received a complimentary letter from Fisher, the Brigade Commander, who had evidently revised his opinion about his fitness as adjutant. The barracks at Hounslow were old and dilapidated and HQ Squadron went into tents at first, as the buildings allotted to it were initially unfit for habitation. The other ranks were on the whole pleased to be there, with the delights of London close at hand. For his part Dick took his new responsibilities very seriously, giving lectures to the machine gunners and the signallers and taking them out on exercises, but he also continued with a full sporting programme. He rode again in the Grand Military Gold Cup, but the 1926 winner was Lumsden, whilst Dick himself came off when Annie Darling shied at a fallen jockey four fences from home.

Dick decided to take part of his annual leave in Ireland that May, timing it to coincide with the Irish National Hunt meeting at Punchestown. Just as he was due to travel, the General Strike was called by the Trades Union Congress and the regiment was put on full standby to take whatever action might be necessary to keep essential services going and prevent civil disturbance. All leave was stopped and the men were confined to barracks, with one troop placed on half an hour's notice. To Dick's relief he was then given permission to take his leave, enjoying enormously his first trip back to Ireland since the regiment had left the country four years earlier, even though he was only there as a spectator. Shortly after his return the strike was called off. The regiment had not been involved, much to Houston's disappointment, his restlessness whilst it was taking place infuriating Dick's successor as adjutant, Alex McBean.

The latitude shown to him by Houston over his leave may have had an impact on how he behaved to others. In general he was developing a reputation as a keen disciplinarian who did not tolerate disobedience, but he could also be very human. One day a very junior subaltern in his squadron, Kenneth 'Kate' Savill, who would later admit that Dick made him quake much of the time, requested permission to go to London for lunch and was told emphatically no. As Savill had already asked a girl to join him at the Cavalry Club and could not afford to let her down, he took a chance on not being found out. Unfortunately the lift at the club was broken, so Savill was compelled to use the stairs on his way out and, to his horror, whom should he see at the bottom but his squadron commander! Dick smiled and never said a word, then or later.

At the end of the summer, the War Office once again changed its mind and ordered the regiment to prepare for Egypt in December. Dick was not to accompany them, at least initially, as he had been selected as a candidate for the Staff College and needed to attend a course of preparatory lectures in London and at much the same time to take his promotion exams, which were held at Woolwich. The latter were passed with a good overall score of 70 per cent and a top score of 80 per cent in military law. The Staff College exams, not held until the end of February 1927, promised to be much more challenging, but in the event Dick found them easier than he had expected. Unfortunately so did all the other candidates, which concerned him greatly. 'I can only hope and pray for the best', he wrote in his diary, 'but shall be v. disappointed if I haven't qualified.'

In the meantime he had to rejoin the regiment and on 7 March his mother saw him off at Croydon by aeroplane. After a very bumpy crossing to Le Bourget, on which he came close to being sick, he caught the overnight train to Marseilles, where he boarded the new Messageries Maritimes ship, the *Champollion*, bound for Alexandria. On his arrival there the local Thomas Cook office supervised his transfer on to a train for Cairo, where he was met by a welcoming party of Lieutenant Colonel and Mrs Houston, accompanied by Eldred and the mess car.

Egypt had been occupied by the British since 1882 and had become a protectorate in 1914, providing a secure base for operations against the Turks in Palestine, Trans-Jordan and Syria during the Great War. In 1922 the country became notionally independent, but defence and the protection of foreign interests remained the responsibility of the British Government, which still kept a large body of troops in the country. The majority of these were to be found in three formations, the Canal Brigade, responsible for and mostly located along the Suez Canal, the Cairo Brigade, based in the capital but with one battalion in Alexandria, and the Cavalry Brigade, also in and around Cairo. The other components of the Cavalry Brigade were the 3rd and the 15th/19th Hussars.

The barracks into which the regiment moved at Helmieh were even worse than Hounslow, with poor huts, potholed roads and no facilities for sport. Houston responded immediately to the challenge and set his men to transforming the place, refurbishing the huts, mending the roads and building tennis courts, a football pitch and a hockey ground. When Dick arrived he was immediately placed in charge of creating the gardens. Polo, played during the winter months, was still taking place, but the regiment's ponies had not arrived in good condition after their sea voyage and it was to be some time before the 12th Lancers were able to compete on even terms with the best.

Dick's main concern was to bring HQ Squadron back to the high level of efficiency in which he had left it, as he felt that his second-in-command had let standards slip, in spite of the fact that one of his machine-gun troops and the signals troop were lying in first and second place in the Bongo Beaker. He instituted parades for the machine gunners and signallers from 0630 to 0815 hrs every morning, which he thought would give the officers and men a good appetite for breakfast, and stepped up the training schemes. Having worked hard to recover lost ground, he was sorry to have to hand over the squadron to Lumsden, taking command of B Squadron instead.

Entry to the Staff College occupied a great deal of Dick's thoughts during his first four months in Egypt. For an officer with any ambition to higher command, attending and passing the two-year course was a vital step in his career, whilst failing to enter would probably condemn him to a ceiling of lieutenant colonel at best. In June he learnt that a lieutenant in the Royal Irish Fusiliers in the Cairo Brigade, Gerald Templer, had heard unofficially that he had passed into the college, causing Dick to worry even more. He was delighted to receive a telegram a few days later from his mother to say that he had qualified, as had Lumsden and Russell, but his 5,766 marks[1] were not enough for automatic entry and he still needed the all important nomination. With places limited for the cavalry, news that Claude Nicholson of the 16th/5th Lancers had secured one of them seemed to him to have lessened his chances. It was therefore with huge relief, nearly a month later, that he received another telegram from Minnie to tell him that he had got into the next course, due to begin in January 1928.[2] It had been announced by this time that Houston would be returning to Tidworth to take command of 2 Cavalry Brigade, so it was Charrington, his successor, who told Dick that he could depart from Egypt by the beginning of November, in order to take leave before the course began. To make his happiness complete, Dick was promoted to major on 6 September.

Dick's youngest brother Jack, who had recently left Oxford, arrived that September to stay with him for the remaining weeks of his posting and to travel round Egypt seeing the sights. Unfortunately his visit coincided with a virus which swept though the regiment, a high fever that brought down both brothers, almost all the officers, and many of the men. Dick was out of hospital in a few days, but Jack was incapacitated for nearly two weeks, ruining his plans. The two of them instead took a fortnight in Alexandria to recuperate, the sea air and plenty of sailing restoring them to health. At the end of October Dick handed over B Squadron and gave a dinner for all the officers in the mess. 'I shall miss everyone enormously', he wrote in his diary, 'and I do hope they write to me sometimes.' He had served continuously in the regiment for nearly twelve years and it had become his home, but he was now to take a significant step forward which would lead him in new directions.

Dick and Jack sailed from Alexandria in the venerable old P&O liner *Kaiser-i-Hind*, disembarking in Marseilles and travelling back to England on the P&O special train and then by ferry from Boulogne, the first time that Dick had been there since 1919. With more than two months ahead before he was required to start at the Staff College, Dick had two priorities for his leave. The immediate one was to buy a car and his choice was a model from the Star Motor Company,[3] for which he paid the princely sum of £325. The second was to get in as much hunting as possible before the course began in late January.

Three days after arriving back in the country, Dick spent a day with the Blackmore Vale, during which he encountered Lettice St Maur. This was not their first meeting, indeed they had spent some time together at the end of the previous season shortly before Dick went to Egypt. They had a common interest in riding and in particular in hunting and Dick had ridden Lettice's horse, Bron, in the Blackmore Vale point-to-point only two days before he left to rejoin the regiment. When he heard subsequently that she had won the Ladies' Race on Bron in the South-West Wiltshire point-to-point, he had cabled his congratulations and followed up with a letter, a brief correspondence ensuing between the two of them, entirely devoted to equestrian matters.

Lettice was born in 1902 to Lord Percy St Maur,[4] a younger son of the 14th Duke of Somerset, and his wife, Violet White, the daughter of the 2nd Lord Annaly, and she grew up at Maiden Bradley, the seat of the Somersets. Both her parents had died, her father when she was very young, her mother only while Dick was away in Egypt. She had two sisters, Helen, born in 1900, and Lucia, born in 1906, and the three of them had at one time gained something of a reputation for high spiritedness, being known in society collectively as 'Hell Let Loose'. Helen had been married since 1924 to Major George Gosling, 'Squeaker' to friends and family, who had served in the Army during the Great War and won the Military Cross. They already had three children and lived in a large house near Bicester, Stratton Audley Park. Lucia was still single and very close to Lettice. Their mother had rented Horsington Manor, near Stowell Hill, since 1925 and the two girls were still there, enjoying the season's hunting with the Blackmore Vale. Lettice in particular was a most accomplished horsewoman.

Before Dick's departure for Egypt and during his stay there, he and Lettice had been no more than friends with a common interest in riding, but very quickly something more significant began to blossom. This was not, however, the first time that Dick had been attracted to a member of the opposite sex. Shortly before the regiment left Ireland in 1922 he had been briefly infatuated with a young woman called Betty Malcolm. Although she came over to England from time to time, he was initially away at the Small Arms School and then the Cavalry School and was able to see her only infrequently. That November she became engaged to Henry Somerset, a cousin of the Duke of Beaufort, and they were married in the following month. She and Dick remained good friends, however.

Then at the Blackmore Vale Ball in January 1926 Dick had met Veronica Morley, who was only 17 at the time, and was much taken with her. They spent some time together and he met her parents, who lived at Biddestone Manor in Wiltshire, and subsequently escorted her to a number of social occasions. She was not a good correspondent and it was well over a month after he had arrived in Egypt that he first received a letter from her, a possible indication that the relationship was not as close as he thought. It may therefore have been no great surprise that during the summer, as he was waiting for news of his entry to the Staff College, he heard she had become engaged to a subaltern in the 11th Hussars. He was thus to some extent on the rebound when he arrived back in England.

Throughout November and December Dick and Lettice were in each other's company almost daily, sometimes alone and sometimes with either or both of Jack and Lucia. Dick also introduced her to his mother and grandmother. Lettice was a woman of very determined character, as was Minnie, and they did not always see eye to eye. On 8 December, having just driven over to Camberley to have a look at the Staff College, Dick wrote in his diary: 'A terrible row over Lettice whom I simply adore.' The circumstances can only be guessed at, but two days later he wrote again: 'Mother and I have made it up, but I am very sore over it & worried & told Lettice out hunting today, she was terribly nice about it, & I hope that I may have a chance.' By the following week Lettice was dining at Stowell Hill and all seemed to be well again. She went off with Lucia to spend Christmas with the Goslings at Stratton Audley, but was back in time for the New Year festivities.

On 5 January 1928, following a successful day's hunting, Dick proposed to Lettice. 'When nearly home,' he wrote in his diary, 'I asked Lettice to marry me, she said why didn't you say something weeks ago! I am <u>terribly</u> happy.' Not wasting any time, the following day they went up to London and selected an emerald engagement ring at Cartier, following which Dick was progressively introduced to her family, notably her much loved Aunt Dora (Lady Ernest St Maur) and the Duke of Somerset and his immediate family at their house at Maiden Bradley. The engagement was formally announced on 9 January.

officers of the 12th Lancers, including Victor Cartwright and Alex McBean, and Nicholson and MacMillan from the Staff College. The evening started with drinks and an early dinner at the Berkeley, followed by the C. B. Cochran/Noel Coward revue This Year of Grace at the London Pavilion. Barron had then laid on a late supper at the Savoy, to spice up which he had recruited a number of young ladies from the revue. Ogilvy maintained subsequently that Dick had not enjoyed the last episode of the evening one bit, but Dick himself said in his diary that it went very well and that he retired to bed at 3.00 in the morning. He was still hung over on the morning of the wedding more than a day later!

Dick and Lettice were married at 2.15 in the afternoon of 18 April at St Mark's, North Audley Street. Dick had recovered from his headache and Lettice looked, according to him, like 'a lovely dream'. She was given away by her brother-in-law, George Gosling, Selby was the best man and the reception was held at 180 Queen's Gate, the home of close family friends of the St Maurs, the Makins, where there was barely room for all the guests. The newlyweds got away shortly afterwards to catch the boat train to Folkestone on the first stage of their honeymoon, their destination being Lake Como, where Dick's Uncle Richard and Aunt May had made the Castello di Urio available to them.

The ten days on Lake Como were spent quietly, walking and visiting the local sights, after which they moved on to Venice, staying at the Danieli, which Dick thought both noisy and rather expensive. After a few days of culture, including the opera, and gondola trips, they returned by the Orient Express, arriving back on 6 May. A week later they moved into Brownhill, two days before the Staff College reassembled. The subsequent combination of hard work and long hours, not helped by hound exercise (which Lettice much resented), made Dick very tired, especially as he was now playing polo again and spending such time as he could improving the garden.

Two days before the end of the summer term in late July, Lettice announced that she was expecting a child. Michael was born early on the morning of 5 February 1929. Dick's mother and grandmother and Lettice's sister Lucia motored up immediately to see the baby and Minnie managed to upset Lettice by her comments on the choice of name, but in all other respects the family were very happy. However, as a new member of the family arrived, another was shortly to depart. Dick's beloved grandmother, Frances McAdam, fell ill about a month after Michael's birth with a kidney infection. Her condition deteriorated and she died on 12 May at the age of 82. Although Dick was deeply saddened, Minnie was the most affected, as she had lived with her mother since her separation from Walter in 1909. The two women had been very close, running the hospital at Greenhill House together during the Great War and then creating an entirely new home at

Stowell Hill, where Minnie continued to live until her own death sixteen years later.

Dick's second year at Staff College was in many ways a repetition of the first, though unlike his contemporary John Harding he never suggested that it was a waste of time. The students went further afield than before, Dick going with a small party to visit the battlefields of Flanders and Picardy, taking part in a North-West Frontier exercise in Snowdonia and spending a few days in and around Portsmouth aimed at familiarizing the Staff College students with the Royal Navy. He rode Dash o' White again in the Grand Military Gold Cup, although the handicapping weight proved too much for the horse, which came in a distant ninth out of seventeen starters. Dick had much more success on Wavering Down, a horse belonging to Herbert Lumsden, which he rode to victory in the Staff College Lightweight Race, the Army Point-to-Point and the Aldershot Open Cup. Annie Darling by this time had been put out to stud, beginning a new equine career in which she foaled a number of outstanding horses.

Dick's final term at Camberley was substantially concerned with combined operations, with him leading a large syndicate which from time to time included visiting officers from the Royal Navy and the RAF. He was mortified when Henry Curtis, the member of the directing staff concerned, said that his plan was a poor one, feeling his syndicate had received misleading guidance, but at the end of the course the Commandant, Major General C. W. Gwynn, told the division that they had all done exceptionally well.

Dick had enjoyed the Staff College and what he learnt there certainly informed his military thinking. There are some hints of this in his notes on military history. He admired Robert E. Lee's use of cavalry for information and communication during the American Civil War and felt that in future the cavalry arm should be primarily trained for close reconnaissance, a role which was easily transferable to the armoured car. He thought Lee and Stonewall Jackson were the two greatest Civil War commanders, 'Both always *thinking* war, studying, reading history.'[3] Of Napoleon's marshals he rated Davout the best: 'Ney brilliant with definite orders and under Nap himself, but timid and useless when holding an independent command. Davout never beaten, brilliant at Jena, the chief share of the military victory due to him, a good disciplinarian and the only well-bred one of the lot!'[4]

The contacts Dick made at Camberley were to prove invaluable to his career, especially during the Second World War. He made some very good friends, notably Harding and Templer, the three of them unquestionably numbering among the finest soldiers of their generation. His quality was already apparent to his contemporaries, although there was one discordant note. 'Chink' Dorman-Smith, one of the cleverest officers of the year above, but in many ways something of a maverick, formed a low opinion of him, dubbing him 'Dreary McCreery'. Many years later, their respective roles would bring them into conflict and it was Dick who would come out on top.

Dick had known for many months before he left the Staff College to what job he would be going and it was one of the best available. The fear of many graduates was that they would be in a junior position pushing pens at the War Office or at one of the Home Commands, but Dick had been personally selected by Houston to become brigade major of 2 Cavalry Brigade at Tidworth, the chief staff officer of a formation, even if it was a small one.[5] Having served as adjutant of one of its then constituent units some years earlier, this was something he could take to like a duck to water. Moreover, he had already familiarized himself with the brigade, spending a week of his summer leave there. It was even more attractive in that it was an independent formation rather than part of a larger division, under the direct control of Southern Command. After a break over Christmas and the New Year, spent largely with Lettice's sister Helen at Stratton Audley and hunting with the Bicester, Dick arrived in Tidworth on 11 January 1930. Lettice, Michael and the nurse followed to take up residence at their new home, Muir House.

Dick was at 2 Cavalry Brigade for nearly four years, initially under Houston and, from October 1931, under Brigadier F. B. 'John' Hurndall, who also became a good friend. The constituent units of the brigade were the 1st King's Dragoon Guards, the Queen's Bays (2nd Dragoon Guards) and the Royal Scots Greys (2nd Dragoons), all regiments with which Dick would be associated in his future career. This was a frustrating time for the British Army, with stringent budgets resulting in a lack of investment in new equipment, mechanization taking place at a snail's pace (the KDG were not to lose their horses until 1935, the Bays in 1937 and the Greys in 1941, the last regular cavalry regiment to use them in action), a progressive reduction in headcount and even limitations on training. In the autumn of 1931 for instance, it was announced that for the following year there would be none of the traditional yeomanry training camps with which the regular cavalry were always involved as trainers and mentors, and nothing higher than brigade exercises for the regulars themselves. Against this background the years took on a familiar pattern, with troop and regimental training in the spring and summer, followed by brigade training each September. Dick had also to accompany the brigade commander on 'staff rides' and war games, specific training exercises for commanders and their staff officers.

There was an important addition to the staff of 2 Cavalry Brigade in March 1931 with the arrival as staff captain of His Royal Highness Prince Henry, Duke of Gloucester, third son of the king. The staff captain was the right-hand man of the brigade major, responsible for the administrative side of the staff work. The duke was to work closely with Dick and they became good friends, although on the first occasion he came to drinks with the McCreerys he somewhat outstayed his welcome, remaining unexpectedly for dinner. Prince Henry had served as a regular soldier for a number of years in the 10th Hussars.

Dick's duties meant that there was less time for racing and polo, although neither went completely by the board. He was appointed to the Grand Military Race Committee, which was charged with organizing the annual meeting at Sandown Park and was a member on and off for most of the rest of his life. He rode at the meeting himself every year except 1932, when he was ill, coming in fourth on Hikari in the Grand Military Handicap in 1930 and riding Canute in the Gold Cup in both 1931 and 1933, finishing runner-up on the latter occasion. There was one new racing-related project which he pursued with great enthusiasm, the construction of a new race track at Windmill Hill, just outside Tidworth.[6] He and Willoughby Norrie, now commanding the 11th Hussars which was attached to 2 Cavalry Brigade as an extra regiment, worked on the course themselves with a number of volunteers. The first meeting was held on 4 March 1931 when Dick was beaten by Norrie by a short head in the heavyweight race, possibly the occasion on which Norrie remembered Dick's ripe language! They had by this time attracted 420 members and the course took a sizeable sum for entrance.

On the family side Lettice gave birth to their second son, Robert James, always known as Bob, on 10 November 1930. Otherwise the years fell into a pattern, with Christmas and the New Year spent at a combination of Stowell with Minnie and Stratton Audley with the Goslings, whilst Lettice used to go to Littlehampton for a beach holiday in the summer, a part of the world which she knew well as her mother had lived there before moving to Horsington. It was also conveniently close to old friends of her family, Bernard Fitzalan-Howard, the Duke of Norfolk, and his sister Rachel at Arundel Castle.

Just as Frances McAdam's death had followed Michael's birth, so now there was another death in the family, this time from a completely unexpected quarter. On 19 February 1931, Dick received the awful news that Jack had gone under a train at Euston station, dying later in hospital. Jack had been quite unlike his three brothers, with no ambition to pursue a military career and only a modest interest in hunting. His childhood had perhaps been more difficult than theirs as he had been still at home during the period of Minnie and Walter's separation and likely to have been more affected: he had even been made a Ward of Court at one point. He did not have the same relationship with his father that his three older brothers had enjoyed and, possibly because she was more remote from the battle between his parents, had become more closely attached to his grandmother than his mother, indeed a photo of the former was the only one he displayed when at Eton. He had doubtless been greatly affected by her death, but he had not supported Minnie at all during her last weeks, much to Dick's disappointment.

After leaving Oxford, Jack had become a playwright. As gainful employment at the same time he became private secretary to a man called Victor Hawker, with whom he had formed an emotional attachment which went a long way beyond the normal relationship with an employer, although Hawker was married with three children. Jack's first play, The Force of Circumstance, was put on at the Grafton Theatre early in 1931. A post-Chekhovian study of family life in Victorian England, it received good, if not ecstatic notices from the critics.

Then on 15 February 1931 Hawker died following a terrible motor accident, with Jack at his bedside. Jack went down to Tidworth immediately afterwards to stay with Dick and Lettice for a night, 'v.tired & broken' according to Dick's diary, but he returned to London on the following day, accompanied by Da to keep an eye on him, especially as he had taken to drinking too much. Dick and Lettice went to see the play on the day after that and enjoyed it, whilst Jack seemed more cheerful. Other friends rallied round, but it was not enough to save him. Dick, deeply upset, gave evidence at the inquest, the coroner returning a verdict of 'suicide while temporarily of unsound mind'. Minnie was in California visiting Selby and was unable to attend the funeral.

In 1929 Selby had decided to resign his commission and emigrate to California, where he worked for the McCreery Estate Company. At the end of 1932 Dick and Lettice, together with Rachel Fitzalan-Howard, set off to visit him. They left Southampton on a German ship, the TS *Bremen*, on 9 December and arrived in New York via Cherbourg five days later. After 24 hours in the city, having visited the top of the Empire State Building and the Cotton Club in Harlem, they took the train to Washington, to attend a diplomatic reception in the White House. They then travelled on to Chicago, where there was eight inches of snow, and on to the warmer climate of New Mexico to visit the Grand Canyon. On the evening of 23 December they arrived at Oakland, where Selby met them and took them across the bay on the ferry.

Most of the rest of their visit was spent in California, being regally entertained by Selby and by Uncle Richard and Aunt May at their estate at Hillsborough. Selby took Dick round San Francisco, showing him many of the buildings on which the McCreery Estate Company had mortgages, although with the Great Depression having entered its fourth year many of them were worth less than the loans for which they were the security. After a few days skiing in Yosemite, they left for Southern California, where they saw all the sights, including the Chinese Theatre and the RKO studios in Hollywood. The intention was to visit the McCreery Ranch on the way back north, but floods had made it inaccessible, much to their disappointment. On 30 September Selby saw them off by train to Omaha, Chicago and New York, whence they sailed in the SS *Aquitania*, arriving back in Southampton on 10 February 1933. Just over three months after their return, Selby himself was married in California to Josephine Grant, a member of a prominent and wealthy old San Francisco family. He and Jo paid a return trip to Europe as part of their honeymoon, entertained in London and at Stowell by Dick and Lettice.

Dick's appointment as brigade major came to an end in October 1933 and it was time for him to return to some regimental soldiering. The 12th Lancers were still in Egypt, so on 13 November Dick and Lettice, with the two children, their nanny and a draft of 48 new recruits for the regiment, embarked on the TS *Nevasa* for the voyage to Alexandria.

Chapter 9

The Colonel

Dick had been away from the 12th Lancers for six years, during which time the regiment had been through the enormous changes demanded by mechanization. The conversion had begun in May 1928, when B Squadron lost its horses and commenced training with the 3rd Armoured Car Company of the Royal Tanks Corps. On 1 January 1929 the squadron took over the armoured cars on which it had learnt, Rolls Royces of the 1920 and 1924 patterns with the Vickers .303 machine gun as their sole armament. These were mechanically very reliable, and once fitted with sand-tyres specially developed by the regiment they proved highly desert-worthy. The last of the horses, apart from the officers' chargers, went at the end of 1929, replaced by the Rolls Royces, augmented in a few troops by the slower and less reliable Crossleys. Now the regiment was fully mechanized, although it still needed nine months before all squadrons were fully trained. Apart from some lorries, none of the vehicles had wireless sets, communication taking place by semaphore.

In September 1931 Charrington had handed over command to Paul Hornby, the last commanding officer to have served in the regiment before the Great War.[1] Hornby had spent twelve years away from the regiment, in the Somaliland Camel Corps and the Egyptian Expeditionary Force during the Great War and then back to Somaliland and the Sudan Defence Force, before returning in 1926. Dick had hardly had time to get to know him before leaving for Staff College, so there was initially none of the close relationship which he had formed with his two predecessors, although they subsequently got on very well and Dick particularly admired Hornby as a trainer of men. On his arrival at Helmieh, on 26 November 1933, he was immediately appointed to the command of A Squadron and at 0545 hrs on the very next morning set off on a three-day reconnaissance of the roads in the Nile Delta, bivouacking at night. The winter months were ideal for training schemes of all sorts, the focus being on reconnaissance, both in the Nile Valley and further out in the desert, where it was clear that armoured cars were of much greater military value than horses, and on building road blocks, protecting convoys and cooperating with the RAF – all functions which would take on great significance when war came. Dick himself had to learn not only to drive the vehicles but to act as the gunner.

Lettice disembarked in Egypt already many months pregnant and on 24 February 1934 their third son, Jonathan, was born at the Anglo–American Hospital. Some weeks beforehand Minnie and Lucia arrived to help Lettice after the birth, the two of them also taking advantage of their visit to see something of the country. Dick took his mother up the Nile for a few days to Karnak, Luxor and the Valley of the Kings and Lucia went on an expedition with a number of friends to St Catherine's Monastery in Sinai. Minnie later travelled up to Palestine and Syria, where Dick joined her briefly to visit Damascus, Baalbek and Beirut, before breaking away to take part in staff exercises in Palestine.

In May Dick and Lettice went home on leave, but he was back in Egypt by the end of July, Lettice joining him later without the children, who remained at Stowell with their grandmother. Lettice had a friend with her, Bryony Johnson, and the three of them took a week in Palestine and Trans-Jordan, where they visited Petra. At the end of November the 12th Lancers' long stay in Egypt came to an end when they were relieved by the 11th Hussars, who took over their armoured cars.

To complete the exchange, on their arrival at Tidworth the 12th Lancers took over the 11th Hussars' former barracks and their armoured cars, which in this case were Lanchesters. These had six wheels instead of four, which gave them good cross-country performance in the softer conditions of England, and they mounted three machine guns, including one .50 calibre. However, although generally robust and better armoured than the Rolls Royces, they proved to be unsuitable for one of the key functions of an armoured car regiment, reconnaissance – they were too big to turn round on narrow roads. In an attempt to remedy this deficiency a rear driving position was installed, but it made the vehicle very unwieldy.

In January 1935 Dick began a ten-week course at the Senior Officers' School in Sheerness, a 'hideous place' according to his diary. The SOS had one very important function, to prepare majors for command of a battalion or regiment, in which it was largely successful. It also attempted to provide them with a common military doctrine, but in this it was markedly less effective. The school ran a pack of beagles, which provided some good exercise over the featureless country of the Isle of Sheppey, intersected by its numerous ditches, but Dick took every opportunity to get away for some proper hunting at the weekends.

Whilst Dick was at Sheerness, he heard that he was to get command of the 12th Lancers in succession to Hornby in the coming September. His immediate reaction was to feel sorry for the only other candidate, Cuthbert Rawnsley. Rawnsley had joined the regiment two years before Dick, was senior to him on the Army List and had had a good regimental career, but Dick's quality made him the obvious choice. He certainly had the support of

Birdwood, as well as that of Mike Houston, who had recently been promoted to major general and appointed Inspector of Cavalry at the War Office, which brought him into regular contact with the 12th Lancers (still considered to be cavalry in spite of having lost their horses).

Dick formally took command on 7 September. He and Lettice moved into Candahar House in Tidworth just in time for him to begin planting bulbs for the following spring. Lettice was in her element as the wife of the commanding officer and over the next few years – and indeed even after Dick left the regiment – would remain very closely involved with its affairs. She was instinctively interested in people of all ages, took the trouble to get to know about them and their families and kept in touch after they had moved out of her direct orbit. She was a natural enthusiast and a great organizer, so her new role played very much to her strengths. Within a month of Dick taking command she had formed a Wives' Club which arranged concerts, lectures, jumble sales and even a 'husbands' night', the success of which was only marred by the beer running out. Many generations of 12th Lancers and their wives looked up to her and considered her their friend, notwithstanding the increasingly elevated rank of her husband.

For Dick the appointment came at a good time, just as the regiment moved into its autumn programme of manoeuvres. His first such exercise in command resulted in a letter of thanks from Sir Cyril Deverell, then GOC-in-C (General Officer Commanding in Chief) of Eastern Command and destined to become Chief of the Imperial General Staf (CIGS) within the year, so he was already coming to the notice of some of the key people in the Army. Mechanization was still a matter of considerable debate and Dick attended a conference at Aldershot at which Sir Archibald Montgomery-Massingberd, Deverell's predecessor as CIGS, spoke on the subject, saying that conversion to armour would now come fast for the cavalry. Dick never questioned the argument in favour of mechanization and he spent much time improving the regiment's handling of its armoured cars and looking at new equipment. The deficiencies of the Lanchester meant that alternatives were already being considered and Dick went to the Morris factory to drive a prototype of the company's new armoured car, being favourably impressed by its speed and handiness, a complete contrast to the lumbering Lanchester. (It had its own deficiencies, however, which would become apparent once it was in full use.)

The end of November brought with it a major surprise: the 12th Lancers, less one squadron, would be returning to Egypt at the end of the year. This development arose as a result of increasing tensions with Italy, which had invaded Abyssinia at the beginning of the preceding month. The League of Nations condemned the invasion, but its sanctions against the aggressor were already proving futile, whilst the secret Hoare–Laval Pact, put together by Britain and France to attempt to buy off Italy with the annexation of part of Abyssinia, would before the end of the year be cast aside due to adverse public opinion. In the meantime, there was a serious concern that Italy would seek to expand its African empire by moving against Egypt from Libya, where its local garrison had been significantly increased. At the same time, trouble was brewing between the Arabs and the Jews in Palestine. There appeared to be no alternative to the War Office augmenting its establishment in the Middle East, at least on a temporary basis, and the 12th Lancers knew the territory well, so were an obvious choice to include among the reinforcements.

Immediately putting aside the normal pattern of peacetime soldiering in the UK, Dick had a busy month bringing the regimental HQ and the squadrons destined for Egypt up to their full complement, deciding on which officers would remain behind at Tidworth, attending a long briefing at the War Office with his adjutant, Frank Arkwright, and re-equipping according to the appropriate tables for active service. The 11th Hussars were still in Egypt, so there were no spare armoured cars there and the 12th Lancers had to supply their own, which were duly prepared for shipping. On the last day of the year the regiment embarked from Southampton on the TSS *Vandyck*, a fine modern liner specially chartered for the voyage and much more luxurious than the usual troopships. They were seen off by the wives, who were not permitted to accompany them on what was seen as a temporary move.

After an unprecedentedly comfortable voyage, the troops disembarked at Alexandria on 10 January 1936 and entrained for Cairo, where they moved into their old camp at Helmieh. This was the home of the 11th Hussars, but that regiment had already moved to the Western Desert, leaving only a caretaker party behind. On 26 January C Squadron moved up to Mersa Matruh, followed by Dick and the RHQ, joining the Mobile Force – often referred to in moments of exasperation as the Immobile Farce – which was commanded by Brigadier Friend. Accommodation was in huts and tents and the facilities were, as usual, very sparse, but football, hockey and cricket pitches were soon constructed, sea bathing was encouraged and the officers arranged with the Alexandria Boat Club for some boats to be brought along the coast for them to sail. The largest of these was renamed the *Vandyck*, in honour of their pleasurable voyage out.

Very shortly afterwards Mike Houston arrived in his capacity as inspector of cavalry, in company with George Weir, GOC British Troops in Egypt, and John Dill, then the Director of Military Operations at the War Office and already recognized as one of the up and coming soldiers of his generation. They were followed within a month by Deverell himself. The activities of the Mobile Force and others in the Western Desert were of considerable interest to higher authority in the light of uncertain relations with the Italians and much of the experience gained at the time would have beneficial consequences some years hence, when Italy actually invaded Egypt. This included desert reconnaissance expeditions, one of which, to Siwa Oasis, was undertaken by Dick and four of his officers – Harry and Frank Arkwright, Tony Warre and Arthur Gemmell. Houston also came along for the ride. The journey, in two Hillman cars and three Leyland lorries, took five days, ignoring the direct desert road and instead taking a circular route across some difficult passes and sandy desert which provided a challenge to the vehicles. In spite of some mechanical difficulties, the party arrived back without serious mishap.

A number of more warlike exercises were mounted by the Mobile Force, which now included not only the 12th Lancers and the 11th Hussars in armoured cars and the 8th Hussars in light Ford trucks, but also two battalions of the Royal Tank Corps equipped with light tanks and a battery of the Royal Horse Artillery. Dick was impressed with Vyvyan Pope of the RTC, who commanded half the force against Friend with the other half in an exercise which saw Friend's HQ put to flight and his own capture only avoided by a very fast retreat.

In mid-March C Squadron went forward to Sollum, on the Egypt–Libya frontier, to be relieved at Mersa Matruh by B Squadron: they later swapped places. The troops preferred Sollum, as there were proper barracks 800 ft up on the escarpment where the weather was cooler, and the bathing was particularly good. Dick made a number of trips there, his friend John Combe of the 11th Hussars taking him on one occasion up to the frontier near Fort Capuzzo. Most of his time continued to be at Mersa Matruh, where RHQ was located. Unlike at Tidworth or even in Cairo, there was no possibility of creating a garden as there was nothing but sand. Dick, however, was insistent that the Prince of Wales's feathers, the crest which had adorned the space outside the mess in each of the regiment's stations, usually in white flowers, should be replicated and ordered that it should be made out of white desert snails, of which there were thousands to be gathered. Rodney Palmer of his RHQ pointed out him that the snails were probably alive, but a brief inspection seeming to indicate otherwise, Palmer was ordered to get on with the job and many hours were spent by a fatigue party collecting and laying out the shells. By the next morning the crest had disappeared – the snails, clearly of nocturnal disposition, having gone absent without leave, some even invading the colonel's desk! Palmer was summoned for an explanation, but after a while even Dick saw the funny side.

Before being put on notice to go to Egypt, Dick had been looking forward to the polo season, in which it seemed that the regiment stood a serious chance of winning the Inter-Regimental Cup for the first time since 1914. The move to Egypt had temporarily dashed his hopes, but with his own short leave imminent and having placed his best players amongst the officers left behind at Tidworth, it now seemed possible to compete. Leaving Lumsden in temporary command, he set off by plane to Brindisi on 30 May and then took the train to Paris and another plane from there to Croydon. The next two weeks were spent getting in as much practice as possible with the team, the other members of which were Andrew Horsburgh-Porter, George Kidston and Dick Hobson. Because of the likelihood of missing the season, both the regiment's and Dick's own ponies had been sold before they left for Egypt, but Hobson still had his and the generosity of other officers ensured that the 12th Lancers were well mounted. The team met the 3rd Hussars in the first round on 22 June, winning easily 14–1. A much closer match with the 16th/5th Lancers resulted in an 11–7 victory, followed by a good fast semi-final against the Royal Inniskilling Dragoons, won 8–4.

The opposition in the final came from an unexpected quarter, the Royal Navy, which had never won before – indeed a cavalry regiment, or possibly the Royal Horse Artillery, was always expected to take the honours. As underdog the Navy was the firm favourite of both Press and public, its team including Lord Louis Mountbatten. The day of the final was exceptionally wet. The 12th Lancers appeared to have the advantage in the first chukka, despite only scoring one goal. Honours were even in the second, but the third and fourth chukkas went the Navy's way and at the end of the fourth a collision between Hobson and Heywood-Lonsdale of the Navy cost the former a 40-yard hit and the latter a damaged knee. The Navy secured the goal and were now leading 4–1. For the last two chukkas the Lancers threw caution to the wind and attacked incessantly, rewarded by three goals to bring them level at the start of the sixth. Keeping up the pressure they ran out 6–4 winners, the last two goals being scored by Dick himself. The celebrations involved drinking four bottles of champagne from the cup and, although the Press made capital out of Heywood-Lonsdale's injury, subsequent letters from him and Mountbatten made clear that it had not affected the result.

Three days later, after further celebrations with the Norfolks at Arundel Castle, Dick set off back to Egypt, travelling straight on to Mersa Matruh in time to make the necessary preparation for the regiment's return to Cairo, as a decision had been taken to evacuate all but the frontier gendarmerie from the Western Desert in a goodwill gesture to the Italians. The 12th Lancers moved into barracks in Abbasia formerly occupied by the 8th Hussars. As relations with the Italians had improved, the units brought out during the Abyssinian crisis were now ordered back to the UK. Dick decided nevertheless to bring Lettice out for a short stay and she was in Cairo for rather less than a month, returning to England in haste and earlier than planned when the boys fell sick with what was suspected to be tuberculosis: happily it was a false alarm. The regiment itself sailed from Alexandria on the *Laurentic* at the end of November and arrived back in England just in time for the abdication of its former Colonel-in-Chief, Edward VIII.

1937 was a complete contrast to the year in Egypt, the rhythm of peacetime soldiering reasserting itself very quickly. The major change was the replacement of the Lanchesters with the Morris armoured cars Dick had seen earlier. His appreciation of their nimbleness was deserved, but in every other way they were inferior. They had an open turret, and armour which was even lighter than the old Rolls Royces, whilst the main armament was the ineffective Boys anti-tank rifle and the secondary armament the Bren gun, a good infantry weapon, but unsuitable for the role. The other ranks were unimpressed and called the vehicles 'suicide boxes'. Dick, as usual, made the best of a bad job and instituted a training regime to take account of the cars' virtues and deficiencies, which was to bear fruit when they eventually saw action in 1940.

It was by now clear that Dick was a commanding officer of the highest quality. To the subalterns he was an awesome figure who did not suffer fools gladly. Some, like Rodney Palmer, were never entirely comfortable in his presence, while Kate Savill later said that he was always rather alarmed by him: 'I usually expected criticism and it was often a delightful surprise and relief when instead of a rebuke one got a friendly smile instead.'[2] George Kidston remembered that he worked his officers for longer hours and much harder than most regiments, at the same time allowing them to participate in whatever sport they enjoyed, but recalled that he could be very frightening to anyone who failed to do his job properly. He demanded the highest standards of even the more senior officers, encouraging one who was not taking his work seriously to send in his papers and threatening another with dismissal if he did not move from his house, a long way from Tidworth, to be close to the regiment, as his frequent absences were having an adverse impact on the efficiency of his squadron.

In many regiments the commanding officer was a distant figure to the other ranks, but not in the 12th Lancers. Freddie Hunn,[3] who joined up in 1937 just after the regiment's return from Egypt, remembered that he was very popular with the men, as was Lumsden subsequently. He recalled that everyone in the regiment looked up to Dick, in spite of the fact that he was, on the whole, soft-spoken and gentle. There was no need for him to be a martinet as the regiment was already well-disciplined and there was great pride among all ranks in being a member. Dick participated with them regularly in one event, the monthly regimental 7-mile cross-country run from Tidworth around Tidworth Pennings and back. Hunn, who was a very good runner and usually won the race, admired Dick's efforts going up the initial steep Clarendon Hill in spite of his limp, but remembered that he would then like to cut across so as to be able to run in with the winner!

There were other lighter moments, including an occasion when the Duke of Gloucester came to dinner whilst the regiment was in Egypt. The all-male party – Lettice was in England – decided to move on to a night club and, once there, Dick was ordered by Prince Henry to dance with a well-known cabaret artiste called 'Jelly Belly' in honour of her act. When Dick protested that he was the senior officer present, the Duke replied that he was in Cairo in his capacity as Colonel of one of the regiments based there and was thus himself the senior. Threatened with disclosure to Lettice if he did not proceed as ordered and, worse still, to her sister Helen who loved to gossip, Dick saw no alternative but to comply. Not renowned for small talk, all he could think of to say to 'Jelly Belly' was 'Do you know Tidworth-er?'[4] It was an occasion of which he was occasionally reminded by Lumsden, Russell and others present if he ever became difficult!

A number of officers, notably Kidston and Horsburgh-Porter, were close to Dick due to their common participation in polo. The same team as in 1936 contested the Inter-Regimental Cup the following year, only to be beaten in the second round, although it was some consolation that the regiment won the Subaltern's Cup. In 1938, Dick's last season with the regiment after a career which had begun in 1919, the team went right through to the Inter-Regimental final, to be beaten 10–8 by the Royal Scots Greys after leading 7–4 at the end of the fourth chukka. In 1937 Dick was also selected to represent the Army against Australia, whose team consisted of the four highly talented Ashton brothers, who had won 17 matches out of 22 on their previous visit to England. On this occasion there was a fast and very good game, from which the Ashtons emerged the winners by 6–5 after extra time.

During 1937 Dick came into contact for the first time with a man who was to play a major role in his professional life. Just as they benefited from mentors when they were junior officers, the rising stars in the British Army needed patrons if ever they were to achieve high command. Patronage had actually been the scourge of the Army between the wars, successive CIGSs giving important jobs to their favourites rather than to the most deserving. The system depended on the judgement of those conferring patronage, which in some cases had been sadly lacking. The man whose attention Dick now attracted certainly did not lack judgement. Alan Brooke was widely admired by his seniors and his contemporaries as an officer of the highest capability. A gunner himself, at the end of 1937 he was selected for command of the new Mobile Division, the forerunner of the armoured divisions of the future, and although the 12th Lancers were not part of the formation, the regiment cooperated closely with it as the armoured car regiment of

Southern Command. When Brooke was appointed to command the Anti-Aircraft Corps, he wrote to Dick to thank him for all his help and support. He had formed a high opinion of the young lieutenant colonel, whom he would not forget when the opportunity arose.

In 1938 Dick's time as commanding officer came to an end. In Egypt he had written to Lettice: 'I cannot imagine who talks such rubbish about my only staying with the regiment about 2 years in command. I am sure to stay for my four years, unless I get the sack, as I am so young; even at the end there is *no* chance of a brigade. I am bound to leave to do a staff job first.'[5] He was wrong about the term as he left less than three years into his appointment. He was right about the staff job. In May 1938 he heard officially that he was to become the GSO1, or chief staff officer, of 1 Division at the end of July.

For Dick, leaving the 12th Lancers was a desperate wrench, the only consolation being that he had a very high opinion of his successor, Herbert Lumsden. He was dined out in the mess a week before he handed over, being carried to bed by Rodney Palmer at 12.30 and suffering a serious hangover as a result. The Old Comrades reunion took place some days later, attended by many old friends, including Bill Truman and Dick's first squadron commander, Willy Styles, while Birdwood gave a most appreciative address. At the church parade Dick very nearly broke down during his speech and was said to have shed tears subsequently. The regiment had been an anchor for the whole of his adult life, always there even when he was at Staff College or on secondment to 2 Cavalry Brigade, but now he was being forced to part from it.

Chapter 10

Alex

In spite of his accurate prediction to Lettice that he would not get a brigade as his first appointment after commanding his regiment, Dick was disappointed not to do so, mainly because Hugh Russell was chosen at much the same time to command an armoured brigade in Egypt. Birdwood queried the preference for Russell with Lord Gort, by then the CIGS. It was clear from Gort's reply that Russell had caught his own eye, demonstrating the power of patronage, but just as Gort's career was to stall in 1940, so Russell's went little further.[1] For Dick, on the other hand, going as GSO1 to 1 Division was probably the most significant career move in his life, as it brought him into direct daily contact with the General Officer Commanding, a man who was to have a huge influence on his later advancement and who was himself to become one of the two best known British generals of the Second World War.

Even by 1938 Harold Alexander had enjoyed a stellar career. Born in 1891 and commissioned into the Irish Guards in 1911, he had commanded two of his regiment's battalions during the Great War and, during the German offensive of March 1918, had assumed temporary command of a brigade at the age of 27. Shortly after the Great War he led the Baltic Landeswehr, fighting the advance into Latvia of the Bolsheviks, driving them back into Russia and thereby earning the admiration of his troops, who were largely Baltic Germans. Following rapid advancement, he was appointed in 1934 to the plum job of command of the Nowshera Brigade, one of two conducting campaigns on the North-West Frontier, his fellow brigadier in the Peshawar Brigade being Claude Auchinleck, the coming man in the Indian Army and some seven years his senior. Alexander was promoted to major general at 45, at a time when the average age for such appointments was nearly ten years older, and shortly afterwards he was appointed GOC of 1 Division, one of only five regular UK-based infantry divisions in the British Army.

Alexander's rise had been seemingly effortless. There were those, however, who were doubtful about his abilities, including his former instructors at the Staff College, Brooke and Montgomery. The latter, in many ways his complete antithesis as a soldier, regarded him as a triumph of style over substance. All agreed that his interpersonal skills were excellent and that he was imperturbable in adversity, while it also became evident that his instinct was of a far higher order than his intellect. He relied heavily on his subordinates, both as commanders and staff officers, as he disliked detail and he tended to look for ideas from others rather than conceiving them himself, although after assimilating them he would always make the final decision and it would usually turn out to be the right one. He and Dick, whose intellect was of the highest quality and whose grasp of staff duties was first-class, were thus almost certain to make an excellent team.

Although Dick was not to take up his appointment formally until the end of July 1938, when he was simultaneously promoted to colonel,[2] his first visit to 1 Division in Aldershot was on 2 June, just over a week after he had received the news. He was there again on numerous occasions in June and July, as he needed not only to be briefed by the outgoing GSO1, Tom Hutton, but also to provide input into the divisional exercises, which had begun by his start date. Hutton told him that his job would be to ensure that Alexander was kept out of the way and only appeared when he had to take command. As Dick wrote later: 'He presented me with a paper on the subject. What would have been much more useful to me would have been to find that some of the exercises were prepared, at any rate in draft form, but all I found were the actual subjects of the exercises. This meant that I had a very busy time ahead of me, especially as I was still commanding my Regiment for the next 2 months.'[3]

Dick's appointment was in every way an accolade. A cavalryman by training and inclination, his only practical experience of staff work was as brigade major to a cavalry brigade, whilst his more recent experience of working with the Mobile Division was limited to the armoured car role. His acquaintance with the infantry came from his time in the trenches with the dismounted companies and the theoretical knowledge picked up at the Staff College. His selection as the chief staff officer to an infantryman in an infantry division was thus remarkable and he often wondered what Alexander thought about being presented with him, yet they got on well from the start. Dick's first note on his new chief in his diary was 'Alexander is quick and good' and it was evident very quickly that their skills were complementary. Hutton had actually been quite accurate in his advice, Dick writing subsequently: 'At quite an early stage I realised that my divisional commander was a man who liked to decentralise, and although he gave the direction he expected me to do most of the detailed work.'[4] The first major exercise for which Dick was entirely responsible came just over two weeks after he took up his new role. He had been concerned that, as a cavalryman used to operating on a wide front, he would tend to give the infantry brigades too much to do: in the event it went very well.

The advance notice of his new appointment had given Dick and Lettice time to look for new accommodation. After inspecting houses in the

Aldershot area they bought one called Runwick, just outside Farnham. It needed extensive repair and decoration, but by early September the family was able to move in. From a gardening perspective the timing was good, as planting spring flowering bulbs could begin immediately, and the autumn was the best season for preparing new herbaceous borders and shrubberies. In such spare time as he could afford, Dick threw himself enthusiastically into the necessary work.

In the wider world the political background was by now deeply concerning, with Germany making hostile moves towards Czechoslovakia, resulting in the Munich Agreement at the end of September and the annexation of the Sudetenland by the Germans. Dick and most of his contemporaries thought that war was inevitable, despite Neville Chamberlain's declaration of 'peace for our time'. The pace of training was given added urgency as Aldershot Command, of which 1 Division formed part, had already been identified for conversion to a corps in any expeditionary force which Great Britain might have to despatch to the continent. For Dick this meant a lot less time hunting and a lot more preparing schemes, the major one of which was the Winter Exercise, scheduled to begin on the Berkshire Downs at the end of the following January. This required frequent reconnaissance trips with Alexander, which enabled Dick to get to know his commander well. He was fascinated to find that Alexander, a talented artist, would take pencil and paper with him to sketch the details of some tactical problem. Alexander, for his part, tested Dick by making various suggestions and seeing how he would react. A less agreeable feature of these journeys was the requirement to sit in the back of the GOC's staff car, where with windows closed due to the cold weather and no other ventilation, Dick frequently fell victim to his old enemy, travel sickness.

The end of November brought with it a family tragedy when George Gosling, Lettice's brother-in-law, died after a short illness, leaving Helen with a young family.[5] Lettice sprang into action to help where she could, while Dick found that he had been made an executor of the will, demanding his attention when he could least afford it. With a hectic period leading up to Christmas, it was with some relief shortly before the New Year that he was able to get three weeks' leave, taking Lettice and the two older boys for their first winter sports holiday to Crans Montana in Switzerland. They stayed there for a fortnight, joined by a number of friends, and the whole family developed a great enthusiasm for skiing and sledding, so much so that they left their luges in the care of the hotel on the assumption that they would return the following year. They were not to know that it would be another seven years before they would put on skis again.

It was probably just as well that Dick was acclimatized to snow as eight inches fell on the Berkshire Downs during one of the days of the Winter Exercise. He plunged back into the training programme, but there were now other distractions, not all of them military. As a cavalryman, he was an obvious choice to organize a number of activities in which the horse featured strongly, such as the Aldershot Polo Club and the Aldershot Horse Show, one of the largest in the country. He was also made chairman for the year of the Hurlingham Polo Association, the governing body for the sport in the United Kingdom. In March 1939 he decided to have another crack at the Grand Military Gold Cup, riding Twelfth Lancer, one of the numerous progeny of Annie Darling. The horse was an excellent jumper, but not as determined as his mother. Dick had a good ride, but pulled up two fences from the finish when it was clear that he would have no chance of a place. It was to be his last competitive steeplechase.

The week of the Grand Military Meeting coincided with Hitler's invasion of Czechoslovakia, after which the pace of preparation for war accelerated through spring and summer. In May Alexander went to France with Dill, now the GOC-in-C of Aldershot Command, and Henry 'Jumbo' Maitland Wilson, the GOC of 2 Division, for three days of meetings with their French opposite numbers, commenting on his return that the Maginot Line looked impregnable. At the end of that month Dick himself accompanied Alexander to France on a battlefield tour around Cambrai and Arras, where he had been wounded in 1917. There were no fewer than 60 senior officers on the tour, many of whom, including Alexander, had fought in the Guards Division at Bourlon Wood during the Battle of Cambrai and were able to lecture their colleagues on the subject. Back in the UK, exercises continued apace, including some for the whole of what would, in the event of war, become I Corps. For Dick much of the emphasis turned to mobilization, with reservists being recalled to the colours to bring all units up to full strength, whilst a plan was drawn up to get the whole division over to France within three weeks of a declaration of war.

In August Lettice took the boys on a seaside holiday to Thorpeness in Suffolk, where Dick managed to get away for a long weekend. He was back in the office four days later, just before the announcement of the German–Soviet Non-Aggression Pact, which convinced even the doubters that war was imminent. As the countdown began, Dick found himself spending long hours in the office finalizing the plans, sleeping there on a camp bed on many nights. When war came all his efforts paid off and mobilization went very smoothly, although Dick had to hold a special exercise to induct all the new divisional HQ personnel. Equipment shortages remained, particularly of vehicles, the division's second line transport being largely requisitioned from civilian sources, former laundry vans mingling with the regulation army lorries.

The Advance HQ left Aldershot on 12 September to make arrangements for the division's arrival in France and its transportation to the assembly area. On 19 September Dick said the first of many wartime goodbyes to Lettice and drove down to Southampton, where the Main HQ embarked on the *Ulster Monarch* and crossed to Cherbourg. Travelling at the same time was 1 (Guards) Brigade, while 2 and 3 Brigades were in France by 25 September.

The division concentrated initially around Laval, with the divisional HQ at Evron, moving thence to its permanent location at Bersée, between Douai and Lille. By the end of the first week of October, despite frequent accidents as the drivers sought to cope with driving on the right and unfamiliarly cambered roads, the division had relieved a French division along the frontier with Belgium between Bachy and Camphin-en-Pévèle, just to the south of the Lille–Tournai road. It was what Dick described as 'very ugly sugar beet country'. He wrote to Lettice that the divisional HQ was based in 'a very nice chateau, but their water supply is running out, so we shall not get baths and the W.C.s are frightful.'[6] Much of his time was spent accompanying Alexander on inspections of the division's positions, which had been prepared to some extent by the French, with one line of widely spaced block houses and a rudimentary anti-tank ditch.

During the autumn and winter of the 'Phoney War', the British Expeditionary Force, commanded by Gort and consisting initially of Dill's I Corps and Brooke's II Corps, with Ronald Adam's III Corps arriving in early 1940, had one major priority, to improve these defences, engaging in a great deal of digging and the construction of innumerable concrete pill boxes. Large-scale exercises were impossible as the French were afraid that they would spoil the countryside. The original orders in the event of a German offensive were to advance into Belgium as far as the line of the River Escaut, but in November the French C-in-C, General Gamelin, proposed 'Plan D', whereby the Allies would take up positions even further forward on the River Dyle. Gort, although reluctant to do so, accepted this as an order from a superior officer, much to the dismay of Dill and Brooke, both of whom felt that abandoning prepared defences for a line which had not even been reconnoitred would lead to disaster – exactly what did happen. In planning for this Alexander and Dick were frustrated, as were all the British commanders and their staffs, by the impossibility of liaising with the Belgians, who were holding fast to their neutrality.

The tedium of the 'Phoney War' was broken only by a number of visits from dignitaries, including the secretary of state for war, Leslie Hore-Belisha, and the King, who arrived to inspect the division on 5 December. Perhaps more usefully, arrangements were made for one brigade group at a time to be transferred to Lorraine, where the French Third Army was in contact with the Germans on the border with the Saar, allowing units to gain experience of patrolling and coming under artillery fire. Dick's main concern on a personal level was to resume the flow of cakes which had made his life more bearable in the Great War and to obtain some books for his men, who were very prone to boredom. Lettice duly obliged.

In mid-October the 12th Lancers arrived in France, moving to Arras where they were to provide local defence for the BEF GHQ. Selby was with them. Dick had not seen him since early 1937, when he and Jo had come over to Europe on a visit shortly after Dick arrived back from Egypt. Immediately after the declaration of war Selby decided to rejoin the Army and, on his arrival in England, was taken on by Lumsden as second-in-command of a squadron, reverting to his old rank of captain.

Although Dick was delighted to have Selby nearby, he was dubious from the start about his decision. His brother seemed to be on good form when he arrived to join the main body of the regiment from a temporary job organizing reinforcements, but at the end of November Dick's fears were proved well founded when Selby was admitted to a military hospital in Dieppe, suffering from what was probably jaundice and feeling very sorry for himself. Dick went down to see him, to be told by his brother that he was sure he was not strong enough to stand the winter and that he hated the armoured cars. Dick met Lumsden, who agreed Selby was not really fit for active service and should probably be put in front of a medical board with a view to being invalided out. Dick wrote to Lettice: 'I <u>always</u> knew that it was a mistake Selby hurrying over here, but I didn't realise that, having had every luxury for the last 8 years, and living in a good climate, he would crack up so soon!'[7] Jo had by then arrived in Paris, but in early January 1940 Selby was shipped back to England, where a medical board duly found him unfit. Jo returned almost immediately to California, but Selby remained in London, off and on, until the spring of 1942.[8] Dick did feel slightly ashamed of his brother's behaviour, although also very sorry for him.

In mid-December Dick was told by Alexander that he was probably going to move on to a bigger job, but was asked by him to keep it quiet from everyone until it was confirmed. On 11 January 1940 he heard officially that he was to take over 2 Light Armoured Brigade. His successor as GSO1, William 'Monkey' Morgan, arrived two days later and Dick was back in England by the following evening.

Alexander wrote to Dick shortly afterwards: 'It was very sad to see you go – and although I am delighted for your sake, it makes your loss here none the less. I have enjoyed our partnership enormously and am most grateful to you for all your able and excellent work which has now been fittingly rewarded.'[9] The seventeen months spent as Alexander's right-hand man had done Dick an enormous amount of good in terms of experience as a senior staff officer and understanding of infantry operations. Most importantly of all, it had confirmed him, in Alexander's own words written long afterwards, as a 'trusted friend and companion whose wise advice and companionship meant much to me.'[10] A happy combination of circumstances was to bring them together again, just at the time when Dick needed it most.

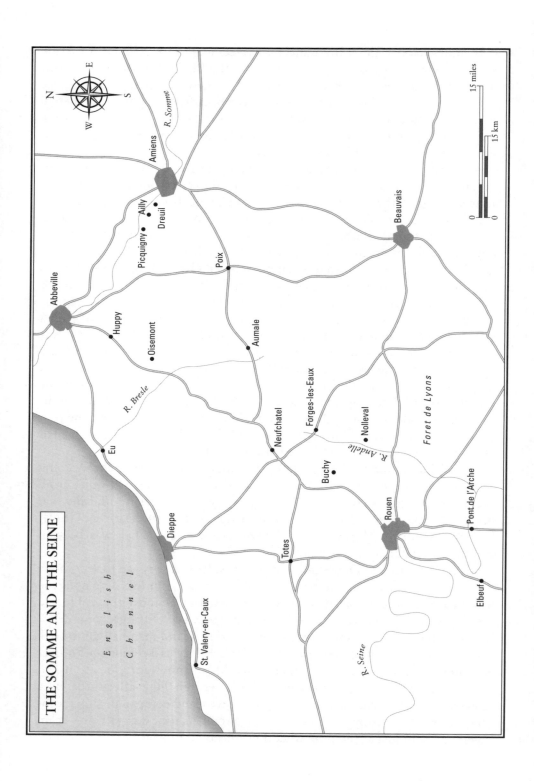

THE SOMME AND THE SEINE

Chapter 11

The Somme and the Seine

fter a brief meeting with Lettice in London, Dick travelled straight to Saffron Walden, where his brigade was situated. However, on telephoning the HQ of his superior formation to announce his arrival he was told to take a week's leave, much of which he spent at Runwick in bed with a temperature. It was not until the afternoon of 22 January that he arrived back at Saffron Walden and was able to take stock of his new command.

2 Light Armoured Brigade was a major component of 1 Armoured Division which, until a month before Dick's appointment, had been the sole such formation in the United Kingdom. It was still the only one which was even close to being fully equipped, as 2 Armoured Division at the time comprised barely more than a divisional HQ. This compared with the six complete and highly trained panzer divisions which Germany had deployed against Poland in September 1939 and the four more which would be available by the time it launched its assault on France and the Low Countries in May 1940.

That this situation had been allowed to develop was an indictment of the parsimony of the British Government and the reactionary attitude of the Army establishment towards armoured fighting vehicles, both of which had persisted throughout the inter-war years, squandering the leadership in armoured warfare which Great Britain had established by 1918. The voices of the small band of tank enthusiasts had gone almost unheard until 1931, when 1 Brigade Royal Tank Corps was created, although even this small formation was experimental in nature and did not achieve permanent status until 1934. It was only at the end of 1937 that the Mobile Division, with which Dick had cooperated so enthusiastically in the first half of the following year, was formed and later renamed 1 Armoured Division.

The division comprised three subordinate formations, the other two being 1 Heavy Armoured Brigade and 1 Support Group. All the light tanks were in Dick's brigade, which was formed of three cavalry regiments mechanized in the 1930s, the Queen's Bays (2nd Dragoon Guards), the 9th Lancers and the 10th Hussars. Dick knew all their commanding officers, respectively George Fanshawe, Christopher Peto, who had been a fellow student at Sandhurst in 1915, and Charles Gairdner, who had been brigade major of the Cavalry Brigade in Cairo during Dick's time there in 1936. Dick's own brigade major from early May onwards, John Anderson, described the brigade as a 'family party', such were the close friendships that existed amongst the cavalry officers. The cruiser tanks were to be found in the other armoured brigade, whose units were all battalions of the Royal Tank Regiment and whose background and traditions were thus quite different. Whilst it would be highly misleading to describe the RTR officers as professionals compared with amateurs in the cavalry, Roundheads and Cavaliers might not be too far from the truth. The Heavy Brigade was likewise something of a family party, its commanders in the first half of 1940 both being former members of the RTR, first Vyvyan Pope, whom Dick had admired in the Mobile Force in Egypt, and then John Crocker.

The armoured fighting vehicles in these two brigades themselves reflected the historic lack of interest in armour by the military hierarchy. The light tanks in Dick's brigade had been developed in the early 1930s by Vickers Armstrong. By 1940 these were mostly the Mark VI variants, A and B, but although they were robust little vehicles with a fast maximum speed of 35 mph, they were under-armoured and under-gunned, their armament consisting of one .50 and one .303 machine gun. The other tank, initially confined to the 'heavy' brigade, was the cruiser A13, in both its Mark III and more heavily armoured Mark IV variants. This had as its main weapon the quickfiring Ordnance 2-pounder, with the right shells a moderately satisfactory anti-tank gun, but not suitable for use with high-explosive ammunition. The A13s were, in theory at least, a match for the PzKpfw IIs and IIIs equipping the German panzer divisions, but were far from reliable. They were also in short supply and there were still a number of the older and more cumbersome A10s in use.

The third of the three components of the division was 1 Support Group, which theoretically contained all the artillery, infantry and engineers. By the time that Dick arrived, however, the two regiments of Royal Horse Artillery had been sent to join the BEF and had not been replaced. There were two regular rifle battalions, but these were also shortly to be removed. Other than the engineers, which at one point became divisional troops before reverting to the Support Group in the field, the only other unit was a territorial infantry battalion, which was in the course of being converted into a combined anti-tank and anti-aircraft artillery regiment. Motor transport for 1 Support Group was thin on the ground and even incorporated the vehicles of a travelling circus, complete with barred lion cages! It was this and other deficiencies which led to its commander, Freddie Morgan, describing the division subsequently as 'more of a basis for argument than an instrument of war.'[1]

Dick's first priority was to relocate his brigade from Essex to the area in South Dorset and Hampshire where the rest of the division was concentrated and where he was much closer to the HQ of his divisional commander, Roger Evans, at Breamore House near Fordingbridge. He and Lettice decided that they would rent a house near his own HQ at Wimborne for two months and she moved down from Runwick shortly afterwards. However, they found the new accommodation uncomfortable and Lettice returned to Runwick after the letting period, while Dick stayed at the King's Head in Wimborne.

The following weeks were spent in a variety of exercises and training schemes for the various units and TEWTs (tactical exercises without troops) and conferences for the officers. During March, however, the War Office decreed that the organization of armoured divisions would change with immediate effect. Instead of the two armoured brigades differing in both nomenclature and equipment, they would now become identical: 1 Heavy Armoured Brigade was renamed 3 Armoured Brigade and 2 Light Armoured Brigade became simply 2 Armoured Brigade. All the cavalry regiments and RTR battalions would have three squadrons, each of four troops of 3 tanks, plus 4 tanks for the squadron HQ. With 4 more tanks in the regimental or battalion HQ, this resulted in a war establishment of 52 tanks. Adding the 10 tanks at Brigade HQ, which were mostly A10s, the full complement for each brigade worked out at 166 tanks, all of which were intended to be cruisers. In practice there were nothing like enough cruiser tanks available to equip the division to these levels, so light tanks continued to provide nearly half the establishment. By the time the division departed on campaign, Dick reckoned that each regiment in his brigade had 20 light tanks and about 22 cruisers, woefully short of what was intended.

Dick experienced much more difficulty in converting his brigade than Pope and Crocker. First of all his men had to be retrained on cruiser tanks, with which they were completely unfamiliar. There was not enough time to do more than give the crews basic instruction on driving, maintenance and the use of the 2-pounder gun. Dick tried to fit in as much training as possible for the three regiments at the range at Linney Head in Pembrokeshire, during which he drove a cruiser across country himself and found it an exhilarating experience. Secondly, the units of the two brigades had different strengths in personnel, those of the RTR numbering 30 officers and 573 other ranks, whilst the cavalry regiments ran to 24 officers and 492 other ranks. The new standard establishment of 31 officers and 546 other ranks meant that, whilst Pope and Crocker could get rid of their worst performing men, Dick was compelled to bring his brigade up to strength by taking draftees from the training regiments, many of whom subsequently proved to be of poor quality. There was a particular shortage of specialists, notably drivers and mechanics, the latter having little familiarity with the cruisers.

All this put Dick under considerable pressure, although this was relieved by two competent brigade majors in succession, Archie Little and, shortly before leaving for France, John Anderson. Anderson was later to say of Dick that 'he inspired utter devotion among old friends and new ones alike and, at times, considerable alarm as well! At heart the gentlest & most sensitive of men, he could nevertheless "explode" in a frightening way "out of a blue sky" and with a surprising violence of language! Those who knew him well took note of a somewhat wintry smile which was the danger signal & the storm blew up very quickly indeed. I was reduced to tears by him, but within ten minutes he was seeking me out to say how sorry he was.'[2]

On 3 May the division received the warning order for a mid-month move to join the BEF in France. Exactly one week later the Germans struck in the west, making immediate gains in the Netherlands and Belgium, whilst the BEF, faithful to Gamelin's Plan D, moved forward from its prepared defences to the Dyle Line. Having been inspected by the King on 14 May, the division began its move to the Continent without any artillery except the composite 101st Anti-Tank/Anti-Aircraft Regiment, which had a dozen 2-pounder anti-tank guns but nothing heavier than Lewis guns for its anti-aircraft batteries. Worse still, the two rifle battalions had been moved at short notice to 30 Brigade, hurriedly assembled under Dick's great friend, Claude Nicholson, and destined for a heroic, but in the end fruitless stand at Calais, which would see most of the survivors incarcerated for the duration.[3] There was thus no infantry in the division. Morgan lost most of his HQ to Nicholson, the newly arrived replacements lacking any practice in working together, but with only one unit and the division's engineers under command, 1 Support Group was doomed to irrelevance.

Somewhat bizarrely, therefore, it was the Support Group which left first for France, although there may have been some logic in it providing air cover, however paltry, with its Lewis guns. It was followed by 2 Armoured Brigade, which, in spite of nearly three weeks' warning, was still lacking some vital equipment and adequate ammunition. For example, although all the tanks had dischargers for smoke bombs, there were no such bombs available and these were sorely missed when the time came to attack the enemy. Notwithstanding the deficiencies the Brigade HQ and the Bays sailed on schedule, arriving at Cherbourg on 20 May, with the 9th Lancers and 10th Hussars disembarking the next day. What followed was four weeks of extreme confusion, heroic but futile endeavour and ultimately total failure.

By the time that 2 Armoured Brigade had concentrated at Pacy-sur-Eure, east of Evreux, on 22 May, the situation for the Western Allies was dire, as Evans explained to his brigadiers at a conference that afternoon. On the previous day the first and only successful tank attack against the Germans had taken place near Arras, but it had proved only a temporary respite for the BEF, the French First Army and the Belgian Army, which had been cut off from the rest of the French forces. The German panzer divisions had reached the English Channel near Abbeville on the night of 20 May and had crossed the Somme at various points, although the panzers had swung north towards Boulogne and Calais, leaving their infantry to establish a defensive flank along the river. There was no immediate hope of 1 Armoured Division achieving its original objective, which was to join up with the BEF. Evans was under orders instead to cooperate with the French, with a view to stopping any further incursions south of the Somme, eliminating the existing bridgeheads and crossing the river as quickly as possible. With this end in mind, the Bays were ordered forward to the Forêt de Lyon and thence to the Somme, across which they would establish a bridgehead through which the other two regiments would pass.

From the outset these orders seemed to Dick to be impossible to execute, in the absence of any infantry or artillery other than whatever the French could supply. He nevertheless instructed the Bays to move forward on 23 May, although they were unable to reach the Somme that day largely because of heavy congestion on the roads. Dick met Fanshawe in Aumale that evening and gave orders to reconnoitre a number of bridges over the river between Amiens and Abbeville. When patrols were sent forward, including one from brigade HQ, they found all of them to be either destroyed or in the possession of locally strong German forces. More encouragingly Dick now acquired some infantry in the shape of the 4th Battalion, the Border Regiment (4 Border), which had been separated from its parent brigade whilst on line of communication duties. An attack was planned on the crossings at Dreuil, Ailly and Picquigny by the Bays and one company of 4 Border.

At 0630 hrs on 24 May a liaison officer arrived from the division to inform Dick that the French were planning a large attack themselves. In the event this developed into a fruitless artillery duel, but Dick decided to postpone his own attack to take advantage of the distraction. The Bays then advanced along the river and two platoons of 4 Border managed to cross it at one point, but with a 40 ft gap in the bridge it proved impossible to support them and they were withdrawn. Enemy resistance increased and it soon became apparent that without any artillery support and bridging equipment a crossing was impracticable. German shells landed around the 9th Lancers, from whose position Dick was watching the action. One of the officers, Derek Allhusen, recalled that he was completely unperturbed, talking to Peto as if nothing had happened.

On the next day patrols were again sent to the crossings, but the situation was found to be unchanged. That evening orders were received to move 18 miles west to Oisemont, where 2 Armoured Brigade came under command of the French 2e Division Légère Mécanique (2 DLM), the intention being to combine with it to mount an attack on the large German bridgehead at Abbeville. Attending a conference at the HQ of General Berniquet, the French commander, Dick found to his horror that 2 DLM consisted of a few armoured cars and motorcyclists and about 400 men carried in trucks, so any cooperation in the attack would be very limited. Shortly before the attack was due to begin, directed on the village of Huppy, Berniquet arrived with the news that the French artillery were otherwise occupied and proposing a delay. By that time the 10th Hussars had begun their advance and Dick was out of radio contact with them.

The attack duly went in with very limited artillery and no infantry support, which inevitably led to disaster. It was not helped by heavy rain which had made the ground very sticky for tanks. Both the Bays and the 10th Hussars fought bravely but took heavy losses from well sited and concealed German anti-tank guns, losing respectively about 15 and 22 tanks, a significant proportion of their armour. The light tanks were already proving to be highly vulnerable. On the next day General de Gaulle's 4e Division Cuirassée de Réserve (4 DCR), equipped with 120 tanks, of which 40 were well armed and armoured Char Bs, and supported by 3,000 infantry, tried again. Only on 28 May was this division able to break through the defence and force the Germans back across the river, although an attempt to cross was foiled on 30 May. Dick was nevertheless highly impressed by de Gaulle, the only French general in this campaign for whom he subsequently had any time. As he later wrote: 'It was most interesting to watch his method of control from his H.Q. Many French tank officers had by then lost their tanks and these were employed in motor cycle combinations as Liaison Officers to keep touch with tank units. A constant stream of these officers flowed in and out from his Command Post and he appeared to keep excellent control in this way... Gen. de Gaulle's verbal orders for his attack on the 28th May were decisive and clear and inspired everyone with confidence.'[4]

By this time 1 Armoured Division was in a sorry state, Crocker having lost nearly as many tanks as Dick in an attack by 3 Armoured Brigade on another part of the Abbeville bridgehead. The only uncommitted unit thus far in 2 Armoured Brigade was the 9th Lancers, so Peto was put in command of a composite regiment comprising his HQ and two of his own squadrons, with a third made up from the Bays and the 10th Hussars, whilst the remainder of those two regiments was withdrawn to near Rouen to refit, the broken-down tanks being transported further back to the divisional workshops at

Louviers. The dismounted men were formed into Motor Transport squadrons. The composite regiment was left under the command of 51 (Highland) Division, which had arrived in the area after a long journey from Lorraine, where it had been serving on the Maginot Line, and which now took over a 12-mile front near Abbeville.

The dispersal of his units made command very difficult for Dick. As his failure to contact 10th Hussars before the attack on Huppy demonstrated, radio communication was unreliable, so the only alternative was to visit the regiments and even squadrons personally. Anderson remembered that he 'kept going literally night & day contriving to be where it mattered all the time ... when not in some fairly primitive armoured vehicle on reconnaissance or in personal command he was driving his own staff car, night & day, at high speed, since no driver could go fast enough for his liking! I ventured once to say to him "I don't know how you go on driving all the time like this", to which he replied quite simply "you'd get tired – I don't!"'[5] Dick must have had tremendous reserves of energy, as he wrote to Lettice on 26 May that he had only had an hour's sleep on two of the preceding four nights and again on 29 May that he had spent the previous night with only two hours dozing in a chair. He was well looked after by his batman, Bryant, who had worked for Dick privately before the War.

On 4 June the last British and French troops were evacuated from Dunkirk, freeing up the German divisions for a concerted attack south of the Somme. The composite regiment engaged the enemy very effectively in support of 51 Division east of the River Bresle, Peto and his HQ capturing 2 officers and 40 men whilst covering the division's withdrawal, but Peto himself was seriously wounded in the hand on the following day and handed over to his second-in-command. Up until this time the only engagement had been with German infantry divisions on which even the cruiser tanks took a toll, in spite of them needing increasing maintenance as their tracks were wearing very thin. On 7 June, however, the Germans threw two panzer divisions into the battle and by that evening they had reached the area of Forges-les-Eaux. Crocker was ordered to hold the River Andelle north of Nolleval, but his units were so depleted that one squadron of the Bays was placed under his orders, together with some still functioning 'runners' from both Dick's and the Divisional HQs.

On 8 June orders were received for Dick's MT squadrons and all remaining personnel not in tanks to fall back across the Seine, whilst the composite regiment was withdrawn from command of 51 Division and began to make its way south to rejoin the brigade, just in time to avoid being cut off with the Highlanders.[6] It saw some more action against German medium tanks near Buchy: one troop leader fired no fewer than 50 rounds at the Germans without any apparent effect, as he only had 'plugged-shell' available, normally used for training and able to penetrate no more than 20mm of armour. The regiment crossed the Seine that evening, but not without difficulty due to the officiousness of the French at the crossing points, which required Dick's personal intervention. With the remnants of 3 Armoured Brigade doing likewise, the whole of 1 Armoured Division was now behind the river with the exception of the Support Group, whose engineers and anti-tank gunners had been overrun, leaving only scattered parties to escape. Morgan himself was in a party which had joined up with the composite regiment.

Whilst Dick admired the officers and men of the French armoured divisions, the same could not be said for their infantry. His opinion had not improved over the previous few days, during which he had seen them retreat in confusion from the advancing Germans, attributing their performance to the debilitating effect of French politics over many years and their recent exposure to German bombing. He was later to write: 'There was no indication of any defensive preparations having been made on the left bank of the SEINE; the bridges were ready to blow but there were no entrenchments anywhere. The folly of rushing up French Divs piece-meal into the open country between the SEINE and the SOMME was now apparent. The French Inf simply marched on into the woods to the South-West.'[7] At least all his own troops were now behind the next water barrier, poorly defended though it might be, as were those of 3 Armoured Brigade. The bridges at Elbeuf and Pont de l'Arche were blown on the night of 8/9 June.

On the morning of 9 June Dick was summoned to an urgent conference at Divisional HQ south of Elbeuf. Following much 'clicking of heels and shaking hands', he found himself placed under the command of General Petiet of the French 3 DLM, which was ordered to hold the line of the Seine. The 10th Hussars and 150 men operating as MT squadrons covered the river from Louviers to just short of Pont de l'Arche and the Bays and a similarly sized party did the same from Pont de l'Arche to Elbeuf. The 9th Lancers remained in reserve.

On the morning of 10 June the Germans crossed the river at St Pierre-du-Vauvray, east of Louviers and the situation appeared critical. Dick brought up the 9th Lancers, who plugged the gap but reported that the Germans were moving south towards Gaillon in large numbers. By the end of the day it was apparent that the enemy had also established a strong bridgehead at Vernon and Dick made it clear to Petiet that he could no longer employ skilled tank drivers as infantry when it was quite obvious that the line of the Seine could not be held. He agreed to leave 9 light and 6 cruiser tanks to act as Petiet's reserve, whilst withdrawing the MT squadrons to the Le Mans area, where such broken-down tanks as were fit to be repaired had been sent.

In the event the Germans turned towards Paris and over the next two days the remainder of 2 Armoured Brigade withdrew without interruption to Le Mans to complete its refitting.

Arriving at the new brigade area on the evening of 14 June and believing that he would be staying there for some days, Dick was just unpacking his kit properly for the first time since arriving in France when he was summoned to divisional HQ about 20 miles away. There Evans told him that there had been a major development. Alan Brooke had arrived in France two days earlier to take command of the remaining British forces there[8] and had rapidly concluded that further participation in the campaign would be futile and that only a rapid evacuation would serve the national interest. Supported by John Dill, now the CIGS, he had obtained permission from a reluctant Churchill to commence the operation. Dick was ordered to load his remaining 14 cruisers and 24 light tanks on to a train at Le Mans bound for Cherbourg and to send his B Echelon transport and all personnel to Brest by road. The tanks failed to arrive, never getting further than Caen, but the rest of the division, less its transport, which was left behind at the port, embarked satisfactorily and Dick himself sailed for England on 16 June.

Chapter 12

Q and Bumper

Dick disembarked at Plymouth early on the morning of 17 June and proceeded immediately to 2 Armoured Brigade's new camp at Longbridge Deverill in Wiltshire where, in Anderson's words, he 'at once set about siting the Brigade H.Q. defensive layout in complete detail, weapon by weapon, with fields of fire, etc.'[1] The camp was far from satisfactory and Dick began a series of improvements, setting an example by spending hours digging trenches himself. It was some time before he felt able to take the leave to which every man in 1 Armoured Division was entitled.

He could now reflect on the last month. In almost every respect it had been a complete debacle. One relief was that the losses of men in the brigade had been relatively slight: 7 officers and 25 other ranks had been killed, 6 officers and 63 other ranks wounded, and 5 officers and 28 other ranks were missing. Of greater concern was the loss of equipment, with all the tanks and 'soft' transport either destroyed or left behind in France, together with most of the warlike stores. The men had come out with their personal weapons and kit, but not much else.

Perhaps more important than the material losses was the knowledge that the British forces were in most ways no match for the Germans. Their tactics were poor and their equipment was inferior. However, a number of valuable lessons had been learnt. Foremost amongst these was the confirmation that committing armour to an attack without either infantry or artillery support was a recipe for disaster. This had in reality been understood long before the division left for France, making its commitment to the campaign, incomplete in such a fundamental respect, an act of near criminal folly. Unfortunately, and precisely because of the lack of these key ingredients, the experience had done nothing to improve the British Army's appreciation of how to use its armour and it would be some long time before either its organization or its tactics were to meet the demands of modern warfare.

Other lessons were also learnt. One was that the light tanks were so vulnerable as to be obsolete, their armour penetrated even by relatively light anti-tank weapons. The cruisers had not been markedly inferior to their German counterparts in this respect, but the 2-pounder gun was inadequate with the type of solid shot ammunition in use at the time. On the other hand, whilst the light tanks went on week after week with hardly any mechanical problems, the cruisers were subject to constant breakdowns, many of these associated with their tracks wearing out very quickly. Their problems were exacerbated in Dick's brigade by its recent conversion to A13s and the consequential inexperience of its mechanics.

The priorities for Dick were now to re-equip and to retrain. The first of these was delayed by the continuing demands of 2 Armoured Division, which was still incomplete: with the possibility of invasion looming, it was vital to have at least one fully operational armoured division. Slowly the replacement tanks began to arrive, still A13 Mark IVs to begin with, followed by the Mark V 'Covenanter', which proved to be unsatisfactory as its engine had a tendency to overheat. The improved Mark VI 'Crusader' also began arriving later in the year: it was destined to be the main tank employed by the British Army until early in 1942, although it too was never wholly reliable. Like all the others, it used the 2-pounder gun which was increasingly inadequate as an anti-tank weapon against better armoured German tanks and was incapable of use with high-explosive ammunition.

In the meantime training had to progress without armoured vehicles, the MT squadrons formed in France remaining in place. There was a great deal of frustration during the summer as the Battle of Britain took place and fears grew about invasion, improvisation being the order of the day. Much of Dick's own time was spent on TEWTs, mostly on Salisbury Plain and the surrounding hills. He had acquired a dog of uncertain origin called Beetle, who would accompany him on these exercises. According to Anderson, Beetle's 'nervous energy was in inverse proportion to his master's, although his will-power was just about as great. On long, striding walks and tactical reconnaissances on the Wiltshire Downs it was Beetle who called the tune & dictated the overall pace, defying his owner's exhortations to greater speed &, what is more, getting away with it every time!'[2] Dick as usual was indefatigable, covering great distances to keep in touch with his troops, often riding alone on his motorcycle, as he was concerned about the amount of fuel needed for the staff car.

The campaign in France and Belgium had exposed the failings of a number of commanders and highlighted the qualities of others, so many changes now took place at the senior levels of the British Army. A number of officers who were judged to have done well were advanced, Alexander and Montgomery being amongst those promoted to corps command, but the most significant appointment was that of Brooke to Commander-in-Chief Home Forces. Brooke was on his way to becoming the most influential British general of the War and was already identifying the men who would lead the armies of the future, although at this stage and for some time longer he was inclined to despair of the lack of talent. He visited the brigade twice during the summer, on the first occasion telling Dick how splendidly the 12th Lancers had performed in France. Many in the regiment thought that it was not only Lumsden, but also Dick in the years before, who had instilled in the regiment the qualities which made it the outstanding reconnaissance unit of the campaign. Lumsden had been awarded the DSO and promoted to the command of a brigade. In his reply to Dick's letter of congratulation, he wrote: 'I feel that I was extremely lucky to have been in command when the fighting started as that was what I wished for most in the world. But without all the hard work that had gone before and over a period of many years it would not have been possible to take the same risks and escape with so few casualties.'[3]

In September it was announced that Dick, too, had won the DSO for his leadership in the field. As he wrote to Lettice, it showed that at least Roger Evans had been satisfied with his performance. Evans himself, however, was one of those who had not found favour and was replaced by Dick's great friend, Willoughby Norrie. Much to Dick's pleasure, his recommendation of Anderson for a DSO also went through at the same time as his own.

With some uncertainty about Dick's movements, Lettice remained at Runwick. She was expecting their fourth child later in the year and, partly for this reason, Dick was becoming increasingly concerned about the location of their house, which was in an area crowded with army establishments and thus likely to be a prime target of the Luftwaffe. Although Stowell was very much closer to Dick's HQ, Lettice was seldom there; her relationship with Minnie was going through a difficult patch, with Dick playing the peacemaker whilst sympathizing entirely with his wife. With Stowell not an option, he encouraged her to stay with her Aunt Dora at Wilcot, which was not too far from Longbridge Deverill. He was even more delighted when she elected to take a house at Polzeath for the duration of the school summer holidays, down in Cornwall and likely to be far away from any German bombing. Dick was able to join the family for an enjoyable six days' leave in the middle of August.

The HQ of 1 Armoured Division was located near Dorking, about 90 miles away from Longbridge Deverill, but the visits there at least enabled Dick to drop into Runwick on the way. His concerns about its safety grew when bombs dropped in the area at the end of September, just after the family had returned from Cornwall, and they had to take refuge for the night in the cellar. The brigade moved in due course from Wiltshire to Surrey to join the rest of the division, with its HQ at Hindhead. Dick was able to spend some more time at Runwick, but insisted that Lettice should move to Wadley Manor, the home of her friends Josephine and Rupert Craven, for the birth. She eventually drove up there with Lucia on 17 October, arriving at the house one hour before their daughter Sarah was born. Dick was delighted to have a daughter and enchanted with her once he was able to visit.

By this time the brigade was being gradually re-equipped with tanks and during the autumn Dick was required to spend many days in South Wales visiting each of his regiments during their training at Linney Head, but contriving to drop in at Wadley on the way there or back. On one of these journeys he was diverted instead to attend a cloth-model demonstration at Longford Castle, near Salisbury, which preceded a full-scale exercise during the following week by Montgomery's V Corps. The exercise was to involve 1 Armoured Division, under V Corps just for its duration, and 4 Division plus an army tank brigade. In the event it turned out to be something of a disappointment, 4 Division finding itself in difficulty whilst crossing Salisbury Plain at night and grumbling that it had been delayed by two of Dick's regiments. However, the preliminary demonstration was notable for the first sign of Dick's feelings towards Montgomery, evidenced in his diary with the words 'What an unpleasant man Monty is!' Dick also found Monty's two-hour long talk at the subsequent conference rather tedious.

On 12 December Dick returned to his office from addressing new recruits at the 10th Hussars to find a telegram informing him that he had been appointed to command 8 Armoured Division with the rank of acting major general and ordering him to take up his appointment without delay. Two days later he was on a train bound for Yorkshire, where his new command was forming. At the age of 42, this was a considerable accolade and it is easy to see the hand of Brooke in the appointment. It was also, albeit in an indirect way, due to Churchill. The Prime Minister had been greatly impressed by the German use of panzer divisions in the invasion of France and demanded from the War Office that Britain move closer towards parity with its enemy. 'I asked the other day,' he wrote to his Chief Staff Officer, Hastings Ismay, on 5 August 1940, 'for a forecast of the development of the armoured divisions which will be required in 1941 – namely five by the end of March and one additional every month until a total of ten is reached at the end of August 1941.'[4] At the time, there were just two armoured divisions in the United Kingdom, one of which was due to leave for the Middle East as soon as circumstances permitted, while 7 Armoured Division was confronting the Italians in Egypt. Plans were put in place to create a number of others, the timetable largely dictated by how fast the factories could produce the tanks. In September 1940 6 Armoured Division had already been formed under John Crocker, followed by 8 (November 1940), 9 (December 1940), 11 (March 1941) and Guards (June 1941) Armoured Divisions. This was short of Churchill's target and in fact the British would never get anywhere near the German total – it was the entry of the Soviet Union and the United States into the War that would ultimately achieve the required balance on the Allied side.

Important developments were taking place alongside the raising of the new armoured divisions. In the summer of 1940 Vyvyan Pope had been appointed to the new post of Director Armoured Fighting Vehicles at the War Office, with a key part of his role being the procurement of new tanks in conjunction with the Ministry of Supply. Pope was the ideal man for the job, one whose experience in armour went back to the early 1920s, and he brought a great deal of energy to setting up the infrastructure for the expansion, but he was to be foiled in his main objective, the installation in the new tanks of a 6-pounder gun. The counter-argument to what might have made a great difference to the war in North Africa in 1941 and early 1942 was that there was no design for a tank to accommodate such a gun and that it was better to continue producing those mounting 2-pounders than suspend production for six months while the factories were re-tooled.

One other appointment made in early 1942 would have a more immediate impact on Dick. This was another new role, Commander Royal Armoured Corps, and the man to hold it was Lieutenant General Giffard le Quesne Martel. Known to all as 'Q', Martel was an interesting, but on occasion a difficult man. He was neither a cavalryman nor a former member of the RTR, but a Royal Engineer, although his experience with armour went back right to the beginning, when he was a staff officer at the HQ of the Tank Corps in 1916. Subsequently he had designed one of the forerunners of the tracked infantry carriers, had commanded the engineer component of the first experimental mechanized force, had been instrumental in the introduction of the Christie suspension now used in the current generation of British cruiser tanks and had overseen the development of the first infantry tanks, better armoured but much slower than the cruisers. He had recently commanded an infantry division in the BEF and in June 1940 had deployed Matilda II infantry tanks in the only successful British armoured attack against the Germans near Arras.

Martel asked the War Office for a charter for his new role, but this turned out to be too difficult to draw up and it remained somewhat ambiguous. It was certainly agreed that he was responsible for developing a common operational doctrine and the tactical training regime within the armoured divisions. On the other hand, whilst he believed that these divisions were under his operational control, this was never understood by their commanders, let alone by their superiors in Home Forces and its various commands.

For Dick these issues were of secondary importance, as he had to get to grips with forming his division and bringing it up to readiness for active service. The HQ had opened initially on 4 November at Risely Hall, near Ripon, and was temporarily under Brigadier A.G. 'Kench' Kenchington, who simultaneously held the command of 24 Armoured Brigade. Dick had met Kenchington during the latter's previous appointment as BGS AFV Home Forces. He was seven years older than his new GOC and might easily have resented the new arrival, especially as Dick was a cavalryman whilst Kenchington was from the RTR. However, although Dick thought he talked too much he seemed to be amenable.

In October 1940 the structure of the armoured divisions had changed yet again. Each armoured brigade now had its own battalion of motorized infantry, partly balanced by the infantry element of the support group being reduced to a single battalion. The establishment of tanks remained unchanged, but an armoured car regiment had been added. Dick immediately began a tour of inspection, finding that his units were scattered across the whole of Yorkshire. In addition to Kenchington's brigade, comprising the 41st, 45th and 47th RTR and the 1st Queen's Westminsters (later renamed the 7th King's Royal Rifle Corps) and based around Leeds and Harrogate, there was 23 Armoured Brigade under Brigadier W. F. 'Wallie' Morrogh, with the 40th, 46th and 50th RTR and the 1st London Rifle Brigade (later the 11th Rifle Brigade) at Whitby, and 8 Support Group under Brigadier H. M. 'Stan' Stanford in various other locations. The armoured cars of the 2nd Derbyshire Yeomanry were at Stamford Bridge. Dick thought the units very variable in quality, Kenchington's tank battalions being markedly superior to Morrogh's.

To his great pleasure Dick found that his GSO1 was Harry Arkwright of his own regiment and the two of them and Denys Buckle, the assistant adjutant and quartermaster general, got down to work on the first task, the training schedule for the coming months. This was issued only two days later and laid out a schedule of individual, troop and squadron training until early May, followed by a progression of exercises involving whole battalions, then brigades and finally the complete division. The objective was to have the whole formation fit to take to the field by 1 July. Dick's overall priority was to find the best ways for all arms to work together and he proposed to hold a series of discussions for all the senior officers and staff, covering the employment of the motor battalions, the support of the armour by the field artillery, the use of the divisional engineers and of the anti-tank and anti-aircraft batteries and cooperation with the RAF, all areas which had been deficient in France.

Dick continued to press home the lessons he had learnt. On finding that there was a tendency for the armoured brigades to look at their new tanks admiringly, but not to use them and continue to train on the older models, he wrote to all commanders: 'This is unsound. By all means train drivers on training vehicles until they have reached the necessary standard, but our mobilisation vehicles are not there to look at – they must be used. One of the outstanding lessons about the employment of the 1st Armoured Division in

France was the impossibility of handling equipment and weapons well if the troops are not thoroughly familiar with their use.'[5] His main concern was to have sufficient men trained in time for his July deadline. Equipment was also in short supply, with a dearth especially of infantry carriers and 3in mortars for the two motor battalions, both of which Dick thought would be very good, but only if they had the necessary tools of war. Other shortages included only one gun per battery for the 73rd Anti-Tank Regiment and no live ammunition for the 5th Regiment, Royal Horse Artillery, which was in any event training on 4.5in and old French 75mm guns, pending the issue of the new 25-pounders.

Martel came for his first visit on New Year's Day 1941 and Dick was impressed by him then and at a subsequent conference at Camberley: he was only too keen to help remedy the deficiencies in his division. Brooke was also taking a close interest and paid his first visit to 8 Armoured on 26 February, writing in his diary: 'Found the division going on well under Dick McCreery.'[6]

By that time the division was poised to move south to the area around Chippenham, with the divisional HQ at Lackham House near Laycock. With the location of Runwick a continuing concern, Dick had been wondering whether or not to bring the family north and had already insisted on Eldred bringing up Beetle, but he now urged Lettice to look for a house as close as possible to his new HQ. After a number of false starts, she was offered a temporary tenancy of Bewley Court, a medieval manor house on the outskirts of Laycock and about twenty minutes' walk from Dick's office. It belonged to Arthur Gemmell of the 12th Lancers and was occupied by his wife Rosemary, who was happy to let it for six months.

Dick was now serving under Alexander again in Southern Command, or so he thought. Martel had a somewhat different idea. On 5 May he wrote: 'Armd. Divs are lodgers in Commands. Commands cannot order them to move to new localities or give them operational roles without reference to G.H.Q., which means H.Q. R.A.C., but these proposals can be solved by mutual discussion.'[7] In practice this system never really worked, as the GOC-in-Cs held a different view, arguing very reasonably that, in the event of invasion, they would become army commanders and would need to have complete authority over all the formations in their areas.

Martel was also at odds with a more formidable opponent in the shape of the prime minister. Churchill wished to have direct involvement in the development of the armoured divisions, writing to the Secretary of State for War and the Minister of Supply on 24 April: 'I propose to hold periodical meetings to consider tank and anti-tank questions, the first of which will be at Downing Street on Monday, May 5, at 11a.m. These meetings would be attended by the C.I.G.S, A.C.I.G.S., and General Pope should come, and

General Martel and his Armoured Divisional Commanders should also be invited…I am particularly anxious that all officers attending the meeting should be encouraged to send in their suggestions as to the points which should be discussed, and to express their individual views with complete freedom. I contemplate, in fact, a "Tank Parliament".'[8]

This was a problem for Martel, for whom Churchill was unsound on armoured matters as he had been listening too closely to the views of one of the armoured division commanders, Percy Hobart. Like Martel, 'Hobo' was one of the early tank pioneers, but he was an even more difficult man who had run foul of his superiors while commanding the Mobile Division in Egypt and been forcibly retired. He was reinstated after a petition to the King, with the support of Churchill. Spurning the offer of Martel's role, he instead accepted the command of 11 Armoured Division. Hobart had long been a proponent of an 'all tank Army', which was now anathema to Martel and others who considered that armies should comprise all arms, although there was continuing debate about the appropriate balance.

Martel now feared that Churchill would be influenced by Hobart. His solution was to hold meetings with all his divisional commanders before each meeting of the Tank Parliament, specifically so that they should agree in advance their views on the agenda and speak as one. The majority of the GOCs – Dick, Norrie, Crocker and Brocas Burrows of 9 Armoured Division – were content to play along with this, but Hobart was not. Dick, who was broadly in accord with Martel, described Hobart's attitude before one meeting as tiresome: Hobart was indeed quite prepared to voice his own opinions, even if they were contrary to those of his colleagues. In the event Churchill realized after four meetings that he was not getting the open expression of views he had asked for, and decided not to proceed with the 'Parliament'. It was unfortunate that it could not be made to work, as the prime minister's support was invaluable and some good might have come of the debate. In the longer run it did Martel no good and probably contributed to his being sidelined the following year.

At the end of June, 8 Armoured Division moved to the South-Eastern Command area, with its HQ at Brockham, between Dorking and Reigate. The tempo was now rising, with Dick exceptionally busy, visiting units, running ever more complex exercises and spending time down at the tank range at Linney Head. He was invariably accompanied by his ADC, Tom Powell and occasionally by Harry Arkwright or the GSO2 (Ops), Harry Floyd, a contemporary at Eton with whom he built a close rapport. Rollie Charrington, who had commanded 1 Armoured Brigade in Greece, was invited to lecture the officers on the experience gained in a brief campaign which had been as unsuccessful as that in France and Oliver Leese came to stay for two days to pick up some tips prior to forming Guards Armoured

Division. Dick managed to take a week's leave in early September, based at Bewley Court and largely spent relaxing by riding, playing tennis and going on blackberrying expeditions with the children, with a visit to Stowell thrown in for good measure.

On his return, all his energy was focused on the main event of the year, Exercise 'Bumper'. Bumper was the largest Home Forces exercise held to that date, involving two 'armies', each of two corps, with between them 3 armoured divisions, 9 infantry divisions, 2 army tank brigades and an independent infantry brigade. The background hypothesis to the exercise was that Britain had been invaded by the Germans, whose landings in the north-east and on the south coast had been repulsed, but who had established a firm foothold in East Anglia. The 'German Sixth Army' was provided by Eastern Command under Lieutenant General Laurence Carr, the defenders being Southern Command under Alexander. Carr was given two armoured divisions, Alexander only one, 8 Armoured. Brooke supervised the whole exercise from Oxford, whilst Montgomery was the chief umpire.

Dick attended the first conference on Bumper at Alexander's HQ at Wilton House, near Salisbury, on 19 September and four days later held his own divisional conference. Alexander's final pre-exercise conference took place on 28 September at his new temporary HQ near Reading and at 0030 hrs the following morning 8 Armoured Division began moving from Surrey to a position in Oxfordshire west of Bicester, concentrating there by 1100 hrs. The 'intelligence' indicated that the 'Sixth Army' had begun to move rapidly south-west from a line running from March through Ely and Newmarket to Sudbury. Alexander ordered V Corps, with 8 Armoured Division under command, to establish a defensive line roughly along the A5 trunk road from Stony Stratford to St Albans and brought the Canadian Corps into the Chilterns, from where he could move it as the situation demanded. On the left flank was the 8 Armoured Division position, which extended beyond Stony Stratford to Bicester, but there was a vulnerable gap between it and the neighbouring 48 Division.

Contact between the two armies was established that day, when the 'Germans' made a successful attack in the St Albans–Luton area, establishing a salient there, but Dick's troops saw no action. On the following day 2 Canadian Division recovered the salient, whilst units of 9 Armoured Division were encountered by Dick's reconnaissance regiment, the 2nd Derbyshire Yeomanry, advancing towards Buckingham. The armoured cars fell back, but not before suffering losses. Having failed to find the gap in Alexander's line, 9 Armoured Division mounted a frontal attack against 8 Armoured Division, but Dick had one priceless advantage. He was in the middle of Bicester Hunt country, where he had a thorough knowledge of the ground from many hunting seasons spent with his sister-in-law at Stratton Audley, which was on his front line. He positioned his troops in well-concealed positions, on which the opposing armour stumbled with disastrous results. In the words of one Canadian observer: 'The road at CAVERSFIELD was full of Covenanter tanks flying the red and yellow flags denoting "out of action". Another thrust at Brackley, where 8 and 9 Armd Div tanks had watched each other across the OUSE for some time, had a similar result.'[9] Dick's own casualties were estimated at only 10 per cent.

On the following day, 1 October, as the Canadian Corps pushed the 'Germans' back towards Hitchin, 9 Armoured Division again tried to advance, but lacking good intelligence allowed 8 Armoured Division to strike on its flank and rear, destroying Lumsden's 28 Armoured Brigade and sending the whole division back in confusion, its HQ only just avoiding being overrun. On 2 October, 8 Armoured Division crossed the Ouse and advanced rapidly towards St Neots, finishing off the enemy 27 Armoured Brigade on the way before being withdrawn into reserve. At 0630 hrs on 3 October Brooke brought the exercise to a close.

Dick's reputation was considerably enhanced by his performance during Bumper. In the subsequent conference Brooke criticized Alexander, unfairly in the latter's opinion, for dispositions which had lent too heavily on his right flank, rather than on the left where Dick had shown how much damage could be achieved in open country, but he commended Dick and the other armoured commanders for their handling of their divisions. Alex was unstinting in his praise, writing to Dick: 'Now that Bumper is over and we have had such a great success, just a line to thank you for the grand part you have played in it. Thanks to your brilliant operations near Oxford we were able to gain the initiative and secure success.'[10] Martel also sent a letter: 'I must just write you a note to congratulate you and everyone in the Division on your great success during manoeuvres. The Commander-in-Chief was particularly impressed with your handling of the Division throughout the Exercise, and particularly on the 1st and 2nd Oct.'[11]

Bumper unquestionably marked Dick out as a senior officer of great potential to Brooke, who within two months would be the Chief of the Imperial General Staff. As far as Alexander was concerned it confirmed Dick not only as an outstanding staff officer, but also as a commander who had the ability to handle a complex formation in the field. For Dick himself, however, change was just around the corner. As he wrote in his dairy on the day after the exercise closed: 'A v. satisfactory end up to my comd. of the Div.'

Chapter 13

Adviser

The first intimation of a change had come in August 1941, when Martel put forward a proposal to create a number of Armoured Corps Headquarters. Dick responded, accepting that there was a need to lift the burden of dealing with the multiplying number of armoured divisions and army tank brigades from HQ RAC, but challenging Martel's argument that each new Armoured Corps HQ should effectively take operational control of two or more armoured divisions. His letter throws some light on his own thinking at the time:

> It does not appear necessary to form a group of two or more Armoured Divisions to develop their technique in Armoured fighting. I think that the technique of Armoured fighting, except in exceptional circumstances such as the Western Desert, is an Armoured Division affair or, more often, an Armoured Brigade affair. Again, operational control of say two Armoured Divisions does not appear to be very likely except in a very open theatre of war.
>
> It strikes me that what a Corps Headquarters wants to learn much more than the control of two Armoured Divisions is the combined handling of an Armoured Division and a Motorised Division ... Surely one of the outstanding lessons of the fighting in Russia is the failure on many occasions of the Germans to get up sufficient infantry in time to back their Panzer Divisions. The reported reduction of the tank battalions to two, thereby increasing the proportion of infantry, again points to the importance of using infantry in sufficient numbers to back up tanks.
>
> It does seem that all Corps commanders should be able to handle an Armoured Division and that these proposals are really for helping in training. The Corps Staff of a mixed Corps of Armoured and Motorised Divisions surely need not be entirely Royal Armoured Corps Staff. In fact, by forming these Armoured Corps Headquarters there does appear to be a danger of retarding the spreading throughout the Army of a tactical doctrine for handling Armoured Divisions.[1]

Martel was almost certainly motivated by his continuing desire to get operational control of all the armoured formations, whilst Dick believed strongly that the only possible solution to success in armoured warfare was a proper balance of all arms, and particularly the mix of armour and infantry. In the event, it was not Dick's view which counted, but Brooke's, and the C-in-C was strongly opposed to Martel's idea, supported by Montgomery and others. The result was a watered-down version which Martel described as a bad compromise. Three Armoured Group HQs were formed, one in each of Northern, Eastern and South Eastern Commands, their role being to advise the respective GOC-in-Cs on the organization, manning, training and deployment of their armoured formations, but not to have any direct operational control themselves. The new Armoured Group Commanders retained their existing rank of major general. Dick himself was appointed to 2 Armoured Group,[2] based in South Eastern Command and responsible for overseeing his old 8 Armoured Division, 5 Canadian Armoured Division and 25 and 31 Army Tank Brigades, with a watching brief as well over Guards Armoured Division and 34 Army Tank Brigade in Southern Command.

Dick held his final conference on Bumper on 8 October, writing to Lettice that day: 'Everyone is still very pleased with themselves, I hope they won't think they are too good, but this morning I told them how much we all had still to learn! I don't think my new job is going to be very exciting, this winter it will purely be a training job... We have found a new home for our "Group H.Q." south of Dorking. A hideous Victorian house, but fairly comfortable.' Trashurst, as the house was called, turned out to be very suitable for the small HQ which Dick set up with Harry Arkwright later that month. There was no suggestion of Lettice and the family coming to live nearby, indeed at almost the same time they moved into what was to be their home until shortly before the end of the War, College House at Stanton St John, north-east of Oxford. This was close to her sister Helen at Stratton Audley, very convenient for the boys' preparatory school, Cothill, near Abingdon, and not too far from Eton, where Michael was due to start in 1942. Runwick was let for the long term and one of the consequences of these changes was that it was no longer possible to keep on Eldred, who had been with Dick, as soldier and civilian, for more than 20 years. He went off to work in a factory in Grantham to Dick's regret, even though Eldred had driven him mad on many occasions.

Dick found himself reporting directly to the GOC-in-C South-Eastern Command, Bernard Paget. In mid-November, however, a number of changes at the top of the army were announced. Brooke was to replace Dill as CIGS, whilst Paget would succeed him as C-in-C Home Forces. Relieving Paget would be Montgomery, until then GOC of XII Corps, which now brought Dick into regular contact with a man he would come to know well during 1942 and 1943. Martel was initially firmly in the picture, but in December he went to Egypt to learn more about Operation Crusader, which had been mounted during the previous month by the newly formed Eighth Army and had, after some potentially disastrous reverses, eventually succeeded in driving the Axis forces out of Cyrenaica.

Dick's activities in his new role followed much the pattern that he had expected, with a heavy emphasis on training. He had confidence in Charles Norman, his successor at 8 Armoured Division, an old friend with whose tactical ideas he was in general agreement and who needed the minimum of supervision. Only just arrived in the UK, 5 Canadian Armoured Division required more attention. The very small size of the regular Canadian peacetime army meant that it lacked the backbone of professional soldiers who still filled the most important positions in its British counterparts, but what it lacked in experience it made up for in enthusiasm and Dick soon formed a good working relationship with the Canadian Corps Commanders, Andrew MacNaughton and his successor Henry Crerar, and grew to admire their men. He also saw a lot of Oliver Leese at Guards Armoured Division. He had known him from afar at school and rather better at Staff College, where Leese had been in the Senior Division when Dick arrived. Their relationship was always good and Dick was also able to use his remit with Guards Armoured to continue his association with Alexander, in whose Southern Command it was located.

Dick, as so often, found himself constantly on the move, visiting Bovington to inspect the AFV School and to see demonstrations of new tanks, watching combined services landing craft exercises in Scotland, lecturing to other HQs on the use of armour, visiting public schools to encourage their pupils to apply to join the RAC and holding innumerable TEWTs. He saw a great deal of Montgomery, particularly just before and after the many exercises which were held in South-Eastern Command. Dick tended to be exasperated by the sheer length of the GOC-in-C's summing up in the conference held after each exercise, although he was compelled to admit after one of them that it had been a tour de force. He was particularly irked on one particular occasion by Montgomery using his material without an appropriate attribution. 'I made out some notes for Gen. "Monte" [sic]', he wrote to Lettice, 'and he gave them out almost word for word at a big conference yesterday, which he held on last week's exercise! All the audience listened to his words of wisdom, & thought how much he knew about armoured divisions.'

Towards the end of January 1942 Martel returned from his visit to the Middle East and Dick, who still respected his views although he did not always agree with them, was keen to hear his findings. Martel had not been at all happy with what he heard about Operation Crusader. The strategic objective of Norrie's XXX Corps, the capture of the important Axis airfield at Sidi Rezegh, had been correct, but 7 Armoured Division's formations had been dispersed and, whilst 7 Armoured Brigade and the Support Group had captured the objective, 22 Armoured Brigade had been detached and had suffered badly in a battle with Axis armour, as had the independent 4 Armoured Brigade. The lack of concentration had meant that the division was driven away from Sidi Rezegh with considerable loss and it was only Rommel's decision to dash for the Egyptian frontier, where he had been repulsed, which saved the situation. The only way in which 4 Armoured Brigade, equipped with American Stuart light tanks, had found itself able to engage the enemy was to charge, as the range and penetration of its guns was so poor and its only advantage lay in speed.

Martel came back with a few positive conclusions, notably that Norrie's command function had worked well, but overall he was critical. 'As regards tactics in detail,' he later wrote, 'there had not been enough co–operation between the tanks and other arms. In fact the division needed a larger proportion of these arms. There were cases of tanks charging home like cavalry in bygone days and being shot to pieces in the process by artillery. A careful plan and artillery support was needed at every stage.'[3] He was clearly now much closer to Dick's point of view and the upshot was a radical reorganization of the armoured divisions in Home Forces, the initial work on which started at the end of February, although it was not concluded until May. There were two important changes. The first was that one of the two armoured brigades was replaced by a lorried infantry brigade, reducing the tank establishment from 340 to 201. The second was that the support group was abolished and, in its place the artillery and engineers were put under their own HQs, the former commanded by a brigadier, whereas the senior gunner hitherto had been a colonel acting in an advisory capacity. There were further changes made as the war progressed, but they were minor and the new structure would in essence remain in place for the duration.

Just as Martel left Egypt to return to England, events in Libya took a serious turn for the worse. On 21 January Rommel launched the Axis forces back into Cyrenaica. The initial blow fell on 1 Armoured Division, which had arrived relatively recently, but had temporarily lost Lumsden, its GOC since early November, who had been wounded in the post-Crusader advance. His replacement, Frank Messervy, barely had time to get to know his division. The Support Group was overrun, whilst neither the tanks nor the tactics of 2 Armoured Brigade proved a match for the Germans and it was forced to retire after heavy losses. Eighth Army made an undignified retreat to the Gazala Line, where it dug in.

Churchill was taken aback by this reverse, putting enormous pressure on Auchinleck, the C-in-C Middle East, to strike back, an impossible task given that his forces were in general disarray and that his only available armoured division was no longer an effective fighting force. Brooke was gravely concerned about the performance of the armour in the desert. On the very day of Rommel's attack he wrote to Auchinleck: 'I am worried... that you have not got a first-class armoured force officer on your staff...There is a colossal amount of work for him in the re-equipping and reforming of your armoured divisions and army tank brigades, and in the provision of general advice on armoured matters.'[4] Brooke saw Martel for a report on his visit five days later and on 4 February he wrote to Auchinleck again: 'I do hope that you will reconsider the advisability of appointing an armoured forces major-general on similar lines to your chief gunner and sapper.'[5] On February 14 Auchinleck responded, asking for a major general AFV (armoured fighting vehicles) to be sent if one could be spared. One could and it was to be Dick.

Dick was notified on 24 February that he was probably to go to GHQ Middle East, but it was 20 March before he departed. On 3 March he was briefed by Brooke, who warned him that 'he might have a difficult furrow to plough,'[6] but there was still much unfinished business to resolve at 2 Armoured Group before he could finally leave the country. For Dick it was not an ideal time, as Lettice was expecting another baby in the summer, but he was keen to get close to the action. Except for three months in the summer of 1943 and a brief visit in early 1945, he would be overseas for the rest of the war.

The journey to Cairo took a week by a very circuitous route. Having parted from Lettice on 20 March at Waterloo,[7] Dick left Poole Harbour on a BOAC Boeing 314 flying boat in the company, among others, of Lord Beaverbrook, who was on his way to the United States. The plane called at Foynes in the West of Ireland and then Lisbon, where the party, all in civilian dress, motored out to Estoril for a bath and lunch at the Park Hotel. The next stop was Bathurst in The Gambia, whence Beaverbook and the flying boat flew off across the Atlantic, whilst Dick and some of the other passengers changed to a conventional aeroplane. Their route took them via Freetown in Sierra Leone and Marshal in Liberia to Takoradi and Accra in the Gold Coast and thence on the 'reinforcement route' via Kano and Maiduguri in Nigeria and El Fasher and Khartoum in the Sudan, reaching Cairo on the afternoon of 27 March, where Dick was met by his new GSO1, Bill Liardet.[8] It had been an exhausting journey, but he had managed to fend off airsickness with frequent pills.

Auchinleck was away at the front when Dick arrived, so he reported instead to the Chief of Staff, General Corbett. Corbett, like Auchinleck himself an Indian Army officer, was an unimpressive man and Dick wrote in his diary that he was 'not v. struck by him'. The good news was that the director of military training was his old friend and fellow whipper-in from Staff College, John Harding, with whom he had an excellent relationship –

just as well as the two would have to work closely together. Also away from Cairo at the time was another Staff College contemporary, Eric 'Chink' Dorman-Smith, who had been employed by Auchinleck as a senior staff officer, albeit with an unspecified role. It was partly to counteract what Brooke saw as Chink's influence that Dick had been sent to Egypt. The CIGS later wrote of his concerns about Auchinleck: 'I was beginning to be suspicious that "Chink" Dorman-Smith, one of his staff officers, was beginning to exercise far too much influence on him. Dorman-Smith had a most fertile brain, continually producing new ideas, some of which (not many) were good and the rest useless.'[9] There had been no love lost between Dick and Chink at Camberley and the seeds were now about to be sown for conflict between them.

It was several days before Auchinleck returned to Cairo, during which Dick ploughed through the copious files he had inherited and visited some of the armoured formations and units located around Cairo. His initial meeting with the C-in-C on 3 April went well, Dick writing to Lettice subsequently: 'There is no doubt he is a fine man. He was friendly. I am dining with him tonight.' This was in fact not their first meeting as Dick had been introduced to Auchinleck by Alexander at a dinner in April 1939. Auchinleck suggested that Dick should go up to the front immediately and he left on the following day.

Dick spent a week on the move, travelling initially to meet Brian Robertson, the deputy adjutant and quartermaster general at Eighth Army's Rear HQ at Buq Buq, not far from Sollum where he had spent much time in 1936. From there he moved on to the Main HQ at Gambut and then to Norrie's XXX Corps HQ behind the Gazala Line. On the following day he saw 4 Armoured Brigade and Messervy's 7 Armoured Division, before travelling across the desert to XIII Corps to meet its commander, 'Strafer' Gott, with whom he was favourably impressed. He spent nearly two days with the now recovered Lumsden at 1 Armoured Division before returning to Gambut for a meeting with Neil Ritchie, the Army commander. Having inspected the tank replacement centre there, he went on to look at the RAC transit camp at Mersa Matruh, eventually arriving back in Cairo on the evening of his seventh day away.

Dick had learnt a lot during this trip. Two significant changes had occurred within the armoured divisions in the Western Desert, one good, the other of dubious value. On the positive side, the formations were now partially equipped with the new American M3 Lee/Grant tank. This was much better armoured than the Crusader and, more importantly, its main armament was an excellent 75mm gun, which was capable of firing not only armour-piercing shells at a velocity which could penetrate the armour of most German and Italian tanks, but also high explosive shells, which were able to destroy the formidable German 88mm anti-tank guns from a safe distance. Mechanically it was also far more reliable than the British Crusader, which was just as well as one of Dick's responsibilities was to provide an adequate supply of tanks fit for battle to the units on the front. It had one disadvantage, that the gun was mounted in a sponson on the right-hand side of the vehicle, giving it a limited traverse and making a 'hull down' position more difficult.

The other change was equally significant, but its value was a matter of debate. As in the UK the organization of the armoured divisions had changed. The common factors were the demise of the support group and the exchange of a motorized infantry brigade for the second armoured brigade. However, whereas in the UK the artillery and engineers had become divisional troops, in the Middle East they had been allocated to the two brigades. The top divisional gunner and sapper were still advisers, not commanders, and the brigades were brigade groups, effectively 'all arms' mini-divisions themselves. The limited supply of Lee/Grants meant that in four of the brigade groups in the theatre the armoured regiments still employed one squadron of Stuarts to two of Lee/Grants, whilst in the remaining two there was one squadron of Lee/Grants and two of Crusaders.

Dick was never persuaded of the value of brigade groups, except in a wholly independent form. In a divisional context he felt that their presence encouraged the dispersal of force, believing that the whole division was the more effective weapon to deploy. As the campaign developed, this would become a significant issue.

GHQ Middle East was responsible not only for Eighth Army in the Western Desert, but also for Tenth Army in Persia and Iraq, the object of Dick's next visit. In the spring of 1942 there was considerable concern about any further advance that summer by the Germans into the Soviet Union, threatening the Caucasus and, much more significantly from the British perspective, the oilfields of the Persian Gulf. A large force had been assembled to defend the area, both British and Russian, and the former included 252 Indian Armoured Brigade Group. Dick met the Army commander, General Quinan, in Cairo for a briefing on 16 April and left eleven days later, flying to Habbaniya in Iraq and then driving on to Baghdad and Mosul, where the armoured brigade was located. There he inspected the units, which included the 14th/20th Hussars, and was taken to see the lay of the land. He moved on to Kirkuk before returning to Baghdad, where there were discussions about a number of topics, one decision being to enhance the army's armoured capability by bringing the HQ of 31 Indian Armoured Division from India to take over 252 Armoured Brigade and an as yet unspecified motor brigade.

Back in Cairo a week after he had left, Dick found numerous issues on his desk, the most pressing of which was the painfully slow expansion of armour in the theatre. In the late summer of 1941 it had been decided to convert 1 Cavalry Division to armour. The division's Household Cavalry and yeomanry regiments had come out to Palestine with all their horses at the beginning of 1940, but found that there was no chance of employment for them in their traditional role. From the units 10 Armoured Division had been formed, but the conversion was still not complete, due largely to the lack of tanks, the priority for which remained with the front-line divisions. There was as yet no motor brigade and the divisional troops were thin on the ground, with a total absence of artillery. Dick thought that the human element was good, but progress towards creating a full division remained frustrating.

Dick's other concerns were training, in conjunction with John Harding, and liaison with his opposite numbers in the various services. There were also various tactical theories being advanced on how to deploy the armour most effectively, most of which he could not support. One of the more bizarre of these was the 'cow-pat' theory, which posited the establishment of a number of supply bases located forward of the Gazala Line but south of the Axis forces, in which strong armoured forces would be based, supported by infantry and artillery. These, the theory held, would draw the enemy out from his fixed defences, whereupon he could be destroyed. Dick, supported by the Director of Military Intelligence Freddie de Guingand playing the role of the enemy, demonstrated in a war game that this would result in the Axis being able to concentrate overwhelming force against each individual base, wiping them out one by one. It was precisely the sort of dispersal of strength which Dick deplored.

This was a minor victory in what Dick was fast recognizing was an impotent role. Although he was invited to attend the C-in-C's major conferences he was not a member of the inner circle, which was dominated not by Corbett but by an increasingly influential Dorman-Smith, and Dick's views were often disregarded. On the family side letters from Lettice arrived infrequently, although the Duke of Gloucester brought several with him when he visited the theatre, and there was one scare when he received a cable from Lettice to say that Bob had had an operation to have a kidney removed, but was doing well. Follow-up cables reported that he was out of danger and Dick took comfort after consulting a colleague from the RAMC, who reassured him that the loss of a kidney should not have any adverse effect on quality of life.

In mid-May Dick paid another visit to Eighth Army, spending all his time with Norrie, Lumsden and Messervy, discussing their dispositions. Gott's XIII Corps held all the fixed defences of the Gazala Line with the bulk of the infantry and an army tank brigade, positioned behind minefields running south from the Mediterranean coast. Norrie's XXX Corps was to defend the desert flank with almost all the armour, Lumsden's 1 Armoured Division lying astride one of the main east–west desert arteries, the Trigh Capuzzo track, Messervy's 7 Armoured Division dispersed further south in the open desert. 1 Free French Brigade, positioned in a well-defended box at Bir Hacheim, and 3 Indian Motor Brigade to its south-east both came under Messervy's command.

Back in London, Churchill's impatience with the lack of movement was growing and signal after signal went out to Auchinleck pressing him to take the offensive. The reply was inevitably that the C-in-C would do so when he was completely ready, but that this was unlikely to be much before the end of May. On the night of 26/27 May, Rommel struck first.

Chapter 14

Crisis in the Desert

Rommel's armour swept round the desert flank and turned north, with a view to driving a wedge between the static British infantry divisions and the rest of Eighth Army. Although it had been spotted by the armoured car screen its strength was unexpected, consisting as it did of 15 and 21 Panzer Divisions, 90 Light Division and the Italian Ariete Armoured Division. The result was that 3 Indian Motor Brigade was overwhelmed and 7 Motor Brigade, the infantry component of 7 Armoured Division, was pushed back to the east. Messervy's divisional HQ was overrun and he himself was taken prisoner: although he subsequently escaped in the confusion, it was some time before he was able to re-establish contact. The first two armoured brigades encountered, 4 and 22, took heavy losses, but as the Germans pressed on they were given time to recover. By the time the Germans reached the Trigh Capuzzo track, the British were waiting for them and Lumsden attacked with his 2 Armoured Brigade, whilst the Germans also came under fire from 201 Guards Brigade in its defended box at 'Knightsbridge'. Meanwhile the Free French held out at Bir Hacheim.

Though caught napping, this was not yet by any means a disaster for the British. The Lee/Grants came as a particularly unpleasant surprise to the Axis, holding off the leading 21 Panzer Division with their superior range. Running out of momentum and with his supply lines cut, Rommel was close to defeat, but his response was masterly. Turning due west towards his own static front line, he destroyed 150 Brigade[1] and pulled back all the attacking formations into a defensive position against the minefields, known as 'the Cauldron', from which he cut a passage to his own lines for supplies. Ritchie's response was sluggish. A quick attack on the Cauldron might well have settled the issue in the British favour, but it was not until the night of 5/6 June that a concerted operation was mounted by 22 Armoured Brigade and two Indian infantry brigades. The planning and execution were both poor and the result was a fiasco. The Free French evacuated Bir Hacheim after a heroic stand on the night of 10/11 June and on the following morning Rommel broke out of the Cauldron. Bolstered by PzKpfw III Js, which were a match for the Lee/Grant, he won the subsequent tank battle conclusively, in spite of heroic efforts by Lumsden, who found himself commanding two armoured divisions when Messervy was once again cut off. By 18 June

Eighth Army was in pell–mell retreat to the Egyptian frontier, leaving a garrison at Tobruk which was surrounded and eventually surrendered on 21 June. Futile attempts were made to try to stop the advancing Germans and Italians at Sollum and Mersa Matruh, but by the end of the month the army was back on the El Alamein Line. By that time Messervy had been sacked, as had Ritchie, and Norrie was to follow them a few days later. Auchinleck himself took direct command of Eighth Army

Back in Cairo as the battle developed, Dick had been seething with frustration. 'I am fit and well,' he wrote to Lettice on 27 June, 'but, needless to say, during these last few weeks I have hardly enjoyed being a spectator and feeling that I can do so little.' 'Herbert', he continued, 'has been magnificent... he ran nearly all the fighting for the first two weeks... he was always calm, encouraging and thinking ahead.' The see-saw nature of the battle had been highly confusing. Leaving the Sunday morning service in Cairo Cathedral on 31 May, Dick had found himself standing next to Auchinleck, who told him that it was too early to be sure, but he thought that they might be on the brink of a great victory. Optimism continued to reign right up to 18 June, then their hopes plummeted.

On the following day Dick had been up to the Western Desert, arriving at Sidi Barrani to find the army moving through on its way east. 'The most extraordinary sight,' he wrote later, 'with traffic of every description packed nose to tail, frequently double banking, nearly all moving eastwards towards the Delta. Tanks, bulldozers, staff cars, bren gun carriers, recovery vehicles, and lorries of every type were moving inextricably mixed up.'[2] He saw Ritchie, Norrie and Lumsden and was back in Cairo to brief Auchinleck on the tank situation before the C–in–C left to take personal charge of the battle on 25 June, accompanied by Dorman-Smith, who had recently been appointed to the position of Deputy Chief of the General Staff (DCGS). The losses of tanks at Gazala and on the retreat had been enormous. At one stage at the beginning of the battle the numbers had been reduced from 300 to 70 and Dick now had to ensure that these were replaced as quickly as possible.

Dick had been taken aback by the attitude at GHQ, writing in his diary on 29 June: 'C.G.S (Corbett) more gloomy than usual, all sorts of preparations going on for the defence of the Delta.' There were signs of panic, as secret papers were burnt and women and children were evacuated to Palestine and the Sudan. Dick had not agreed with the attempts to halt the Germans at Sollum and Mersa Matruh, where outflanking through the desert was almost inevitable, but was now adamant that Eighth Army should stand and fight in its new and intrinsically strong defensive position. In Norrie's words: 'He was emphatic that it would be very wrong to discuss withdrawing to the Nile and that we should make a "do or die" stand at

Alamein with no further retirements. I entirely agreed and expressed this view officially.'[3]

The next month was to prove one of the most trying of Dick's military career. One of the consequences of 'the flap', as the mood of panic at GHQ was called, was a proposal to close the base workshops at Alexandria and move the most valuable plant and machinery to Haifa. 'I was absolutely opposed to this,' wrote Dick later. 'These workshops were turning out some six tanks a day after repair and base overhauls and every good running tank was needed up with the Armoured Brigades. I argued that it was far better to have another 50 or 100 tanks now to fight with, even if we lost the equipment in the base workshops as a result. I felt that if we lost Alexandria we would certainly require no base workshops for some considerable time afterwards!'[4] In this at least he got his way.

The workshops themselves were not always functioning at peak efficiency and were particularly dilatory in preparing the tanks for Dick's old 8 Armoured Division, which he went to Suez to greet on its arrival in the country. Dick had a number of set-tos with the director of mechanical maintenance, so much so that the latter complained to Auchinleck. The Division's 23 Armoured Brigade was equipped with Valentines, designed as infantry tanks but expected to perform in the cruiser role. The urgency to bring the brigade into action meant that they were sent up to the front eleven days after arriving in Egypt, before being modified for desert conditions and without their wireless sets being properly netted. On 22 July the brigade was ordered to support an attack by 6 New Zealand and 161 Indian Brigades on the western end of the defensively important Ruweisat Ridge. Armed with the old 2-pounders, capable of a maximum speed of 15 mph, and with their crews unversed in desert warfare, the Valentines were no match for the Germans. By pure luck they overran a Panzergrenadier battalion and came within yards of the Afrika Korps HQ, but swift action from anti-tank guns and 21 Panzer Division overwhelmed them and by that night the brigade had effectively ceased to exist. Just 7 Valentines remained of the 106 which had gone into battle. One consequence of this operation was the general loss of confidence in the armoured formations among the infantry divisions, and particularly the New Zealanders.

Both Lumsden and Raymond Briggs, the commander of 2 Armoured Brigade, were wounded during the weeks of fighting which later became known as the First Battle of El Alamein, as was Alec Gatehouse, who had temporarily succeeded Lumsden at 1 Armoured Division, but all were back in action relatively quickly. Dick's former adjutant Frank Arkwright, however, was killed in action leading a yeomanry regiment, an event which affected Dick deeply. On a much more positive note, Dick learnt on 6 August that his fifth child and fourth son, Charles, had been born on 30 June. The cables sent to him by both Lettice and his mother had gone by air mail and taken over five weeks to arrive.

By this time Dick was locked in conflict with his C-in-C. As he wrote to Lettice on 28 July: 'I have had my worries lately, people who know nothing about it advising my boss on all sorts of points of organisation without me being consulted. I had a real set-to with my boss 2 days ago and I hope that I have cleared the air a bit. I cannot be just a "yes" man, and did not come out here just to sit in our office whilst others give most unsound advice on matters they know nothing about!' The 'unsound advice' was coming from one quarter only, Dorman-Smith, but it was finding a ready acceptance in Auchinleck. The background was one in which the C-in-C was urgently seeking new ideas on how to break what looked like deadlock, having succeeded in stopping Rommel, who was himself now at the end of a very long line of communication and unable to press any further attack due to lack of supplies. The issue was one which was spectacularly demonstrated in the attack on Ruweisat Ridge – the apparent inability of the armour to cooperate effectively with the infantry. The solution proposed by Dorman-Smith was the extension of the 'all-arms' brigade groups to carry out the sort of operations which had been used by the 'Jock columns'[5] with some success in the early days of the Desert War against the Italians, effectively carrying out 'hit and run' raids rather than mounting a concerted offensive. Auchinleck had a history of leaning towards such battle groups and he and Dorman-Smith had written a paper on the subject in 1938 when the former was the DCGS in India and the latter the director of military training.

Most of the senior officers were against them. Messervy, now in Cairo as acting DCGS in the absence of Dorman-Smith, presented a paper disagreeing with battle groups which had the support not only of Dick, but also of Wilfred 'Tommy' Lindsell, commandant at the Senior Officers' School during Dick's time there and now the Principal Administrative Officer. Auchinleck tore it up in a fury. Bernard Freyberg and Leslie Morshead, who as the GOCs of 2 New Zealand and 9 Australian Divisions had the luxury of appeal to their governments if they were ordered to undertake a reorganization of which they did not approve, declared that they would refuse to implement any such proposal, preferring to fight as complete divisions. Dorman-Smith then proposed the creation of 'mobile' divisions, by which every division would be reorganized to comprise one armoured brigade and two infantry brigade groups. This might have been a good idea and indeed Freyberg later reorganized his division on much the same lines, albeit with the artillery and engineers as divisional troops. Dick, like others, felt that to do this in the middle of a battle, when all the training had been for the current organization, was madness.

The last straw for Dick came when Dorman–Smith proposed that each armoured regiment should be formed of four squadrons rather than three, to make the regiment better able to withstand losses after a major engagement. This was not as simple as it sounded and would result in serious disruption as men were moved about between units and sub-units and then trained in what would inevitably be new tactics. This would apply particularly to any regiments arriving in the theatre from the UK, where no such reorganization was contemplated.

On 16 July, having sounded out all the armoured commanders, who were entirely like minded, Dick began work on a memo arguing against the various reorganizations and he met Corbett three days later to discuss it, writing about the CGS in his diary with evident surprise –'he agrees to a lot!' On 26 July he was summoned to Eighth Army HQ with John Harding to confer with Auchinleck, who was not in a good mood. Arriving after a very bumpy flight, he found the C-in-C 'v. angry with my memo, and he bullied me for over an hour, but I stuck to my pts.' In the face of Dick's intransigence a decision was reached to send out a questionnaire to all the armoured commanders seeking their views. Harding, who had been due to fly to the UK to give Brooke a full update on the situation in Middle East Command, was to delay his departure so that the results could be taken into account. This actually suited Dick, who was certain of how his RAC colleagues would react, but it made his position with Auchinleck very precarious. 'So I have won the first round!' he wrote in his diary, but there was serious uncertainty as to whether he would come out on top in the match.

In the meantime, and unknown to Dick, significant developments were taking place in the UK, whose consequences would shake the whole of Middle East Command. On 16 July Brooke obtained Churchill's approval to go to the Middle East to see the situation for himself. Although it was clear that the Axis advance had been stopped, he was concerned about what would happen next, particularly in the light of a proposal by Auchinleck to give command of Eighth Army to Corbett, whom Brooke did not know but doubted would be suitable. Because a high-powered delegation was due two days later from the USA, the visit had to be deferred until the end of the month. By this time the prime minister had decided that he would come as well, staying in Cairo before going on to meet Stalin in Moscow. Brooke set off on 31 July so that he could spend a day in Malta, whilst the prime minister flew on the following day. The two men arrived in Cairo within an hour of each other on the morning of 3 August.

Dick was unaware of the impending arrival of the two most important figures in the British war effort until two days beforehand and it was a while before he met either Brooke or Churchill. In the meantime nothing had changed, and when he visited the C-in-C at Eighth Army's Tac HQ on

6 August he was subjected to 'another long bully' and threatened with dismissal if he did not toe the line, which he resolutely refused to do. That evening, however, he was treated to a talk with Churchill and on the following morning he had a meeting with the CIGS, whom he found 'v. helpful & encouraging!' On 8 August he accompanied Churchill and Brooke on a visit to 8, 9 and 24 Armoured Brigades. Dick travelled in the PM's car and wrote later: 'I had picked him up at the British Embassy and we had only gone 100 yards when he said, "Now don't forget I am the Prime Minister and you must be absolutely frank. In your opinion what is wrong?" I did not find this difficult to answer.'[6] Churchill was somewhat indiscreet, as Dick's diary recorded: 'He told me a few secrets about changes in comd!'

Much had indeed been going on in the meantime. It was by then common ground between the prime minister and the CIGS that Auchinleck should go, as should both Corbett and Dorman-Smith. Churchill offered the C-in-C's job to Brooke, who declined it on the grounds that he would give better service in his current role. The two men decided on Alexander as Auchinleck's replacement and a signal was sent for him to fly out to Egypt immediately.

It is a fair assumption that Dick had wind of Alexander's appointment from his conversation with Churchill and he would have been entitled to assume from this and Brooke's encouragement that his own career was reasonably safe, albeit not necessarily in his current appointment. What he did not know was that the CIGS already had other ideas for him, Brooke writing much later in his *Autobiographical Notes*: 'It now remained to find a successor... as Chief of Staff. I at once thought of Dick McCreery, who I had sent out to the Auk as his Adviser on Armoured forces... I knew his ability well and I also knew that he had acted as G.S.O.1 of the 1st Division...I therefore decided to suggest him to Alex as soon as he arrived.'[7] Unsurprisingly Alexander leapt at the suggestion.

It was because his new appointment was so unexpected rather than because he was concerned about his future that Sunday, 9 August 1942, was one of the most extraordinary days of Dick's life. He was sitting in his office in the 'Pink Pillars', the GHQ building in Cairo, when he was visited by Angus Collier, the deputy military secretary, responsible within Middle East Command for all senior appointments. He came, in Dick's words, 'to say that General Auchinleck[8] had decided that he did not need an M.G.R.A.C. at GHQ and that he was recommending to the War Office that I should go home to command an armoured division, and I would be replaced by a Brigadier. In other words I would be politely sacked.'[9] An hour later Alexander walked into the office to say that he wanted Dick to be his chief of staff. He asked Dick to come over for tea and a chat at the British Embassy, after which Churchill invited Dick for a post-dinner drink and kept him talking until after midnight.

Chapter 15

Chief of Staff

'**G**eneral Staff conferences are going on with no sign of a change!' wrote Dick in his diary on 11 August, but he himself was seeing Alexander every day to prepare for taking over, although his own appointment did not formally start until 23 August. Auchinleck's hopes of a measured transfer of authority were abruptly disrupted by the arrival in Cairo of the man who would instantly become the dominant figure in the theatre. Churchill's original intention had been that 'Strafer' Gott, who was by then the most experienced general in the Western Desert, would assume the command of Eighth Army, but Gott was killed on 7 August when the plane in which he was travelling was shot down by German fighters. Tragic though this was it was also providential, as there is evidence that Gott was not only tired, but also as bereft of new ideas as Auchinleck. The man who was sent for to replace him was Montgomery, who arrived on 12 August. Disregarding the agreed timetable, he went up to the front on the following day, from where he sent a message that he had assumed command. Auchinleck was furious, but could do nothing about the fait accompli.

Two days later Alexander took over as commander-in-chief and immediately moved the GHQ out of Cairo to a site on the edge of the desert at Mena, close to the Pyramids, where most of the staff was accommodated in tents. Dick welcomed the move: he had been staying in a room in the Turf Club, which had not been entirely to his taste, and he disliked the atmosphere of the old GHQ building. The new site was not only more comfortable, markedly cooler at night, but also engendered a far more businesslike approach.

Although recognizing the importance of his new job and looking forward to working for Alexander, whom he knew he complemented well, Dick was disappointed that he was to continue on the staff rather than in the field. This was in spite of the fact that the appointment had brought with it promotion to acting lieutenant general, although, as he wrote to Lettice, 'later for various reasons I may come down again to Maj-Gen... It is rather sad, however, still being stuck to an office stool for a lot of my time.'[1] His first week was interrupted by the reappearance from Moscow of Churchill and Brooke, who both took up a lot of his and Alexander's time agreeing the organization of Middle East Command, which was to hive off a new Persia and Iraq Command to 'Jumbo' Wilson, but to retain Palestine, Transjordan and Syria, as well as Sudan and the Horn of Africa. It was necessary to agree the appropriate allocation of troops to Wilson, which was not easy against the background of demands by Montgomery. The Eighth Army Commander had already persuaded Alexander to send up the newly arrived 44 Division, overruling the latter's own staff, who considered that it was not yet acclimatized to the desert, and he was to do much the same for 51 (Highland) Division, reformed after the debacle at St Valéry and disembarking at Port Tewfik that very week.

On a more positive note, a reorganization of the armoured divisions took place to reflect broadly the same structure adopted earlier in the year in Home Forces, the only significant difference being an increase in the field artillery regiments from two to three. Out went brigade groups for both armoured and infantry divisions, the artillery, engineers and supporting services all becoming divisional troops under their own commanders. On one principle all the senior officers, including Alexander, Montgomery and Dick, were united: in future all types of division would fight as complete formations. Montgomery's immediate order to Eighth Army, that all plans for a withdrawal to the Delta would be scrapped and that it would stand at El Alamein and defeat Rommel there, was also entirely in line with Dick's thinking, although at Churchill's express command measures were put in place to defend Cairo and the line of the Nile, lest Rommel should break through.

At the top of the many pressing issues confronting Montgomery was the appointment of corps commanders. Three would be needed since one of his first demands, made on the day of his arrival to John Harding, now the DCGS, was the creation of a new *corps de chasse*, to be composed largely of armour and used as a reserve for a major offensive. Within days Harding came up with a proposal to revive X Corps and incorporate within it three armoured divisions – 1, 8 and 10 – and 2 New Zealand Division. A commander would be required for the new formation as well as one to replace Gott in XIII Corps, whilst Ramsden in XXX Corps was unacceptable to Montgomery.

Montgomery had by then already sent for Brian Horrocks from the UK and it was his original intention to appoint him to X Corps. Horrocks had commanded 9 Armoured Division in England, but was himself an infantryman and had no experience of armour in action. Dick felt very strongly that the right man for X Corps was Lumsden, who had commanded 1 Armoured Division with distinction at Gazala and had also fought in the July battles, although he had been as exasperated as Dick with Auchinleck's employment of armour. Dick strongly recommended Lumsden to Alexander and Montgomery, but the latter did not know him well and was dubious about his record, preferring as always to trust only those of whom he had personal experience. As soon as Horrocks arrived in Cairo, Dick met him to advance the case for Lumsden and found him in ready agreement. Horrocks subsequently claimed that it was he who persuaded Montgomery to accept this arrangement and indeed this is likely, as Montgomery was unlikely to listen to Dick. When Alexander, accompanied by Dick, paid his first official visit to Eighth Army in his capacity as C-in-C, Lumsden was confirmed in command, somewhat against Montgomery's better judgement. Dick recorded later that when he saw Lumsden on the following day 'there is no doubt that he was worried. He gave me the clear impression that he would not get on with General Montgomery. Certainly the two never hit it off.'[2] This would all come home to roost in due course.

Montgomery's demand for 44 Division was justified by his decision to fight a defensive battle against Rommel at the earliest opportunity. This came less than three weeks after his arrival, when the Panzerarmee Afrika was launched through the minefields just north of the Qattara Depression with a view to outflanking Eighth Army to the south. Finding 7 Armoured Division in its path, it hooked north towards the Alam Halfa Ridge. Montgomery had anticipated this, his anti-tank guns well dug in and his armoured brigades in hull-down positions from which they were forbidden to emerge in the kind of senseless charges to which they had been accustomed. After two days of battering his head against a brick wall, Rommel found the initiative passing to the British and a day later he began to withdraw, bombed by the RAF and shelled on his flanks by ground forces. It was a vital victory, which bought Montgomery breathing space to prepare for his future offensive at El Alamein.

By this time the relationship between Montgomery and Alexander had become clear and it was not by any means the normal chain of command. Montgomery was absolutely determined to do things his own way, depending on Alexander to provide him with the tools for the job and to keep the War Office and the politicians, particularly Churchill, off his back, while leaving all military decisions to him. Although Montgomery welcomed Alexander's position as a buffer between him and higher authority, his opinion of the C-in-C's military skills, formed when he had taught him at Staff College and unchanged by subsequent events, was not high and this frequently translated into rudeness towards his superior, verging at times on insubordination.

For Dick and the staff of Middle East Command, this was very difficult to bear. The relationships between them and the individual members of Montgomery's staff, now led by Freddie de Guingand, were for the most part very good, but they resented deeply the Eighth Army Commander's cavalier attitude towards their chief and his occasional interference in matters which did not concern him, such as the selection of officers for command outside his own army. Dick himself was made of sterner stuff than Alexander and was not going to be bullied. Brigadier A. F. 'Fish' Fisher, then in command of 2 Armoured Brigade and himself a former 12th Lancer, was visiting Montgomery's HQ one day and saw that Dick's car was just outside his caravan. 'I kept well out of the way. But one could not help overhearing a heated conversation taking place in the Caravan. I cannot remember the exact words but the gist of the remarks were – that if Monty was not going to obey orders he received from G.H.Q. there would be a vacancy for a new Commander of the 8th Army. Few people other than Dick would have been able to say this to Monty when he was at the height of his success in the Desert.'[3] Charles Miller, Major General Administration later in the campaign, wrote subsequently that 'Dick's characteristic loyalty and singlemindedness caused him to show outspoken resentment at Gen Montgomery's disloyalty to Gen Alexander – but these were brushed aside by Gen Alexander's tact – "keep your eye on the ball" was a favourite remark.'[4]

As Dick was later to concede, such an approach may have rankled, but it worked. In an appreciation of Alexander written after the War, he put these words into the C–in–C's mouth: 'There is only one active army in my command and Montgomery is in command of it. The essence of my job here is to support him in every way I can, to handle all the political problems involved with many allies, and let Monty get on with the battle.' Dick described Alexander's attitude as 'typically unselfish', but in practice the C–in–C had no other option in dealing with a very difficult and sometimes wayward subordinate.

That Dick was prepared to stand up to Montgomery did not go down well with the latter. Charles Richardson, Eighth Army's GSO1 (Plans), was later to recall that 'Monty disparaged McCreery, in my view unjustifiably'[5] and personal relations between the two men were cool for the rest of Dick's career. For his part, Dick never really liked Montgomery and deplored his showmanship. On the other hand, there was a higher level of professional respect on each side than either Montgomery's disparagement or Dick's hidden dislike and his public criticism of Montgomery a decade and a half after the end of the war might suggest. Just after Montgomery's arrival in Egypt he asked for Dick to carry out some unspecified job, which may even have been a corps command, and in March 1943, as the campaign in North Africa was moving towards its climax, Montgomery proposed to Alexander that Horrocks should be sent back to the UK as an experienced corps commander for the invasion of France and that Dick should take his place. When Horrocks was later badly injured, he endorsed the decision that Dick should succeed him. Like many others, he also regretted him stepping down in due course as Alexander's chief of staff, although his criticism not long beforehand that Dick was out of touch with the practical side of battle fighting was unfair. Dick, for his part, always gave Montgomery full credit for restoring the morale of Eighth Army and was later to write to Lettice that he was certainly the best person to command the Allied ground forces in Normandy on and after D-Day.

In the meantime, the two men had to work for the common goal and to that end Dick did not spare himself or others. Brigadier George Davy, the director of military operations at GHQ Middle East, wrote later that 'he drove the staff and services very hard indeed so as to ensure the success of the Eighth Army, and nobody could drive people harder than he if he wanted!'[6] As David Hunt, then a GSO2 (Intelligence) at GHQ Middle East, was to find along with many others, Dick's restrained manner and his seemingly soft voice could be misleading: 'When displeased about anything he would curse in the same slightly quavering rather refined voice, never raised above a murmur, but mixing complaints and threats with curiously old-fashioned but signally pungent blasphemies and obscenities.'[7]

Davy expressed both admiration and affection for Dick and such sentiments were replicated at all levels. Dick's new Personal Assistant, Patrick Stewart from the 11th Hussars, wrote in his diary ten days after joining GHQ: 'Because he works so hard, is so impatient & apparently helpless, he inspires much affection and loyalty.'[8] The helplessness on which Stewart remarked probably referred to one side of Dick's nature which only occasionally manifested itself, an apparent inability to tackle quite small and mundane practical tasks (changing an electric plug for example, or a tyre). It was certainly not a characteristic of his approach to bigger issues.

Through September and into early October, Dick's preoccupation remained with bringing Eighth Army up to full strength, working closely with the Lieutenant General Administration, Tommy Lindsell. In addition to getting the Highland Division and other formations up to the front, the major task was to prepare in newly established workshops the 300 Sherman tanks which President Roosevelt had presented to Churchill and to organize training on them.[9] Although somewhat inclined to catch fire on being hit, these were outstanding armoured fighting vehicles, mechanically reliable and armed with an excellent dual-purpose 75mm gun, which gave the British for the first time parity with their opponents. There were not enough Shermans to equip fully all the formations: including replacements, about 300 Crusaders, a third of them with an improved 6-pounder gun, and 200 Lee/Grants provided most of the balance, whilst 23 Armoured Brigade was still equipped entirely with Valentines. Some 200 Stuarts also remained on the establishment, the majority in 7 Armoured Division's 4 Light Armoured Brigade.

Dick was still required to participate in innumerable meetings. Some of these were with politicians, notably Richard Casey, an Australian who had been appointed by Churchill as Minister of State Resident in the Middle East and was effectively the prime minister's eyes and ears on the spot. Others were held with the RAF, whose AOC-in-C, Air Chief Marshal Sir Arthur Tedder, was reluctant to cede any operational control of his force, although Montgomery improved cooperation enormously by having the HQ of the Western Desert Air Force co-located with his own. Last but not least, Alexander was responsible for relations with the Dominions and with Allies, both the Free French and the Greeks having brigade-sized formations in Eighth Army, and Dick was pulled into the various discussions taking place about their deployment. In spite of his concerns about being deskbound, Dick was able to make frequent visits to Eighth Army, to discuss preparations with Montgomery and his staff and to visit the subordinate commanders. New arrivals from the UK included Oliver Leese to replace Ramsden at XXX Corps, which would bear the brunt of the forthcoming battle, and Harry Arkwright to act as Montgomery's own advisor on AFV(armoured fighting vehicles). John Harding left GHQ to command 7 Armoured Division.

On the night of 23/24 October Montgomery launched Operation Lightfoot, his major set-piece battle designed to destroy the Panzerarmee Afrika. Whilst XIII Corps in the south was restricted to feint attacks with a view to keeping a large part of the Axis armour there, the first part of the main advance was undertaken on a 10-mile front by four of the five infantry divisions in XXX Corps, which from north to south were 9 Australian, 51 Highland, 2 New Zealand and 1 South African. The infantry was given a clear objective, to advance through the belt of minefields and fixed anti-tank defences and seize Miteirya Ridge and the area to its north-west. Two corridors would then be created, one between the Australians and the Highlanders for 1 Armoured Division to pass through and establish itself on another key feature, Kidney Ridge, the other between the Highlanders and the New Zealanders for 10 Armoured Division to cross Miteirya Ridge into the flat desert beyond. The armour would then provide a defensive shield against counter-attack by the Axis armour whilst the infantry engaged in 'crumbling' operations on the flanks to wear down the enemy and create the conditions for a break-out.

The infantry advance, preceded by the heaviest artillery barrage since the Great War, was substantially successful. However, Lumsden's divisions were delayed in their advance by the relatively slow clearance of the minefields by the sappers, the poor visibility caused by sand and dust and congestion in the corridors. Neither 1 nor 10 Armoured Division was able to reach its objectives, largely because of hidden minefields and anti-tank defences in much greater depth than anticipated. The former was forced to deploy either side of its corridor, whilst the latter sheltered behind Miteirya Ridge. Although further small advances were made by the infantry in the next 24 hours, a new attempt to break through with the armour was equally unsuccessful.

At 0200 hrs on 25 October Montgomery was awoken by de Guingand to be told that the battle was in a state of crisis. Not only was there no further progress, but confidence had broken down between the infantry and armoured division commanders. Lumsden and Leese were both summoned to Montgomery's HQ, where the army commander told Lumsden in no uncertain terms that he should follow the plan and then rang Alec Gatehouse of 10 Armoured Division to order him to fight his way out across the Miteirya Ridge. This proved impossible, due to the strength of the German 88 mm guns on the reverse side of the ridge. Under New Zealand command, 9 Armoured Brigade had penetrated beyond, but found itself hopelessly exposed and in due course forced to retreat.

The battle had now reached a stalemate, although 'crumbling' operations continued, with particular success by the Australians around the Tel el Eisa feature in the north. A reshuffle took place in XXX Corps, with the New Zealanders moving into reserve and the South Africans sidestepping into their place, themselves relieved by 4 Indian Division. Montgomery's staff began to draw up a new plan, Operation Supercharge, which proposed a concentrated attack due east along the coast.

Back in Cairo Dick had been watching developments with mounting concern. He was much later to write a trenchant criticism of both Montgomery's plan and his use of armour, but Alexander had approved Operation Lightfoot and there is no evidence of Dick trying to have it changed in any way or even doubting its effectiveness at the time. On the evening of 26 October he had over an hour with Brigadier Julian Gascoigne, who had just returned from XXX Corps HQ.[10] In his diary he wrote: 'He says that Gatehouse and Herbert have been very sticky and that the name of the armour is *mud*. Early on the armour could have got through.' Dick was later to act as an apologist for the armour and, indeed others were subsequently to accept that their stance was understandable, even realistic, but at the time this was a clear manifestation of much going wrong.

Alexander was also seriously concerned, as was Casey, who was poised to report failure to the prime minister, so on 29 October the two of them and Dick went up to Montgomery's HQ for a conference to discuss 'Supercharge'. Dick did not even mention the visit in his diary, writing instead about the heroic action of 2nd Rifle Brigade in defending 'Snipe', an area on one side of Kidney Ridge, against large numbers of German tanks: neither does it feature in his later published recollections. Alexander did record it in his own memoirs, however, and the impact it made: 'The Eighth Army commander appeared to have favoured an attack from as far north as possible. But Dick McCreery, as an experienced armoured commander, was emphatic that it should go in just north of the existing northern corridor. There is no doubt at all in my mind that this was the key decision of the Alamein battle, nor have I any doubt that Monty was suitably grateful to my Chief of Staff.'[11]

There is no record anywhere of Montgomery's gratitude! Moreover other accounts, whilst recognizing Dick's urging of this new direction of attack, do not ascribe all the credit to him. The rationale behind his advice was that new intelligence had shown that the majority of the German element of Rommel's army was now positioned in strength along the coast, but that the Italians, who would be much more vulnerable to attack, were situated further south. This intelligence, derived from Ultra, was available to both GHQ Middle East and to Eighth Army, where Montgomery's gifted GSO1 (Intelligence), Bill Williams, had come to exactly the same conclusion as Dick, although he and de Guingand had so far failed to convince their chief. De Guingand confirmed later that 'McCreery also felt that "Supercharge" might work better further south, and we discussed the matter together.'[12]

Charles Richardson, who had joined de Guingand and Williams in advocating the change in plan, remembered that when the staff met Dick, 'the subject of the axis was then raised; McCreery, who approved of the proposed change, volunteered to discuss it with Montgomery, only to be warned off with some vigour by Freddie. The Chief of Staff had now learnt that such acts of persuasion stood no chance of success when conducted by outsiders, particularly if attempted by McCreery, whom Montgomery invariably disparaged; they must be handled *à deux* at the right moment by one of Montgomery's own team. The delegation departed and Freddie soon pulled it off.'[13] Certainly later that day it was de Guingand who rang Dick to let him know that Montgomery had changed his mind. Dick was delighted, as was Alexander. The correct interpretation of events thus seems to be that, whilst Dick had undoubtedly come to the conclusion on his own that the axis of advance should be changed, had convinced Alexander that it was necessary and had advanced the argument in the conference with Montgomery, the Eighth Army staff had reached an identical conclusion and, doubtless encouraged by Dick's concurrence, had finally convinced Montgomery to change his mind.

Supercharge was launched on the night of 1/2 November, just after Dick had returned from a flying visit to Palestine to lecture at the Middle East Staff College in Haifa. The operation was directed by the New Zealand Division HQ and used that division's artillery and engineers, but took three infantry brigades from other divisions under command as Freyberg's own infantry, other than the 28th Maori Battalion, was recovering from the earlier battles. Pole position was taken by 9 Armoured Brigade, which was effectively sacrificed to draw the teeth of the German armour, whilst the infantry expanded the shoulders of the salient. The armoured cars of the 1st Royal Dragoons were the first to get behind the enemy, on 2 November, but it took further infantry attacks before 1 Armoured Division could break through comprehensively on the night of 4/5 November, followed by 7 Armoured Division. Dick was with Alexander visiting Eighth Army on 4 November and arrived back at GHQ at 1700 hrs. Half an hour later Montgomery telephoned to say that a great victory was in sight.

If Dick had kept his counsel on any doubts about Montgomery's plan for Lightfoot, he was unable to contain his frustration over the subsequent pursuit, as the Germans withdrew in good order, leaving their Italian allies to their fate. George Davy later wrote: 'Dick could not have influenced the events after the battle and he and I alike failed – at our respective levels – to overcome the inertia in the desert. We shared the feeling of frustration and exasperation as Rommel crept away.'[14] Dick felt that, in his determination to have no subsequent reverses, Montgomery took forward far too many troops. On 14 November he was astonished to find an enormous traffic jam at the Halfaya Pass near Sollum, with 1 Armoured Division's tank transporters packed together nose to tail, whilst up on the escarpment 7 Armoured Division kept running out of petrol. Alexander suggested to Montgomery that it might be possible to send a mobile force to cut off Rommel at El Agheila, just as O'Connor had succeeded in doing to the Italians in February 1941. Montgomery replied that if anyone thought he was going to be the fool to get a bloody nose for the third time they were very much mistaken.

Montgomery was indeed only too aware of the reverses to earlier victories in the desert, but his caution meant that the pursuit became a litany of missed opportunities to strike a decisive blow at the retreating Germans. Not for the last time, he was demonstrating his seeming inability to finish off a defeated enemy. On the other hand, between Lindsell and Eighth Army's DA & QMG, Brian Robertson, the arrangements were put in place to ensure that the increasing length and vulnerability of the lines of communication were not going to be a major cause of bringing an end to the advance, as they had been in the past to Wavell and Auchinleck and twice to Rommel.

One after another the old battlefields of the desert war were passed and Eighth Army entered Benghazi on 19 November, although it was another full month before it was able to overcome the defences at El Agheila. During that time it became apparent that Montgomery wanted to get rid of both Lumsden and Gatehouse. With barely room for two corps in the advance towards Tripoli and with Miles Dempsey having been called out from the UK to take over XIII Corps in Egypt, Montgomery was determined to give

X Corps to Horrocks. His view of the performance of X Corps at El Alamein fully justified this in his own mind, but many of his critics thought he was prejudiced against the cavalry, whose senior officers he saw as amateurs. When Dick dined with the newly sacked Lumsden on 30 November he found him very bitter about Montgomery. Dick suspected that the animus between them might have had its origin during the retreat to Dunkirk, when Montgomery was commanding 3 Division and Lumsden the 12th Lancers, providing intelligence on German movements. Brooke, Montgomery's corps commander at the time, later put paid to this theory, but admitted that he had never got to the bottom of the troubled relationship. He himself admired Lumsden greatly and gave him another corps command on his return to England.[15]

Dick was also saddened by the decision to disband 8 Armoured Division, which he had formed and trained in 1941. It had never fought as a division and its constituent parts were now needed as reinforcements. Also disbanded was 24 Armoured Brigade, still under the command of 'Kench' Kenchington, the RTR battalions being dispersed elsewhere, although the other founder member of the division, 23 Armoured Brigade, was by now a significant independent component of XXX Corps.

On 23 January 1943 Eighth Army entered Tripoli, by which time change was in the air for Alexander and Dick. GHQ Middle East was now 1,000 miles away from its only army, whose success had been followed by the necessity to set up a military government in the newly occupied territories. The burgeoning geographical extent of the C-in-C's responsibilities was made that much more apparent by a trip which he and Dick made in the first week of the New Year over much the same distance in a completely different direction, to Sudan and Eritrea.

At the other end of the Mediterranean the Allies had landed in French North Africa on 8 November, but First Army had made slow progress in expelling the Axis from Tunisia, which had been seized from the Vichy French. With Montgomery now poised to enter the country from the south, the need arose for coordination between the two armies and this was endorsed by the Casablanca Conference. General Eisenhower, who commanded Allied Forces, had no battlefield experience and it was agreed that Alexander should take overall command in the field.

On 18 February Alexander handed over Middle East Command, shorn of its responsibility for Eighth Army, to Jumbo Wilson and was duly appointed to the command of the new 18th Army Group, taking Dick with him as his chief of staff.

Chapter 16

Victory in Tunis

'I hope to get a change of job sometime this year,' Dick wrote to Lettice on 27 January 1943 in the knowledge of the decisions made at Casablanca, 'but I must stick to Alex as long as he wants me. He knows that he will give me a fair deal. I may even get something like Herbert had out here' (a corps command). There was, as it happened, no question of Dick leaving Alexander at this juncture. Brooke wrote subsequently: 'I must confess that I had some doubts as to whether Alexander would have the ability to handle this difficult task. I had, however, great faith in his Chief of Staff, Dick McCreery, and I hoped that between them all would be well. The battle of Tunis proved the accuracy of this forecast, but I have never felt that McCreery received all the credit due to him for the part he played in these operations.'[1]

As the chief of staff to an army group commander, rather than to a C-in-C of a major overseas command, Dick took a step down in rank to major general, whilst his erstwhile deputy James Steele, who took over from him, moved up in the opposite direction. It is apparent, however, that both Alexander and Dick saw this as a temporary arrangement until the campaign had reached a successful conclusion, and that not only Alexander, but more importantly Brooke, in whose gift it lay, had promised him a field command in due course. In the meantime there was tangible recognition of his contribution to Middle East Command when Dick was made a Companion of the Bath. Alexander's citation made clear his opinion.

As my Chief of Staff since August, 1942, Lieut.-General McCreery has been actively involved, in general, in the re-organization of Middle East Forces, and in particular, in the preparation of plans for the successful Eighth Army offensive which commenced in October. That the re-organization has been completed rapidly and smoothly is, in large degree, due to the leadership which he has given the whole staff both general and administrative.

The preparation of the plans for the Battle of Egypt threw a heavy load of responsibility on him for a considerable period beforehand, and it is no exaggeration to say that its success was greatly influenced by the completeness and exactness of the preliminary arrangements. General

McCreery during this time was the guiding planner and controlling co-ordinator. He worked strenuously and advised wisely. He relieved me of much anxiety.

When operations started he continued to be of the greatest assistance to me, displaying qualities of forethought and patience which has meant so much, particularly during the critical opening days of the offensive. I have no hesitation in saying that by his work and influence he contributed greatly to the victory of the Desert Army.

Although 18th Army Group was not to be formally constituted for another ten days, Dick left Cairo on 8 February and travelled via Malta to Allied Forces HQ in Algiers. There he stayed with Walter Bedell Smith, Eisenhower's chief of staff, whom he thought 'v. nice and capable' and with whom he was to establish an excellent working relationship. Fortunately there was one member of Eisenhower's multi-national staff, Jock Whiteley, whom he already knew well, both from Staff College and more recently as BGS (brigadier general staff) to Ritchie at Eighth Army, and he was briefed extensively by him before meeting Eisenhower, whom he found very talkative. He also met Harold Macmillan, the British minister of state resident in North Africa, whose chief Foreign Office adviser, Roger Makins, was an old family friend in whose parents' house Dick and Lettice had held their wedding reception. On 11 February he left for Constantine, where the new HQ was established. Some 3,000 feet above sea level, it proved to be bitterly cold in the tents used as accommodation, with a very poor temporary mess in a local café.

Leaving Charles Miller, the Major General Administration, to organize the 70 officers and 500 other ranks who had come to join the HQ from Cairo, followed in due course by a number of Americans and French, Dick left on the following day to visit First Army. This formation was very different to Eighth Army. Created to command the disparate British and American troops who had landed in North Africa in November 1942, and subsequently the French who had declared for the Allies after some difficult moments, it had had a gruelling winter. Balked almost at the gates of Tunis by the lightning speed of German reinforcement, it had found itself fighting in the mountains in often appalling conditions of wet and cold. Moreover, relationships between its commander, Kenneth Anderson, and his Allied subordinates had not always been good, the French determined to establish their independence in their own territory and their self-esteem after the bitter defeats of 1940, the Americans suspicious of the British and nettled by comments about their inexperience. Anderson's character, dour, occasionally irritable and often incapable of establishing a rapport with his fellow officers of any nationality including his own, had not helped.

Dick found Anderson worried by his difficulties with Allies and with the military position. He was more heartened by meeting Charles Allfrey of V Corps – 'a grand chap' – and Charles Keightley, a fellow cavalryman and old friend who had been AA&QMG of 1 Armoured Division in 1940 and was now GOC of 6 Armoured Division. He was back in Algiers on 17 February to welcome Alexander on his arrival to take up his new role. The two of them left on the following day to visit II US Corps, where they found what Dick described as 'an atmosphere of gloom'. The commanding general, Lloyd Fredendall, was away on a visit, but the two British officers quickly realized that there was no effective plan or coordination on his front.

Fredendall's absence was understandable as II US Corps was under attack to the south. Von Arnim, the German commander in Tunisia, and Rommel, still facing Montgomery but anxious about his rear, had launched a coordinated attack with two panzer divisions on the American positions at Gafsa and Sidi Bou Zid on 14 February forcing their way through the passes in the Eastern Dorsal range of mountains and driving the Americans back in confusion. Further attacks were made over the next week, pushing the defenders, many of them in a state of panic, back though the passes in the Western Dorsals at Sbeitla and Kasserine and threatening the Allies' supply bases at Tebessa and Le Kef. Anderson hurriedly sent British reinforcements to stem the tide and the Germans were held at Thala and Sbiba, with von Arnim and Rommel, whose own coordination had been poor, eventually conceding failure on 22 February – but it had been a very close run thing.

Alexander was far from impressed by Anderson's handling of the situation, asking Montgomery for Leese to replace him, but the latter was still needed in Eighth Army. As a result Alexander put Anderson on a much tighter leash than Montgomery, relieving him of II US Corps and XIX French Corps and placing them under his own direct command and giving each nationality its own well-defined sector, whereas they had previously been intermingled. The other deep impression made on Alexander was the poor planning and training of the Americans and their generally low morale, although a number of individual units had fought well. He expressed his concern over Fredendall to Eisenhower, who had reached the same conclusion and had him replaced at II US Corps by George Patton, a strong leader with very high standards who rapidly took a grip on his new command. Alexander also insisted on the Americans setting up a battle school, which was largely staffed in the early days by British instructors and NCOs, some from Eighth Army.

The reorganization of First Army and direct operational control of the Americans and French provided a great deal of work for Dick, helped in part by the HQ's relocation to Ain Beida, south-west of Constantine on the road to Tebessa and better placed for visiting the front. David Hunt described it as 'the smallest and certainly the most efficient HQ that I ever served on in the whole of the war.'[2] It was still in the mountains and still very cold, with both offices and accommodation under canvas, but it stood in a very attractive location in a fir wood. Dick had little free time whilst he was there, but when he did he enjoyed walking through meadows full of spring flowers, including carpets of wild jonquils. For his numerous journeys in an open car, Alexander had lent him a spare wool-lined airman's jacket, but he still had to wear three jerseys every evening to keep warm.

The main reason for Rommel's withdrawal from the Kasserine area was his growing concern over Eighth Army's progress in the south. On 6 March he launched what would be his final attack in Africa, against a well-prepared Montgomery at Medenine. For the Germans and Italians this was a repeat of Alam Halfa, as their tanks made little impression on the well-sited defences, incurring serious losses. On 9 March Rommel left Tunisia on sick leave, never to return, and the newly styled German–Italian Panzer Army retreated behind the defences of the Mareth Line. Montgomery began his assault on this formerly French defensive system on 20 March, but failed completely to crack it open. It required a long flank march by the New Zealanders and Free French, followed by 1 Armoured Division, to threaten the Axis rear and compel von Arnim to order a retreat.

Alexander's forces in Tunisia were in almost constant action, with the intention of cutting the Axis retreat from the south and forcing their formations in the north back into an ever smaller area around Tunis and Bizerta, but the resistance, established in carefully sited positions in the semi-circle of mountains around the Plain of Tunis and the various passes across the Eastern Dorsals, was strong and well led. Very little progress was made at first, indeed there were a number of setbacks, including an individual one when Dick's invaluable personal assistant, Pat Stewart, was seriously wounded while out with an American reconnaissance patrol.[3] Dick spent much of his time visiting the various commanders, both with Alexander and by himself. He was delighted by the arrival of John Crocker to command the newly arrived IX Corps, the more so as Crocker's BGS was 'Babe' MacMillan, Dick's Sandhurst and Staff College contemporary. The corps became operational on 24 March, but its first operation, mounted on 8 April by 6 Armoured Division and 34 US Division in an attempt to break through the Fondouk Pass and cut off the retreating Italian First Army, ended in failure when the Italians escaped the trap.

II US Corps experienced much the same result in its attempts to take the El Guettar defile further south, to bring pressure on the Germans to withdraw from their positions opposite Eighth Army at Wadi Akarit. Like Crocker, Patton failed to break through, and after Montgomery had succeeded in forcing the Germans' position by a stunning outflanking movement through the hills by 4 Indian Division, the Americans also failed to cut off their retreat. Dick liked and admired Patton and spent a lot of time at his HQ, but he was not an easy subordinate for Alexander. Dick often had to call on the assistance of Patton's more diplomatic deputy, Omar Bradley, to couch the C-in-C's orders in such a way that they would be palatable. On one of these visits, Dick came as close to the actual fighting as he had been at any time since France in 1940, near enough to see the German guns in action. Although Patton himself had by this time transformed the organization of his corps and was full of confidence in his ability to beat the Germans, Dick continued to be surprised by the ineffectiveness of some of his formations, noting particularly in his diary that 34 US Division was 'hopeless' and 1 US Armored Division 'useless, morale v.low'.

Dick's role was not confined to planning or operations: he was also required to smooth relations between the nationalities, particularly the British and Americans. The Americans were inclined to bridle at attempts by the British to tell them how to fight, but although Alexander had influenced the removal of Fredendall and set up a British-led battle school for them and although he was critical in private, he himself was the essence of diplomacy to their faces and Dick followed his lead. Others were less guarded and a serious instance of Allied dissention came when Crocker criticized the performance of 34 US Division at Fondouk to some visiting Americans in the belief that he was speaking off the record, only to see it published. Eisenhower was angry with Crocker and furious with the censors who had let it through, whilst both Alexander and Dick had to pour oil on the troubled waters.

A bigger problem was the bad feeling between the two British armies, who now met each other for the first time. The origins of this lay with Montgomery, who positively encouraged his men to regard themselves as superior, not difficult after their victorious fighting advance across North Africa. In Dick's words:

> My headquarters now had to contend with the rivalries between the Eighth and First Armies. Unfortunately, Monty in his build-up of the Eighth Army had led everyone to adopt a very intolerant attitude to others, and Allies. This was a great pity when close cooperation between the two wings of 18th Army Group was about to begin. Certainly the inflated ideas of the Eighth Army made my life much more difficult in the last few weeks of the African campaign.[4]

Following Montgomery's success at Wadi Akarit there was no natural defensive line for von Arnim until the range of hills just north of Enfidaville, to which he retreated in good order. It was clear that further progress on this sector by Eighth Army would be difficult, if not impossible, and thus one of its formations, 1 Armoured Division, was transferred to IX Corps, which was due to play the major role in the final battle for Tunis. The contrast between the tanned and healthy desert warriors, lauded at every step by the press and the BBC, and their compatriots, pale from their winter in the mountains and without a victory to their name, could hardly have been greater. The men of 1 Armoured were informed that 6 Armoured Division and 46 Division, whom they were joining in IX Corps, had fought very hard and would be sensitive to any criticism, but tensions nevertheless developed. Oliver Leese, visiting First Army's HQ, was taken aback by the very evident resentment of Eighth Army, particularly as articulated by Anderson.

The Axis forces were now penned into a relatively small area in the north-east of Tunisia and Alexander and Dick began to plan the closing moves in the campaign from their new HQ, which had moved at the beginning of the second week of April to a site next to some Roman ruins at Le Kef. Here they were much closer to the front, although visits to Eighth Army still had to be made by plane. For this phase II US Corps and XIX French Corps were brought back under First Army, although Alexander continued to exercise tight control over Anderson. In the initial plan only one American division was to be used. Patton and Bradley protested strongly to Eisenhower, who recognized that it was vital for public opinion in the USA that Americans should be seen to be playing a major role in the victory. The solution was to transfer II US Corps from the most southerly to the most northerly sector of the front, adjacent to the Mediterranean, and to give it the responsibility for taking the key city of Bizerta. At the same time Bradley replaced Patton, who left to command Seventh US Army for the invasion of Sicily.

The pace of life intensified for Dick, who was on the move almost every day, visiting the various formations and agreeing their plans for the forthcoming operations. Inspecting the newly arrived 1 Armoured Division, led by Raymond Briggs, one of the last survivors of the pre-Montgomery armoured commanders, he was delighted to find a number of old friends. There were in particular many familiar faces in Dicks's old 2 Armoured Brigade, whilst the armoured car regiment was the 12th Lancers, whom he had not visited since just before El Alamein.

On 16 April Alexander issued his orders for Operation Vulcan, timed to commence on 22 April and to involve the whole of First Army, the intention being finally to get out of the mountains and onto the plain, from where the assault on Tunis would be markedly easier. The fighting was extremely hard, but eventually V Corps managed to take its long-desired objectives, including the notorious Longstop Hill, IX Corps made progress in the south and II US Corps surprised Alexander by the success of its advance in the north. The way was now open for the final attack.

Andrew Buchanan McCreery, Dick's grandfather.

Isabelle ('Belle') McCreery, Dick's grandmother.

John Loudon McAdam, the great road-builder and Dick's great, great, great grandfather.

Walter McCreery, Dick's father.

Emilia ('Minnie') McCreery, Dick's
mother, shortly after her wedding.

Dick with his nanny/governess, Catherine Stay ('Da').

Dick, Bob and Selby as children.

Dick at Eton.

Walter driving his three sons and his chauffeur Henri in the Lozier.

The newly commissioned Dick at Bilton with his youngest brother Jack.

Dick at the head of a troop of the 12th Lancers.

The officers of the 12th Lancers on Telegraph Hill on 9 April 1917, two days before Dick was wounded. They include (from left) Dick (2), Alex McBean (3), Bruce Ogilvy (4), Cuthbert Rawnsley (6) and Frank Spicer (11).

The Greenhill House nursing staff during the Great War. Seated (from left) are Dick's grandmother, Frances McAdam (3), Minnie (5) and Da (6).

Dick mounted shortly after the Great War.

Dick's brother Bob, drawn not long before
his untimely death at the hands of the IRA.

Minnie in the Great War.

The officers of the 12th Lancers at The Curragh in 1921. In the top row Dick is on the far left; Selby, wearing a black armband for Bob, is 2 from right. Front row (from left): Lt Col Fane (3), Frank Spicer (5) and Cuthbert Rawnsley (6).

Stowell Hill, built for Dick's grandmother in 1922–3 and his own home from 1945 onwards.

Dick on his all-time favourite horse, Annie Darling, winner of the Grand Military Gold Cup in 1923.

Dick and Selby (back to camera), on the British Army polo team, meeting King George V and Queen Mary on the occasion of one of two matches against the US Army in June 1925.

Lettice shortly before the wedding.

Dick and Lettice at the Sparkford Vale Harriers point-to-point in March 1928, just before their wedding.

Lettice, Michael and Bob standing on the right with her two sisters, Helen and Lucia, in the centre and Helen's husband, George Gosling, second from left.

Dick and Lettice clowning around at Brownhill.

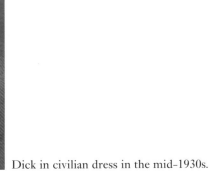

Dick and Lettice at Brownhill with Mike Houston.

Dick in civilian dress in the mid-1930s.

The Staff College Draghounds being led out by Charles Miller, Claude Nicholson and Dick.

Dick on Canute, winning the Military Hunter Chase at Sandown Park in 1933.

Dick in uniform in the mid-1930s.

Dick, Lettice and Rachel Fitzalan-Howard with guides in the Grand Canyon in December 1932.

Dick and Bob painting the garden shed.

Dick and Lettice with Michael and Bob on the beach.

The officers of the 12th Lancers at Tidworth in 1935. They include (from the left): Back: Tony Warre (1) 'Kate' Savill (2); Middle: Andrew Horsburgh-Porter (1) Dick Hobson (3) Arthur Gemmell (5) George Kidston (7); Front: Frank Arkwright (2) Hugh Russell (3) Paul Hornby (4) Field Marshal Lord Birdwood (5) Dick (6).

Dick standing in front of one of the regiment's Lanchester armoured cars in the Western Desert in 1936.

Digging a Leyland lorry out of the sand on the desert reconnaissance expedition to Siwa Oasis.

Dick playing polo in the 1930s.

The winners of the Inter-Regimental Cup at Hurlingham in 1936. Dick holds the trophy, followed by Andrew Horsburgh-Porter, George Kidston and Dick Hobson.

As expected, Eighth Army had ground to a halt, its attempts to penetrate the hills north of Enfidaville blocked by vigorous German resistance. On the night of 28/29 April Montgomery made his final attempt to get though with the newly arrived 56 Division, but it was a disaster. On 30 April Alexander and Dick visited him to discuss the future of the campaign. 'Left 0630 for 8 Army,' wrote Dick in his diary. 'C-in-C had long conference with Monty. Decided to abandon major ops of 8 Army due to great difficulty of ground, & 7 Armd. Div and 4 Ind Div & 201 Gds. Bde. all to come & join 1st Army.' Dick had been pressing Alexander for some time to engineer the transfer of more formations from Eighth to First Army, but the C-in-C had been reluctant to force such a dramatic move on his powerful subordinate. Now he found Montgomery offering to do just that, indeed the Eighth Army commander took all the credit for the plan to finish off the war in North Africa. In addition Horrocks was sent to command IX Corps, where Crocker had been seriously wounded. Dick was dubious about Horrocks's abilities as a corps commander, but there was no obvious alternative, as Leese, like Montgomery himself, now had his mind on planning the forthcoming Sicily campaign.

The centrepiece of Operation Strike, planned by Alexander and Dick to deliver the *coup de grâce* to the Axis, was an assault by IX Corps straight down the road from Medjez el Bab to Tunis. This brought together two longstanding First Army formations and two which were newly arrived from Eighth Army: 4 Division and 4 Indian Division, respectively on the right and the left of the road, were ordered to crack the German defences on a 3,500-yard front and thereby create a breach in the defences for 6 and 7 Armoured Divisions to pass through. Horrocks planned the usual daylight attack, preceded by a heavy artillery barrage, but on the insistence of Francis Tuker, the GOC of 4 Indian Division, it was launched in the dark at 0300 hrs on the morning of 6 May, achieving a significant element of surprise. By mid-morning the armour was able to move through and, although it failed to capitalize on the disintegration of the defenders on the first day, on the second it found little resistance. The armoured cars of the Derbyshire Yeomanry from 6 Armoured Division and the 11th Hussars from 7 Armoured Division, symbolically representing the two British armies, entered Tunis together on the afternoon of 7 May: at exactly the same time 9 US Division occupied Bizerta.

Mopping up took another four days during which the British cleared the Cape Bon peninsula and, with XIX French Corps advancing speedily from the south, surrounded the remaining Germans and Italians. Von Arnim found himself cut off and surrendered to Tuker's troops and on 12 May Field Marshal Messe of the Italian Army sued for an armistice on behalf of all the Axis forces. Hostilities ended formally at 1220 hrs the following day and later that afternoon Alexander sent his famous message to Churchill: 'Sir, it is my duty to report that the Tunisian campaign is over. All enemy resistance has ceased. We are masters of the North African shores.'

By any standards this was a triumph. Some 238,000 prisoners were taken, a greater number than at Stalingrad, whilst the Allied strategy, to start on the road to ultimate victory by clearing the Axis out of Africa and thereby establishing dominance in the Mediterranean, had been triumphantly vindicated. Moreover, in spite of Montgomery's vainglorious claims, the triumph was unequivocally Alexander's.[5] His critics would later say that he could have achieved it faster, but it could hardly have been more unambiguous.

Alexander's skill lay in welding together an Allied team out of the disparate formations which he had inherited and giving it the confidence to succeed. As Dick was to write later; 'It is sometimes said that great leaders of men, like great racehorses, are somewhat on the lazy side. They always have something in reserve for the emergency which tests a man's calibre. That would certainly be true of Alexander. He abounded in physical and moral courage, but he conserved his energy for the great occasion.'[6] This happened in front of Tunis, but it would not have worked without Dick, of whom Alexander wrote in his despatches: 'His scientific grasp of the whole sphere of military matters made him of the greatest assistance to me throughout my period of command in Africa.'[7] Brooke was one of many who felt that Dick had not been accorded the credit due to him for his part in the victory. Dick's only claim for himself came in a letter to Lettice: 'This time, anyway, I feel that I have had some small hand in this success.'[8]

Dick was being characteristically modest. During the final stages of the Tunisian campaign Alexander had demonstrated more grip of military operations than he had done at any time before and he was not to do so again until just before the end of the war. The main ingredient of the C-in-C's success was a highly talented chief of staff, who deployed the intellect which he himself lacked. There was a very marked contrast between his performance in this campaign and the one which followed shortly afterwards in Sicily, in which he proved unable to control either of his army commanders, Patton and Montgomery. Montgomery was the first to recognize this, writing later in a characteristically forthright way: 'Alexander... is not clever and requires a C.G.S who knows the whole business and will get on with it... Given such a C.G.S. he is excellent. But without such a C.G.S nothing happens.'[9]

Alexander had told Dick in late April that he would like to keep him on, but went on to say that it would not be fair to him, with which Dick did not disagree. The C-in-C was as good as his word. The day after the end to hostilities was Dick's last one at 18th Army Group. On 15 May he left for

Algiers, driving there in leisurely fashion and seeing many of the Roman sites on the way. Having taken leave of Eisenhower and his staff, he flew out from Maison Blanche airfield four days later, stayed two days at Gibraltar, delayed by the reports of fog in England, and eventually arrived back at Hendon early on the morning of 22 May.

Dick reported immediately to the War Office, but was able that afternoon to travel down to Oxford by train to be met by Lettice and all the family except Michael, who later arrived from Eton. For the next four weeks he was based at College House, but he was required to make a number of visits to London. Brooke was abroad, but Dick met Archie Nye, the VCIGS, and Sandy Galloway, the Director of Staff Duties, and had a long interview with James Grigg, the Secretary of State for War. It was clear that there was no immediate job for him, and this was confirmed when he eventually saw Brooke on 22 June, although he was greatly encouraged by the meeting. 'The C.I.G.S. was in very good form and very nice. He said that he did not want me to think that I was being forgotten, and I think there is no doubt I shall get a Corps. I gathered from him that it may be some little time before all the changes are made. As you know the P.M. has to have a hand in it all. I am in General Paget's[10] mess, and he also obviously wants me to have a good job, so all should be well.'[11]

After meeting Brooke, Dick had gone down to GHQ Home Forces, which was at Wentworth Golf Club with its offices in the clubhouse and the senior officers' mess in an elegant residence close by. His immediate task was to give a series of lectures on the North African campaign, which took him all round the country, talking to army, corps and divisional HQs, the Staff College, training organizations, groups of independent units and even schools. He delivered twenty-four of these lectures over thirty days, often two a day, a daunting task for one who was far from adept at public speaking, but they were at least interspersed with welcome breaks at College House.

On 24 July he heard that he would be taking over VIII Corps from Herbert Lumsden. He found this very awkward, as his hopes for his best friend in the Army were nearly as high as for himself, and whereas VIII Corps had been nominated as one of the components of Second Army for the future invasion of Europe, II Corps District, to which Lumsden was now appointed, was a static formation with administrative responsibility but no operational role. Four days later Dick travelled up to York, to be met by Lumsden for a briefing over dinner at the Station Hotel, after which they went to the HQ at the nearby Claxton Hall for the formal handover.

Dick had got what he wanted, command of a corps destined for what was becoming known as the Second Front. What is more, it was a predominantly armoured formation, designed with much the same role in mind as Montgomery's corps de chasse and incorporating both Guards and 11

Armoured Divisions, the latter still commanded by Percy Hobart, the former by Alan Adair, an old friend of Dick's from Cairo in the 1930s. The third component was 15 (Scottish) Division, but during Dick's four weeks in command, two of which were spent on exercises held by the armoured divisions and one on a study week for the senior commanders of Second Army, he had no opportunity to visit it.

On 5 August, just before leaving for the study week, Dick heard that the honours for services in Tunisia had just been announced and that he was to be made a Knight Commander of the Bath alongside Anderson, now his immediate superior as GOC-in-C of Second Army. This was a tremendous accolade, reflecting Alexander's appreciation of his services and undoubtedly endorsed by Brooke, and it put him well ahead of any of his contemporaries. A few days later it was announced that he had also been appointed an Officer of the Legion of Merit by the Americans.

There was a further surprise to come on 24 August. Dick's diary records 'Tel from 21 Army Gp that I have to leave at once for my old haunts. Probably someone has been wounded.' Under orders to travel as soon as possible, he travelled down from Claxton Hall to College House to pick up some essential items of kit, before going on to the War Office, where he was told that Horrocks had been seriously injured in a 'tip and run' German air raid and that he would be taking over X Corps with immediate effect. Moreover, he was informed, the corps would be in action within weeks.

Dick's delight at the prospect of command of a corps on active service was only tempered by his sadness for Lettice and the family, who had been looking forward to him remaining in the UK until well into 1944. He was able to treat her to Jack Buchanan's latest show in the West End followed by dinner in a smart restaurant where they ate 'an excellent grouse'. On the following day she saw him off at Hendon.

Chapter 17

Avalanche

There was no repeat of Dick's first meandering wartime journey to North Africa. Instead he was given top priority for transport, arriving in Algiers on 23 August, less than 24 hours after leaving England. That afternoon he saw Eisenhower, Alexander and Humphrey Gale, AFHQ's Chief Administrative Officer, and dined with Bedell Smith in the evening. On the following day he met Macmillan and Makins for a briefing on the political situation and settled down to read the plan for Operation Avalanche, the proposed landing by Allied Forces on the mainland of Italy at Salerno.

The political background was complex and had exposed a strategic rift between the Allies which would impact on the Italian campaign as it developed. The British, notably Churchill, saw it as an end in itself, with the prize being a drive into the Po Valley and then through the Ljubljana Gap in Slovenia into the Hungarian and Austrian plains. The Americans, led by the Army Chief of Staff George Marshall, but with Roosevelt in full accord, were clear that the only way to defeat the Germans was an attack on the heart of the Reich in north-west Europe. For them Italy was a diversion, valuable in drawing off German divisions from France and useful in giving gainful employment to the enormous resources the Allies had accumulated in the Mediterranean until the summer of 1944, the earliest time an invasion of France could be mounted – but it was not the route to victory.

At the tactical level Dick was far from happy with what he read. X Corps was to come ashore at the northern end of the Bay of Salerno, with two divisions to the south of the eponymous town and a force of British Commandos and US Rangers to the north and further along the Amalfi coast. All the beachheads would be overlooked by mountains, whose passes the corps would have to force to get into the Plain of Naples. On Dick's right would be VI US Corps, landing near the Roman ruins at Paestum. For the task in hand, his resources looked very thin, but the major constraint, as always in amphibious operations, was the availability of landing craft. Dick knew that 1 Airborne Division was in the theatre and decided to ask for a parachute brigade to fly in simultaneously. With this in mind he went on the next morning to Mostaganem, west of Algiers, for his first meeting with Lieutenant General Mark W. Clark of Fifth Army, under whose command

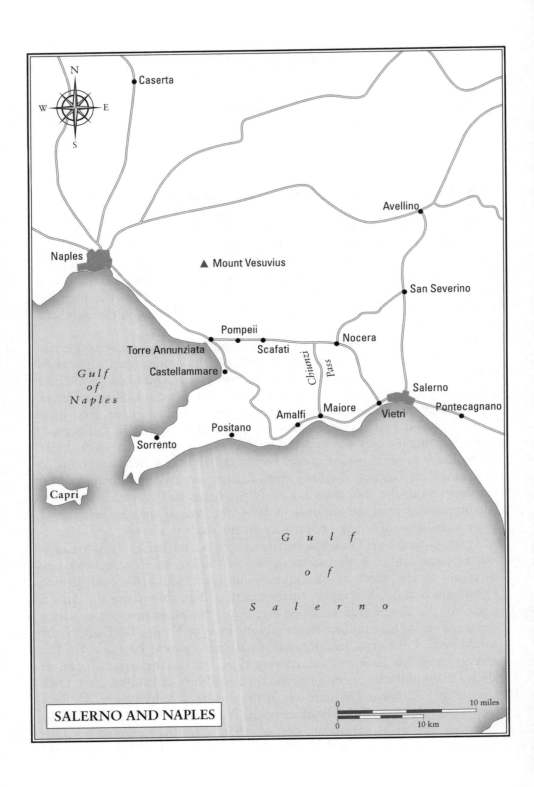

SALERNO AND NAPLES

he would be operating. He was met by a large US Military Police guard of honour and by Clark's chief of staff, Al Gruenther, to whom he warmed immediately. He was not so sure about Clark himself, especially when the army commander rejected the proposal for the parachute brigade.

Clark was to play a major role in Dick's career, both during and after the war, and their relationship was not always easy. He was a relatively young man himself, less than two years older than Dick. He had seen action in an infantry battalion in the Vosges during the Great War and, like Dick, had been wounded, in his case by shell splinters. He had done well between the wars, attending both the Command and General Staff School and the Army War College and becoming an instructor at the latter in 1940. By the time the United States entered the war Clark had reached the rank of brigadier general and was serving as assistant chief of staff at the Pentagon. There he came under the watchful eye of Marshall, who was every bit as influential as his British counterpart, Brooke, in the selection of officers for high command. This was not Clark's first experience of Marshall; he had impressed his superior some four years earlier with the clarity of his planning for manoeuvres. He was also a close friend of Eisenhower's and accompanied him on his first visit to London in early 1942, during which he made a strong impression on Churchill, who nicknamed him 'the American Eagle'. When Eisenhower assumed the role of Commanding General, European Theatre of Operations, US Army, Clark joined him, initially to lead II US Corps.

Subsequently Clark became the first US general officer to set foot in French North Africa, as the leader of a clandestine mission landed from a British submarine on an Algerian beach to meet French officers sympathetic to the Allied cause. Immediately after Operation Torch he was instrumental in persuading Admiral Darlan, the French Commander-in-Chief, to reject the Vichy Government and declare for the Allies and thus, by the end of 1942, his stock was riding high. When Fifth Army was formed in early 1943, he was an almost automatic choice to be its commanding general.

In spite of their close friendship, Clark was in many ways the antithesis of Eisenhower. Whereas the supreme commander subordinated national interest to Allied harmony and was invariably the most diplomatic of men, Clark was blunter with his allied counterparts and subordinates, put the United States first and had an innate distrust of the British, although this did not extend to the virulent Anglophobia displayed by a few of his countrymen. He had disapproved of placing US troops under British control during the Tunisian campaign, though he had no such thoughts when X Corps was later brought into Fifth Army. Whilst Eisenhower was personally modest, Clark went to the same lengths as Montgomery to promote himself to his troops and, through the press, to the American public. Another trait which he shared with Montgomery was to insist on his own orders being followed to the letter, but to be selective on occasion in his interpretation of orders given to him.

To Dick, who never sought the limelight, Clark's showmanship was anathema and he was dubious from the start about his military ability. Their approaches to battle were quite different, Dick relying to a great extent on intelligence and reconnaissance before selecting a weak point in the enemy's defences and applying the maximum pressure there, Clark preferring to probe extensively on a wide front, thereby in Dick's opinion incurring many unnecessary casualties. Even at this stage of the war the British were conscious of their limitations in manpower, whilst the Americans had no such concerns. The latter, usually preferring to attack an objective frontally, could not understand why the former tended to adopt an indirect approach, which might take longer but which cost fewer lives.

The meeting with Clark at an end, Dick set off to visit the formations under his command. He went first to Bizerta, where he saw Horrocks in hospital before going to inspect 46 Division. This Territorial formation had arrived in North Africa in January 1943 and was actively engaged in the Tunisian campaign from then until the end. The GOC, who had arrived to take command on the very day of Dick's visit, was an old friend from Staff College, John 'Ginger' Hawkesworth, who had previously commanded 4 Division, which had also played a major role in the battle for Tunis. Dick knew his record, which included leading an infantry brigade with distinction during the retreat to Dunkirk in 1940, and had every faith in his ability. He also liked the look of his brigadiers.

Most of the rest of the corps, together with its HQ, was situated 400 miles away around Tripoli, but Dick now had the exclusive use of a two-engined plane, piloted by a charming Frenchman. His other infantry division was less well known to him, although it had joined Eighth Army just before the end of the Tunisian campaign and fought briefly and unsuccessfully near Enfidaville. 56 Division had begun life as 1 (London) Division, a first-line Territorial formation which had originally recruited exclusively from in and around the capital. One of its three brigades had been lent to another division for the Sicily campaign and was now refitting, replaced on a temporary basis by Julian Gascoigne's 201 Guards Brigade. As 56 Division would be fighting in relatively open country south of Salerno, it had also been given its own armour in the shape of the Shermans of the Royal Sots Greys. Dick knew the GOC, Douglas Graham, only slightly as a brigade commander in the Highland Division from El Alamein to Enfidaville. He was some five years Dick's senior in age, but had a sound reputation.

These two divisions would make up the main landing force as the early stages of the battle were likely to be predominantly an infantry affair. As soon as circumstances permitted, Dick proposed to bring ashore his old friends of 23 Armoured Brigade, now commanded by Harry Arkwright and formed of the same three battalions of the RTR that had served under Dick in 8 Armoured Division in 1941.

For the break-out Dick had 7 Armoured Division, under the command of Bobby Erskine since John Harding had been seriously wounded shortly before the capture of Tripoli. Whereas Hawkesworth had been in the division above Dick at Staff College, Erskine had been in the one below. He had also been BGS at XIII Corps through much of 1942, so Dick knew him well and liked him. The main infantry component was 131 Brigade which, like 168 Brigade in 56 Division, consisted entirely of three battalions of the Queen's Regiment. Somewhat confusingly, both were popularly known as 'The Queen's Brigade'.

To carry out landings on his left flank, there were two further formations. One was the Commando Brigade of 2 and 41 (Royal Marine) Commandos under Brigadier Bob Laycock, which would land at the small town of Vietri sul Mare, just to the west of Salerno. On the commandos' left would be a force of three battalions of the US Rangers under Colonel William Darby, which would land at the town of Maiore, along the road to Amalfi. The Rangers and the Commandos were both in Sicily, so Dick had no time to visit them, although he saw the two commanders at the final briefing conference at Clark's command post at Mostaganem on 31 August.

Dick described this conference, which ran for five and a half hours, as 'endless speaking', but conceded that it was very well run. Charles Richardson, who had been transferred from Eighth Army to act as Clark's Deputy Chief of Staff (British), recalled the contrast with Montgomery's conferences, at which the Eighth Army commander would give a prominent lead, indeed do most of the talking himself. Clark, by contrast, sat in the background and the scene was set by his Head of G.3 (Operations), Donald Brann. He was followed by Lieutenant General Ernest J. Dawley, Commanding General of VI US Corps, whom Richardson recalled as a 'ventriloquist's dummy' completely dominated by his staff.[1] Dawley was followed by Dick. 'I thought his performance was excellent,' wrote Richardson later. 'We all felt that he had worked out very firmly in his own mind how his corps battle should develop after the assault landing, and clearly he was not in the hands of his staff. This impression remained with me as the battles continued.'[2]

The conference over, Dick returned to Tripoli to continue to put the final touches to his plan and to see the amphibious training being carried out there and at Bizerta. He may not have been dominated by his staff, but he got on with them very well and they were unquestionably important to him, two of them in particular. His BGS was R. B. B. B. 'Cookie' Cooke, late of the 17th Lancers, in which regiment he had been an exact contemporary of Dick's brother Bob. Dick had known Cooke from the inter-war years and had come across him more recently as the Brigadier RAC of First Army. He was to remain with Dick for most of his tenure with X Corps and be a tower of strength. Even closer to him on a daily basis was his ADC, Captain (later Major) Hugh Vivian Smith, whom he knew personally and had interviewed in London prior to his departure.[3] Smith was to serve with him for an even longer period but, unlike Cooke, Dick found him exasperating at times, yet he tried so hard and was so likeable that he kept him on.

The other key person in Dick's life for the next few weeks was Commodore Geoffrey Oliver, who commanded the Northern Attack Force of warships and transports and was thus responsible not only for getting the troops ashore, but also for supporting them with naval gunfire once they were there. Dick immediately struck up an excellent relationship with Oliver and his senior officers. He spent time looking over the various types of landing craft and was entertained in the wardroom of the command ship, HMS *Hilary*, which not only flew Oliver's broad pennant but would also serve as Dick's Main HQ until it was safe for it to be relocated ashore.[4]

After a final visit to see Hawkesworth in Bizerta, Dick and his senior staff embarked on the *Hilary* on the evening of 5 September and set sail at 1230 hrs the following day. The vessel made slow progress initially due to having been bunkered with sub-standard Indian coal, but an infusion of Welsh coal held in reserve allowed her to increase her speed and make her rendezvous with the rest of the enormous convoy on time. They were spotted by enemy reconnaissance planes on 8 September, but that evening there was apparently excellent news on the BBC that the Italians had agreed to an armistice. Orders went out immediately that any Italian troops were to be treated as friendly unless they acted in a hostile manner and the news swept round the attackers, with many immediately assuming that opposition to the landings would be slight.

On the following morning such assumptions proved hopelessly optimistic. In the early hours of 9 September the ships reached their allotted positions for disembarkation and the troops transferred to the assault craft. The initial naval bombardment was due to start at 0315 hrs, but an hour earlier the accompanying destroyers reported that they were being engaged by coastal batteries and were given permission to respond. It was already clear that the Germans were prepared for the landings, indeed they had come to the same conclusion as the Allies that this was the furthest point north at which air cover could be delivered from Sicily. The timing of the Italian surrender had come as a surprise, but plans had already been formulated for such an eventuality and the Germans reacted to the news with speed and ruthlessness, disarming their former allies and, where any resistance was

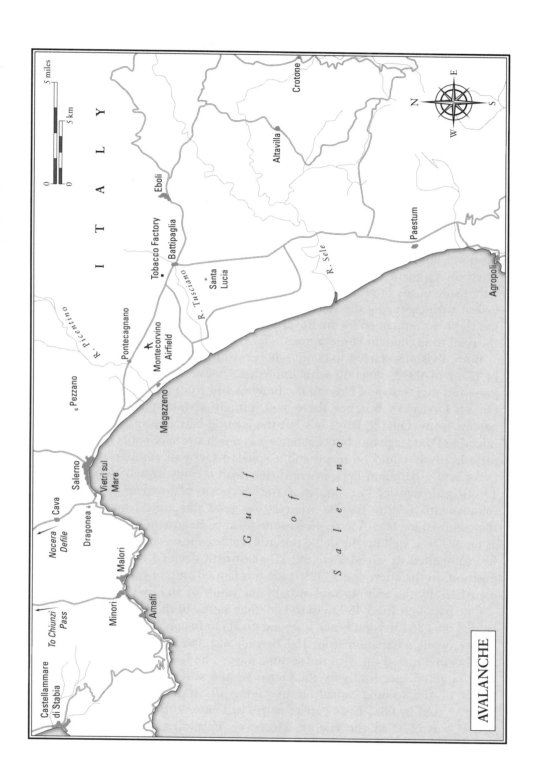

met, dealing with it summarily. The only major German formation on this stretch of coast, 16 Panzer Division, had been on the alert since the previous afternoon and was able to respond immediately, whilst reinforcements were called up. From the bridge of the *Hilary* Dick could see demolitions taking place at the oil storage depot at Salerno and realized that surprise had not been achieved.

Hawkesworth had decided to land on a one-brigade front, with his 128 Brigade chosen as the initial assault force on the beach opposite the town of Magazzeno, followed as soon as it had secured a lodgement by 138 Brigade, whilst 139 Brigade remained in reserve. The main objective for 46 Division was the town of Salerno itself, through which Hawkesworth expected to pass to join up with the commandos on the other side. He also planned to take the town of Pontecagnano on the road from Salerno to Battipaglia. At 56 Division Graham opted to land two brigades simultaneously on beaches either side of the mouth of the River Tusciano, with 169 Brigade on the left tasked with capturing the key Montecorvino airfield, whilst 167 Brigade on the right, accompanied by the Royal Scots Greys, would take Battipaglia and the road from there to Pontecagnano. 201 Guards Brigade was to follow later.

Both divisions started to come ashore within 10 minutes of the planned H-Hour of 0330, meeting with immediate resistance both from machine guns and mortars sited close to the beaches and from artillery further away. On 46 Division's beaches there was initially serious congestion on the narrow front. On 128 Brigade's left the leading battalion managed to push inland to Pontecagnano, but resistance was much stronger on its right, where little headway could be made and a spirited German counter-attack with tanks sent a battalion back in confusion with serious losses. Nevertheless, 138 Brigade managed to come in to the beaches as planned and was ordered to move into Salerno. At first progress was good and contact was made with the commandos from Vietri, 46 Reconnaissance Regiment even penetrating as far as Cava, well up the defile towards Naples. Heavy artillery and mortar fire compelled its withdrawal and Hawkesworth decided to consolidate his position. In the afternoon 139 Brigade was landed and, in spite of numerous casualties, by the evening substantially the whole of 46 Division was ashore.

One battalion from 46 Division had gone astray in the early morning and landed on a 56 Division beach, causing great confusion as 169 Brigade came ashore, while a battalion from 167 Brigade also landed in the wrong place and became mixed up with the second wave. The large LSTs of the Greys were targeted specifically by the Germans and several were hit, only two-thirds of the leading squadron managing to land. Progress was made, however, and by 0825 hrs a carrier patrol had entered Battipaglia, reporting that it was clear of the enemy. Moreover, Brigadier 'Lou' Lyne of 169 Brigade considered that he was strongly enough established to attack

Montecorvino airfield, where his troops found a great number of aircraft on the ground and destroyed them most satisfactorily. However, they could not secure the whole airfield and dug in facing the Germans across the runway. In the afternoon 201 Guards Brigade began to come ashore.

On the left both the Commandos and the Rangers had landed without difficulty. Laycock established his HQ at Dragonea, a small village on the flank of the Molina Pass, leading via Cava to Nocera and Naples, which he intended to dominate from the high ground. Darby had done even better. Regarding speed as the essence, he had gone hell for leather up the road towards the Chiunzi Pass, which led down very steeply to Pagani, at the far end of the Nocera defile. His advanced patrols reported that they could see as far as Castellammare on the Bay of Naples. There he dug in and, having also cut the coast road to Amalfi, effectively denied the Germans the ability to outflank the Allies on their left. The Rangers and Commandos also joined hands on the road from Maiore to Vietri.

Dick had received a bewildering array of signals throughout the day, some very hopeful, others indicating that the resistance was going to be tougher than many (although not Dick himself) had anticipated. At 1800 hrs he went ashore for the first time, meeting both Hawkesworth and Graham and returning to the *Hilary* at 2300 hrs. There he issued orders for the following day: 46 Division was to capture Salerno completely, hold the defile north of Salerno to enable the port to be opened and complete the occupation of its planned beachhead, whilst 56 Division was to capture Battipaglia, take the whole of Montecorvino airfield, and, like its sister formation, secure its beachhead. Dick was worried, however, about his right flank and when he saw Clark on the following day he asked for the corps boundary to be altered in his favour, to which the army Commander acceded. Dick did not know it, but this exacerbated a problem which was not then apparent but would emerge within the next 48 hours – the extent of the gap between the two corps, bisected by the River Sele.

VI US Corps, which had only landed 36 US Division on the first day, had established itself successfully, but not without being badly knocked about. Plans were now made to move into the gap and at the same time to land Dawley's reserve, 45 US Division. A force was despatched to cross the Sele, but it failed to reach the town of Eboli or the nearby Ponte Sele, the latter a significant crossing point. In the meantime, enemy reinforcements were arriving to bolster 16 Panzer Division, both from Calabria, where Montgomery was moving very slowly up the toe of Italy, and from the north. The noose was tightening about Fifth Army.

Dick was only too aware of the increasing strength of the Germans. 201 Guards Brigade took Battipaglia in the early hours of D+1, but the battalion which then occupied the town was thrown out again on the following morning. The Guards found themselves battling for control of a tobacco factory, a natural bastion which lay on the road to Salerno, whilst the Germans were also attacking strongly around Santa Lucia on Dick's vulnerable right flank, their advance only broken up by accurate fire from the divisional artillery and the Royal Navy. The airfield at Montecorvino was finally cleared after three days of hard fighting, but was initially impossible to use as it was overlooked by German guns. In the Commandos' sector the battle swayed backwards and forwards, with control of the hill above Vietri, nicknamed Commando Hill, being lost and then regained, whilst the enemy was infiltrating 46 Division's front north and east of Salerno. The Rangers, on the other hand, beat off an attack on their position with relative ease. The beachhead, moreover, was now secure and, despite the continuing uncertainties, Dick decided to bring his Main HQ ashore on the morning of 12 September. A skeleton staff had set up the site two days earlier in an orange grove near Pontecagnano, but Dick had preferred to use the facilities of the *Hilary* until he was absolutely sure that the corps was there to stay. By 14 September he was sufficiently confident to bring ashore 23 Armoured Brigade, which he now used as the core of a force to secure his right flank around Santa Lucia against an attack by the Germans from the gap between the two corps.

That Dick was fully in control of his battle was clear to all, including the war correspondent of the *Daily Express*, who wrote about how he had met 'a thin, tall and softly spoken man with a deceptively mild appearance. I found it reassuring hearing him explain the battle. It is this sense of professionalism that runs right through the Army now. We would hold here, and here, and here, he said, but not here, and for this reason, and with that plan in view. It was succinct and clear and mathematical without either optimism or pessimism.' Dick's 'scientific' grasp of a battle or even a wider campaign was remarked upon by many who served with him, from Alexander downwards, and it was never displayed to better advantage than at Salerno.

Clark was not so confident. A strong counter-attack was mounted by the Germans against VI US Corps on the afternoon of 13 September, leaving 45 US Division at risk of being cut off. Although his divisional commanders remained resolute, Dawley himself proved unequal to the situation, so Clark effectively took command of the corps himself. By the following afternoon, the situation was so dire that he asked Admiral Hewitt, the American commander of the naval task force, to prepare two plans, one for the evacuation of VI US Corps to the British sector, the other the reverse. When he heard about this from Commodore Oliver, Dick was furious. Charles Richardson, who had noticed like many others that whenever Dick was deeply concerned he would lower his voice to a whisper, was visiting his HQ at the time and heard the volume drop significantly. Dick had actually seen Clark that morning when there had been no mention of such a plan and he now sent a signal to say that, as it had not been discussed, there was no possibility of it happening.

Alexander, following the battle from Hewitt's flagship, supported Dick's stance and Clark's plans were dropped. To bolster the position the C-in-C arranged with his naval and air force counterparts for two British battleships to be brought in to shell the Germans and for bombers to be diverted from other operations, whilst Clark ordered 82 US Airborne Division to drop first one and then a second parachute regiment into the American beachhead to bolster the defences. Perhaps more significantly, a major part of the German attack found itself in a dead end between the Sele and one of its tributaries, causing their whole offensive to grind to a halt. By the following day Clark, who had in the meantime displayed considerable personal courage in leading his troops on the ground, had recovered his nerve and was now determined to stay put.

The crisis had passed and the Germans had lost their last chance to push the Allies into the sea, but there were many days of bitter fighting ahead. On 15 September Alexander visited both corps, accompanied by Clark and Air Marshal Coningham, AOC of the Desert Air Force.[5] Dick took them to the HQs of 46 and 56 Divisions and 169 and 201 Brigades and then gave them a picnic lunch on the beach. The C-in-C was delighted with Dick's handling of the battle, but unimpressed with Dawley. He conveyed his views on the latter to Clark, who agreed that he would have to be relieved, but it was some days before Eisenhower took the decision to replace him with Major General John P. Lucas.

On the following day, the arrival of 7 Armoured Division's 131 Lorried Infantry Brigade allowed Dick to begin the process of shifting his weight to the left. He described his situation in a signal to Darby: 'I am strong on my right in front of 56 Division, but the situation in the SALERNO area is NOT satisfactory, owing to the shortage of troops and the fact that some Inf Bns are now very tired... The most dangerous sector for the enemy to attack is at VIETRI.' He instructed the Rangers to thin out in the hills to the east of Castellammare in order to be able to attack the main road to Naples if the situation demanded.

On 18 September came the first signs that the Germans were withdrawing on the right when Battipaglia was firmly occupied at last and 56 Division's reconnaissance regiment found the road clear right into the hills at Olevano. With VI US Corps now in control to the south, having both brought in 3 US Division and joined up with the leading elements of Eighth Army, Dick was able to shift his weight to the left yet again, positioning 56 Division to advance up the main road to San Severino, the alternative entrance to the

Plain of Naples, whilst concentrating the remainder of the corps on forcing the direct route through the Nocera defile. The rest of 7 Armoured Division was landed and preparations made for it and 46 Division to attack from Vietri through the defile, with the Rangers and 23 Armoured Brigade coming down from the Chiunzi Pass to cut off the enemy's retreat.

Before this could happen there were two notable events for Dick. The first came on 19 September when he received the news from his staff that some of the reinforcements shipped over from North Africa were refusing to join the units to which they had been assigned. The story behind this had begun five days earlier during the crisis, when urgent requests were sent to Tripolitania District to send any men who were available from the reinforcement and transit camp there. A draft of some 1,500 was put together and picked up by three Royal Navy cruisers. The majority of the men were Eighth Army veterans, most of whom had served in Sicily in either 50 or 51 Divisions and had been sick or lightly wounded. They were told that they were returning to their units, but found themselves instead at Salerno. Many of them, from Scottish or north-east English regiments, were thoroughly dismayed by this, not least because it was by then known that their original divisions would be returning to the UK. When they were ordered to report to 46 and 56 Divisions as replacements for battle casualties, they refused to do so. The majority were in due course persuaded to march off, but some 350 remained behind, in no mood to comply. It appeared that X Corps had a mutiny on its hands.

On hearing this, Dick decided that he would appeal to the men personally and drove down to their transit camp. Climbing onto the bonnet of his jeep, he told them that he was shocked by their action, but had been briefed on their grievances and understood that there had been a 'cock-up'. He undertook to see that all of them were returned to their units as soon as possible, but said that for the moment they were urgently needed by X Corps. To boos and jeers he told them to think it over, otherwise there would be serious consequences. As a result another 50 men agreed to follow their orders. It was an extremely busy day for Dick and he was due to meet Clark at Vietri, so he had to leave, giving instructions to his staff to try and persuade the others before taking the necessary action. More agreed to return to duty, but 192 were left, who were duly arrested and tried for mutiny.[6]

The second event was one which nearly cost Dick his life. It took place on 20 September on a part of the front on which the Germans were retreating before 56 Division. His diary recorded it succinctly:

'Got ambushed this am. West of PEZZANO. I was on the ground with Hugh S. when both armd Cs and my dingo[7] were hit with A. tk guns, we had to walk home 2m! A few bullets near me! V. stupid to go so far, but thought recce patrols ahead. An Italian warned us too! Hugh is hopeless at present!'

Smith told the full story later (see Appendix I) and, indeed, it was always known afterwards as 'Hugh's Little Ambush'. Dick had been given to understand that 56 Division's reconnaissance regiment had relieved the equivalent unit in 46 Division, but whereas the latter had withdrawn, the former had not arrived to take its place. Although this was some excuse for his lack of suitable precautions, the incident was also characteristic of his frequent decisions to find out in person what was happening as close to the front line as possible. An old friend, Wilfred Lyde, spotted him driving his own jeep at a time when the battle was not going well, 'his calm, almost casual manner... an inspiration to everyone.'[8] There were to be many instances later in the campaign when divisional and brigade commanders found their corps commander well forward of their own positions, indeed up with forward observation posts or even the leading infantry companies.

The X Corps offensive to push the Germans back through the passes began on the night of 22/23 September, with attacks by 46 Division towards Nocera and by 56 Division up the road to the north towards Avellino. There was fierce fighting in the hills on either side of the two routes, with pockets of Germans holding out until the last moment and delaying the capture of both villages and high ground. Cava was taken on 24 September, but 46 Division made slow progress until two days later, when it appeared that a withdrawal of more than local significance was taking place. By the morning of 27 September the leading vehicles were in Camerelle, just short of Nocera, and plans were issued for the final break-out.

On the following day the tanks of 7 Armoured Division burst through as far as Scafati, 23 Armoured Brigade, which had come down the Chiunzi Pass, reached the sea at Castellammare, and 56 Division passed through San Severino. By 29 September the line ran from Torre Annunziata around the southern flank of Mount Vesuvius to Sarno and at 0930 hrs on 1 October the armoured cars of the King's Dragoon Guards reached the centre of Naples. The first great city of mainland Europe had fallen to the Allies.

Chapter 18

River and Mountain

'The last two nights,' Dick wrote to Lettice on the day Naples was liberated, 'I have had a pleasant site alongside some world famous ruins.' At Pompeii his HQ was not far behind the forward troops, who were mostly bypassing Naples in response to Clark's determination to keep pushing forward as fast as possible. Although delayed by demolitions, X Corps reached the River Volturno by 5 October and closed up to the south bank on a 20-mile front three days later. Reconnaissance patrols reported that all the bridges had been destroyed and that the Germans had dug in on the other bank in strength, so an assault crossing would be necessary.

Positioned on the right at Capua was 56 Division, where it was in contact with 3 US Division, part of VI US Corps. It had been reinforced by 168 Brigade, back again after its exertions in Sicily, but had lost its GOC, Graham having broken his shoulder when his jeep tumbled into a bomb crater. For the next three months it would have four brigades rather than the usual three and it acquired an excellent GOC in the shape of Gerald Templer, whom Dick was delighted to have under his command.[1] Elsewhere, 7 Armoured Division was concentrated near Santa Maria la Fossa, and 23 Armoured Brigade opposite Cancello, whilst 46 Division extended the line from there to the sea. Both the Commandos and the Rangers had been transferred out of the corps, Dick writing warm letters of thanks and congratulation to their commanders.

'The Volturno is the very devil,' wrote Dick in his diary on 9 October, 'v. high banks and after the recent rains over 6 ft deep everywhere.' It was also, in his sector, over 100 yards wide for most of its length and flowing at 4 miles per hour. The steep and slippery banks rose to 20 feet on the northern side, where a belt of trees gave good cover for the defenders, who were also well protected by minefields: it was thus a considerable obstacle. The enemy's stand on this river, albeit a brief one, was to give the Allies a serious jolt. From Eisenhower downwards, many believed that the Germans would now conduct a withdrawal to the line of the Apennines north of Florence, where intelligence reports had been received of fixed defences being constructed. On the enemy side, even Hitler was in favour of a withdrawal north of Rome, arguing that the southern half of the peninsula would be impossible to hold after the desertion of the Italians, and he was supported in his view by both

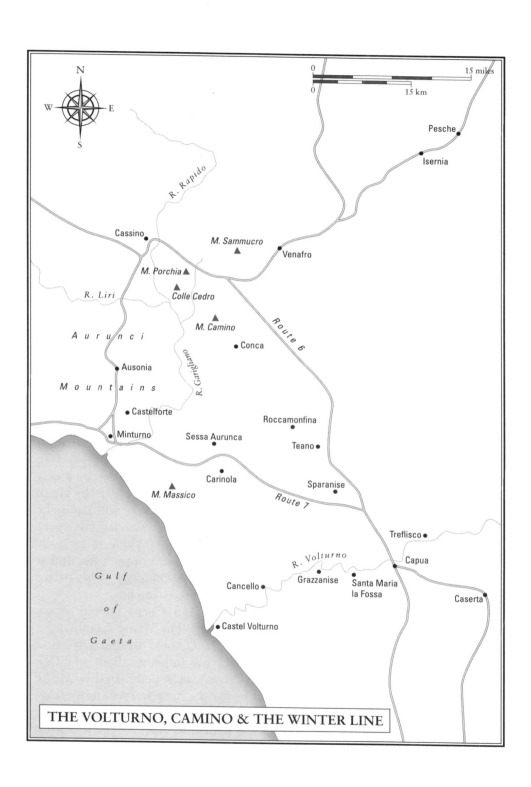

THE VOLTURNO, CAMINO & THE WINTER LINE

the OKW (Armed Forces High Command) and Rommel. Neither he nor the Allies had reckoned with the stubbornness of the man who would, over the next year, conduct the one of the most skilful withdrawals in military history. Field Marshal Albert Kesselring believed that the topography of Italy offered unparallelled opportunities for defence and he was loathe to let the Allies advance so far north that they could use the captured territory for bases to bomb Germany. In defiance of his orders he began the preparations of defensive lines much further south, the first of which to the west of the Apennines lay along the Volturno. Kesselring regarded it as only temporary, but he needed to buy time there while he prepared a much stronger line to the north.

For several days Fifth Army remained halted, although its time was well spent in bringing up boats and bridging equipment, building rafts and giving the inexperienced soldiers some very basic training in river crossing. Dick had by now adopted Montgomery's practice of locating a small Tactical HQ as close as possible to the front line, with the Main HQ situated further back and a Rear HQ, dealing largely with supplies and reinforcements, further back still. His mobility was greatly assisted by the use of a motor caravan, which housed both his personal office and his sleeping quarters. He described it to Lettice: 'My caravan… has a good desk all down one side, lots of room for my photos, etc., two cupboards with shelves & hanging room for coats each side of the door (at the back) & a bed down the other side which in the day is an excellent sofa seat. At the front end, in a separate compartment with a sliding door, is a basin, looking glass, etc. All most complete, the only crab I have is that I am always banging my head on something as I cannot stand upright.'[2] He was now looked after by a new batman, Wagstaff, who arrived during the Volturno battle, as well as by Hugh Smith, who, he wrote 'is definitely improving, but I think he will always be a better businessman than a soldier.'[3] Dick's time was largely spent preparing his corps for the forthcoming battle, but he was able to get away for one day to attend the liberation thanksgiving service in the cathedral at Naples, going on afterwards to meet the Cardinal Archbishop in his palace with Clark, and then to visit the Roman ruins at Herculaneum.

Clark's orders were that X Corps and VI US Corps should attack simultaneously on the night of 12/13 October. The Army Commander arrived at X Corps HQ on the morning of 12 October to find Dick in a pessimistic mood. Not for the last time, Dick was unhappy about an attack along a whole front rather than concentrated on a weak point. In this case he believed that a much better plan would be for the Americans to move first, as the river was much narrower in their sector and the ground significantly less marshy on the other side, and for the British to cross on the following day when some of the enemy reserves had been drawn away. He asked Clark to walk with him alone in a nearby field, so that he could express his very strongly held opinion without embarrassing his staff. After a vigorous debate, Clark rejected his proposal and gave an unequivocal order to go ahead with all the crossings at the same time. Having lodged his objection, Dick accepted it, although he made it clear how difficult it was for him to receive from an American commander an order to British troops with which he fundamentally did not agree. This did nothing for the relationship between the two men, which would come under further strain as the campaign developed.

The crossings began at 2050 hrs. On the far left 46 Division put two brigades in DUKWs (amphibious vehicles) successfully across the river near its mouth at Castel Volturno, accompanied by two squadrons of tanks from 23 Armoured Brigade in LCTs, but a battalion crossing further upriver proved fruitless. The division now found itself in flat countryside criss-crossed by numerous canals and drainage ditches, which offered excellent possibilities for defence, but little opportunity for attacking tanks. The fighting developed into an attritional infantry battle, but with a 5-ton ferry working well reinforcements could be passed across and the Germans were pushed back. On 17 October Dick was able to make his first crossing of the river in this sector.

In the centre 7 Armoured Division, whose crossing was intended to be diversionary, managed to get a foothold by the evening of the first day opposite the village of Grazzanise, the small bridgehead then reinforced by anti-tank guns ferried over by a large raft. Work was begun on a 9-ton Bailey bridge, but the site came under immediate artillery fire from the Germans and it was not until 1600 hrs on 16 October that it was completed. At much the same time a ford was found which proved suitable for waterproofed tanks and by the end of that day a full regiment was across.

56 Division, starting its battle before Templer's arrival and temporarily under the command of Lou Lyne, was markedly less successful than the others in its own crossing at Capua. The assault boats were mostly sunk by heavy mortar and artillery fire and the crossing was temporarily abandoned, while the few troops who had reached the far bank were withdrawn as they could not be adequately supported. On the division's right 3 US Division had made a successful crossing and was building a 30-ton bridge at Treflisco, so Dick asked if the corps boundary could be shifted for 56 Division to use it. Clark obliged, whilst at the same time making clear his disappointment with the division's performance. On the morning of 15 October, 201 Guards Brigade crossed and occupied the high ground to the north in support of the American advance and, on the same day, a successful crossing was made at last at Capua: two days later work was begun on a new 30-ton bridge for the rest of the division. Now 56 Division was able to form up for an advance to

the west of Route 6, which led towards Cassino, whilst Dick decided to pull 46 Division in from the canal country and send it along Route 7 towards the mouth of the River Garigliano. Heading towards the same objective was 7 Armoured Division, following a route parallel to the coast.

Dick had been working at a frenetic pace throughout the battle, visiting all his formation HQs and many individual units almost daily and calling on Lucas at VI US Corps and Lucian K. Truscott, the Commanding General of 3 US Division. Numerous dignitaries, including Alexander, turned up at his own HQ, Clark bringing with him Henry Morgenthau, the US Secretary of the Treasury, who was on a tour of the theatre. On 21 October Eisenhower arrived to invest Dick formally with the Legion of Merit. Ever modest, Dick found this acutely embarrassing as 'there was a veritable battery of cameras at very short range.'[4]

The advance now gathered speed temporarily and by 31 October 56 Division had taken Teano, 46 Division had occupied Carinola and 7 Armoured Division was poised to break through the gap between Monte Massico and the sea. On 1 November Dick had his first glimpse of the Garigliano from an OP near Sessa Aurunca and advance patrols reached the river a few days later. Only one obstacle remained before the whole corps could close up to it and it was a formidable one. Rising out of the plain to the left of Route 6 was the massif of Monte Camino, which was held in strength by the Germans. This would have to be taken before any further advance towards Cassino by Fifth Army was possible.

Monte Camino anchored the southern end of the Bernhardt Line, a series of strong defensive positions which bulged out from the main Gustav Line between Castel di Sangro and a point on the Garigliano opposite the Aurunci Mountains. The strongest German positions in Fifth Army's sector were on and around the 1205m Monte Sammucro to the north of Route 6 and the 963m Monte Camino to the south. Lucas ordered 36 US Division to take the former, whilst Dick gave the latter to Templer, who did not take long to realize that this would be an exceptionally difficult nut to crack.

The only possible approach for 56 Division was from the south, the objective being the peak itself, on which stood a chapel: it was accordingly named Monastery Hill. A mule track lay northwards up a valley towards the mountain before bending away towards the north-west. On either side was a ridge. The one on the left was christened Bare Arse Ridge with typical British military humour, that on the right Razor Back Ridge, a good description of its physical properties. From positions on these the Germans were able to enfilade the mule track. There was no possibility of motor transport, indeed it was even difficult to bring equipment and supplies to the start point of any attack because of the condition of the mountain road from Teano. From Roccamonfina, many miles to the south, it was impassable even to jeeps. Mule companies now assumed great importance, which they would continue to hold well into 1945.

With such difficulties, Templer explained to Dick at a divisional commanders' conference on 4 November, he could only maintain one brigade forward in a direct attack, although he could at least secure the left flank at the same time. Because the topography of Razor Back Ridge was so unsuitable, the most promising alternative was Bare Arse Ridge, which did not lead directly to Monastery Hill, but would allow the attackers to sever the Germans' supply route from the north-west. He selected 201 Guards Brigade for the job. Dick spent the following day on 56 Division's front and was able to appreciate the problem. He was thus extremely irritated to be told that afternoon by Clark, who had not been to see for himself, that he should have taken the mountain already.

At 1630 hrs on 6 November, 201 Guards Brigade began its advance, preceded by an artillery barrage on the assumed German positions on and below Bare Arse Ridge. At its foot 3rd Coldstream Guards took the first objective, the small village of Calabritto, while 6th Grenadier Guards then passed though and had some success, taking the intermediate summit of Point 727 and establishing itself on the slopes of the highest summit, Point 819. The ground conditions, mud and boulders, were appalling and the battalion came under severe machine-gun and mortar fire, finding itself effectively pinned down with little cover, most of its officers dead or wounded, and little hope of receiving food, water and ammunition. A company from 2nd Scots Guards arrived as reinforcements but no further progress was possible. On 8 November the Germans began a series of counter-attacks which pushed the Grenadiers back and although the Coldstreamers moved up to relieve them on 11 November, their position was clearly hopeless. Templer went forward and realized the futility of any further attack. He later recorded what followed:

We were in a jam. To take the ultimate summit at that moment – without further replenishment and without some new factor in the method – was quite impossible. At the same time, to withdraw from the near summit of that awe inspiring mountain – and in those weather conditions – in the face of the enemy might be practically disastrous. I decided that it was the proper course of action, knowing the reception which my thinking would receive at the American Army Headquarters.

I got onto Dick on the blower from the bottom of the mountain. He told me that he was just about to attend an important conference at Army Headquarters and that he could not possibly fail to be present. I argued with him in veiled phraseology for some minutes. Eventually he realised that my predicament must take priority over the conference – however important it was – and he said that he would be with me in a couple of hours. When he arrived I stated my case in more detail and guaranteed to him that I would be able to get to the top in a couple of weeks time at a second attempt, – and knowing the ground up top as I then did. He immediately gave authority for me to withdraw down to the valley – though a bit doubtful I think whether this difficult tactical operation would be successful without heavy casualties. In the event the withdrawal was carried out on the night 14/15 November, and as a result of immensely careful planning, there was hardly a mistake.[5]

It was quite clear to me at the time that Dick realised what hell he was going to have to undergo from Mark Clark. And he did, – having accepted the whole responsibility for the decision on to his own shoulders. I have never admired any man more than I did at that moment.[6]

Dick rated Templer highly as a great fighter and it was very clear that the latter had been personally far enough forward to get the full picture, so he took little convincing. The meeting between the two men was held at 1230 hrs on 13 November and Dick met Clark at his own Main HQ at 1730. Dick's diary records: 'He accepts situation and 3 Div is really in the same state.' Clark himself wrote later that the situation was a severe disappointment and that he himself directed the withdrawal. The first assertion was understated, as in truth he was furious – this was after all the same division which had failed in its first attempt to get over the Volturno. The second was palpably inaccurate, except inasmuch as he was approving a fait accompli. His view of both Dick and the British in general plumbed new lows, although he had to accept that the Americans were not doing any better.

Templer was as good as his word, except in the matter of his timetable, which was elongated by a few days to make sure that much bigger resources were at his disposal, assisted by the construction of a proper jeep track. Dick had brought over 139 Brigade from 46 Division to secure the concentration area, whilst the survivors of 201 Guards Brigade were ordered to move up a third ridge parallel to Bare Arse. Clark had added the artillery of II US Corps to that of X Corps and 56 Division. Templer thus had 436 guns at his disposal, which fired off 17,000 shells from 1730 on 1 November to 1200 hrs on the following day, preceded by heavy bombing from Allied planes.

In clear starlight on the evening of 2 November 167 Brigade advanced up Bare Arse Ridge and 169 Brigade attacked Razor Back Ridge, previously thought too difficult. By first light on the morning of 3 December, 169 Brigade had taken Razor Back and was moving on Monastery Hill. 168 Brigade had retaken Point 727, but were still being held up by concentrated fire from Point 819. The monastery itself was captured and then lost again.

In very heavy fighting it took until 6 December for the Germans to be pushed off Bare Arse Ridge and for Monastery Hill finally to fall to the attackers, and 10 December before the whole massif could be said to have been cleared. The Germans fell back in good order towards Cassino and to new positions on the western bank of the Garigliano.

Dick himself took a 5-mile walk over the battlefield three days later and met all the 56 Division brigadiers to congratulate them, after which he could focus on future operations. He had by this time lost 7 Armoured Division, which was on its way back to England, retaining 23 Armoured Brigade as his only armour, so he was compelled to spread his forces more thinly than he would have liked along the Garigliano, which looked even more formidable than the Volturno. On 17 December he received a visit from Alexander and Alan Brooke, who was on a tour of all the British forces fighting in Italy. Brooke had already seen Eighth Army and now spent a day meeting Dick's HQ staff and the senior commanders in X Corps and then visiting the scene of the recent battle. 'The C.I.G.S had a most successful day on our battlefields,' Dick wrote to Lettice, 'he rode up the "mule track" on a quiet horse and saw a lot of the ground. He was pleased with what the Corps had achieved.'[7] Brooke himself recorded later: 'I had found more life on Dick McCreery's Corps' Front than I had found on the rest of the Italian front and I was impressed with the way he was running his corps.'[8]

Chapter 19

The Winter Line

1943 ended on a relatively quiet note at X Corps, the quartermasters doing particularly well to produce what Dick described as 'excellent & plenteous Christmas fare'. Morale among the troops was high, but there was a serious sense of frustration within the senior levels of the Allied Armies in Italy (AAI), as Alexander's command was now styled. On the right of the line Eighth Army had made rapid progress up the Adriatic coast and had successfully broken through the Gustav Line beyond the Sangro at its seaward end, reaching Ortona before the end of the year, but had now come to a complete halt in appalling weather. Montgomery had gone back to England to assume command of 21st Army Group, handing over to Leese.

Fifth Army had also slowed to a crawl. On a positive note, it had now been reinforced by General Alphonse Juin's French Expeditionary Corps (FEC), which had already distinguished itself by some vigorous actions along the tops of the Apennines. However, VI US Corps only completed the capture of Monte Sammucro on 17 December and still needed to take the German positions on the last hills before Cassino in the New Year before any more general offensive could be mounted on the Winter Line, as the German defensive positions were collectively referred to by the Allies.[1] In the first week of January it launched an attack on one of these, Monte Porchia, and 46 Division was ordered to protect its left flank, earmarking 138 Brigade for the task, with its objective being the hill of Colle Cedro. The attack began on 4 January and the brigade soon found that it was attracting the full brunt of the German response. The Americans were repulsed from Monte Porchia initially and it was only two days later that 46 Division, with 139 Brigade relieving its sister formation, could take Colle Cedro, but the division had incurred heavy casualties for what had been billed as a support operation.

Dick was now busy planning X Corps' role in a major assault on Fifth Army's sector of the Winter Line – later it would be known as the First Battle of Cassino, although the corps would be operating many miles away from that unfortunate town. He had sited his Main HQ at Sparanise, close to the fork between Routes 6 and 7, allowing him to use the former to visit Hawkesworth at Conca and the latter to see Templer at Sessa Aurunca. The weather was awful. On New Year's Day a gale, accompanied by rain and sleet with snow on the higher hills, completely swept away the mess tent. Better news lay in the appearance at HQ that day of the GOC of 5 Division, which would shortly bring X Corps up to full strength and move into position over the next ten days on the far left of the corps in great secrecy, taking 201 Guards Brigade under command.

After a long odyssey to India, Persia and Syria, followed by participation in the campaign in Sicily, 5 Division had been one of the first two to land on the mainland of Europe at Reggio di Calabria, six days before 'Avalanche'. It had subsequently advanced on the far left of Eighth Army, next to its boundary with Fifth Army, being moved in early December to take part in the bitter fighting in the Adriatic sector. With that front closed down for the winter, it was available for further operations. Its GOC was Gerry Bucknall, who was to be relieved by Philip Gregson-Ellis in the middle of the forthcoming battle in order to take up a corps command in England. Both had been in Dick's year at Staff College.

Clark's overall plan was for successive attacks by the formations of Fifth Army on a long front, from the mouth of Garigliano to well up into the Apennines north of Cassino. He had identified the Liri Valley, which carried Route 6, as the most attractive route to Rome, but proposed that X Corps should draw in the enemy's reserves on Fifth Army's left before Geoffrey Keyes's II US Corps mounted a frontal assault across the Liri's tributary, the Rapido, which ran down from the north past the town of Cassino. Crossing this river successfully would force open the 5-mile wide entrance to the valley. In his determination to see Rome taken by Americans, Clark arranged that this would be undertaken by 36 US Division, followed up by 1 US Armored Division. Further attacks to the north would be undertaken by II US Corps' third formation, 34 US Division, and the FEC. Convinced that the whole operation would draw Kesselring's reserves south in the first few days, Clark also planned an amphibious landing by VI US Corps at Anzio, some 60 miles up the coast from the current front line, with a view to cutting off the enemy's retreat and, more importantly to him, taking Rome.

In spite of the fact that the attacks were to be successive rather than simultaneous, Dick was unhappy with the plan. He once again felt that there was a serious dispersal of force rather than a concentration at one particular point, advancing the argument that this should be near the coast and not into the Liri Valley, which would be heavily defended. He was particularly critical of the single division attack across the Rapido: Keyes had agreed with him initially, wanting the two corps to combine in an attack though the Aurunci Mountains, but the American had been persuaded that the topography forbade such an operation. When Al Gruenther and Charles Richardson visited Dick to discuss the plan he expressed his concern, the volume of his voice dropping to an ominously low level. 'As we left', wrote Richardson later, 'Dick McCreery's voice, still a whisper but choked with emotion followed us to our jeep: "It's not on! Tell your Army Commander he will have a disaster."[2] And so it proved to be.

Dick's own plan, forced on him by Fifth Army against his better judgement, split his corps in two. Two of his divisions, 5 and 56, followed by 23 Armoured Brigade, were to cross the Garigliano first and establish a strong bridgehead on the other side, exploiting through the Aurunci Mountains towards Ausonia if circumstances permitted, but primarily accomplishing Clark's main objective of drawing in the German reserves. Two days later 46 Division would attack, crossing the river south of the junction between the Liri and the Rapido, but its role was quite different, to protect the flank of 36 US Division in its assault. The plan was issued on 10 January, Dick held a corps coordinating conference three days later and a final conference two days after that, attended by Clark who according to Dick's diary 'said some nice things about 10 Corps.'

The operation was launched on the night of 17/18 January. 5 Division crossed in complete silence on a two-brigade front, 17 Brigade actually sending one of its battalions out to sea in DUKWs before looping round to land on the coast north of the Garigliano's mouth. The rest of 17 Brigade and the two leading battalions of 13 Brigade made more conventional crossings, but whereas the former found itself stuck in minefields in the triangle between the river, the coast and Route 7, the latter was able to make substantive progress towards the division's main objective, the town of Minturno. As day broke on 18 January, both brigades were in exposed locations, but a bridgehead of sorts had been established. Over the next two days both 15 Brigade and 201 Guards Brigade were fed in to bolster the position.

Templer also took his division across the river on a two-brigade front, in this case supported by the full weight of his artillery. 167 Brigade met some resistance and only one battalion achieved its objective, but 169 Brigade, with 40 (Royal Marine) Commando in support, had no such difficulty and quickly established a bridgehead, which was soon strong enough to take 168 Brigade as well and to link up with 5 Division. Dick now had a firm foothold north of the Garigliano.

The Germans were taken completely by surprise. Their observers had not noticed the concentration of 5 and 56 Divisions, whose guns had been brought up by night, camouflaged and then left unmanned. The only formation in the area was 94 Infantry Division which was rocked back on its heels. For the Allies it created a brief opportunity which was not to be repeated. In the words of the talented commander of XIV Panzer Corps, Frido von Senger und Etterlin, in whose sector the operation took place: 'The thrust by the British X Corps against 94 Inf. Div. had special significance, for if it had led to a breakthrough, the entire German front would have been rolled up from the south.'³ If Clark had listened to Dick about concentrating the attack near the coast and had positioned a strong force to exploit the initial success, it could have gone either up Route 7 towards Anzio and Rome or through the defile formed by the River Ausente to Ausonia and thence into the Liri Valley. Neither would have been easy, but for many hours there was nothing of substance in the way. However, other than 23 Armoured Brigade, Dick had no more resources and the opportunity was missed.

This did not mean that Clark had not achieved his objective. On the contrary, von Senger's appeal to Kesselring for help resulted in the latter ordering both 29 and 90 Panzer Grenadier Divisions from their positions south of Rome down to the Minturno area as quickly as possible, the former to block the Ausente defile, the latter to prevent any further advance up Route 7. Kesselring's immediately available reserves had been committed, just as Clark wanted.

On 19 January 46 Division also tried to cross the river, but was spectacularly unsuccessful. Unlike 5 and 56 Division, which had used DUKWs and other relatively robust small craft, 46 Division was forced to rely entirely on rubber boats, as all the other available DUKWs were on their way to Anzio. Moreover, whilst the river had been flowing relatively slowly close to its mouth, at the division's main crossing point it was narrower but much faster flowing, the volume increased not only by the nearby junctions with the Rapido and another river, the Peccia, but also by the opening of sluice gates further north by the Germans. In the fast current, the frail craft proved exceptionally difficult to handle and a number were swept away. Swimmers were sent across with ropes attached to cables, but even with the help of these the boats were unmanageable, many becoming waterlogged. By this time the Germans had realized what was happening and had begun to react.

With a single company on the far bank, Dick ordered it to be evacuated and further attempts to be abandoned, although he also instructed Hawkesworth to carry out a feint crossing on the night of 20/21 January to draw the defenders away from 36 US Division. This division duly attacked then and again two nights later, with disastrous results, much as Dick had predicted.⁴ Keyes felt let down and Clark was once again very angry with what he saw as a lack of determination by the British. The facts were clear, however – 46 Division could not have succeeded with the equipment it was forced to use. With that exception X Corps was the only part of Fifth Army to break though the Winter Line, both 34 US Division and the FEC having fallen short of their objectives in the north. It was Clark's refusal to exploit success on Dick's front, almost certainly because he wanted the glory to lie with the Americans rather than the British, that condemned the whole operation to failure.

The landings at Anzio went ahead as planned on 22 January, notwithstanding that the condition originally imposed by the planners, that a breakthrough should have been achieved to the south, had in no way been fulfilled. They were a success at first and VI US Corps managed to establish itself ashore without difficulty, not least because of the absence of 29 and 90 Panzer Grenadier Divisions from the area. Lucas, however, proved to be excessively cautious and just dug in, allowing Kesselring not only to bring down reinforcements from the north, but also to call back 29 Panzer Grenadier Division as von Senger's front stabilized. The beachhead became, in Churchill's words, 'a stranded whale'.

Dick was still faced with a great deal of fighting to hold the positions he had captured. On 21 January, the arrival of 90 Panzer Grenadier Division allowed the Germans to mount vigorous but ultimately unsuccessful counter-attacks on 5 Division, in an attempt to drive a wedge through Minturno to the Garigliano. Meanwhile, 17 Brigade remained pinned down in the minefield close to the sea, although the divisional engineers managed to get a 9-ton bridge across the river behind them, while work started on preparing for vehicles the railway bridge carrying the main line from Naples to Rome, which had been badly damaged. No bridge was available to 56 Division, which was forced to continue to use rafts and attracted considerable artillery fire. Its hold on the key Damiano ridge was proving tenuous and it failed to break through to its objective of Castelforte.

Dick crossed the Garigliano for the first time on 20 January when he visited the Tac HQs of both 13 and 15 Brigades, running an artillery gauntlet in both directions. He decided to bring 46 Division's 138 Brigade into the bridgehead directly after the aborted crossing, in order to consolidate his line on the right of 56 Division, with another brigade following a few days later, but he had to leave the third brigade on the near side of the Garigliano along the stretch where the west bank was still held by the Germans. Dick asked for II US Corps to take over this sector, but the request was rejected by Clark. By 24 January, it was becoming clear that 5 Division was in no state to mount an offensive and that the troops in 56 Division were very tired. Although Dick received a modest reinforcement in the shape of 2 Special Service Brigade, formed out of 9 and 43 (Royal Marine) Commandos, it was not enough to mount more than local operations.

The Germans clearly remained concerned by the X Corps foothold to the north of the Garigliano and took all necessary steps to keep it bottled up there. The corps intelligence summary on 2 February reported that units from no fewer than 12 German divisions had been identified opposite the corps, whilst the German defences had been strengthened to a point where, without further resources, Dick's options were very limited. Gradually the fighting settled down to patrolling and small-scale actions.

The situation at Anzio had by now become very serious, with the Germans mounting strong attacks on the beachhead. On 30 January Dick was ordered to send a brigade up there immediately and chose 169 Brigade from 56 Division, which arrived at Anzio on 3 February. He received 1 Guards Brigade from 6 Armoured Division as a replacement, only to be told that the rest of 56 Division would be following its departed brigade. Templer wrote later to Dick that he had hated leaving X Corps, but he formed a very high regard for Truscott, who relieved the hapless Lucas at VI US Corps within a fortnight of 56 Division's arrival there.

In spite of these tribulations Dick himself remained in good heart. Gregson-Ellis, a personal friend, wrote in a letter to Dick's mother, Minnie, thanking her for a consignment of books for the troops, that he had never seen him look better, whilst Lieutenant Colonel Lord William Montague-Douglas-Scott,[5] a friend of Lettice's, wrote to her that he looked fitter and less close-drawn than he had during the Salerno battles. Dick himself claimed that this was because he was getting plenty of exercise climbing mountains to visit his various units. He moved his Main HQ to Templer's former site at Sessa Aurunca, from where he could reach them faster. On the professional side he was delighted that Alexander's new chief of staff was John Harding, recovered at last from the injuries he had received before the capture of Tripoli.

Change was now in the air. In mid-February and again in mid-March Bernard Freyberg's New Zealand Corps, which had relieved II US Corps opposite Cassino itself, made two disastrous attempts to force the German positions, the first one preceded by the destruction of the monastery by heavy bombing. After these failures, Alexander decided to shift his weight significantly from the Adriatic, where little further progress looked possible, to the southern sector, moving Eighth Army's boundary to include Cassino and the Liri Valley entrance and bringing XIII Corps and II Polish Corps south. Fifth Army would then comprise II US Corps, which would relieve X Corps, and the FEC.

At the end of February 46 Division, which had been continuously in action since the previous September, began to be relieved by the newly arrived 4 Division prior to leaving for the Middle East to rest and refit. After that 5 Division was also relieved in order to go to Anzio to replace 56 Division, which followed its former partner for a well-earned rest. For the first and last time since the departure of the Rangers, this move brought an American formation under Dick's direct command in the shape of 88 US Division, which had just completed several months' training in Morocco. Its arrival was followed by that of 4e Division Marocaine de Montagne from the

FEC, releasing 4 Division back to Eighth Army and 23 Armoured Brigade to V Corps on the Adriatic coast. On 31 March X Corps itself transferred from Fifth Army to Eighth Army.

Clark wrote a fulsome letter to Dick:

> On the occasion of the separation of 10 Corps from Fifth Army, I wish to tell you what a privilege it has been for me to have had your corps under my command and how much I value my personal association with you during the period in which we have been fighting together.
>
> The association of Fifth Army with yourself, your staff and the units of 10 Corps brought us from the shores of Africa to your present position north of the Garigliano River. Despite many difficulties encountered in the bitterly opposed Salerno landing, the subsequent expansion of the beachhead and the severe fighting later in the mountainous area north of Naples, the 10 Corps under your leadership has consistently fought with a courage and determination which have resulted in wresting many square miles of territory and inflicting severe losses on him. At the same time the entire corps, following the example of its commander and staff, has demonstrated a spirit of cooperation towards the other components of the Fifth Army, which has provided perhaps the most impressive example thus far of the fighting solidarity of the United Nations, and has proved conclusively to the Nazi enemy the futility of his efforts to sew discord among them.
>
> May I express to you the keen pleasure which I have had in our personal association during these past months, and my regret that our official relationship is being interrupted at this time. My staff joins me in wishing the very best of fortune to you and the members of your staff. We shall follow your future activities with great personal interest and hope to be able to see you frequently as time goes on.

Dick wrote a generous reply. The truth was that the relationship was not as portrayed, although it never came near to breaking point. Clark had been deeply frustrated by what he had seen as X Corps' failures at the Volturno, Monte Camino and the Garigliano, notwithstanding that they were hugely outweighed in the balance by the successes. At one point he was moved to describe Dick as a 'feather duster', almost as inappropriate a description as it is possible to imagine. Dick did not dislike Clark, but he thought him vain and he doubted his military skill. On the other hand the two staffs had got along very well, indeed Al Gruenther was deservedly popular at Dick's HQ, and there was no animosity in general between the British and the Americans as there had been on occasion in Tunisia. Nevertheless both Dick and Clark were almost certainly relieved by their separation. They were not to know that the relationship would be resumed before the year was out.

Dick's staff certainly deserved some respite and their reward was for the corps to take over the quietest sector of the Winter Line, high up in the Apennines, allowing the Polish Corps to step to the left. Before Dick himself went there he was able to take his first leave since arriving back in the Mediterranean in August 1943. After two days in Naples, including a visit to the opera, he left for Sorrento. Vesuvius was in full eruption and the site of one of his former HQs had been engulfed by lava, while fine ash was covering everything from Torre Annunziata onwards. He spent a lot of time reading (one book which he particularly enjoyed was Arthur Bryant's *The Years of Endurance*, about the early stages of the Napoleonic Wars, which resonated strongly with those British who had experienced 1940–42) and otherwise relaxing and he was back at his old HQ on the evening of the fifth day in time to pack up for the move into the mountains.

The new Main HQ was at Pesche, a small village close to Isernia, which allowed him access to all sections of his long front, albeit by very winding mountain roads. At the beginning of April the only fighting troops in the corps were the King's Dragoon Guards, giving rise to a quip by some wag at Eighth Army HQ that Dick was holding the front in his sector 'with a squadron of armoured cars and a volley of oaths'! Gradually the various formations and units which would now comprise the corps assembled, and they were a very mixed bag. The most sizeable formation was 2 New Zealand Division, but this was in the course of recovering from its bitter experiences at Cassino and was hardly fit for battle. The others were all smaller, respectively 2 Parachute Brigade, 11 Canadian Brigade Group, 24 Guards Brigade Group and, for the first month, 28 Brigade, whilst the corps also recovered its own guns, 2 Army Group Royal Artillery (2 AGRA), which had been lent to the New Zealand Corps for the Cassino battles.

The most intriguing new member of the corps was 1º Raggruppamento Motorizzato, an Italian co-belligerent formation which was given the rather more impressive title of Corpo Italiano di Liberazione on 17 April. Formed of volunteers from elements of the Legnano and Messina Divisions in the old Italian Army, with an infantry and a Bersaglieri regiment each of approximately brigade size and other infantry components, its own artillery, engineers and services, it was not dissimilar to a British division in size and was armed, clothed and otherwise supplied entirely by the Allies. Dick went to visit it and liked what he saw, particularly the Alpini battalion, which was well suited to the country in which they were all now situated. The formation had seen action in December 1943, when it had participated effectively in the battle for Monte Lungo as part of VI US Corps, and its commander, Lieutenant General Umberto Utili, was generally well regarded.

Smallest of the new units to arrive at X Corps, but closest to Dick's heart, was the 12th Lancers, which would in due course provide an additional armoured car regiment. Now commanded by 'Kate' Savill, it had to put away its armoured cars for the immediate future and join the King's Dragoon Guards as Hermonforce, named after the KDG's CO. Hermonforce took over part of 24 Guards Brigade Group's sector and began immediate patrolling as infantry.

Dick did an immense amount of driving and walking through the mountains over the next two months. The journeys were made more difficult by the poor quality of the roads and his front was huge for the forces he deployed, stretching as it did from about 10 miles north-east of Cassino along the upper reaches of the Rapido and then over the watershed to the Sangro, following that river through Castel di Sangro to near the village of Pizzoferato, its boundary with V Corps on the Adriatic. Dick had few days off, but one he particularly enjoyed was a visit with Cooke to General Guillaume, the commander of the Moroccan Goums. He was invited to ride by horse up the track to Monte Camino, where the French unveiled a memorial to those who had died there during the battle. After speeches, Dick making his in French, he enjoyed a typically excellent lunch at Guillaume's HQ, at which he sat next to General Georges Catroux, one of the first senior officers to declare for de Gaulle and now the Governor General of Algeria. 'A v. vital personality,' wrote Dick in his diary.

X Corps was to play no part in the early and critical stages of Operation Diadem, in which Alexander launched Fifth and Eighth Armies at the Winter Line on 11 May. II US Corps and the FEC broke out of Dick's Garigliano bridgehead at last, the former driving up Route 7 with the objective of meeting US VI Corps south of Anzio, the latter carrying out one of the most stunning advances of the campaign, through and over the Aurunci Mountains, turning the German flank in the Liri Valley: this gave Dick great pleasure as he admired the FEC enormously and was delighted that X Corps had created for them their jumping-off point. He wrote a letter of congratulation to Clark, who replied to say that, flying over the area: 'I could not help but give a prayer of thanks for the fine pioneer work which 10 Corps did for Fifth Army in obtaining the bridgehead from which we debouched.'

XIII Corps was the battering ram at the door of the valley, forcing the Rapido and capturing at last the town of Cassino, whilst the Poles restored their national pride by taking the monastery. Von Senger and the Tenth German Army commander, von Vietinghoff, were both on leave and rushed back to find that the Allies had broken right through the Winter Line and, with I Canadian Corps also in the field, were poised to attack the last defensive line across the Liri Valley, after which there was nothing until beyond Rome. At the same time Truscott ordered a breakout from Anzio. To his dismay and that of many others, only part of his force was sent to cut off the retreating Germans at Valmontone, Clark ordering a switch in direction towards Rome, which he was determined to liberate in person. A great opportunity to destroy the German Tenth Army was missed.

On 25 May Dick flew to Eighth Army's Tac HQ to meet Alexander and Leese and to be given orders for X Corps' future participation in the campaign. In the centre of his sector, the CIL had already taken a long contested position across the Sangro as the Germans withdrew, whilst Dick met Freyberg to put his division on notice to move. X Corps Main HQ relocated on 28 May to Venafro and on the following day to near Cassino. On 1 June the corps joined the Allied advance.

Chapter 20

The Tiber Valley

T he next four months, as the AAI advanced from the Gustav Line to the Gothic Line, tend to be dealt with briefly by most historians, as they lack the drama of Salerno, Cassino or Anzio. For those involved, the advance was no picnic. The Germans were as skilled as ever in their withdrawal, mining roads and tracks, demolishing bridges and embankments, blowing up passes and cuttings and leaving unpleasant booby-traps everywhere. Moreover, at well-selected positions they dug in with the intention of forcing as long a delay as possible. The Allies had no alternative but to move with caution and, although their progress occasionally developed a momentum and fluidity which was unusual in the Italian campaign, they continued to be hampered by the topography, which favoured the defenders.

In Dick's case, this period demonstrated his skills as a corps commander probably better than any other. Divisions, independent brigades and smaller units arrived and left with great rapidity. Set-piece attacks for the whole corps, such as on the Volturno and the Garigliano, were almost non-existent, being replaced by brigade, battalion or even company-sized actions which responded to the requirements of the situation. All this required a great deal of flexibility, a focus on priorities and very close liaison with the divisions under command. Dick's various HQ's, and especially his Tac HQ, all moved very frequently, but there was never a moment when he and his staff were not in complete control of their situation.

The first two weeks were chaotic in terms of the command structure, the only consolation being that the Germans were at this stage in headlong retreat. On the very first day, 1 June, the CIL and Hermonforce were transferred to V Corps, leaving X Corps effectively just with 2 New Zealand Division and a single squadron of the 12th Lancers, but Dick was shortly to lose the New Zealanders into army reserve. Brief appearances in the corps were made by 4 Division, 1 Canadian Armoured Brigade, 7 Armoured Brigade and 25 Tank Brigade, none for more than a few days. However, towards the end of the first week of June both the composition of the corps and the direction of its advance became clearer. It was to take under command 6 Armoured Division and 8 Indian Division, the former moving on the left up the east bank of the Tiber north of Rome, skirting the Sabine

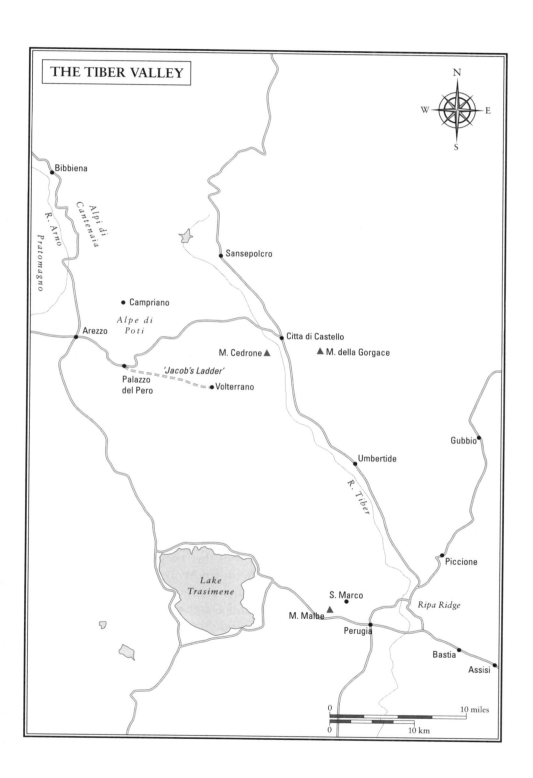

THE TIBER VALLEY

Hills with its intermediate objective as Narni, the latter pushing forward on the right, using relatively minor roads on an axis Alatri–Subiaco–Rieti–Terni. Both divisions would then advance side by side on Perugia. The 12th Lancers were restored to X Corps in their entirety and ordered to protect the right flank.

X Corps was now one of five advancing up the Italian peninsula towards the Gothic Line, which ran roughly from Pisa to Rimini. On the coast heading towards Leghorn and Pisa was Willis D. Crittenberger's IV US Corps and next to it, heading through Tuscany towards Siena, was Juin's FEC. Both of these were still in Fifth US Army. The left hand corps of Eighth Army was Sydney Kirkman's XIII Corps, moving to the east of Lake Bolsena and the west of Lake Trasimene, with its final objective as Florence. On its right, with orders to take the whole of the Tiber valley, to Perugia and beyond, was X Corps, whilst on the other side of the Apennines on the Adriatic coast was Wladislaw Anders's II Polish Corps.

Dick now had two new formations with which to familiarize himself. As a former armoured division commander the more straightforward of the two from his perspective was 6 Armoured Division, which he had come across frequently in Tunisia. The GOC, Vivyan Evelegh, had commanded 78 Division during that campaign, so was personally known to Dick. The division's 26 Armoured Brigade contained two lancer regiments, the 16th/5th and the 17th/21st, together with a yeomanry regiment, the Lothians and Border Horse. There were not one but two infantry brigades, 1 Guards Brigade, which had come under Dick's command for a brief period in February and March, and 61 Brigade, which had just joined and consisted of three battalions of the Rifle Brigade. The division had made rather heavy weather of the breakthrough in the Liri Valley, but Dick was confident that it could now do what he wanted.

On the other hand he had no experience of Indian divisions. He was soon to learn that the only significant difference between these and their British infantry counterparts was the composition of the troops. About two-thirds of the men in each division were from the Indian Army, which provided two battalions in each of the three brigades, the reconnaissance regiment, the machine-gun battalion, all the engineers and a large part of the services. The artillery, except in the case of 8 Indian Division the anti-tank regiment, were all from the British Army, as was one battalion in each brigade. The overwhelming majority of the commissioned officers were also British, although Indian officers were now beginning to come through at an increasing pace.

A long spell in Iraq had meant a slow start to the war for 8 Indian Division, but it had been in Italy on the Adriatic coast since the previous autumn, had fought on the Sangro and was the division which had crossed the Rapido in the breakout through the Winter Line, thus achieving, albeit not without great difficulty, what 36 US Division had failed to do in January. The GOC was Dudley 'Pasha' Russell,[1] whom Dick had met socially in Cairo in 1942. Dick visited the division for the first time on 5 June, writing in his diary, 'they seem a jolly good show'. Not only did this initial impression prove right, but he very quickly came to admire the men in this Indian division and two others as well.

Terni and Narni were both reached against light opposition on 13 June. The crossings over the Tiber's tributary, the Nera, had been destroyed and it took valuable time to construct Bailey bridges, but on 15 June the advance was underway again, 6 Armoured Division making very good progress and capturing Todi. The 12th Lancers reported that Rieti was clear and by the next day their armoured cars had gone right through Spoleto and were in Foligno. On 17 June 8 Indian Division found Assisi in the hands of Italian partisans and Dick was able to visit the Basilica of St Francis two days later to marvel at Giotto's frescoes. His Tac HQ was moving daily and on the day of the visit to Assisi was relocated to just south of Perugia, where it was already apparent that the Germans had turned to face the corps and were contesting any further advance.

The Albert Line ran east and west of Lake Trasimene and was intended to stop or at least delay both X and XIII Corps. In X Corps' sector it ran along the top of the hills north of the road between Perugia and the lake, incorporated the hilltop city itself and then ran for 5 miles to the north-east along the Ripa Ridge, a 1,000 ft high escarpment between the Tiber and the River Chiascia which blocked the road into the Apennines. Breaking the line was substantially a job for the infantry, so 6 Armoured Division directed 1 Guards Brigade on the city and 61 Brigade on the hills to the west, whilst 8 Indian Division tackled Ripa Ridge.

Fighting was fierce on the night of 19 June, as the Riflemen attacked the key position of Monte Malbe and the Guards tried to shake up the defences in front of the city itself. Much to the surprise of the latter, on the morning of the following day it was found that the Germans had abandoned Perugia. On the same day the 7th Rifle Brigade took Monte Malbe. 1 Guards Brigade now directed its weight north-west of Perugia, where 3rd Welsh Guards took the village of San Marco with the help of a squadron of the 16th/5th Lancers.

This proved to be the swansong of 6 Armoured Division within X Corps as Leese now decided to switch the division to XIII Corps, which was experiencing difficulty with penetrating its sector of the Albert Line and which offered better country for an armoured division. When Dick flew in his Piper Cub to discuss the move with Leese and Kirkman on 27 June, he learnt that he was also to give up 8 Indian Division, which had endured a very tough fight on the Ripa Ridge, captured on the afternoon of 19 June, but only after the division had incurred heavy losses. The arrival of the Shermans of the 3rd Hussars enabled a brilliantly executed attack to carry the division as far as Piccione, 5 miles to the north, on 26 June, taking the enemy completely by surprise. Dick was very sorry to be losing it.

As a replacement he received 10 Indian Division, a relatively new arrival in Italy, which for a short time took over the whole corps sector. Like 8 Indian Division it had spent much time in Iraq, although it had been hurried to the Western Desert in the aftermath of the disaster at Gazala, only to see its brigades thrown piecemeal into the battle and consequently mauled by the enemy. It had reformed in the Levant, where it had trained extensively for mountain warfare. Its GOC was Denys Reid, like Russell an Indian Army officer, but one who knew Italy well from personal experience. Reid had been captured with his brigade HQ near Fuka during the retreat to El Alamein and had been incarcerated in Northern Italy. Released after the armistice in September 1943, he had made his way on foot through the mountains with a fellow brigadier until they reached the Allied lines. With this and some earlier experience of fighting the Italians at Keren, there was little he did not know about the defensive properties of mountains and his troops were taught all the techniques required to infiltrate and penetrate enemy positions, to capture high ground and to hide in dead ground. The next few months were to prove that they had learnt their lessons well and as mountain troops were as good as the best, until now the Algerians and Moroccans of the FEC.

The loss of 6 Armoured Division did not mean Dick lost all his tanks. The arrival of the 3rd Hussars on 8 Indian Division's front heralded that of 9 Armoured Brigade, whose three regiments of Shermans, the others being the Warwickshire and the Royal Wiltshire Yeomanry, gave him the punch he was to need. With the brigade's tanks in support, 10 Indian Division began the move into the Upper Tiber Valley, which became narrower and more hemmed in by high ground the further north it stretched.

By 2 July the Germans had pulled back completely from the Perugia area and, after some fighting on the intervening hills, they broke contact and withdrew north of Umbertide, partly at least because XIII Corps had now broken through the Albert Line and was moving forward fast, requiring the units facing Dick to conform to their retreating comrades. His next objective was Citta di Castello, which blocked any further progress up the valley. As 10 Indian Division began a series of attacks on the mountain positions in front of and to the east of the city at the end of the first week of July, X Corps received a welcome reinforcement in the shape of 4 Indian Division. This was the most experienced of its type in the theatre, having been in action more or less continuously since June 1940. With experience at Keren, the

Mareth Line, Wadi Akarit and Cassino, it had learnt mountain warfare in the field rather than in training and it was to form an incomparable team with 10 Indian Division, highly suited to the task ahead. Its GOC was an experienced Gurkha officer, 'Hol' Holworthy.

Dick welcomed the addition as his front was about to expand. As well as forcing a route to the top of the Tiber Valley past Sansepolcro and up the mountain pass which carried the main road to Rimini, he was now to divert a significant part of his strength towards Bibbiena, some 15 miles north of Arezzo in the Upper Arno Valley. Dick decided that 10 Indian Division would continue for the time being up the Tiber Valley, whilst 4 Indian Division forced its way across the nearly trackless hills towards Arezzo. Before this happened, Citta di Castello needed to be taken and this was a task for both divisions, with 10 Indian Division taking one by one the strong points to the east of the main road and 4 Indian Division those to the west. Lengthy battles developed for the former at Monte della Gorgace and the latter at Monte Cedrone before the city fell on 22 July, following which the Germans made a general withdrawal to the north.

In the meantime the lack of roads towards Arezzo meant that 4 Indian Division's engineers had to construct a jeep track across the hills to Palazzo del Pero, a few miles short of the town. Nicknamed 'Jacob's Ladder', it was completed in time for Dick to drive up it on 15 July. Two days later 4 Indian Division began its attack on the Alpe di Poti, a line of hills north of the lateral road between Arezzo and Citta di Castello, whose possession was vital to any further advance. Meeting complete success allowed Dick to switch more of his strength towards the advance on Bibbiena, and he moved his Tac HQ to a hill overlooking Palazzo del Pero so that he would be close to the action.

'Cookie' Cooke had now been relieved as BGS by Reggie Hewetson, a gunner officer, whose attention was partially diverted by the preparations necessary for the arrival of a distinguished visitor, known by his code name 'General Collingwood'. This was none other than King George VI, who was making a tour of the Italian front and arrived at X Corps on the morning of 25 July in company with Oliver Leese. The corps war diary described the visit succinctly:

HM THE KING visited 10 Corps landing by plane at PERUGIA airfield this afternoon. He saw comds and tps of 46,[2] 10 Ind and 4 Ind Divs and during his time motored up the 10 Corps Jeep track from VOLTERRANO 4421 by the PALAZZO DEL PERO rd. He was entertained to tea at Tac HQ 10 Corps est 3825 where the Corps Commander received the accolade of knighthood. He left the Corps area at Arezzo shortly after 1800 hrs.

In his letter describing the event to Lettice, Dick was hardly more forthcoming, other than to say that he had dined with Leese that night, sitting next to the King and that 'I was knighted during the tea interval,[3] most embarrassing!'[4] The visit had been arranged so that the King, driven by Leese himself in an open car through Perugia and then by Dick in his jeep up Jacob's Ladder, could be seen by as many of the troops and meet as many of their commanders as possible. He was in his element, delighted to be on an active front and among military people, with whom he always got on well. He was particularly thrilled to be taken to an OP near Palazzo del Pero, where he was able to watch the field gunners of 4 Indian Division fire in support of an attack which was taking place at Campriano, north of the Alpe di Poti.

In addition to losing Cooke, Dick had said goodbye temporarily to Hugh Smith. He wrote to Lettice that he would miss him, as he was so nice, but that he was really rather relieved as Smith was poor at the details which were the heart of the ADC's job, such as knowing the names of the people Dick would be meeting and the whereabouts of the units he was visiting. He was particularly hopeless at map reading, which was very necessary as Dick usually drove himself. Dick had high hopes of his new ADC, Walter Jones. He had been put forward by Andrew Horsburgh-Porter, who was now commanding a new cavalry regiment, the 27th Lancers, which had been formed on a cadre of the 12th.[5] For a time both regiments were in X Corps, but Dick had little time to visit them as they were operating on the right flank up in the mountains.

During one of his rare visits to the 12th Lancers, Dick left one indelible memory with Kate Savill. The two of them were standing outside the RHQ where Savill was telling Dick about how he planned to convert one of the large rooms into a canteen for the men:

> Suddenly a sapper sergeant rushed out and shouted 'Everyone get well clear; there is a huge mine in the cellar that is overdue to go off.' Dick stood his ground and I did the same, though with inward trepidation. Then he said 'You were telling me about the canteen. Let's go in and have a look at it.' And in we went and spent what seemed like an age looking around. All was well, because the sappers de-fused the mine, but I just wonder if he was trying me out!

It is more likely that this was another example of Dick's fearlessness, on which so many commented during the campaign.

In early August there were a number of changes to the composition of the corps: 46 Division joined it for five days, before being transferred to V Corps, and 6 Armoured Division for eight days until it was recognized that the country it was entering was not suitable for tanks. During this time the latter was under the all too brief command of Gerald Templer. Appointed as GOC on 24 July, he was in the course of gingering up the division, which was showing signs of exhaustion, when he was wounded on 5 July as the result of a mine set off by a 1 Guards Brigade lorry on the other side of the road.[6]

Much more significantly, 4 Indian Division was also withdrawn into reserve before following 46 Division to V Corps. Dick had launched Operation Vandal, the advance up the Upper Arno valley to Bibbiena, on a two-division front on 4 August, which involved not only attacking along the valley bottom, but also securing the ranges of hills on each side, the Pratomagno to the west and the Alpe di Cantenia to the east. Now, just over a week later, he was reduced to a single infantry division and 9 Armoured Brigade, which remained with the corps but could only be used on rare occasions. The arrival of the Lovat Scouts, who were specifically trained in mountain warfare but lightly armed, did little to redress the balance.

4 Indian Division had been required for Operation Olive, which saw Leese switching most of his weight to the Adriatic. The Eighth Army commander expected this application of force to carry him right into the Plain of the Po before the end of the year, taking Bologna and rolling up the Gothic Line from the east. The Poles would initially continue their attacks towards Rimini, but the main punch would come from V Corps and I Canadian Corps passing through them on the night of 25/26 August. XIII Corps would pass to Fifth US Army, which had lost not only the FEC but also VI US Corps to the invasion of Southern France. Clark planned to launch his own attack through the mountain passes north of Florence in early September and needed Kirkman's troops until he could bring up more American divisions. X Corps' role was greatly diminished, being effectively to maintain what pressure it could with modest resources on a very wide front and to move into any vacuum created by the Germans in their retreat to the Gothic Line.

This task was made more difficult over the following weeks by further losses. The two yeomanry regiments in 9 Armoured Brigade had been on active service for so long that they were repatriated to the UK, whilst the 3rd Hussars were placed under the direct command of AAI. At much the same time the 12th Lancers were transferred to V Corps.

As is turned out Leese's new offensive, followed in due course by Clark's, drew away some of the Germans formations facing X Corps and the pressure began to come off Dick during late August and September. On 26 August, the day before Bibbiena was entered by a patrol from 10 Indian Division, he was able to get away for a whole day to an officers' rest centre on an island in Lake Trasimene, spending much of the time sleeping on a deckchair, whilst on 19 September he was able to take his first leave since his stay in Sorrento in early April – just five days, of which three were spent in Rome, where he much enjoyed seeing all the sights and during which he had an audience with the Pope. By the time Dick returned, the German withdrawal to the Gothic Line had been completed and he was able to drive all the way to Bagno di Romagna.

Dick's only remaining complete division, 10 Indian, was now itself moved in great secrecy to the Adriatic, where Leese had met considerable resistance and needed further reinforcement. By this time X Corps was down to its lowest level of manpower since it had moved into the Apennines in April. Dick's only formations of any size were 1 Guards Brigade and 2 AGRA. Otherwise there was an extraordinary mix of units, including two anti-aircraft regiments, one retraining as infantry, the other as field artillery, the Nabha Akhal Battalion, an Indian States Forces unit, and 2271 Field Squadron of the RAF Regiment. The armoured cars of the Household Cavalry Regiment and the King's Dragoon Guards remained, as did Skinner's Horse, the 8th Manchester Regiment, and the 1st/4th Essex Regiment, the last three of which had been temporarily left behind by 10 Indian Division. The bottom of the barrel had been well and truly scraped!

For Dick himself, a dramatic change was about to occur. On 28 September he was summoned to a meeting at HQ AAI, where Alexander told him that Leese would be going to the Far East as Commander, Allied Land Forces South-East Asia, and that Dick had been selected to take over from him as the commander of Eighth Army. Two days later he left X Corps en route to his new HQ.

Chapter 21

Army Commander

Leese left Eighth Army on 1 October, having briefed Dick the previous evening. Following Montgomery's example, he was taking with him to India all his most senior staff. George Walsh, his chief of staff, stayed behind to introduce Dick to the remaining staff members and the various commanders, following Leese a week later. Dick had brought with him only his Chief Royal Engineer, two more junior staff officers, his jeep driver, his excellent cook and Walter Jones. His most urgent requirement was a replacement for Walsh and he was delighted to be offered Harry Floyd, who had been serving as BGS of VIII Corps, with four months' experience of the fighting in north-west Europe. Floyd arrived on 20 October.

Dick knew most of the senior commanders already. Charles Keightley was now GOC of V Corps. After leading 6 Armoured Division in Tunisia he had commanded 78 Division in Italy. Just 43 years old, he was the only commander of a British corps on active service to have been commissioned after the Great War. All Keightley's divisional commanders had served under Dick within the last 12 months. Hawkesworth was still leading 46 Division, Reid 10 Indian Division and Freyberg 2 New Zealand Division, whilst Dudley Ward of 4 Division and John Whitfield of 56 Division had both commanded brigades in 5 Division on the Garigliano.

At II Polish Corps, Dick had worked alongside Anders during his sojourn in the High Apennines in the late spring and thought highly of him, while understanding that he brought with him some potentially difficult political baggage relating to his country's circumstances. This left the one formation with which he was not familiar, I Canadian Corps, although he had exercised oversight of 5 Canadian Armoured Division in England in early 1942 and one of its brigades had served briefly in X Corps. He found the corps commander, Tommy Burns, very uninspiring, but liked what he saw of Chris Vokes of 1 Canadian Division and Bert Hoffmeister of 5 Canadian Armoured Division.

Extraordinarily, no announcement was made about Leese's departure or Dick's appointment until about a month after the handover, although by that time Dick had visited every single formation in Eighth Army and many of their constituent units, so his arrival was far from a secret in the theatre itself. The word spread within Army circles elsewhere, Templer writing from

England, where he was still convalescing: 'Do you remember my saying in First Camino (in that wet chestnut wood) that you'd be an Army Comd. soon?'[1] Even Auchinleck, now C-in-C India, to whom Dick had reported on the performance of the Indian divisions, wrote warmly to 'My dear Dick' saying, 'as a former commander of 8th Army myself I am sure I feel it could not be in better hands and I wish you all the good luck in the world,'[2] – a remarkable sentiment from one who had sacked Dick not much more than two years earlier!

Given Dick's successful career as a corps commander in the theatre, the patronage of Alexander and the vital approval of Brooke, the choice appears to have been inevitable. The only other experienced corps commander in Italy was Kirkman, but he was in the middle of fighting an important battle. Dick wrote to Lettice telling her how pleased Alexander had been, and he had met Brooke for dinner as recently as 22 August, the CIGS confiding in his diary how delighted he was to see him.

Dick noted in his own diary on the day of his arrival at Eighth Army: 'Things are very much bogged down and at a standstill at the moment.' In fact Operation Olive had been a tactical victory but a strategic disappointment. It had achieved its first objective, the Canadians crashing through the Gothic Line along the coast, but Leese had failed to provide them with adequate reserves to exploit their success. On the V Corps front, the Germans proved as tenacious in the foothills as they had been in the mountains and the corps ground to a halt in front of the Coriano ridge. 1 Armoured Division, which had been brought up to drive the advance onwards, arrived late at its start point and failed to establish any momentum. It took a combined attack by both corps to shake the defences loose.

With the capture of Rimini by the Canadians on 20 September, Eighth Army was on the threshold of the Po Valley, but it was now faced with what seemed like an endless succession of rivers crossing its path, obstacles which were to prove just as difficult to overcome as the mountain peaks. With heavy rains in the Apennines in these wettest months of the year, the rivers were all in flood, while the low-lying country for which Leese had longed turned out to be a sea of mud. Dick wrote to Lettice two days after he arrived: 'Today we have had over 2 inches of rain, and only four days ago there were another 2 inches here. The Po valley will be an absolute morass, the poor tanks find Italy almost impossible.'[3] Considerable losses had been incurred during Olive, one consequence of which was a decision taken just before Dick arrived to disband 1 Armoured Division to provide reinforcements for other divisions, although his old 2 Armoured Brigade, now commanded by John Combe, remained in Eighth Army as an independent formation.

Alexander ordered Dick to continue the advance along the axis of Route 9, the old Roman Via Emilia which ran straight as an arrow from Rimini to

Bologna. Dick decided that the Canadian Corps should take the coastal sector, whilst V Corps should attack through the foothills. Less deterred than Leese by the terrain to be encountered by the latter, he felt that success there would allow each river to be crossed upstream on relatively firmer ground, so the enemy's flank could be turned. The attacks began on the night of 6/7 October in appalling weather, but the experienced mountain warriors of 10 Indian Division made good gains immediately, capturing Monte Farneto. This forced a German withdrawal and by 19 October 46 Division was in Cesena, 20 miles up Route 9 from Rimini. Two days earlier the Polish Corps had attacked further to the left and seized the heights of Monte Grosso and then Predappio, the birthplace of Mussolini. The Canadians in the meantime moved steadily up the coast road. By 25 October Eighth Army was over one of the larger rivers, the Savio, and approaching the next one, the Ronco, but on the following day, flooding caused by heavy rain washed away all the bridges on the Savio and the advance ground to a halt.

Dick had made a good start, but Bologna remained a tantalizingly distant goal and the failure of Fifth US Army to capitalize on its own successful breakthrough of the Gothic Line in the mountains added to the Allies' frustration. There was no alternative to pressing ahead. Whilst all thoughts of ending the Italian campaign in 1944 had long been abandoned, Alexander was determined to put AAI into the strongest possible position to launch an offensive when the weather improved in the spring. This required a huge effort to penetrate as far as possible before shutting down the front for the winter. After a brief halt to let river levels subside and rebuild the bridges, Eighth Army attacked again, forcing the Ronco near Forli on 30 October and attacking vigorously with 4 and 46 Divisions a week later. By 24 November the latter had reached the River Lamone near Faenza. Dick now launched a coordinated attack all along his front. The Canadians, with Burns replaced as their corps commander by Charles Foulkes, a man much more to Dick's liking, took Ravenna on 4 December, but Faenza, the next major town on Route 9, was not taken by 2 New Zealand Division until nearly two weeks later.

By this time significant developments had taken place, both in the command structure and in the political situation in the Mediterranean theatre. The catalyst for the former was the death of Sir John Dill, the head of the British Joint Staff Mission in Washington, and thereby the senior British representative on the Combined Chiefs of Staff and a key intermediary between Brooke and Marshall. Dill's successor was 'Jumbo' Wilson, who had been Supreme Commander in the Mediterranean since Eisenhower's departure for north-west Europe nearly a year earlier. Alexander, highly acceptable to both Americans and British, was the obvious choice to succeed him, his place being taken by Clark, the senior of the two Allied army commanders. Dick thus found himself back under Clark's command in 15th Army Group, as AAI was now renamed. When he saw Clark a few days later, he found him delighted by the promotion, his pleasure only tempered by one great fear, that he might be an army group commander who would never fight a big battle. One piece of good news was that the new C-in-C's successor at Fifth US Army was Lucian Truscott, who had led VI US Corps brilliantly from the South of France to Alsace: he was immensely popular with the British and Dick personally rated him very highly. He was, moreover, a cavalryman, and they spoke the same language. Dick later described him as 'Very professional. Very frank and forthright. No "ifs" and "buts" for him',[4] which description might just as easily have applied to himself.

With five US infantry divisions and one armoured division in Italy, and one more infantry division promised for early 1945, together with the Brazilian Expeditionary Force and the transfer of 6 South African Armoured Division from Eighth to Fifth Army, Truscott had enough troops to form two strong and well-balanced corps and in early 1945 XIII Corps, with Kirkman somewhat bruised by his experiences under Clark,[5] reverted to Eighth Army. This was just as well, as Dick had been losing formations fast in an unexpected direction.

During the autumn of 1944, the Germans evacuated Greece to avoid being cut off in the Balkans by the advancing Red Army. The vacuum was filled initially by 2 Parachute Brigade, 23 Armoured Brigade and the Greek Mountain Brigade, the last of which had been fighting in Italy under the Canadians, and later by 4 Indian Division. In December the communist-led ELAS resistance movement rebelled against an order to disarm and fighting broke out in Athens and other cities. The British commander on the spot, Ronald Scobie, called for reinforcements, the first of which to arrive in early December was 139 Brigade from 46 Division. As the situation deteriorated, it was followed by 4 Division and then the rest of 46 Division, whilst HQ X Corps, now under Hawkesworth, was sent to control the military operations. Over a short course of time Dick had lost a significant proportion of his strength and he was to see none of it return other than Hawkesworth's HQ and 2 Parachute Brigade.

This seriously exacerbated a problem which Dick was already feeling deeply, the sheer lack of manpower in his army. Great Britain's human resources were very finite: new conscripts were not coming through fast enough to replace casualties on the three fronts on which it was fighting and priority was accorded to 21st Army Group in north-west Europe. Already steps were being taken to create more infantrymen from surplus resources, as the retraining of anti-aircraft artillerymen and the deployment of men from the RAF Regiment had demonstrated in X Corps. Another major problem was desertion, which had become endemic in Eighth Army. The mountains provided a good refuge for deserters among generally sympathetic inhabitants and it was easy to lose oneself in chaotic cities like Naples. Right from the time of his appointment Dick had seen morale as a major issue among troops who had been fighting for a long time in very difficult conditions and he placed a great deal of emphasis on this in meetings with his commanders. He decided to set up a home leave scheme, focused on the front line infantry, which accelerated once the winter campaigning had come to an end and did a great deal to raise morale.

Throughout the battles of October and November, Dick covered considerable distances to visit not only the commanders but also the fighting troops, often going as close to the front line as he could. Keightley was later to write: 'Time and again I had my Corps OP what I thought was pretty forward in the battle, only to find he had his in front of mine.' Dick's style was never to interfere with commanders who were doing their job properly, but to be as well informed on developments as possible so that he could offer advice and assistance should it become necessary: Keightley described him as 'clear, incisive, always helpful'.[6] Many of his subordinates thought that Eighth Army under Leese had verged on the chaotic, but that Dick had brought order to the HQ very quickly. Floyd turned out to be an outstanding chief of staff and the officers already there reacted well to the new regime. The experience of John Bland, Dick's military secretary, was typical. With no knowledge of the new army commander, he had been warned by others to watch his step and decided to play himself in very carefully. He found that he and Dick only talked about essential business for the first few days as each summed the other up, then suddenly there was a great change after which he could talk freely and not just on business, and an understanding developed which was close to friendship.

For the first time in his career, Dick now had a direct relationship with the RAF, which had become an integral part of operations. That this was so was largely due to the legacy of Montgomery who had, from the time of his arrival in Egypt, co-located his HQ with the Desert Air Force. The techniques of air support for ground operations had developed considerably since those early days, but there remained a number of problems. Dick raised these with the AOC, Air Vice-Marshal William Dickson, who was succeeded in early December by Air Vice-Marshal Robert 'Pussy' Foster. The issues came to a head at a meeting on 19 December when Dick was highly critical of the Desert Air Force's allocation of priorities and its commitment to attacks in support of his troops. Foster pointed out that he had certain responsibilities outside Eighth Army, was short of equipment to a point at which he was considering disbanding squadrons and was as concerned as

Dick about losses of personnel, whom he found difficult to replace. What was at times a difficult discussion cleared the air and from then on the relationship developed into a very close one, and the Desert Air Force played an increasingly important role in future operations. Dick demonstrated his own commitment to the relationship by dining in the RAF mess on Christmas Day.

On 26 November, the day before the announcement of the command changes, Alexander held his last Army Commanders' conference, issuing orders to Dick to advance to the line of the River Santerno and, if possible, to secure bridgeheads across it, and to Truscott to attack towards Castel San Pietro on Route 9 south-east of Bologna. In the event the combination of bad weather and a counter-attack by the Germans on Fifth Army's left flank against a recently arrived and inexperienced division put paid to Truscott's operation. Dick, on the other hand, used the occasional spells of dry weather to advance all along his front. The Canadians took Ravenna on 4 December and reached the River Senio on 16 December, the same day that the New Zealanders captured Faenza. By 6 January the majority of the German pockets south of the Senio had been eliminated, although there were still stretches where they held the high embankments along the east bank. The Santerno, however, was a river too far. One major problem affecting the capability of both the Allied armies was a serious shortage of artillery ammunition – by the end of 1944 neither had more than two weeks' supply for full-scale operations. For Dick this was a blessing in disguise, as the troops were exhausted and badly needed to rest, recuperate and train for the year ahead. He was pleased when Clark called a halt to offensive activity.

Dick remained very busy in spite of the halt to operations. On 11 January sixty Members of Parliament arrived for a visit to Eighth Army, where they spent three days. On the day after they left Dick paid his first visit to XIII Corps, which now comprised 1 and 78 Divisions and 6 Armoured Division. The infantry divisions were new to him as was Keith Arbuthnott of 78 Division, but Charles Loewen had been his Chief Gunner in X Corps. The armoured division had been commanded since Templer's accident by Horatius 'Nap' Murray, an infantryman who had served as a brigade commander in Normandy, whom Dick immediately identified as 'a good chap'.[7] The corps was still up in the Monte Grande massif in the Apennines, which required a great deal of driving in open jeeps over frozen mountain roads. Dick developed a serious chilblain condition, one foot swelling up and requiring him to stay at his HQ until it subsided. Clark presented him with a pair of winter boots, 'rubber soles & feet & leather uppers, very ugly, but will take endless thick socks inside!'[8] They did not prove quite up to the job, however, so Dick was delighted to be given 'a splendid pair of huge RAF fleece lined boots'[9] which resolved the problem.

There were a few other distractions, including a ceremonial visit to the Republic of San Marino on 3 February, where he was entertained by the Captains Regent to a large lunch, followed by a reception at the palace. On the following day he presented the Medaglio d'Oro to Bulow,[10] the celebrated partisan leader of the Garibaldi Brigade which had participated in the liberation of Ravenna: Dick noted that there were 'six Amazons on parade'. However, with no major operations planned until the spring and the pressure thus significantly, albeit temporarily, diminished, he felt that he should be able to get away for ten days' leave in England in late February and still return in time to carry out the detailed planning for what he hoped would be the final battle. He wrote to Lettice to say that he expected to arrive on 24 February.

On 12 February Dick flew to Rome and Florence for a series of meetings, accompanied by Hugh Smith, whom he had welcomed back warmly as an additional ADC for his personal if not his military qualities. At midnight on 17 February, two days after his return, he was woken to be given a signal from Brooke to say that his mother, Minnie, was dangerously ill. He brought forward his departure, leaving the following morning for Florence and flying from there to Alexander's HQ at Caserta. A Mitchell bomber had been arranged for him by John Slessor, the AOC-in-C, and he left the next day but had to land in Lyons due to very poor visibility. He finally arrived at Lyneham on the afternoon of Tuesday, 20 February, where another plane was waiting to fly him to Henstridge, the closest airfield to Stowell. Sadly, he was too late to see Minnie, who had died at midnight on the Sunday.

Minnie had played an enormous role in Dick's early life, especially after the separation from Walter, and had been a great support right up to the time of his marriage. He was to say later how much he regretted having seen so little of her after 1933, with two overseas tours to Egypt followed by the War. Minnie and Lettice had not really seen eye to eye for most of this time and Lettice had never really enjoyed her visits to Stowell. However, a more equable relationship developed between the two women during the War, possibly because they had not seen a great deal of each other. The lease at College House was due to come up in the spring of 1945 and Runwick had been sold. During the autumn of 1944 Dick had been working on Lettice to persuade her to move to Stowell, which she was initially reluctant to contemplate, but by the end of the year she had agreed to go there in March as a stopgap, pending a better understanding of Dick's future. Circumstances had now determined that it was to be their home for the rest of their lives.

Minnie's funeral took place in Sherborne on 22 February, attended by many friends, including Mike Houston representing the 12th Lancers, to whom Minnie had devoted much time and among whose officers and men she had been deservedly popular. Dick and Lettice and the two younger children went back to College House on the following day and that weekend picked up the other boys from their schools, from which they had been allowed a week off. Dick's leave was extended to two weeks, spent largely with the family, with only one day at the War Office, during which he met Brooke, other senior officers and the Secretary of State for War. Rollie Charrington was also there, now acting as Brooke's ADC after the previous incumbent had died in an air crash.[11] On 6 March Dick retraced his route back to Italy, seeing Alexander in Caserta and Clark in Florence before arriving back at his own HQ at Cesena.

Chaper 22

The Old Steeplechaser

On two successive days in early April 1945 Dick addressed all the officers in Eighth Army down to the rank of lieutenant colonel. He brought them together in four groups, V and X Corps at Forli and 6 Armoured Division and his own Main and Rear HQs at Cesena on 4 April, the Polish Corps at Castrocaro and XIII Corps, now commanded by John Harding, in the mountains south of Imola on the following day. His purpose was to spell out very clearly his plan for the operation which he would be launching on 9 April, which he believed would lead, alongside Fifth US Army, to the final defeat of the German forces in Italy. Lieutenant Colonel ffrench-Blake, commanding the 17th/21st Lancers in 6 Armoured Division, described Dick's opening words:

> In his quiet, almost apologetic voice, he said that the theatre had been stripped of troops for France; that the army was like an old steeplechaser, full of running, but rather careful; that it was his intention to destroy the Germans south of the Po, rather than allow them to withdraw to further defence lines in the north, on the Adige, and finally within the 'fortress' of the Austrian Alps. The plan was then outlined.

The horse-racing analogy was highly appropriate. Eighth Army was by a long way the oldest of Great Britain's armies, having taken to the field in October 1941 in the Western Desert, where its advances and retreats had been jokingly known as 'the Benghazi Stakes'. From the beginning 2 New Zealand Division had been a component, in Operation Crusader, at El Alamein, across the desert to Mareth and then Enfidaville, and on to the Sangro, Cassino and the Gothic Line: Freyberg himself had been wounded twice. None of the other divisions and few of the smaller formations and units had come all the way from Egypt,[1] but almost all had been fighting in Italy for over eighteen months in a campaign dogged by difficulty, and many had been in Tunisia in the winter of 1942/43. Three months earlier the army had been tired out and even now, after a relatively quiet period, it required very delicate handling. The country ahead, with its high banks and open ditches, resembled a steeplechase course and Dick was determined to ensure that each obstacle should be tackled in exactly the right way. He believed that

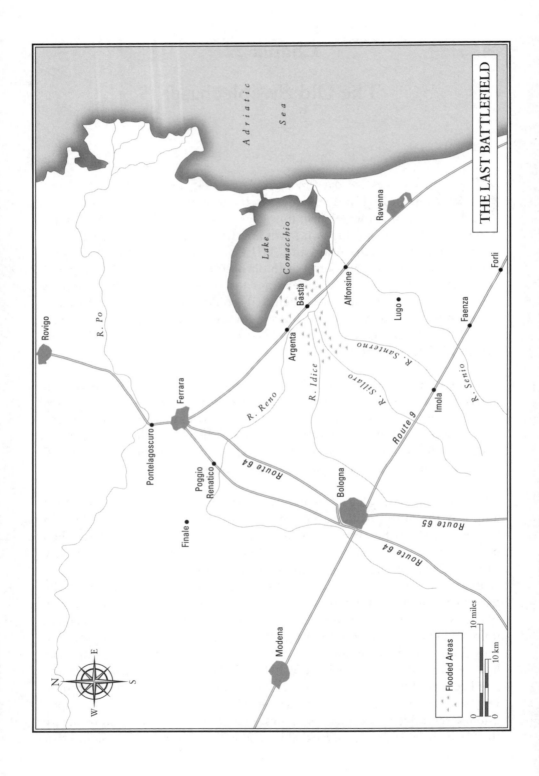

THE LAST BATTLEFIELD

his plan was a good one, but it would only work if the training of the last few months paid off.

Four weeks earlier Dick had arrived back from leave to bad news: I Canadian Corps was off to north-west Europe to join its compatriots in First Canadian Army. Not only were the Canadians outstanding troops under good commanders, but they were among the most experienced at crossing rivers and Dick had rated them very highly in the short time that they had served under him. He had worked hard to establish a rapport, which had been reciprocated. John Tweedsmuir,[2] who had served in Dick's HQ as one of their liaison officers, wrote on his departure: 'You meant a very great deal to them, once you got to know them, and they will miss you', and Foulkes said he felt that there had been complete confidence in the chain of command from Dick all the way through the corps to the private in the front line. After the depredations made on Dick's resources by the troubles in Greece this loss was a hammer blow, as no more formations of division size or above were to join Eighth Army. He had been expecting the return of 5 Division from its refit in the Middle East and indeed the division did land briefly in Italy, but it too was then diverted to north-west Europe.

A few smaller reinforcements did join Eighth Army: 43 Gurkha Lorried Brigade had arrived from Persia and Iraq Command in the previous autumn and there was now another newcomer from that backwater, the 14th/20th Hussars, whom Dick had last seen in Mosul in 1942 and who were desperate to see action before the end of the war. Other arrivals included the Jewish Brigade Group, formed from Jewish settlers in Palestine, and 2 Commando Brigade. There were also three Italian formations, created when the CIL outgrew itself. These were called Combat Groups (*Grupo di Combattimento*) and were, at about 9,000 men, rather larger than a brigade group but about half the size of a full-strength British infantry division. Two of these went to Fifth US Army and three, Cremona, Folgore and Friuli, to Eighth Army. Although Dick was initially dubious about their fighting ability, they proved useful for holding sectors of the front during the quiet period, to allow his more seasoned formations the time to rest and to train out of the line.

Throughout Eighth Army training was going on at full pace and the focus was on river crossings. Five significant rivers lay in its path before the Po itself could be reached, the Reno and four of its tributaries flowing south-west to north-east, the Senio, the Santerno, the Sillaro and the Idice. Apart from the Reno, none of them was particularly wide except in flood, indeed Dick said later that the Senio at certain points was so narrow that it could be jumped, but all of them had high flood banks or 'bunds', wide enough in places to have roads or tracks along the top. These were excellent natural defensive positions, of which the Germans had taken full advantage, turning stretches of them into formidable obstacles. New techniques were developed for tackling the bunds and the rivers themselves, helped by the arrival of specialized vehicles. Many of these had been developed by Percy Hobart, Dick's fellow armoured division commander of 1941, and had been used to great effect in his 79 Armoured Division in Normandy and elsewhere under the generic name of 'funnies'. They included flail tanks for mine clearance, Sherman 'tank dozers' for moving earth, 'Crocodiles', which were Churchill tanks adapted for use as flamethrowers, and AVREs (Assault Vehicles Royal Engineers), which were able to lay bridges over narrow rivers and streams or place fascines to cross ditches – 25 Armoured Engineer Brigade was formed specifically to deploy the last of these.

Two other new vehicles were introduced. The first was the Kangaroo, a turretless Sherman tank, modified for use as an armoured personnel carrier and particularly valuable in bringing infantry up to the front quickly and in supporting armoured attacks. The second was officially named the LVT (Landing Vehicle, Tracked), but was more commonly called the Buffalo or the Fantail. It was a fully amphibious assault vehicle, but unlike a DUKW, which used wheels on land and propellers on water, it was propelled by its tracks on both. Tried and tested in the Pacific, it was able to carry 18 fully armed men, with a ramp at the back allowing easy disembarkation, and it opened up some exciting possibilities. Given the terrain on Dick's front, Clark allocated to Eighth Army all 400 Buffaloes received in 15th Army Group.

Other than the AVREs and some of the Buffaloes, most of the 'funnies' were operated by 9 Armoured Brigade, now commanded by 'Cookie' Cooke, who set up a training centre on Lake Trasimene. Dick flew down there on 15 March and was able to see them in use, many driven by RASC drivers supplied by his resourceful director of supply and transport, Brigadier Joe Divers. Also, 9 Armoured Brigade demonstrated its Sherman DD (Duplex Drive) tanks. By means of collapsible canvas screens inflated by compressed air, they became fully amphibious, powered through the water by two propellers connected to the tanks' engines.

In addition to 25 Armoured Engineer Brigade, which was to be employed in the initial assaults, and the divisional engineers of each division, there were also two Army Groups Royal Engineers, 22 AGRE in support of V Corps and 16 AGRE in support of the Polish Corps and later XIII Corps. These were primarily concerned with bridging, an enormous number of Bailey bridges being prepared to move into place as soon as a bridgehead had been gained on the river or canal in question. The Po, the only river that was exceptionally wide, was expected to pose problems. An enormous bridge nicknamed 'the Po Special' was designed by South African engineers, who carried out full-scale construction trials on the sand dunes near Ravenna.

With the advent of better weather, Dick was able to fly more often to visit his own front, Clark's HQ and the training areas. The C.47 Dakota used by Leese had gone with him and Joe Cannon, the American commander of the Allied air forces, was no longer willing to supply such a large plane for personal use. Instead, Pussy Foster arranged for Dick to be provided with a Beech Model 18 Expeditor, a twin-engined plane with a two-man crew and seats for six passengers. This aircraft had something of a reputation for crash landings, but Dick flew thousands of miles in his without any serious incidents. Almost more valuable to him was his other form of air transport, the 'whizzer'. This was an Auster, used most frequently by the artillery as an Air Observation Post, but also by both the Army and the RAF for short range communication. Graham Lampson,[3] who served on his staff before going as a liaison officer to Clark, marvelled that Dick was able to fold his long frame into the tiny cockpit, but to Dick it was an invaluable piece of equipment. He relied heavily on good aerial reconnaissance, studying the RAF photographs daily,[4] but now for the first time he was able to see 'over the hill' himself, recalling the moment in 1921 when the CO of the 12th Lancers, Bill Truman, had put the idea in his mind. He went up frequently to look at the German defences and, more importantly, to get a clear view of the country which lay immediately behind them.

During March a major problem emerged. II Polish Corps would play a vital part in Dick's plan and, unlike most of the other formations in the army, it was getting larger, due to Anders's success in recruiting ethnic Poles who had been conscripted into the Wehrmacht, but had subsequently deserted or been captured. In addition to those enrolled in Italy, some 11,000 were sent from Normandy and both 3 Carpathian and 5 Kresowa Divisions were able to add a third brigade to their existing two. There now arose, however, serious doubts about the Poles' commitment to the battle. The conclusions of the Yalta conference, at which it was agreed by the Allies that their country would fall into the Soviet Union's sphere of influence, had profoundly dismayed them. Most damagingly, a large part of pre-War Eastern Poland would actually be incorporated into the Soviet Union. A sizeable proportion of the corps originated from this area, particularly from cities such as Wilno and Lwow, and the compensating award by the Allies of German land in Silesia, Brandenburg and Pomerania was of no interest to them. A number of Poles actually committed suicide in protest and Anders himself was shattered by the news. He threatened to withdraw his entire corps and, when Dick met him just prior to his leave, he was not prepared to listen to him, and even suggested that his men might be made prisoners. Alexander and Clark made personal appeals with little effect, so Dick went to see him again shortly after his return.

Dick wrote later: 'When I visited him he said "how can I ask my soldiers to go on fighting, I must withdraw them from the line." I replied that there were no troops to replace them, and that a 10 mile gap would be opened up! Anders remained silent for a moment and then said "you can count on 2nd Polish Corps for this coming battle, we must defeat Hitler first."'[5] Anders himself was later to say that he had expected Dick to argue with him and to talk him round by making excuses about the decisions at Yalta, but in the event he was shaken by his simple down-to-earth response: 'All my pent up emotions and anxieties, all the complexities, all the many pressures and arguments and counter-arguments had been reduced by one single sentence to one single physical consideration, the crux of a ten mile gap… In the end I knew in my heart what I had to do. If we who were fighting for a free Poland did not fight in this battle not only would we ruin the Allied victory in Italy, but we would forfeit the chance of our continuing to fight for our independence… I told McCreery that we would fight on.'[6] This was a fine example of Dick's deep understanding of his fellow man. As a sign of his confidence in the Poles, he placed 43 Gurkha Brigade and 7 Armoured Brigade in their corps, much to Anders's satisfaction.[7]

Shortly before Dick went on leave to the UK, he had flown with Keightley and Foulkes to Clark's HQ in Florence to meet Marshall, who was on his way back from Yalta. Dick found the US Army Chief of Staff very interesting on the world situation. He was left in no doubt that Italy was a secondary theatre in the eyes of the Americans, who were now calling the strategic shots. However, Marshall emphasized that it remained vitally important to keep as many German divisions there as possible, to prevent them from being sent to reinforce the fronts facing the Anglo–Americans and the Russians now closing in on the heart of the Reich. Kesselring was ordered back to Germany in March 1945 to become Commander-in-Chief, West, but his successor at Army Group C, Colonel General Heinrich von Vietinghoff-Scheel, who had commanded Tenth German Army with great distinction since the very beginning of the Italian campaign, still deployed 23 German divisions, almost all at full strength, and four Italian Divisions of the rump Fascist state. The latter were of very dubious quality, but this could not be said of the Germans: in particular the one Panzer, two Panzer Grenadier and two Parachute divisions were amongst the best still available. The Allies could only deploy 17 full-strength divisions, but with a large number of additional brigades, commandos and the Italian combat groups, the two sides were roughly at parity in infantry and armour, although the British and Americans had many more guns. Moreover, the Allies derived a huge advantage from their overwhelming air superiority, whilst the Germans suffered from a chronic shortage of fuel.

Marshall would probably have been content for 15th Army Group to remain on its line for the rest of the war, provided that it threatened the Germans so much that no sizeable formation would be permitted to slip away. Alexander took an entirely different view and in this he was supported to the hilt by Clark, Truscott and Dick. All of them were unanimous that the Germans should be comprehensively defeated south of the Alps, but Clark made it clear that the key role would be filled by Fifth US Army, attacking out of the mountains with Bologna as its primary goal. Eighth Army would play a supporting part, attacking first, much as X Corps had done on the Garigliano, and drawing away the enemy reserves.

Dick was having none of it and, much as Clark had found with Alexander, the latitude available to an army commander was much greater than that accorded to a corps commander. He decided from the beginning that, whilst obeying Clark's orders in principle, he could also fulfil his own objective, which was to destroy the German divisions facing him before they could withdraw over the Po. Having cleared his lines with Alexander first, he began to formulate a plan which would deliver much more than expected by Clark, who continued to believe that Eighth Army was worn out. Dick conferred closely with Truscott, who agreed with him that between the two armies they could achieve a much better result,[8] and they found a ready ally in Al Gruenther. Clark's Operations Instruction No. 4, issued on 24 March, brought the plans of both armies together as agreed by their commanders, although Dick was irritated to read that it still envisaged Fifth US Army launching 'the main effort' of Fifteenth Army Group.

Dick's own plan, codenamed Operation Buckland, was nothing short of masterly. In conformity with Clark's orders a strong force, comprising the whole of II Polish Corps and 2 New Zealand Division from V Corps,[9] was to attack in the direction of Bologna parallel to Route 9, forcing a crossing over the Santerno and then the Sillaro. This the enemy would be expecting and would take measures to counter it, achieving Clark's objective of drawing some of the opposition away from Truscott. The Germans also had a consistent fear of a full-scale seaborne landing further up the Adriatic coast, north of the mouth of the Po, but Dick never contemplated this, although he did decide to mount a limited attack on the spit of land separating Lake Comacchio from the sea, which would keep the enemy on his toes. This deception, aided by conspicuous naval activity around Ravenna visible to German spotter planes, worked well. Von Vietinghoff kept one of his strongest formations, 29 Panzer Grenadier Division, in the Venice/Treviso area until well after the Allied offensive had started.

What the Germans were not expecting was that a significant part of Eighth Army, 8 Indian, 56 and 78 Divisions from V Corps, with the Cremona Group, two armoured brigades and a tank brigade[10] in support, would attack north towards Ferrara. On their right would be the great and apparently impassable area of Lake Comacchio, whilst to the west of the lake the Germans had flooded the country on both sides of the River Reno where it ran parallel to Route 16 to Ferrara, just before the road reached the town of Argenta. The gap between the waters was very narrow, little more than 2 miles wide. Dick's plan, conceived as a result of the many flights in his 'whizzer', was to send as strong a force as possible across the water in Buffaloes, turning the German left flank on the north-east side of the Reno near Bastia and thereby unlocking the door to the Argenta Gap. Once the gap was forced, the road to Ferrara would be open and he would release 6 Armoured Division, until then kept in army reserve, in a pincer movement to join up with the Americans and cut off the retreating Germans south of the Po.

Of his remaining formations, 10 Indian Division also remained in reserve, ready to be inserted into the battle as soon as the front was wide enough to admit it, as did 2 Parachute Brigade, which was prepared to drop behind the Argenta Gap defences if necessary. The Folgore and Friuli Groups and the Jewish Brigade Group would threaten the German flank from the mountains south-west of Route 9. Dick also planned to activate XIII Corps as soon as the number of formations in V Corps grew too large for Keightley to control effectively.

One piece of unexpected good fortune had come the Allies' way. Although the autumn of 1944 had been exceptionally wet, causing immense difficulties to Eighth Army in its attempt to cross rivers which were invariably in spate, there had been very little rain since the end of January and the water levels had dropped significantly. This was to help the ensuing operations considerably as the width requiring to be bridged at each crossing was much less than anticipated. However, it had one unfortunate consequence, which was that the water level of Lake Comacchio, shallow at the best of times, had fallen to such an extent that it had exposed large areas of slime. When the operation was mounted by 2 Commando Brigade on the evening 1 April to take the spit of land separating the lake from the Adriatic, it was found that the Buffaloes attacking from the lake side were next to useless, unable to get a grip on either water or earth. Stormboats were quickly substituted and the Germans were taken by surprise, as they were by an assault crossing of the Reno on to the base of the spit. By the evening of 3 April the brigade had advanced to the Valetta Canal, connecting the lake to the sea, and was threatening Porto Garibaldi on the far side. The use of some landing craft strengthened in German minds the threat of a larger seaborne landing.

There was one more important move to be made before Dick launched full-scale operations. In his flights in the 'whizzer' Dick had been able to see the Argenta Gap in the distance and to work out in his own mind how to force it. Now in the knowledge that the lake itself was impassable to the Buffaloes, it was necessary to confine their use to the inundations. From the air Dick had seen a wedge of dry land just south of these but north of the Reno. For the Germans this was not a high defensive priority, as they assumed that any landings there would lead to a dead end, blocked from advance by the floods. To Dick, however, it was just the springboard he needed to get the Buffaloes into action. On the night of 5/6 April 56 Division's 167 Brigade made an unopposed crossing of the Reno and secured the wedge.

By the eve of battle, Dick was confident of his army's ability to win a great victory and he had instilled this confidence in others. Alexander had just left well satisfied after two days with Eighth Army. Archie Nye, the VCIGS, who had visited the army in late March, wrote to say: 'I came away from Italy with a grand feeling of exhilaration after having seen your troops, who have every right to feel immensely proud of their achievements.'[11] Morale overall had improved enormously since the beginning of the year, boosted by the home leave scheme and the provision of entertainment for troops out of the line, culminating in a race meeting which Dick had arranged for them at Cesena on 10 March and which was long remembered by those attending. The highly focused training had given the troops great confidence in their ability to overcome the obstacles ahead and at the 17th/21st Lancers ffrench-Blake recalled the thrill of excitement which ran through the soldiers when they heard the plan.

The old steeplechaser was ready for its last race.

Chapter 23

The Last Battle

The weather on Sunday, 8 April, was exceptionally windy and the Allied airfields on the Adriatic coast were all out of action. Dick was relieved when Clark came on the telephone to reassure him that the forecast for the following day was fine, as good flying conditions would be critical. Dick's other major concern was that von Vietinghoff would withdraw from the Senio to the Santerno before the start of the battle and that the heavy punch he had planned would land on thin air. He had no need to worry. The German commander had indeed proposed a withdrawal, which would have been tactically sound, but he was prevented from executing it by a direct order from the OKW, inspired by Hitler himself, who insisted that there should be no retreat and that Army Group C should fight to the death on its existing front.

That afternoon Dick was visited by Wilfred Lyde, an old friend and fellow officer from the 1st Reserve Regiment of Cavalry at The Curragh in 1918. Lyde wrote later that, on entering Dick's caravan, 'I noticed that he was reading a Bible. Little did I realise what it meant to him, he was obviously finding some strength to help him bear the strain of the final battle of the River Po, with the consequent casualties, which started the following day.' He and Lyde talked about their mutual interest in hunting, racing and polo and Lyde recalled, 'when I left he thanked me, I felt it was a great privilege if I had helped a little to ease the great strain he was bearing.'[1]

The next morning was still, exactly as the meteorologists had predicted. Dick had found a good OP in a ruined house in the village of Celle, just south of Route 9 and close to the front line. An unglazed window provided a fine view along the fronts of both the Poles and the New Zealanders for the numerous VIPs, including Clark, Cannon and Foster, whom Dick had invited to watch the first phase of Operation Buckland. This was in the hands of the air forces. Cannon had made available to Eighth Army not only the Desert Air Force and its American equivalent, XXII US Air Support Command, with their medium and fighter bombers, but also 825 Flying Fortresses and Liberators of the Fifteenth US Air Force, normally employed on strategic bombing missions over the Reich. The heavy bomber pilots had no experience of supporting ground attacks and Dick had hoped that there might be a rehearsal, but Cannon had decided that it was not necessary. The

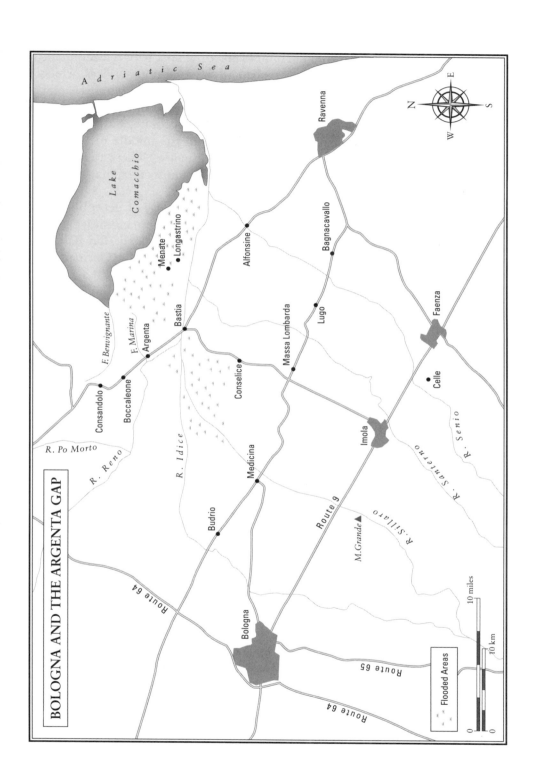

BOLOGNA AND THE ARGENTA GAP

Adriatic Sea

Ravenna

Lake Comacchio

Menate
Longastrino

Alfonsine

Bagnacavallo

F. Benvignante

F. Marina

Argenta

Bastia

Massa Lombarda

Lugo

Faenza

Consandolo

Boccaleone

Conselice

Celle

R. Po Morto

R. Reno

R. Idice

Medicina

Imola

R. Senio

R. Santerno

Budrio

Route 9

M. Grande ▲

R. Sillaro

Route 64

Bologna

Route 65

Route 64

10 miles

10 km

Flooded Areas

N E S W

0
0

intention was for the heavy bombers to blanket the area between the Senio and the Santerno, where the Germans had all their support services, whilst the actual defences would be hit by the medium and fighter bombers, now highly experienced in such actions. When the first wave of heavies arrived punctually at 1350 hrs most of their aiming was accurate, but to Dick's horror one group released its bombs straight into the middle of a Polish brigade forming up for the attack, causing 160 casualties. There were a few 'shorts' also in the New Zealand and 8 Indian Division sectors, but they did little serious damage.

The next phase was an excellent example of Dick's use of deception. At 1520 hrs an artillery barrage from over 1,000 field, medium and heavy guns opened up, targeting the bund defences. The barrage stopped after half an hour and was followed by a wave of fighter bombers, leading the Germans to expect an immediate attack. This failed to materialize and, after a gap, a second barrage and air attack followed, then a third and a fourth. The last artillery barrage ended at 1910 hrs and, 10 minutes later, just when the Germans were expecting another drubbing from the fighter bombers, these pulled up without firing and the ground attack went in while the defenders still had their heads down. By this time Dick was aloft in his 'whizzer', from which he had a marvellous view from 5,000ft of 36 flame-throwing Crocodiles and even more Wasps, the infantry equivalent derived from the Bren-gun carrier, followed by the assault brigades.

By first light on the next morning 2 New Zealand Division had secured a sizeable bridgehead across the Senio to the south of Lugo and was making excellent progress. 3 Carpathian Division was further behind as the Germans still held the bund on its side of the river and these defences had to be eliminated first. Dick visited Anders, expecting to find him deeply unhappy about the bombing error, but the Polish general was not only philosophical about the casualties, but actually requested further heavy bomber support. On the right 8 Indian Division, with the Churchills of 21 Tank Brigade in support, was a mile and a half beyond the river to the north of Lugo, whilst the Cremona Group had put in a good attack to take the small town of Alfonsine on the far bank. The heavy bombers made their second bombing run that afternoon and there were more 'friendly fire' incidents, Freyberg being particularly indignant, although his casualties from this direction remained light. He may have suffered precisely because he had made such good progress, his forward brigades reaching the Santerno before nightfall.

By the morning of 11 April the Poles also had two brigades across the Senio and the New Zealanders crossed the Santerno, the engineers in their wake being quick to erect Bailey bridges. At the same time 80 Buffaloes, crewed by men from the 27th Lancers and the 755th US Tank Battalion,

Dick consulting a map with members of 2 Armoured Brigade's staff in an orchard near Abbeville in June 1940.

Dick demonstrates one of 8 Armoured Division's tanks to Free French Major General Petit.

King George VI inspects 8 Armoured Division on 13 June 1941.

Alexander and his Chief of Staff relax during one of their numerous flights around Middle East Command.

Eisenhower decorates Dick with the Legion of Merit near the Volturno, with one of 'a veritable battery of cameras' just behind.

Brooke (3 from left) visits X Corps with Alexander on 17 December 1943.

Dick riding in the Apennines in the spring of 1944.

General Guillaume, commander of the Moroccan Goums, dedicates the memorial on Monte Camino.

Dick with Oliver Leese, his superior at Eighth Army.

Dick drives with the King and Leese though the streets of Perugia during the former's visit to X Corps on 25 July 1944.

Dick is knighted at his Tac HQ at Palazzo del Pero 'during the tea interval'.

Lettice with Michael, Bob, Sarah, Jon and Charles in 1943.

The new Commander Eighth Army in his caravan.

Alexander with his ground and air commanders, Joe Cannon (Mediterranean Air Forces), Mark Clark, William Dickson (Desert Air Force) and Dick.

Clark and Dick with Wladyslav Anders.

Clark, as the new Commanding General of 15th Army Group, being welcomed to Eighth Army by Dick, wearing his RAF flying boots against the cold.

Dick with Bernard Freyberg.

Dick and 'Pussy' Foster watching the bombing preceding the last battle from the OP at Celle.

Dick receives the Distinguished Service Medal from Clark at a ceremony in Klagenfurt.

The end of the War in Italy – Von Senger surrenders to Clark on 4 May 1945, with Dick standing in the background.

Dick inspects a US Forces in Austria guard of honour with Clark at the latter's headquarters in Salzburg.

Al Gruenther (representing Clark), Marshal Konev, Dick and General Béthouart meet the interim Austrian Chancellor, Karl Renner.

Dick with Konev at the races in Vienna in October 1945. On the table is the cup for the race won by Dick's horse Jumbo.

Dick sets an example in one of the tree-felling competitions in Austria.

Dick and Lettice at a children's party in Austria.

Dick's favourite car, the Mercedes 'liberated' south of the Po and used by him extensively in Italy, Austria and Germany.

Brooke's last conference at Camberley. Other than Alexander, most of the key figures in Dick's War are present: he is talking to Montgomery and on the other side of the gangway sit Brooke and Auchinleck. Anderson sits next to Dick and Leese on the gangway seat behind Montgomery. Crocker can be seen over Dick's left shoulder in the same row as Horrocks, with Gregson-Ellis and Laycock further back on the same side.

Dick in his office at HQ BAOR in Bad Oeynhausen.

Montgomery visits BAOR.

Dick watching I Corps manoeuvres: on the left is the corps commander, Ivor Thomas.

Dick with Sarah, Bob, Michael, Jon and Charles in 1949.

Dick with his eldest son Michael outside his house at Kostedt.

The whole family at the Blackmore Vale Meet at Sherborne Castle, on Boxing Day 1950.

Dick at the Installation of new Knights Grand Cross of the Order of the Bath in Westminster Abbey on 24 May 1951.

Dick with Lt Col Allen of the 14th/20th Hussars on the occasion of the award to him of the Regimental Medal on 31 August 1952.

Dick's last steeplechaser, Granville, with Bob in the saddle, winning at Hurst Park in a course record time.

Dick holding his newborn grandson, Luke Meynell, in December 1964: this was his last season's hunting.

Dick in the 1960s.

carried two battalions of 56 Division's Queen's Brigade across the flooded land bordering Lake Comacchio to solid ground near the villages of Menate and Longastrino. The attack achieved complete surprise, outflanking the enemy's left along the line of the Reno and producing 300 prisoners. With 8 Indian Division across the Santerno to the south that evening and 56 Division's 167 Brigade pushing along the north bank of the Reno, the Germans were compelled to fall back towards Bastia, the gateway to the Argenta Gap, to avoid being cut off.

Further good progress was made on the following day when Keightley passed the fresh 78 Division through the Indians to reach Conselice, whilst the Cremona Group continued to advance on the right, getting a bridgehead across the Santerno near the main road to Bastia. By the morning of 13 April both 56 and 78 Divisions were closing in on the bridge over the Reno at Bastia in a pincer movement, led in the case of the latter by the 'Kangaroo Army', a composite force made up of the Shermans of the 9th Lancers and the Kangaroos of 38 Irish Brigade, but it was unable to stop the bridge being blown. This minor setback was accompanied by a more major one, when 24 Guards Brigade sent a battalion in Buffaloes in another flanking movement with the ambitious aim of taking Argenta itself. This time the Germans were ready for them and the force took a heavy punishment, although it did manage to establish itself on dry land. For the first time some of its prisoners were identified as coming from 29 Panzer Grenadier Division, indicating that von Vietinghoff was committing at least part of his reserve.

Progress was far better on the north-west front, where the New Zealanders and the Poles reached the Sillaro respectively on 13 and 14 April, the latter having taken Imola. The Poles managed to capture a bridge over the river intact and both divisions established bridgeheads. With Keightley temporarily frustrated in his attempt to break through the Argenta Gap and needing to concentrate all his efforts in that direction, Dick decided to bring XIII Corps into the battle. An impatient Harding had visited Floyd at Eighth Army HQ every day since the battle began and was delighted to take over responsibility for 2 New Zealand Division at 1800 hrs on 14 April. He immediately ordered 10 Indian Division, waiting in the mountains, to move up behind the New Zealanders, from where it took over a sector of the rapidly widening front two days later.

The other major event of 14 April was the opening of Fifth US Army's offensive, two days late due to fog on its front preventing the use of supporting aircraft. Crittenberger's IV US Corps moved first along Route 64, which ran north to the west of Bologna, launching the excellent 10 US Mountain Division against the last remaining Apennine ridges, supported by 1 US Armored Division and the Brazilian Expeditionary Force. On the night of 15/16 April Keyes struck with the four divisions of II US Corps on a narrow front just to the east along the parallel Route 65 to Bologna itself. Both corps experienced hard fighting, but made considerable progress.

Keightley meanwhile had changed his tactics following the disappointment over the Bastia bridge. Instead, he sent a brigade of 78 Division across the Reno on a Bailey bridge east of Bastia on ground which was held by the Cremona Group. Adding this force to two brigades of 56 Division proved too much for the Germans, who evacuated Bastia, falling back to Argenta. Keightley recognized that the key to forcing the gap was now the capture of the Fossa Marina, a high-banked waterway leading from the Reno to Lake Commacchio and tenuously held at one end by 24 Guards Brigade. His two divisional commanders, Arbuthnott and Whitfield, combined their forces intelligently, but the fighting became intense and it was not until 17 April that the Germans were pushed back and V Corps at last entered the shattered town of Argenta. Further bitter struggles took place on the Fossa Benvignante further north.

Dick now had a very wide front to visit, stretching from the foothills of the Apennines near Monte Grande, where the Folgore and Friuli Groups and the Jewish Brigade Group were edging forward in conformity with the advance of the Polish Corps, to Medecina, a small town between the Sillaro and the Idice which was taken on 16 April by those former comrades from Iraq, 43 Gurkha Brigade and the 14th/20th Hussars, and then to Argenta and the north-west corner of Lake Comacchio. Whilst remaining as close as possible to the battle, he insisted on returning to his Main HQ near Forli every evening to review the day's events with Floyd, Foster and others, flying in his 'whizzer' to his Tac HQ on the following morning, from where he would go on either by air or by jeep.

On 16 April he began a typical day by driving along Route 9 to see Rudforce,[2] a battle group of II Polish Corps which was tasked with driving up the highway itself towards Bologna. From there he moved to the 2nd/10th Gurkha Rifles of 43 Gurkha Brigade and then on to 5 Kresowa Division, which had taken over responsibility for the main Polish advance from 3 Carpathian Division. After that Dick went to see Freyberg at his HQ, finding him 'in v.g form', as his attack over the Sillaro on the previous evening had been very successful, resulting in more than 600 prisoners. Finally he called in on V Corps to see Keightley, with whom he needed to talk about the next phase of the battle.

Keightley was confident of getting through the Argenta Gap within 48 hours, but he needed to move well beyond it before he could achieve the sort of breakthrough that Dick was planning. In particular there were still the Fossa Benvignante and other water obstacles to cross before the way was open to the Po. Further progress was made as Keightley had anticipated and by 18 April V Corps had reached Boccaleone and Consandolo, nearly 5 miles beyond Argenta on the road to Ferrara. Dick now sensed that the time might have come to bring up 6 Armoured Division and summoned Murray to his HQ. Murray wrote later: 'He [Dick] was not prepared to say whether it was possible to break through there, but he wanted me to go forward and meet Lieutenant General Charles Keightley, the commander of V Corps, to see for myself what the position was and report back to him what were my impressions.'[3] Keightley thought that the way was clear, but Arbuthnott, whom Murray also met, was less positive. Murray nevertheless felt that this might be the last chance for the division to get into action and he decided to take it, telling Dick that he was ready to go. Dick placed the division under V Corps immediately, with orders that it should be ready to move at first light on the next day. That evening he went to Bagnocavallo to visit Murray's HQ and that of 1 Guards Brigade and to wish them well.

The move to the front was frustratingly slow as the division's passage through Argenta was made exceptionally difficult by the destruction of the town and competition for the use of the single road with the supply vehicles of 56 and 78 Divisions. When the division reached its jumping-off point in the late afternoon the ground turned out to be still very soft and was far from ideal for armour, criss-crossed as it was by canals and drainage ditches. The infantry was forced to go on foot, rather than in Kangaroos or carriers. The first full day's operations on 20 April, during which the division struggled to get across the River Po Morto, were disappointing, particularly to Keightley, who arrived at Murray's HQ in what the latter described as 'a towering rage',[4] accusing the division of making no progress at all. Dick was also on the ground north of Argenta, where he saw the commander of 26 Armoured Brigade, Neville Mitchell, expressing his own opinion equally trenchantly. Murray responded by going up in his own 'whizzer' and looking at the country ahead, spotting a number of opportunities for exploitation.

On the following day, there was a dramatic improvement. Murray had followed a practice adopted by the armoured divisions in north-west Europe of fighting in regimental groups, each group in this case consisting of a cavalry regiment and a rifle battalion, with attached gunners and sappers: 1 Guards Brigade, composed entirely of infantry, was given the task of reducing the most stubborn defences, whilst the regimental groups were told to follow Dick's explicit instructions, to move on with all speed and give the enemy no rest. The leading group, the 17th/21st Lancers and the 7th Rifle Brigade, broke right through the German line at last and was followed by the 16th/5th Lancers and the 1st King's Royal Rifle Corps. By that night they had made rapid progress along the north bank of the Reno, cutting Route 64 from Bologna to Ferrara and establishing themselves at Poggio Renatico. As they prepared to move out on the next day to close the trap on the retreating Germans, this began to look more and more like a classic cavalry manoeuvre.

In the meantime there had been equally good progress by II Polish Corps and XIII Corps. On the night of 18/19 April the two corps mounted a concerted attack and early on the following morning the New Zealanders entered Budrio, advancing with 10 Indian Division on their right and crossing the last river before Bologna, the Idice. At the same time IV US Corps was sweeping round to the west of Bologna, leaving the defenders perilously close to being cut off. On the night of 20 April, von Vietinghoff evacuated the city, ignoring the orders of Hitler to stand and fight, but a lack of transport and fuel meant that most of his troops were unable to escape the fast-closing pincers. At first light on 21 April 3 Carpathian Division entered Bologna after crushing its old opponents from Monte Cassino, 1 Parachute Division. Two hours later the Poles were joined by 34 US Division from the south.

Dick was now covering great distances to keep in touch with his army. He had a number of visitors, first Harold Macmillan, whom he took to see Anders, ecstatic after what he described as '*une belle bataille!*' and with the divisional flag of 1 Parachute Division in his possession. Alexander arrived on the following day and accompanied Dick to meet Keightley, Murray and 'Pasha' Russell, whose 8 Indian Division was entering the battlefield again on the right of 6 Armoured Division, and then Freyberg. The envelopment of the German formations defending Bologna was now complete, taking place at the appropriately named town of Finale on 23 April, where the advanced patrols of the 16th/5th Lancers met their equivalents from 6 South African Armoured Division. The first Allied Formation to reach the Po itself was 10 US Mountain Division on the evening of April 22. 6 Armoured Division's long-serving reconnaissance regiment, the Derbyshire Yeomanry, and the 5th Royal West Kents from 8 Indian Division arrived on the south bank of the great river within 10 minutes of each other the next day.

Further east V Corps was still meeting opposition as the Germans retreated to the Po, but the destruction of all the fixed and pontoon bridges and the harrying of the ferry landing sites by the Desert Air Force meant that most of the enemy were left with the option of swimming or surrendering. Almost all their tanks, artillery and motor transport had to be abandoned south of the river and the tally of prisoners mounted rapidly. The rest of 29 Panzer Grenadier Division had belatedly arrived only to find that the battle was lost, but that did not stop it from putting up a fight. Notwithstanding, Ferrara was occupied on 24 April and all remaining resistance south of the Po finally crumbled. By the next day V Corps had closed up to the river along a wide front.

For example, in 1281-2 sales included 130 trees from Turville Dean, 1,100 faggots cut in the Park, 100 spokes for cart-wheels and 28 quarters of charcoal. Other sales reported include sheep hurdles made from wattles cut in the manor (362 sold at Thame market in 1342-43 and 17 made and sent to Cuxham for sheep-fold in 1344-45).

Firewood and charcoal were major wood uses everywhere, using the underwood and fallen branches. In the Chilterns they were also an important use of larger wood, and especially of beechwood, and the smoke (and stench) of charcoal burning would have been common in the woods. Beech is not an ideal wood for structural and external work, in contrast to the more durable oak. Even in the beech-rich Chilterns oak is the consistent choice of timber to be found in the cruck farmhouses and the medieval houses of towns like Wendover, Chesham and West Wycombe. Beech is suitable for internal planks and boards but less desirable than oak, so that much beech coppice-wood and branches was sold for fuel or made into charcoal. Such sales were mainly to villages in and around the edges of the Chilterns, and especially in the Vale, but in the southern Chilterns access to the Thames provided an additional market in London. Thus just one example was firewood from the West Wycombe estate sent from Marlow by boat to Southwark, with a load of 14,000 bundles in 1218.[8] In later years, as London's demand grew, this trade became very important and was a major reason why woodland remained a more profitable land-use in the south Chilterns than elsewhere.

A document describing wood-sales on the Stonor estate in 1482 gives a good picture of the range of uses.[9] Wood was sold 'to my master's nailer', to a shoemaker (probably beech to make his lasts), and firewood to the tile kilns. 'Water wode' was sent to London 'for the household', and 'pale tymber' was given to the woodward Saunders for the park. 'Exule and plowyere' (axle and plough ware) were sent to Henley, and tenants were allowed coppice wood: 'Herry Parvin toke 11 load coppice in Bonell Hill to his fyre'. Thirty quarters of 'cole' (charcoal) were also sold.

The different uses and availability of wood in the Chilterns led to some interesting transactions, with local beech being sold for fuel and the proceeds used to buy oak, as at Berkhamsted Park (see pages 133-4) and at Ibstone. Ibstone windmill was built on the ridge above Turville Dean in 1293-94 and the ridge is still dominated today by a very fine mill with a magnificent view (and very steep descent!) down onto Turville village (Plate 85). Some local timber was used for the 1293 mill, but 400 trees from Westgrove were cut to help cover construction costs. These included the big oak standard needed for the central post of the mill. One of the right size was clearly not available locally, and 'the carpenter had to search for a timber-tree for three days in the woods around Wokingham'.[10]

These direct uses of different types of wood for construction and fuel by no means exhaust the nature of woodland resources in the medieval Chilterns. The Chiltern uplands and woods had long been used for various types of pasture. In woodland the more open glades, grassland and rides provided good grazing at various times of the year, and the trees provided shade. Then the seasonal falls of acorns and beechmast provided food for the pigs—the pannage assessment of Domesday Book—whilst the lower bushes, shoots and holly provided winter fodder.

Pressures on the Woodlands

With so many pressures in a limited space, the woodlands were a zone of conflict. All these different uses of woodland resources were not easily compatible, especially if different groups of users claimed rights to the same woodland. Excessive cutting of brushwood and young coppice-wood for fuel could lead to a declining stock of larger coppice. More intensive grazing of woods meant young shoots were eaten and seedlings failed to regenerate, so gradually slowing reproduction of the woodland and degrading it into open pasture land. Coppicing and

79. Poppies at Kimble. This field of poppies is the result of a year's 'set aside', land taken out of cultivation in much the same location as land was abandoned in medieval times.

80. Ree Field, Codicote. This huge field was the open field in medieval times and today captures some of the scale, and contrasts with the smaller meadows and enclosures which are on the other side of the River Ree.

81. The parish church of Fingest. The church of St Bartholomew, Fingest, is an unusual saddleback design with the tower wider than the nave, as in pre-conquest churches.

82. The parish church of Bledlow. The church of Holy Trinity dates from *c*.1200, and has several early 14th-century windows in the chancel.

pasturage do not go together very easily. The population growth of the early Middle Ages, up to around 1300, and the consequent expansion of villages and fields, not only reduced the area of Chilterns woodland but put more pressure on the remaining, still substantial areas. We must remember though that the Buckinghamshire Chilterns would still have had more woods in relation to population in 1348 than most of England in 1086. The pressure of the growing population accentuated the conflicts between uses and between different groups and communities. These conflicts in resource use could be resolved—or fought over—in a whole spectrum of ways. The sharpest conflict was between pasturage and young wood growth, and this was tackled either by attempting to exclude animals from the woods, or by managing the balance through regulation, legal rights and ownership. To understand the medieval Chilterns' woods we need to look at three forms: private or enclosed wood, common woods and wood-pasture commons, and medieval parks or private wood-pasture.

Enclosed Woodland

Private ownership of woodland was the most direct way of eliminating conflicts—other users were excluded and the owner could manage and balance his own use of the wood's resources. To be effective, however, such woodland had to be surrounded by a boundary, both to delimit land ownership and to exclude other users and wandering animals. These wood boundaries were substantial but necessary investments. They usually comprised a wood-bank and ditch, with a strong hedge or a line of trees a little way down the outer face of the bank to give a thick barrier. Hornbeam was often used on such wood-banks in the Chilterns (Plate 105). In the medieval Chilterns the largest private woods were owned by manorial lords as demesne woodland or private parkland. However each holding in the dispersed hamlets and farms of the uplands usually had its own small woods and groves too. As the individual land-market developed (and David Roden has shown it was very active by the 13th century) so parcels of woodland were sold and exchanged in the same way as fields. The charters of Missenden Abbey record many such transactions in the mid-Chilterns, and sometimes explicitly refer to the boundaries and hedges dividing the parcels. For instance when Hugh de Plessis granted woodland to the Abbey in 1277-79 the wood was delimited 'from there directly to the boundary post in the 'le Scires hegge' which divides my woodland from the demesne woodland of Henry Huse'. Similarly in Pyrton parish in the Oxfordshire Chilterns a 1387 agreement involved the whole wood called 'Harlyngruggewode' (in the vicinity of modern Hollandridge farm) 'with the hedges and hays there, and of all the woods, groves, hays and hedges of that parish'.[11]

Many such woods and groves were created out of woodland with common rights, and involved negotiation and conflict. Once again the Missenden charters provide an illustration. On 16 June 1284 the Abbey and Robert Mantel reached agreement over pasturage rights on their lands: the Abbey gave up rights of common pasture on Robert's lands in Little Missenden whilst he surrendered his rights on their land and allowed the Abbey to construct a ditch between the two properties, build a hedge along it, and enclose the 'Hydegrove Wood'.[12] In the countryside to the north of Little Missenden today there is still a Mantle's Farm, Hyde Farm and Hyde Heath.

The ditches and hedges kept out unwanted animals, but the wood owner could still lease pannage and pasture as he saw fit, keeping grazing intensity low and restricting it to specified months of the year or to years of heavy beech mast whilst earning additional income. Thus at Stonor in 1421 the woodward's receipts include pannage fees of £2 10s. 8d., the sale of acorns for 13s. 4d., and underwood sales for 23s.

The real justification of the enclosed wood was, of course, the growth of trees, both standard timbers and, more importantly, smaller coppiced trees. Valuations of demesne woods were usually based on the underwood, whilst medieval documents tend to record spectacular, but infrequent, large-scale fellings of timber trees. Much of the enclosed woodland was clearly more open than high beech-forest because the canopy cannot have been too thick to prevent regeneration and growth. How these woods were managed varied both through time and across the Chilterns. Where the wood was scarce (in the north-east Chilterns) careful management practices and 'coppice cycles' developed early, whereas some of these practices diffused more slowly to the heavily-wooded south-west Chilterns. Coppicing as a way of managing wood growth is very old, and the medieval documents are recording a long-standing practice.

Where woodland was plentiful in relation to demand, timber was simply drawn out as required. It was regarded as a capital resource and heavy felling and sales occurred at times of financial need, when crop income was low or when building bigger structures such as a windmill as at Ibstone. Sometimes storms and gales akin to those of early 1990 provided fellings: after the great storms of 1362 there were big sales from Ibstone, Berkhamsted and Princes Risborough. Neither the large trees nor the coppice were necessarily cut at regular intervals, but there was still careful woodmanship. The *Stonor Letters* record a sale of 1482 where the buyer of the 'Laned Wode', a William Fullard of Watlington, agreed he would cut no tree 'but yf he be above xx [20] ynche at brest heyth of man', and to ensure that 'the vode shalle be ryd at and draute [cut and drawn out] so the young copyse be not hurt'.[13] A sale of wood from Fawley, Hambleden and Turville in 1480 specified 'appultrez, peretrez, crabtrez and all wode of assise of x [10] inche'.[14] By the end of our period the Lewknor estate map of 1598 records: 'They do not fell the wood together but at every fall do glean and draw out only that which is about the growth of 21 years'.

In these reports one can see the gradual adoption of the more regular cropping established earlier in the north-east Chilterns, where coppicing was done in cycles, cutting different areas of wood at steady intervals. Regular coppicing was clearly the practice at King's Walden

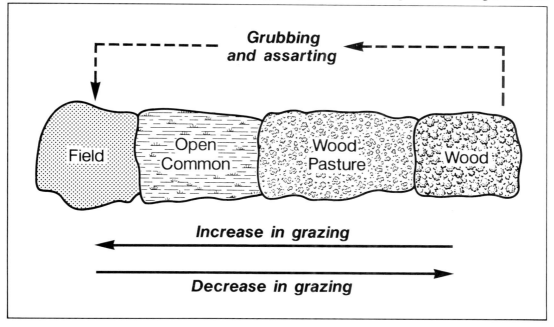

83. The relationship between woodland, pasture and assarting.

The Woodlands of Berkhamsted

Many aspects of the medieval woodland can be illustrated and drawn together by looking at one local landscape in detail. Several parts of the Chilterns would be suitable but let us choose Berkhamsted, partly because it is home ground for the authors but also because it is a good locality in terms of surviving documents and surviving fragments of landscape.[31]

The market town and commuter settlement of Berkhamsted nestles in the Bulbourne Valley of the Hertfordshire Chilterns. It was already an important borough at the time of Domesday Book and became more significant with the royal castle in the medieval period. By 1357 there were 114 shops and tenements in the town. The open fields ran along the lower ground south of the river and to the east of the town, while the demesne fields were on the north bank, west of the castle.

To the south old, steep hollow lanes rise to the plateau and a landscape of individual farms, closes and enclosed woods. 'La Magdeleine', now Marlin, is first mentioned in 1274. A charter of 1294 describes recently cleared land and wood in an enclosure 'Northrudyng' below the wood of 'la Maudelyne', whilst woods at Amberlains Hill (Hamberlins today) and Cock Grove (next to Marlin) are mentioned in later, pre-plantation documents. The major wooded regions were, however, north of the borough. The Park lay immediately north of the demesne fields and castle. Further north on the hillside and plateau was the enormous common wood of the Frith.

The manorial lord controlled not just his demesne wood but also the timber rights from his *boscus forinsecus* or 'foreign wood', the common wood of the Frith lying outside the park. The Frith occupied over 700 acres of the parish at the end of the 13th century but, as noted earlier, this was only part of the vast woodland spreading across several parishes. This would be the 'wood for 1000 swine' in Berkhamsted's Domesday Book entry. The timber, almost exclusively beech here, was reserved for the manorial lord and there are frequent references to it, especially for the mid-14th century when Edward the Black Prince held Berkhamsted as a royal manor.[32] In 1351 he made gifts to the parson of St Peter's of 'three beeches in the foreign wood for fuel'. He also gave his demesne farmer 'seven beeches yearly in the foreign wood for housebote and heybote', and in 1361 he ordered 600 beeches 'to be marked for future use'.

The men of Berkhamsted had rights of pasture in the Frith throughout the year, but they had to share them with other townships. When, however, they turned their pigs into the wood they had to pay pannage dues, despite the fact that the Rector of Ashridge and his tenants were exempt. This anomaly arose from a grant by Edward, Earl of Cornwall, in 1285 to the newly created monastery or college at Ashridge. This gave it lands 'and common of pasture in the wood of Bercamstede called 'le Fryth' for all their beasts; with leave to have their pigs in the said wood in the time of mast quit of pannage; with housebote and haybote and fencing of the said park of Esserugge in the said Fryth wood'. These multiple rights meant that gradually the common wood developed the character of wood-pasture, with pollarded beeches and oaks.

In 1353 the Prince acquired an extra 54 acres of land and 10 acres of wood to enlarge his Park and create a new 'lawn' there. He ordered his Constable to enclose the Park 'with a paling for the preservation thereof and of game there'. To do this he was to sell beeches from the Frith to £20 value and then use the money to buy oak timber for the rails and stanchions of the pale. 'All the beeches are to be cut down in different parts of the wood, as shall be most profitable to the Prince and least wasteful of the wood, and the stumps are to be marked with the axe appointed for the purpose.' As well as the Frith there were also substantial demesne and park woods, for, in 1300, 4,000 faggots were produced from the demesne wood, and in 1354 the Prince's baker was given sufficient beech from the Park or Frith for 'making three "gates" for his bakery, and the residue of the beeches for consumption in the ovens of the bakery'.

90. Woodbank at Frithsden Copse near Berkhamsted. The remnants of a medieval woodbank marking the boundary between the enclosed woodlands of the copse and pasture on Frithsden common.

What can we still detect of this medieval wooded landscape in the countryside around Berkhamsted today? The Park has gone, disparked and converted to fields in the 17th century, as was part of the Frith to create Coldharbour Farm in 1630. Yet many significant elements remain. One can drive or walk up the steep lanes such as Darr's, Durrant's or Hamberlin's to the Cock Grove or Hamberlin's Wood, ancient in much of its character and with old woodbanks that can still be seen. The remains of 'The Frith', in the form of Berkhamsted Common, were saved from enclosure in the 1860s and large areas are now owned and managed by the National Trust. They contain some fine trees known as Frithsden Beeches and Frithsden Copses, described by Dr. Oliver Rackham as 'a rare survival of the medieval Chilterns landscape'.[33] The Beeches are the remnant of old wood-pasture on the north of the Common (Plate 87). At their heart is a group of huge ancient pollarded beeches, with bases up to six and seven feet across. They are surrounded by old (but younger) beeches and then a fringe of oak and birch which has grown up after pasture ceased. Reportedly the beeches were last pollarded in the early 19th century but the bollings must go back to the 17th century.

A few hundred yards to the east are the Copses, given to the National Trust by the historian G. M. Trevelyan. They are old embanked coppice woods separated from the wood-pasture common. The Great Copse was replanted to mark the 1953 Coronation (much to the regret of wood conservationists), but the Little Copse is 'original'. The ditches and woodbanks around the Copse can easily be seen (Plate 90), together with the stumps and remnants of the old boundary hedge. The trees in the Copse are mixed, with much hornbeam and cherry together with standards of oak and the occasional beech. The hedgebank trees are hornbeam and beech and inside there are carpets of bluebells and anemones. Here one can see many elements of the ancient woods of the Chilterns struggling through to the present landscape.

Chapter Eight

Rural Change 1550-1800

Introduction

Sixteenth-century England saw a new vitality, a quickening in economy, society and national spirit. The Tudor monarchy brought a political stability and unity after the conflicts of previous centuries. England's population began to grow rapidly again, and economic growth flowed around a fast expanding London: from a population of about 55,000 in 1520, London grew to 200,000 by 1600 and 575,000 by 1700. The dissolution of the monasteries and abbeys in the 1530s and the rise of a new Protestant England meant that many lands changed hands, and 'new men' led a dynamism that gave the era of Elizabeth, Raleigh and Shakespeare what one writer called 'its spring-like air of expansiveness'.[1] This new progress faltered at times—there was a serious hiccup in the 1580s and '90s when the population grew faster than the food supply, and the next century saw the English civil war and periods of economic depression. But by economic and social change England avoided 'the medieval trap' of a limit to agricultural output.

The Chilterns participated fully in this era of improvement. They were close enough to attract London money and businessmen, and they were well-placed to help supply food and fuel to the growing City. Chiltern farming improved and prospered. The woodlands grew fuel for London. The Chiltern town and inns catered for the travellers and traders.

The Vanishing Open-Fields

Among the first signs of this new era in the Chilterns was the gradual disappearance of open-fields from the Hills and valleys by a process of piecemeal enclosure. This was not the depopulating enclosure for sheep farming, but a change from open arable to enclosed arable. Farmers saw opportunities for more efficiency and improvement if they controlled their own land and reaped all the benefits themselves. Progress could be individual rather than communal. Chiltern farmers knew this from their old enclosed fields, and Tudor writers like Thomas Tusser (brought up at Wallingford) argued the case:

> Good land that is several, crops may have three,
> in champion country it may not so be...

Tusser devoted a whole poem to *A Comparison between Champion Country and Several,*[2] including:

> The country enclosed I praise,
> The t'other delighteth not me!
> For nothing the wealth it doth raise,
> To such as inferior be...

135

The t'one is commended for grain,
Yet bread made of beans they do eat:
The t'other for one loaf hath twain,
Of meslin, of rye, or of wheat.
The champion liveth full bare;
When woodland full merry doth fare.

In woodland, the poor men that have,
Scarce fully two acres of land,
More merrily live, and do save,
Than t'other with twenty in hand.
Yet pay they as much fro the two,
As t'other for twenty must do.

The labourer coming from thence,
In woodland to work anywhere,
(I warrant you) goeth not hence,
To work any more again there...

The very flexibility of the medieval Chiltern field systems meant that they could be readily changed when the time was ripe. And ripe it was. Because there were so many fields and most farmers' holdings were in those closest to their dwellings, consolidation of strips and piecemeal enclosure could take place without challenging the whole communal system or getting everyone's agreement. Consolidation of strips had been taking place for a long time, and once the manorial court stopped enforcing common pasture of the arable, the enclosure of the fields was straightforward. At places like Codicote the Abbot and his monks had departed with the dissolution of the monasteries in the 1530s, and the new manorial lords were keen on improvement. A few decades brought a big change in attitudes. In 1524 at Little Gaddesden on the Hertfordshire-Buckinghamshire border, two tenants were brought before the manorial court for keeping land in severalty in the common fields after the harvest, but after 1550 there was much purchase, exchange and enclosure. Twenty-two exchanges of copyhold land are recorded between 1556 and 1583. Six involved land in Mill Field, and by 1579 a seven-acre piece there is described as 'now inclosed'. Strip by strip, field by field, the common fields contracted.[3] By 1600 at least three of Berkhamsted's common fields had gone, and the story is true across the Hills. Other large common fields were subdivided, as a prelude to further enclosure. For the most part we see only occasional transactions, surveys of holdings at particular dates, but the open-fields shrank and vanished like snow-patches in the landscape.

There were gainers and losers in all this. Those who accumulated in Tudor times were rarely the same families who consolidated in the 15th century, and large tenants and manorial lords gained over small tenants. Holdings became very unequal, and those with the smallest lost out to the new yeoman and tenant farmers as land tenures became more like modern freeholds and leaseholds. It was the little man (or woman, for holdings by females are not uncommon) who was left with strips in the residual common fields as his bigger neighbours agreed to enclose, and his ultimate fate was often as a hired labourer. A detailed survey of Great Hampden in 1653, which is preserved in the Buckinghamshire Record Office, illustrates the pattern.[4] The remaining open fields were only 244 acres in extent, and were clustered at the northern end of the manor below Little Hampden. The larger tenants, like John Lydall with 187 acres and Robert Morton with 179, had most of their land in closes, though they were also still the biggest holders in the remaining open fields. Smallholders like John Knight with his 3½ acres had all their land in the open strips.

   This drawn-out process left its permanent imprint on the landscape. Sometimes fields have been amalgamated since, but many of the closes and their hedges are still there. In some places, as between Harpenden and Kings Walden, it is claimed the fields preserve the reverse-S shape of medieval ploughed furlongs.[5] The piecemeal enclosure proceeded fastest and furthest in the south-west Chilterns, where common fields had been fewer anyway, and more slowly in the north-east. Precisely because it was piecemeal, most localities retained a rump of open-field where agreement had not been reached. These were mainly historical hangovers, of less and less farming significance. In Codicote, for example, although most of the open fields disappeared, a few open pieces still remained in 1800, including a three-strip patch in the middle of Ree Field.

   The real division was between the Chiltern Hills and the surrounding lowlands. In the Vale and along the Thamesside lowlands the open field systems were much more all-embracing, a strong oak hard to tamper with or pull down. Here piecemeal enclosure was impossible. As the open fields disappeared in the Hills but remained in the Vale, the contrast between 'Chiltern and Vale', 'champion and woodland' noted by Leland and others became more marked, and the Chiltern scarp became a great divide in the agrarian landscape.

A Tale of Two Maps

We can see this landscape contrast between the enclosed Chilterns and the open-field Vale first mapped out in Elizabethan times, and there are two lovely examples from the Oxfordshire Chilterns. In Elizabeth's reign map-making made great advances, both in general topographical maps and in detailed land-surveying. The first strand gave us the county maps of Christopher Saxton and others. The second has given us two late Elizabethan estate maps, beautifully drawn and coloured, for Lewknor and for Harpsden.

   The Lewknor map is one of an extensive series of maps commissioned by Warden Hovenden of All Souls College in Oxford, recording the various estates belonging to the College (Plate 98). The Lewknor map was surveyed and drawn by Thomas Langdon in 1598,

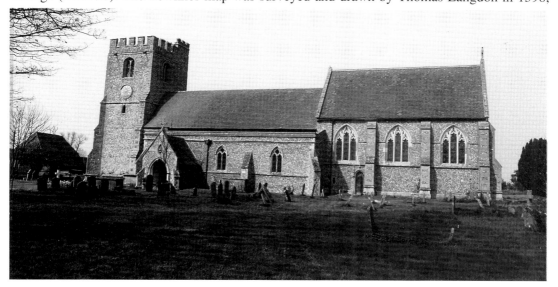

91. The parish church of St Margaret at Lewknor. From medieval times the living of the church was in the gift of All Souls College and the college remains the largest landowner in Lewknor today. On the left the roof of the medieval barn (Plate 71) can be seen.

and has not been reproduced before. All Souls had acquired rights to Lewknor church in 1442, and subsequently acquired further lands there, which they hold to this day. The map shows the open-fields of the village, picking out the strips belonging to the church (the glebe lands) and identifying their size and the landowners on either side. A court roll for 1594 notes that the strips were defined by stakes and merestones which were set down before the spring sowing at Candlemas.[6] The furlongs were made up of these half-acre strips. Many can be identified by name such as Filhole, Woodlande, Stonepitte and Preste Furlonges. In Preste Furlonge on the southern boundary (the right-hand side of the map) the strips of manor and glebe alternate, perhaps reflecting some reallocation. The old enclosures in the village centre stand out clearly, as do the church, and the manor house to the south. Weston Inclosure (in the centre of the map) can still be seen today. The map also shows 'the London waye' at the top (later to be the A40), and running diagonally through the fields is marked 'Hackeman waye' or the Lower Icknield Way. The grazing common of the Chiltern escarpment is marked, including 'Parte of the sheepe comon'. The text around the map records the tithes due from different land parcels, including those from Lewknor Uphill, above the escarpment and not shown on the map.

92. A Harpsden lane. This lane leads down from Upper House Farm to Hunts Green, still very much the same today as it was on the 1586 map.

Lewknor was to remain unenclosed for two more centuries, until 1815, and we will return to its story later.

The second map is a vivid contrast. Made by John Blagrave of Reading it shows the Harpsden valley just south-west of Henley in 1586 (Plate 100). Blagrave was a mathematician, author of *The Mathematical Jewel* (1585) and *The Art of Dyalling* (1609), and produced a small number of estate maps; his elaborate monument is in St Lawrence's church in Reading. His Harpsden map was drawn for Humphrey Forster of Harpsden Manor, and shows a totally enclosed landscape of hedged fields and woods. This landscape remains largely unchanged today with steep lanes and old trees around Hunt's Green (Plate 92). The list of the eight farms and their fields shows the land dominated by three farms of 520, 136 and 116 acres controlling three-quarters of the area, but with three smaller holdings around Hunt's Green. The colouring picks out the different land-uses: yellow/brown stripes for fields ploughed but left fallow; green stripes for the growing crop; light green for pasture and rough grazing; and a dark green for pasture by the river (off our map extract). As yet little is known of the earlier history of this manor, but the names of some of the closes suggest there were once open-fields that had been enclosed. Others have names like Stocking Croft and Upper Croft suggesting old enclosures. It looks like a classic medieval assarted landscape, but we should be cautious and remember that Harpsden Roman villa lay on the hillside just to the south and that *hearps denu* is mentioned in an Anglo-Saxon boundary charter. The wills of several of the 1586 farmers, like John Wydmore of Hunt's Green and William Pearman of Upper House Farm, are preserved in the Oxfordshire Record Office, and Ruth Gibson has studied the subsequent farming history of the valley in detail.[7] She has discovered that parts of the farmhouses shown on the 1586 map still survive, behind later additions and modifications. Bottom Farm (now 'The Old Place') includes a timbered portion with a mid-16th century style of spine beam, whilst the back of Hunt's Farm has a cruck construction that must predate 1586.

Farming Improvements

Throughout the 16th century the Chilterns continued to be dominated by the arable and by corn production. Wheat was the main commercial crop, with barley gradually becoming more important in some parts of the region. Much of the grain went to supply the London market, and was transported through a number of centres. The most notable were Henley in the south, High Wycombe for the central Chilterns, and a number of Hertfordshire towns for the northern parts.

Henley's waterborne links with London made it an excellent collection centre for the Upper Thames Valley, together with Reading and Wallingford. John Leland in the 1530s had written of 'plenty of wood and corne about Henlye'. London depended heavily on Henley's wheat in Elizabethan times: between 1568 and 1573 one-third of all English corn shipped down the Thames to London came from Henley.[8] The records of the London companies show the commercial links in more detail. After a scarcity of corn in London in 1586-87, the Privy Council ordered JPs to assess the quantities of grain in their locality, and, after deducting an allowance for family provision and seed, to require owners to bring the rest for sale 'in open markett'. The returns for the Oxford Chiltern Hundreds survive: for Ewelme the wheat in store was calculated at 943 quarters, and of this 310 quarters were thought to be surplus available for the market.[9]

Malting from barley also became an important trade, probably in the 17th century or even earlier. Richard Blome in his *Britannia* (1673) described the Henley market as 'very considerable for corn, especially barley, which is brought there for their great Mault-trade, there being oft-times sold in one day about 300 cartload of barley'.[10]

The Chilterns were well placed to meet this metropolitan demand, and farmers could make their own choices of crops and rotations on their enclosed farms. Rising demand gave good incomes to the yeoman farmers, which we can still see reflected in the Elizabethan and 17th-century timber-and-brick farmhouses and cottages of the south Chilterns, especially north of Henley. Real improvements in yield came more slowly, for the 'agricultural revolution' was a transformation over two centuries rather than a sudden change.

The continuing arable character of the whole Chilterns region finds confirmation in recent work on marriage seasons.[11] Ann Kussmaul has shown that in arable-dominated regions most people got married in autumn, after the harvest. In pastoral regions the weddings were in spring or early summer, after lambing and calving. There was no strong seasonality in non-agricultural or industrial regions. Although her Chilterns sample is not large, it is resolutely autumn-marriage.

Within this arable character, however, there was much local variation in what was grown and in what proportions. This sprang from that intense local variability of soils that characterises this region. As Thomas Delafield put it in his manuscript *History of Stokenchurch* (1744): 'I believe, a greater variety of soills, and more different forms of the scituation of lands, can hardly be found in any place than in these Chiltern Countrys; and by consequence greater occasions to exercise the Art and Capacity of the Farmer'.[12]

These regional characteristics were becoming recognised in the term 'Chiltern Country', used by many of the county and farming writers of the 17th and 18th centuries. Walter Blith, for example, in *The English Improver Improved* (1652) commented (in a general defence of enclosure): 'Consider the Chilterne countries, and you shall finde, that were it inclosed men would Plow little or no whit less than they doe, because nothing else nor no way else would yeeld the like Advance'.[13]

The pattern of Chiltern farming and its improvements are revealed through writers of the times. For greater detail historians and geographers have recently begun to make use of the mass of surviving probate inventories for 1550 onwards. These list domestic possessions, the crops stocked and sown, farm implements and other indications of wealth and farming practices. Pioneered by Michael Havinden for Oxfordshire, and recently applied on a large scale for Hertfordshire, these studies allow a more reliable picture to be constructed of just how many farmers did what, rather than recording the few innovators.[14] They show that, in Elizabethan and early 17th-century times, Chiltern farmers still followed three-course rotations. They grew wheat and barley, but also considerable amounts of oats and rye because of the acidity of the poorer soils. Sheep were important as an aid to arable production, rather than for their meat or wool. They grazed on the commons and wastes and were folded on the fallow. Pulses were grown as fodder, but in smaller quantities than in the Vale, where waste was scarce.

The inventories reveal that gradually this pattern changed, and grain yields increased, especially in the later 17th century. By 1700 they had increased by some 75 per cent and by 1800 by a further third.[15] The two major sources of this improvement were better preparation of the ground, fertilising the soil, and the use of different fodder crops and foreign grasses that could be used in new rotations.

Chiltern soils benefited enormously from treatment, especially marling, the adding of chalk or lime to the acid surface of clay-with-flints soil. It was an old technique, but now employed with a new vigour and on a large scale. Farmers dug pits in their fields through the clay layer, which might be 20-30 ft. at most, into the chalk. From the base of the bell-pit, shafts might be dug. The broken chalk, sometimes burnt in a kiln to make it into lime, was then spread on the fields. When the pit was exhausted, it would be boarded over and soil put on top; later rotting of the boards and their collapse has left the distinctive depressions in many a Chiltern field. Organic manures were also important, not just in the form of sheep-dung, but as human 'night-soil' brought from London to some parts of Hertfordshire. Shredded rags were also ploughed into the ground, to help lighter soils retain moisture. Throughout the 17th century probates show the increasing role of ground preparation, like that of Henry Tudder of Great Gaddesden, whose £200 include £10 for 'fallowing, stirring, dunging and dressing' the land.[16]

The second element, which probably contributed more after 1700, was the growth of fodder crops such as turnips and swedes and the sowing of new grasses such as clover and sainfoin. The new grasses enriched the soil and provided fodder for animals. Soil was improved, more animals could be kept (important where wastes were limited) and therefore manuring increased, so yields rose. Fodder crops and sown grasses could replace some bare fallowing, making more use of the land and generating complicated rotation patterns. At one time turnips were seen as the key to the agricultural revolution. This is no longer the view.

Although they were pioneered early, and may have been grown in the Chilterns as early as 1670, they were slow to diffuse. Sown grasses probably had an earlier impact. Thus clovers are found in inventories from the 1670s in the Oxfordshire Chilterns.[17]

A single inventory can be used to capture many features of the late 17th-century Chilterns farming. It is for 'Rebekah Harding of Greenfield, widow in the parish of Watlington', dated 18 May 1685. Greenfield is one of the hamlets on the Chiltern escarpment above Watlington village, just south of Christmas Common. The inventory records her domestic goods, her bedsteads and sheets, pewter and brass, her table and cupboards; her 'four flitches of bacon'; her andirons for the fire, with tongs, bellows, spits and a warming pan. It lists 'for barrels and tubs and a salting trough in a room called the drink house', and then moves to the farming goods. These illustrate virtually all the aspects of Chiltern farming. Most of the crops are in closes ('for barley in a ground called Bakers Close £35'), but some are in the common fields of Watlington ('barley in Comonfield'). The crops include wheat, barley, oats and maslin (the mixture of wheat and rye). In Pond Close there was barley, peas, vetches and dills, and 'Clover gras and other gras' is listed. There were about 40 sheep, and 'two dungcarts on the wheels' (Plate 93).

During the 18th century rotations involving turnips and the range of sown grasses became the normal pattern in the Chilterns. This is documented in the County reports between 1794 and 1815, such as Arthur Young's *Oxfordshire*. He instances the Fane estate at Wormsley south of Stokenchurch, where a rotation of (1) turnips, (2) barley, (3) clover or trefoil or ray-grass, (4) wheat was followed. On drier land south of Nettlebed Mr. Dean of English Farm followed a similar sequence: turnips, barley or oats, clover, wheat, turnips, barley or oats, trefoil, wheat.[18] Bare fallowing was now very much the exception on these enclosed farms. Change in the open-field parishes of the Vale and other lowlands around the Hills was much slower. Some agreements for improved farming were successful, especially on the rich greensand loams of the Icknield Belt. As early as 1618 some arable strips in Aston Rowant were put down to pasture as temporary leys, and 'hitching' or fencing part of the bare fallow and sowing grasses was practised in some villages.[19] A lease of 1717, also for Aston, reports that the tenant was to have one ton of rags each year to put on the land, brought from London via Hambleden Wharf. At Lewknor in 1765 the 11 main farmers agreed to a three-year experiment of sowing clover in the spring field after it was cleared, and corn on the fallow land. However it expressly forbade any corn sowing on the hillsides of the sheep-walks. All these changes were, at best, partial tinkering, and in the Vale the full benefits of the new farming methods had to await Parliamentary Enclosure of the open-fields.

Ellis and Kalm

It is time to make the acquaintance of William Ellis of Little Gaddesden. Ellis (*c*.1690-1758) was a former London brewer who began farming in Chiltern Hertfordshire at Church Farm, where 'I occupy my own Farm and the Glebe-land of our Parish, containing in all twenty four inclosed Fields of several Sorts of Soils'.[20] He also became a prolific and influential farming writer, as well as selling advice, new implements like a four-wheel drill plough, and seeds. His books include *The Timber-Tree Improved* (1738), *The Practical Farmer or the Hertfordshire Husbandman* (1732), *The Country Housewife's Family Companion* (1750), and, in eight volumes, *The Modern Husbandman* (1750). For us, however, the most apposite is his *Chiltern and Vale Farming Explained* (1733). Ellis's writings are a real mixture: he is garrulous, he digresses, tells anecdotes and shouts his prejudices; but he is also a shrewd, detailed observer of landscapes and their farming potential, and a vigorous advocate of the new, improved husbandry.

An Inmitacio taken of the goods and Chattels of Reberah
Harding of greenfield widow in the pish of watlington
in the County of Oxon praysed the Eighteenth day
of may 1685

	£	s	d
Imp: of the goods and Chattels in the hous and about home			
Imp: for money and Clothes	5	8	8
Imp: for one bed and beadstead ouer the hall and the rest of the goods in that roome	8	0	0
Imp: for one bead and beadstead and what belonges to it in a Chamber ouer the milkhous	1	10	0
Imp: for fifteene paire of sheetes	3	10	0
Imp: for powter and bras	3	10	0
Imp: for one bead ouer the kitchin		10	0
Imp: for four flitches of bacon	2	10	0
Imp: for goodes in the hall a table and Cubord and Joynt stooles and a forme and a paire of Andirons and fire shouel and tonges and bellows and two spits and three Chaires and on paire of hangers And a paire of dogges and a warming pann	1	10	0
Imp: for barrells and tubs and a saltting trouf in a roome Called the drink hous	1	0	0
Imp: for Eighteene sheepe	6	6	0
Imp: for barley in bodam Close	5	0	0
Imp: for wheat in the Lower grounds	25	0	0
Imp: for three horses	14	0	0
Imp: for three hoges	02	8	0
Imp: for two Dungcarts on the wheeles and three harrowes and the plowes and harroll and the plow timber	2	10	0
Imp: for twoelf bushels of wheat	3	0	0
Imp: for seaventeene bushells of barley	2	9	0
Imp: for hors harnis and halters and Cart rope	1	0	0
Imp: for two Long Carts and the wheels that belong to them	6	15	0
Imp: for barley in Comon foild and at home and Clouer gras and other gras	6	10	6
Imp: for a watter cart and the harroll and a small peell of hey	1	7	0

93. Probate Inventory for Rebekah Harding of Watlington 1685. A very complete list of Rebekah's possessions including furniture, sheets and other household goods, farming equipment and the livestock and crops in the different fields and closes of Greenfield and Watlington.

In *Chiltern and Vale*, Ellis discussed the benefits of good and the 'sad effects' of bad management:

> The Chiltern, or Hilly Country especially, is more concerned in these Subjects, by reason it is mostly enclosed, and consists in diversity of Soils, of clays, Loams, Sands, Chalk, Stony Ground, Hurlucky and Gravelly Grounds, and several other Sorts, that bound more or less with Parts of these Earths. While the fertile Vale or low Country runs chiefly but in little other, than the black Loams or blewish Marly clays in open Fields, that are commonly under one and the same management of Culture; and is easier by far brought into a Tilth or Condition for corn, than this of ours, and with a great deal of less Charge and Trouble.

He recognises that the Vale clays and loams (especially the latter) are inherently more fertile than the Hill soils, but argues that Chiltern soils can give very good returns, if they receive investment, effort, and improvement: 'Not that I pretend to say a Chiltern Man can Farm as cheap as a Vale Man'. The ground needed extra treatment, more ploughing, and other bills were greater. Because of the stony flints, ''Tis therefore computed, that £5 will go as far in a Smith's Bill in the Vale, as 15 will in the Chiltern'.[21] Here Ellis is echoed by his contemporary, Thomas Delafield of Stokenchurch, who enthused:

> after a new plowing one would rather take the Ridges for Causeys Strewed with Stones to walk on, than for Lands to sow corn in: so very little of earth is to be seen among the stones that the Ploughshare in some places turns up. This makes hard service for the horse, and Expensive for the Master, but Profitable to the Smith that repairs the Irons. However these soills often rear plentiful crops of good wheat, often as good, and as much as in deeper Lands. To this the Flints are not a little contribution, by inbuing the nitre of the Air, and by their Proper Salt and Sulphur communicating its genial heat to the seed, by keeping the ground warm and hollow; by sheltering the new spring blade from the extremity of the winter.[22]

Ellis advocates all of the improvements we have seen in action, such as intensive dressings for the 'red clays' or clay-with-flints of the Hills, with both chalk and organic fertilisers: 'Twenty five or thirty Load will well chalk an Acre of Ground, which by discreet Ploughings will last twenty Years'.[23] For farmers within 30 miles of London (Little Gaddesden is 27 miles as the crow flies), he recommends soot purchased in the city:

> And that it may come cheaper home, we commonly carry up Chaff, Corn, Wood, Flour, or timber, and fetch, in Return, Soot in sacks, or loose, in a Cart or Waggon, which now is sold for Six-pence a Bushel, when in Winter, and at Spring, it is sold in London for ninepence. And in this Manner, you may bring down Coal-ashes, Ox or cow's Hoofs, Hog's or Ox's Hair, Trotters, Horn Shavings, Coney-clippings, Pidgeon's or Rabbit's Dung.[24]

He advocates rag dressing for chalky soils, and sheep dung for all soils in Chiltern and Vale. Ellis was also an enthusiast for fodder crops, and for 'resting the Ground chiefly by sowed Grasses' such as clover and lucerne, and not bare fallowing. One of the great gains Chiltern can have over Vale is 'the Enjoyment of the third Year (that with them lies Fallow)', and he admonishes conservative Chiltern farmers

> who are so byassed by their Ancestors Methods ... that many will justify (or at least endeavour it) the third Year's Ground laying Fallow, which indeed is putting the Enclosure almost on the same Footing of an open Vale Field, but this obstinate Absurdity brings them under less Profit, than those that husband their Ground otherways.[25]

Ellis and his writings are fascinating in themselves, but his encounter with Pehr Kalm is even more so.[26] Kalm was a Swedish-Finnish scientist who undertook a visit to England and North America in 1748-51, to look at agricultural practices. Once in England:

I undertook at the cost and request of Herr Vice-President Baron Bjelke, a journey to see Mr.
Ellis, who lived at Little Gaddesden in Hertfordshire. Mr. Ellis was a man who had made a great
reputation for his Practice of Rural Economy, but still more for his many writings on the same
Art, which latterly he had published yearly.

Arriving on 25 March, Kalm and his assistant Lars Ljungstrom spent three weeks at *The Robin
Hood* inn at Little Gaddesden (the inn still survives as a private house). His observations on
England were translated a century and a half later, and include over 150 pages on the Gaddesden
area. Kalm was a careful, scientific observer, and he beautifully records the contrasts between
Chiltern and Vale at that date. He walked the four miles to Ivinghoe in the Vale 'because Mr.
Ellis told us that the appearance of the country and the soil was entirely different from what
there was at Little Gaddesden'. Under a heading 'Evils of the common fields', Kalm wrote:

Today we had manifold proofs of this, what harm and hindrance it is for a farmer to have all
his property in common fields, with his neighbours, and on the other hand what an advantage
to have an isolated farm and possessions all to himself, when he gets to manage and cultivate
them according to his own discretion. Around Little Gaddesden and on all Chiltern-land every
farmer more or less had his own severalties which he afterwards divided into small inclosures
by hedges. There was one inclosure sown with wheat, another with barley, turnips, peas, oats,
sainfoin, clover, trifolium, tares, potatoes, or whatever he wished.

While the field were lying fallow, he could sow it with turnips, feed sheep on it, and afterwards
plough down the remaining bitten turnips, and have thereby a much greater advantage than if
he had left it fallow. In short, he could in a thousand ways improve his property and earn
money. On the other hand, here about Ivinghoe, where the common fields are everywhere in
use, no hedges are seen. Nor are there here any pease or kinds of grass sown as fodder for
sheep, cows, horses and swine ...

Kalm recorded the plants, the trees and the chalk pits, the houses and the women (Kalm
was astonished they did no farmwork, but found them 'very handsome and lively in society').
But he was disappointed in his encounter with Ellis. He found Ellis rather wary and secretive,
and a demonstration of the new drill plough did not impress him. It kept breaking down: 'Now,
the seed would not run; now the mould stuck fast in the hole at the bottom of the funnel; now
the corn was not harrowed well down, so that there were here *frictiones frictionum*'s and less
than a pint of seed was sown in the afternoon. Looking round Little Gaddesden before he met
Ellis, Kalm was amazed to find that ill-cultivated fields belonged to Ellis: '"Mr.Ellis?" I asked
[the farmer], "you must have forgotten yourself, or is there more than one Mr.Ellis?"'

Unfortunately there was not, and Ellis's neighbours were not his most fervent admirers.
Pehr Kalm found a Mr.Williams very much the local model farmer.[27] Ellis himself quoted
Luke, iv, 24: 'No prophet is accepted in his own country', and Kalm certainly caught Ellis at
a period when writing took his energies—the booksellers are reputed to have required 40,000
words a month for the instalment publication of *The Modern Husbandman*. In his time, Ellis
was an influential proponent of improved farming and his reputation deserves some
rehabilitation.

Villages and Market Towns

The quickening tempo of farming life in the Chilterns after 1550 was reflected in much new
building and refurbishment in the villages and towns. Market towns were needed to trade the
produce and provide an ever-expanding range of back-up services. From 1600 the range of
urban crafts and services expanded rapidly, including not only the saddler, the shoemaker and
the blacksmith, but also clothing shops and the services of country physicians and lawyers for
the more prosperous. The inns were very important meeting-places for local business as well

94. Shardeloes, Amersham. The house was built in 1758-66 for William Drake, MP for Amersham, and designed by Stiff Leadbetter and Robert Adam. The house has a fine stone portico with Corinthian columns, facing northwards across the lake.

95. Humphry Repton drawing of West Wycombe Park. Taken from his 1803 book on landscape gardening, it illustrates the panorama after Repton had opened out the view of the lake.

as for travellers, and the towns were studded with an amazing number of them. Later the turnpike roads brought further trade to some of these towns, and along the Thames towns like Taplow, Marlow and Henley attracted wealthy Londoners, sometimes assisted by royal and aristocratic patronage.

This prosperity can be seen in the many buildings which survive from this period. At Watlington, Thomas Stonor, who was lord of the manor, erected the market and town hall in 1664-65, and in 1682 the Drakes of Shardeloes built Amersham town hall. The market hall in High Wycombe was first built in the 17th century too, but rebuilt by Robert Adam in 1761. The better-off tradesmen and landowners built elegant townhouses, though many are refacings of earlier dwellings, and much older structures are often to be found behind the layers. In the 17th century brick became the popular material. Good building stone has always been an expensive import to the Chilterns, and reserved for the grander public buildings and country houses. At first brick was employed to replace the wattle-and-daub fillings between timber structures, but in towns complete brick facings became fashionable. The result is best preserved in the old centres of Amersham, Beaconsfield and Marlow. Appearances can, however, be very deceptive: quite genuine old inns, dating to the 17th century, may have been faced several times, and the half-timbers may be modern mock-Tudor.

Some towns also acquired more specialist, semi-industrial activities. Malting (mainly to make beer) was carried on in a small way right across the region, but the London trade was

96. West Wycombe High Street. The High Street in West Wycombe retained much of its character, especially when this photograph captured it without any traffic at the turn of the century.

increasingly served by two groupings at either end of the Chilterns. Larger-scale malting became identified with particular towns. The Upper Thames barley was malted and traded at Henley and other towns beyond the Hills such as Reading, Wallingford and Abingdon. When John Grant, maltster of Henley, died in 1662 he left 60 quarters of malt in store worth £93, £120 in cash and credits for £180 for 'Maults at London'.[28] Brakspear's Brewery is the last survival of that trade. Wycombe was also an important supplier and a local maltster Thomas Oliffe sent as many as 1,500 sacks a year downriver from Taplow to Queenhithe in the 1730s.[29] In the northern Chilterns, Hertfordshire was a major supplier of London's malt. Tring, Berkhamsted, Hitchin (and Luton across the county line) all had their malthouses, but the industry became focused on towns to the east of the Chilterns, notably Ware which had river access to London via the Lea.

97. Glass jug by George Ravenscroft, *c*.1676. This jug with mould-blown ribbing is an example of Ravenscroft's fine glass-making, and probably came from his Henley works.

For a short period Henley had a glassmaking industry, though its history is still obscure.[30] In Charles II's reign, a London glassmaker, George Ravenscroft, was experimenting with fine crystalline glass. In 1674 he set up a glassworks in Henley, probably attracted by local beech fuel and possibly by the Nettlebed sands and black flints mentioned by Robert Plot. It only lasted 20 years, but produced some fine specimens (Plate 97). Today the exact location of the glassworks has been lost.

Much more enduring were the activities of the water-mills. The Chilterns may lack surface water, but below the spring-line the streams can run swiftly and be good mill drivers. Most notable was the river Wye, with its many medieval corn (and cloth) mills near High Wycombe. They also began to be used for paper-making, and additional mills were constructed in the 18th century around Wycombe Marsh, Loudwater and downriver to Bourne End. The status of the industry was recognised by the award of a Royal Society of Arts gold medal to John Bates in 1787 for inventing a new high quality paper. The 1798 county occupation list (the *Posse Comitatus*) records 16 papermakers and three parchment-makers in Wycombe borough and 75 papermakers in Wycombe parish. These activities, together with the fledgling chairmaking industry, made the Wycombe area 'the nearest thing possible to an industrial valley without locally available coal and iron' (L. J. Ashford).[31]

Other valleys such as the Bulbourne below Berkhamsted also developed such industries, though most came after the canal in 1800, and there were other, more isolated semi-industrial sites. But they were the exceptions: the Chilterns remained predominantly a rural, farming community, and the towns were mainly market centres for that community.

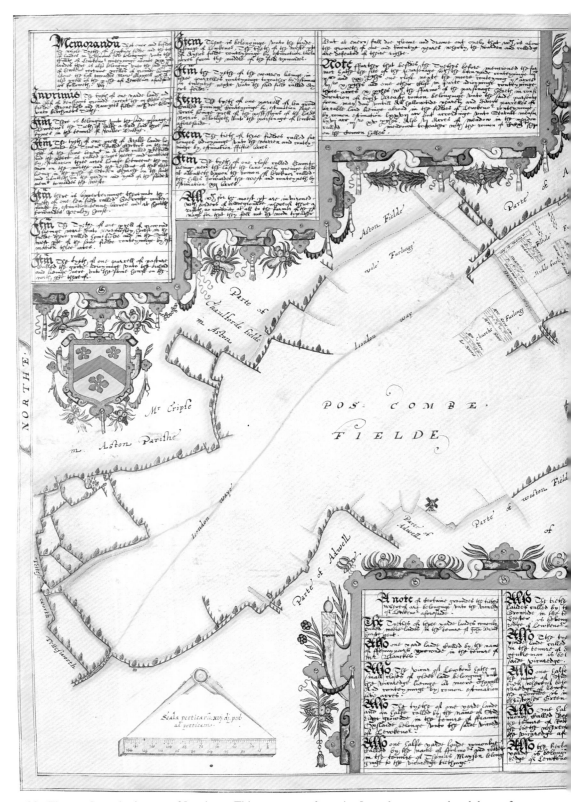

98. Thomas Langdon's map of Lewknor. This map, one of a series Langdon surveyed and drew of estates owned by All Souls College, Oxford, shows the open-field farming with individual strips and furlongs. The text records the tithes and entitlements owed to the college. [All Souls College, Oxford: Hovenden map IV:6.]

Parte of the Comon
of Lewknor called
Beacon hilles

Parte of

Fielde

Lewknor

Fielde

Parte of the Sheepe Comon

Parte of

Sherborne Comon

Parte of

Sherborne Fielde

Fielde

Sherborne

Parte of weston fielde

Parte of Sherborne Fielde

The description of the parsonage impropriate of Lewkenor in the countye of Oxon, to geather with the gleebe landes therevnto belonging being parcell of the possessions of the warden and Colledge of the soules of all faithfull people deceased at Oxon made in September An dni 1598. An Eliz xl Robte Houenden doctor in divinity then warden. by the measure of xvj foote and an halfe to the pch and according to the proportion of xlvm perches to an ynche. by Tho. Langdon.

Item The tythe of one close called Aberfied conteynynge by estimation xx acres belonging unto Pittynners.

The tythes of the groundes called Nutbeame and Wandle being xl yard landes and rontey by estimation xx acres.

The tyth of one fielde called Pottes close conteyninge by estimation xx acres yvell to Pittyners.

The tyth halfe A yarde lienge in divers parcells called Pottes belongynge unto Pittynes.

The tythes of one other halfe yarde lande called Pottes in the tennis of Mr. Elmes near the east on the east.

The tyth of halfe A yard lande called Pottes neere the same towardes the east in the tennis of the Pottes former belonginge unto Pittyners.

The tyth of Jennynges Stroke westerly with And one other Stroke conteyninge by estimation xx acres.

The tyth of one parcell of ground next Mr. meslyn himself in the fielde here called Home Close on the north parte thone of belonginge to Pittyners.

The tythes of ij other fieldes that ys one called Shane fielde and conteyneth by estimation xx acres, the other called close close and conteyneth by estimation xx acres belonginge to Pittyners.

The tyth of one ground called Hurstfield conteynynge by estimation xx acres and one other close under Lewknors Grove conteyninge xxx acres sometymes in Sherborn close belonginge in the tennis of the parsonage and the tennis of Elmes hedge.

The tyth of the one halfe of Ayers close upon the east of the Sherott belonge beleve the hill and conteyneth by estimation xxx acres belonginge unto Pittyners.

Note that about the hilles with in the Pish of Lewknor afforesaide there are sertaine enclosures of arable and medow grounde The tithes whereof are claymed and possessed by the Lord Edmunde Lane by the name of Lewknor vnder the name of Pittyners tythes as followeth.

Three closes of pasture grounde in the tennis of Edmund Lane whereof one is called Grode Close conteyneth by acres Another is called Shanke fielde and conteyneth x acres, the thyrde is called Myers fielde and conteyneth xx acres.

Two close late Madyves now Mr. Lanes conteyninge thereinto being betweene Shankefielde aforesaide on the southe and the groundes of Bartholmewe Tippinge gent on the north and conteyneth xxx acres.

The tyth of ye close called Aignores conteyninge by estimation xx acres belonginge unto Pittyners.

Also the tyth of one close called Twichen in the tennis of Mr. Bartholmewe Tippinge belonginge unto Pittyners.

Parte of weston fielde

Parte of sherborne Fielde

SOUTHE

Country Estates and Parks

The benefits to the upper classes of economic growth found expression in country houses and parks. The Chilterns attracted a lot of this conspicuous consumption, some originating from local farming wealth, but much also from 'outside money', earned in London trading and business, but spent on a country retreat reasonably close to the City. Hugh Prince has calcu–lated that the Chilterns (including Burnham and Stoke Hundreds in south Buckinghamshire) had 250 parks of 10 acres or more in 1768, covering some 23,000 acres. By 1820 this had risen to a peak of around 600 parks covering 37,800 acres.[32] The Chilterns were attractive both because of their accessibility and also their areas of poorer-quality, cheaper land. Thus the sands and gravels around Burnham attracted numerous square, red-brick residences known as 'London Boxes'.

The Chilterns have country houses from every period and style from the 16th to late 19th centuries. As for the town buildings, stone was expensive here, and brick was the main building material. Warm brick is the most typical style, with some stone detail on the grander houses and flintwork on the lesser buildings. Many of the houses and parks are small-scale, often hidden away and unnoticed until one turns a corner and catches a glimpse through trees of a delightful Queen Anne or Georgian manor house set in its garden or park. After 1650 landscape design became fashionable and parks became more ornamental, rather than for the cultivation of deer. Much of the Chiltern landscape—with its bottoms and hills—was unsuitable for the 'grander design' of parks, but equally did not require it, for there were plenty of sites that gave superb vistas with only limited landscape engineering and planting. We think of the manor house at Dancer's End above Tring, with its view over the Bulbourne Gap, or the three country houses around Turville Heath, each with its own panorama in different directions from the ridge.

The Chilterns has, of course, its share of landscaped parks. Many of the more formal 17th-century gardens have been remodelled, but Edmund Waller's Hall Barn at Beaconsfield, built after 1651, retains much of its long straight walks and formal atmosphere. Later fashions encompassed both Gothic fantasy and classical severity. Both are combined in Sir Francis Dashwood at West Wycombe.

Dashwood is fascinating both as a character and because he put his stamp on so many landscape features still to be seen around West Wycombe.[33] Best remembered through distorted tales of Rabelaisian orgies at the 'Hell-fire Club' in Medmenham and West Wycombe, Sir Francis (1708-81) was a many-sided figure. An active politician who held high office, he was also a traveller who brought back styles and art-objects from Italy and the Mediterranean. At West Wycombe he transformed a plain brick house to Palladian style with stone colonnades and porticos, stuccoing the whole. He dammed the river Wye to create a lake in the shape of a swan, and embellished the grounds with statuary from Italy, temples, and a series of follies visible from the house. The mix of classical, gothic and English features made Benjamin Franklin call it 'a paradise'. Outside the grounds, Dashwood gave local employment by quarrying chalk from West Wycombe Hill and improving the road to High Wycombe. He took the opportunity to create a network of small caves there, still an attraction today. Rebuilding St Lawrence's church in 1763, he heightened the tower and topped it with a golden ball, made of copper. There are small seats in the ball, giving a magnificent view over the countryside. At the same time, with a legacy from a friend, he constructed the hexagonal flint mausoleum on the hill east of the church (Plate 99). The lurid tales of orgies and mock-religious ceremo-nies here and at Medmenham are hard to substantiate, and seem to originate in a political smear campaign by Wilkes and others. The reality of Dashwood's Wycombe remains an imposing but rather weird local landscape, one greatly restored by the present Sir Francis Dashwood.

Other Chiltern parks were created or remodelled by the great 18th-century professional landscape gardeners, Capability Brown and Humphry Repton. Brown's enthusiasm for wide vistas and water was not ideally suited to the Hills, but he worked at Moor Park (near Rickmansworth) for Admiral Anson, at Beechwood near Luton for Sir John Sebright, and at Latimer and Fawley Court.[34] His best local example is probably at Luton Hoo, where he worked in the 1760s for the Earl of Bute. Adding 900 acres of woods and fields to the park, Brown diverted the Luton to Wheathampstead road and created an ornamental lake nearly a quarter of a mile wide. Luton Hoo was typical of Brown's style, but his work for the Duke of Bridgewater on the waterless ridge of Ashridge is less so. Only part of his work remains, in the fine avenues and glades of the section known as Golden Valley.

99. West Wycombe: the church and mausoleum. This aerial view shows the hill dominated by Sir Francis Dashwood's reconstruction of the church and the hexagonal mausoleum he built immediately in front of it.

100. John Blagrave's map of Harpsden in 1586. In contrast to the open fields of Lewknor, this map is of a completely enclosed hedged landscape with each field numbered, its owner shown and each farm's holdings itemised. [ORO: Ms.C.17:49(129).]

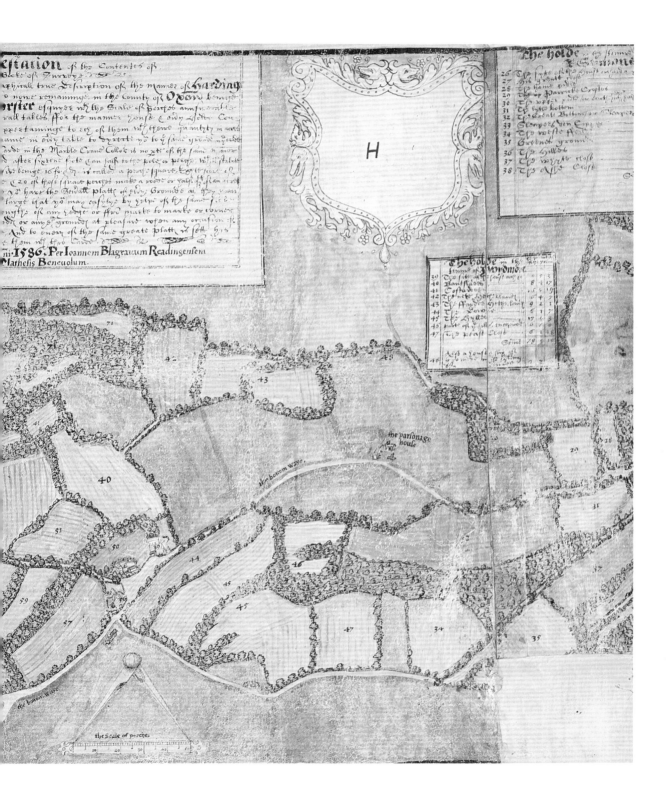

Humphry Repton built on his predecessor's ideas, but his own style drew together more elements of both gardening and landscaping. He favoured banks of trees, rather than Brown's small clumps, and integrated the house and grounds more closely into the local landscape, in a deliberate political statement about the social role of the landowner. Repton worked at several Chiltern estates, including Bulstrode and Stoke Poges.[35] At Shardeloes outside Amersham, he remodelled the water and woodland for William Drake to give the present landscape of wide vistas across the valley from the elegant mansion. At the end of his life he worked on the garden at Ashridge, where his rosery and grotto survive. At West Wycombe in the 1790s he undid some of Francis Dashwood's work, removing some of the statuary and follies and clearing trees to reveal a view of the house. Repton's artistic skills were used in his *Red Books*, sets of watercolour drawings giving 'before and after' scenes that he used to sell his ideas and then presented to his clients. His books on landscape gardening also contain early flip-up illustrations to show his planned changes (Plate 95). Repton's comments on the Chiltern woods give an insight into both his tastes and the pre-1800 nature of the beechwoods:

> The beech woods in Buckinghamshire derive more beauty from the unequal and varied surface of the ground on which they are planted, than from the surface of the woods themselves; because they have generally more the appearance of copses, than of woods; and as few of the trees are suffered to arrive to great size, there is a deficiency of that venerable dignity which a grove always ought to possess.

> These woods are evidently considered rather as objects of profit than of picturesque beauty; and it is a circumstance to be regretted, that pecuniary advantage and ornament are seldom strictly compatible with each other.[36]

Most of these estates and parks have survived to the present day, though often in very different hands. Some are golf clubs (Moor Park), schools (Beechwood Park, Wycombe Abbey) or business colleges (Ashridge), and only a few remain with their original families. But Stonors are still at Stonor and Dashwoods at West Wycombe, though the present generation in both cases has had to fund the renovation and improvement from successful careers in the City and banking.

Chapter Nine

Turnpikes, Canals and Railways

Turnpike Roads

There was an astonishing gap between the end of the Roman period and the mid-1700s when roads with solid foundations were very rarely constructed. Many were simply rights of passage without any recognisable form or definition of purpose, hard and rutted in summer, wet and soggy in winter. The season of the year and the state of the weather became limiting factors in transport, and routeways zigzagged between drier sandy and gravelly soils to avoid the heavier clays, extending journeys and adding to discomforts and delays.

That the system functioned at all is remarkable, but it seems to have done so, until the expansion of business and trade placed it under unsustainable pressure. In 1555 the responsibility of parishes for the upkeep of their roads was formalised (and remained so for minor roads until the County Councils of the 1880s), but this did not work well for the major highways. At this time most goods were moved by pack-horses, singly or in convoys, and some of the old packhorse routes survive because they were bypassed by later improvements. Two such roads in the Chilterns seem to be Collier's Lane, between Stokenchurch and Radnage, and various routes between Henley and Wallingford, such as the 'Pack and Prime'. At Chazey Heath is *The Pack Horse* inn, but there is little documented history to support folk traditions about these roads.[1]

The 17th century saw a big increase in the movement of people and goods, and the old roads became increasingly inadequate. It was most especially the requirements for more wheeled transport—carts, coaches and carriages—which was both cause and effect in the clamour to improve the situation. Stage-coaches and Royal Mail coaches began to run between London and the provinces; coach services from Oxford to London via Stokenchurch and Wycombe began early in Charles II's reign.[2] When Parliament met in Oxford in 1681, the Earl of Shaftesbury noted: 'The road was so full of coaches that there were going down Stokenchurch Hill fourteen coaches and I believe thirty horse at one time'.[3]

Private carriages and wagons began to be used more, and their wheels rutted the surfaces and got bogged down in the mud. Ogilby's *Britannia* (1675), which gave the first detailed instructions on the routes and distances on the roads from London in the form of strip maps, is evidence of this expanding travel, and his technique was much copied in later years (Plate 103).

By 1700 it was clear that new sources of funding were needed for the major routes. The solution was an early form of privatisation, placing the financial burden of road upkeep onto a series of turnpike trusts who would become responsible for the good maintenance of the highways and were authorised by a Parliamentary Turnpike Act to collect tolls.[4] The trustees were no longer local villagers but county gentry often with vested interests in keeping the routes open. They could raise money to carry out improvements usually by mortgaging their future income from tolls.

The map of early turnpikes shows the importance of the capital: it was improving access to this rapidly expanding market that was the principal benefit of the whole system. The roads

101. Milepost at Stokenchurch. Well-hidden on the Beaconsfield-Stokenchurch-Oxford road, it is represented on Davis' 1797 map.

from London to Bristol and the west country (the Great West Road) and to York and Scotland (the Great North Road) outflanked the Chilterns to the south and east, but roads to Oxford, Birmingham and the North-West had to climb over the Hills. A section of Watling Street across the scarp from Dunstable to Hockliffe was turnpiked as early as 1711. Other sections came later, though it is noteworthy how 'patchy' the trusts were, and no single trust looked after the entire length of a major road. A major section of the London-Oxford road via Beaconsfield, Wycombe and Stokenchurch was turnpiked in 1719. The Henley-Oxford road via Bix, Nettlebed and Benson followed in 1736, and the Sparrows Herne trust, linking Aylesbury and Bushey on the present A41 route through Berkhamsted was set up in 1762. Some lesser and cross-country routes were also turnpiked later, such as the Great Marlow-Stokenchurch road

102. Bluebells in spring amongst the high beech trees of the ancient woodland at Ashridge.

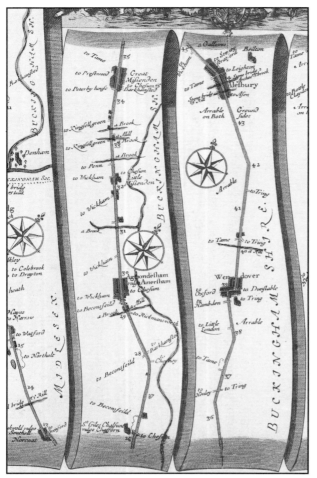

103. Strip map by John Ogilby. Part of the London to Buckingham road giving details of the sections from Chalfont, through Amersham and Wendover to Aylesbury.

in 1791, and the Risborough trust in 1795 following the road from Ellesborough to West Wycombe.

The records of the turnpike trusts provide us with the kinds of task that had to be performed for the upkeep of these highways. The trusts employed 'responsible men' to act as surveyors but they were all amateurs, not the specialist road engineers like Telford and Macadam who were to come later. Their work varied tremendously in quality from place to place. Much of it involved repairing and surfacing the road. Local stones were the most commonly used roadbuilding material, and in the Chilterns this meant flint, which was not an ideal road metal. The flints were brittle and pulverised under the weight of the traffic, producing a thick layer of dust which had to be settled by 'watering' the roads. The Dunstable to Hockcliffe trust mixed the flints with sand because 'it had few stones except flints which ground to powder, but if mixed with sand they cement'.[5] Local travellers however complained that this mixture was loose and heavy. In many cases the flints were not broken down sufficiently beforehand, creating a very rough surface, which Arthur Young described on the Oxfordshire turnpikes as 'calculated for dislocation'.

The turnpike trusts also undertook a programme of re-routing, straightening and widening the roads in order to speed up travel and cope with increased volume. The steep ascents and descents of the Chiltern scarp were difficult and hazardous for coaches and wagons, and needed constant attention. Aston Hill at Stokenchurch was the toughest, and even today the A40 here can be a hard climb. In winter wet, or after one of the intense summer thunderstorms that the Chiltern edge sets off, the road still streams with water, and these north-facing slopes are slow to dry out. The Minute Book of the trust on 2 April 1771 shows that trustees 'ordered that a fence of posts and rails be fixed at the foot of Stokenchurch Hill where the road turns to Aston to prevent accidents'. In 1824 this road was 'found inconvenient' and a new section constructed to be 'more commodious to the public'. The new section is the present A40 descent, whilst the old road survives as a pathway dropping through the tree-clad slopes on the north side (Plate 106).[6] The old *Drum and Plough* inn at the foot of the old road is now a much-rebuilt private house, and its successor, *The Lambert Arms*, stands further along the new road (Plate 107). This same stretch is remembered in a little notebook handwritten in

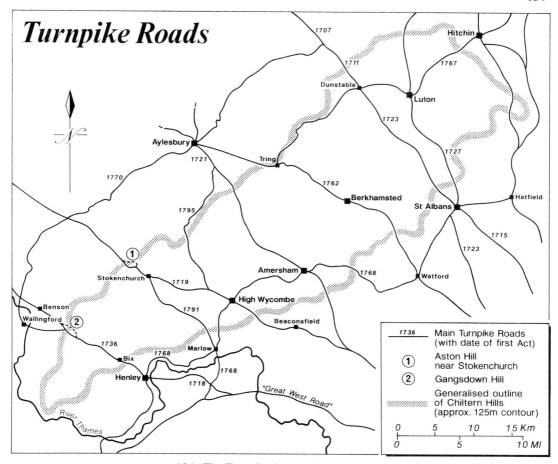

104. The Turnpike Roads of the Chilterns.

pencil by William Bayzard. He was guard on the Mazeppa coach in the 1820s and 1830s and later a janitor at the Radcliffe Camera in Oxford (the notebook is preserved in the Bodleian Library there). He wrote: 'on we go to West Wycombe when a blast to live from the horn and out came our jolly horse and long Jack to give us a pull up a tremendous steep pitch to Stokenchurch ... Change [horses,] put the skid on down Stokenchurch hill very long steep narrow and winding to the "Lambert Arms"—take the skid off and pull up for a glass of that excellent Marlow Beer to Postcombe and Tetworth 42½ miles.'[7]

The Henley-Oxford road also had its difficult stretches, notably the climb from Benson up Harcourt Hill and Gangsdown Hill to Nettlebed. An entry in the *Oxford Journal* for 29 March 1766 reads:

> a bargeman [from Henley?] was bewildered in snow near Harcourt Hill ... and dropped in quite over his head, but had the good fortune to get out again ... Having recovered the road, he found a postchaise which had been left stuck in the snow, and there took up his quarters for the night, which in all probability saved his life.[8]

This line was later rerouted, and again the old road survives as a minor lane and bridlepath. Other turnpikes realigned roads for convenience: the Risborough trust made a new

105. Hornbeam at Herbert's Hole, near Pednor. Hornbeam was frequently used as a hedgerow tree and on woodbanks in the region.

106. The Old Turnpike Road on Stokenchurch Hill. This path through the woods from Stokenchurch to the bottom of the hill was the turnpike road until 1824.

107. *The Lambert Arms* at Lewknor. This inn, now heavily 'Tudorised', was built in the early 1830s as the coaching inn to succeed the old *Drum and Plough*.

114. Railway cuttings in the Chilterns. *Above:* The excavation of Tring railway cutting in 1837 as portrayed by J. C. Bourne in his lithograph. *Below:* Saunderton railway cutting. Excavation methods had not changed greatly when the High Wycombe to Princes Risborough line was upgraded and this cutting was made at Saunderton in 1905.

train as those who had previously travelled by coach or on foot. Those estimates were to prove very conservative because of a social revolution instigated by the railways. Robert Stephenson, who surveyed so much of the Chiltern track, told a select committee on railways on 2 July 1839 that there was 'a class of people who [had] not yet the advantage from the railways which they ought, that is the labouring classes'.[30] By 1844 provision of third-class accommodation at one penny a mile was part of Gladstone's Railway Act and 'people who had never strayed beyond the next town were liberated from the thrall of distance'. The reaction of the upper classes was less than enthusiastic to this new mobility of working men and women. In his novel *Sybil,* Disraeli, who lived in the Chilterns at Hughenden, portrayed the fears and inconsistencies of the members of his class: '... if we nobles do not make a stand against the levelling spirit of the age, I am at a loss to know who will fight the battle. You may depend on it these railways are very dangerous things'.[31] But there was much revenue to be gained and the numbers of third-class passengers increased sixfold between 1849 and 1870 (compared to a fourfold increase in first- and second-class passengers). The initial accommodation may have been spartan but it was infinitely better than sitting outdoors atop a bumpy carriage. It was to improve radically under the 'Apostle of competition', the Midland Railway, which abolished second class altogether in 1874 and then, to the horror of its competitors, upholstered all the seats in the following year. The excursion train gained popularity, especially from the summer of 1851 when the Great Exhibition in Paxton's Crystal Palace provided the opportunity for railways to promote trips for the masses.

The transport of freight by rail immediately challenged both the canal and turnpike trusts. The Grand Junction's main response was a vast reduction in tolls—in three years from 84½d. to 10d. a ton. The canals had their monopoly threatened and prices of fuel dropped as a consequence. The Grand Junction was prompted to improve various sections and it was more aggressive than most in protecting its trade. Similarly, the toll receipts from gates along the turnpikes were halved within a few years of direct competition from the railways. Trains enabled farm produce in particular to be moved for hundreds of miles as cheaply as carrying twenty to thirty miles previously by road. It was to mean the gradual disappearance of the traditional drovers' routes as livestock could now arrive in the market place at the same weight as it left the farm. The new trains were to create a greater demand for milk in the capital— the Aylesbury vale supplied vast quantities of milk especially during the years 1865-66 when cattle plague inflicted huge losses on the urban dairies. The milk vans, which later became known as 'Jersey Lilies', were generally attached to particular passenger trains and the milk was sold on arrival to the London wholesalers for distribution.[32]

The rise of the railway and decline of the turnpike greatly affected many Chiltern towns and villages. The long-distance carriers and coaches were no longer profitable, and the inn trade suffered. Towns on the new railways simply adjusted and grew, but those left off the network or at the end of a minor branch line were hard hit. The gaps in the Chiltern network meant that there were several of these. Henley was now an economic backwater, and its fortunes slumped until the growth of the regatta (which began in 1839) made it a leisure centre in later Victorian times. In the central Chilterns places like Beaconsfield and Amersham lost their long-distance trade, but the lack of a local railway did mean that local coaches and carriers were still needed. The country carrier performed as a vital intermediary between farmers and shopkeepers, and was the most usual means of dispatching bulky parcels and goods to the nearest town or railhead. The reduction in the number of coaches and carriers as a direct consequence of a railway station arriving in a town can be illustrated with a glimpse at the Kelly's *Directory* entries for Chesham. In 1847 there were 14 separate carrying services listed for local destinations and London; by 1891 after Chesham station was opened there were only four of whom G. Caitlin was the only surviving family name. The coach to carry people to and from Watford station before the Chesham line was built awaited the arrival of the 5.30 train from Euston, arriving at Chesham at 8 o'clock in the evening, a full two-and-a-half hours later.

The railways were also to provide opportunities for local employment at a time when the requirement for farm labourers was decreasing. The census return for Princes Risborough in 1881 gives an interesting list of eight railway employees and shows considerable mobility of the workforce: one railwayman came from Maidstone, a clerk came from Scotland, a signalman from Bishopstone and an engine driver from Essex. The other clerk, a platelayer, another signalman and a labourer were all local and almost all of them lived within two streets of the station. But the names of these railwaymen were extracted from long lists of people employed in a variety of occupations which owe very little to the coming of the railways, and the Chilterns did not acquire any major railway towns to rival Wolverton, unless one includes Slough on the GWR in the extreme south. Nowhere in the little towns along the line do we see evidence of an industrial revolution exploding in the Chilterns, with the exception perhaps of the paper mills at Apsley and Nash Mills. While the coalfields and the cities near them were sitting under a pall of factory smoke, the Chilterns remained refreshingly rural. The transport revolution had passed through: turnpikes, canals and railways strode the dominant valleys reducing journey times and costs. But away from these busy thoroughfares there must have been countless rural backwaters that the advances in transport seemed to have passed by. Of course they *had* been affected, but it was to take the 20th century and the motor-car (and bus) to significantly change their world.

115. Horse-drawn 'bus on the Berkhamsted to Chesham Road in the 1880s. This horse 'bus marks the end of an era—passengers from the railway station at Berkhamsted would have a long, slow journey back to Chesham, where the station had not yet opened, and the age of the motor 'bus had yet to arrive.

Chapter Ten

The Chiltern Beechwoods

Introduction

The high beechwoods are the crowning glory of the Chilterns. Captivated by their beauty, it is easy to think of the woods as a natural creation, free of human hand. We have already argued that this is not so. The survival of the Chiltern woodlands, their appearance and ecology, is the result of a long history of management. We have seen that the medieval woods were rather different in appearance to our beechwoods: they were more open and more diverse in species, made up of younger trees, and had much more coppice and underwood. They did not look like today's woods because they were not used in the same way, and it is changes in economic use that lie behind the transformation to today's high beech-forest. The most remarkable and fortunate aspect is that such vast stretches of woodland have survived at all. They may be depleted and altered, having weathered both the medieval onslaught and later changes, but they remain there to grow tall for us to enjoy today. The story of this survival and transformation is an intriguing tale that links the Chiltern woods to the rapid growth of London after 1550 and to the creation of a chair-making industry after this London fuelwood trade collapsed around 1800.

The Thames Wood Trade

The Chilterns wood trade, like the corn trade, was greatly stimulated by the rapid growth of London in the 16th and 17th centuries. Although London was buying vast quantities of the new 'sea-coal' from Newcastle, there was still a rapidly rising demand for wood as domestic and industrial fuel. The rising population also had rising expectations of comfort, and there was much chimney building. The real price of fuelwood rose by 75 per cent between 1540 and 1553.[1] There were sometimes crises of supply, and the City Council had to act. For 16 August 1559 the Patent Rolls note:

> Commission until Christmas next for Thomas Leigh, knight, mayor, and the aldermen of London to provide carriage by water at reasonable rates for 6000 loads of wood stored at Henley, Weybridge and elswhere against the winter, and to take further wood if necessary. The woodmongers restrict the supply to advance the price, and by their consent the said mayor has taken 6000 loads of their store for the use of the city; also the price of water carriage has been unreasonable advanced to more than half of what it was.[2]

Henley was the focus for the Chilterns trade, but did not dominate to the same extent as it did with the corn trade. The high costs of land movement of wood and timber meant that much was handled through many small wharves along the Thames, at Whitchurch and Mapledurham above Henley, and down river at Greenlanes, Mill End, Marlow and Hedsor. The accounts of Thomas West, a trader of Wallingford, for 1572-73 show his wood-sales from wharves between Wallingford and Henley.[3] He sold to the royal household (Queen Elizabeth did not like coal as a domestic fuel), and had difficulty getting payment:

I find that Master Browne and Master Shergent did cawes me to carry 20 loades of talle woode and 10 loades of billetes frome John Melsaides of Mapledorme [Mapledurham] unto the 3 Cranes [wharf] in London. It ys worth 2s 6d or 2s 8d, I trust you will pay 2s 6d. the woode was delivered at the Quene's House. Some ys: £3 15s.

We can get insights into the type and volume of traffic from deeds and probate inventories.[4] In 1677 John Taylor of Henley Park agreed to supply 1,000 loads of billet and stackwood to William Hawkins, a 'woodmonger' of St Margaret's, Westminster for £540, with delivery to the wharf at Greenlanes on the Thames. The 1667 inventory for George Cranfield, a substantial timber merchant of Henley, reveals a diverse trade in billet, hoops and timber suitable for shipbuilding.

The Rawlinson Manuscripts in Oxford contain a volume of papers by the famous 17th-century diarist and Secretary to the Navy Board, Samuel Pepys. Amongst them is a page of c.1688, 'Notes abt [about] Firewood, taken at Henly'. We reproduce it here (Plate 116). He details the different sizes of wood available, and their prices, and adds

my enquiries thereon relate more p'ticularly to beach woode, which is said to burn sooner, clearer, freer from sparkle, and to make a better coale. yt will keep fire longer than those of oake, though oake last longer in ye burning then beach, the measure and price being (as I think they told me) ye same, or near it.

Some, like Robert Plot, thought that this London trade meant that the Chiltern woods did little to relieve the wood shortage of the Vale and lowland Oxfordshire.

The Thames trade was not purely a firewood trade, as George Cranfield's inventory testifies. Daniel Defoe, the author of Robinson Crusoe, recorded in his 1725 Tour of Great Britain that, at Great Marlow:

Here is also brought down a vast quantity of beech wood, which grows in the woods of Buckinghamshire more plentifully than in any other part of England. This is the most useful wood, for some uses, that grows, and without which, the city of London would be put to more difficulty, than for any thing of its kind in the nation.

1. For fellies [wooden wheel-rims] for the great carrs, as they are called, which ply in London streets for carrying of merchandizes, and for cole-carts, dust-carts, and such like sort of voiture, which are not, by the city laws, allowed to draw with shod wheels tyr'd with iron.

2. For billet wood for the king's palaces, and for the plate and flint glass houses, and other such nice purposes.

3. Beech quarters for divers uses, particularly chairmakers, and turnery wares. The quantity of this, brought from hence, is almost incredible, and yet so is the country overgrown with beech in those parts, that it is bought very reasonable, nor is there like to any scarcity of it for time to come.[5]

The Nature and Use of the Woods

The structure of the Chiltern woodlands at this period was little different from that of medieval times, though the management was probably more systematic. To meet the different demands for wood and timber, the woods were mainly 'coppice-with-standards', and the standards were both oak and beech. The different types of firewood—the billet, the stackwood and the faggots—required a range of tree-sizes. Robert Plot commented:

In the Chiltern Country they fell their Under-wood Copices commonly at eight or nine Years Growth, but their Tall-wood, or Copices of which they make tall Shids, Billet Etc. at no certain time; nor fell they these Woods all together, but draw them out as they call it, almost every Year some, according as their Wood comes to be fit Scantling for tall Shids or Billet, cutting every Shid of Tall-wood four Foot long besides at Kerf, and Billet three foot four inches.[6]

123. *The Crooked Billet*, Stoke Row. An old woodland pub up a winding lane north of Stoke Row. Here Silas Saunders had a chair-making workshop attached to the pub.

town became a little industrial centre in its own right, with a strong trade in bowls, brushes, and also the wooden spades that children used to use at the seaside.

Woodland Changes

These changes in the beech wood market after 1800 gradually began to transform the composition and ecology of the Chiltern woodlands. The rapid growth of the chair-making industry kept up the demand for beech after the decline of the large-scale fuelwood trade. Slowly during the 19th century this change began to be reflected in the appearance of the beechwoods. George Peterken suggests that 'perhaps the most interesting conversion from coppice to high forest in Britain occurred in the southern beechwoods'.[31] The village and town 'chair factories' demanded larger, timber trees; these were more economical to transport and would then be sawn up at the workshops. The local turners and woodland bodgers required smaller wood of the billet-type, so there was a complementary demand, met by what became known as the 'Chiltern selection system'. This meant drawing out scattered timber-trees from mixed size woods, whilst smaller wood was thinned and used by bodgers.

This was still a different pattern of demand from the pre-1800 woods. Coppice woods now had a very small market (except as an environment for sporting game), though one exception was the woods around Bix and Nettlebed where the coppice continued to be used to fuel the tile kilns.[32] The growing role of the chair-making factories increased demand for larger timber, and far more trees were left to grow tall and become 'high forest' woodland.

124. Samuel Rockall of Summer Heath. Samuel Rockall is putting the finishing touches to a turned leg on a wheel lathe. In the 1930s, Rockall was one of the last bodgers, and his tradition of craftsmanship was much extolled by H. J. Massingham in his writings of the 1940s.

There is much we still do not understand about the details of the transformation, and it would be interesting to discover a set of estate or business accounts linking the beechwoods with the chair industry. In the early 19th century the chairmaking industry gradually moulded the existing woodlands to its new needs. Where clear-felling and replanting took place, it was to create even-aged, high timber, and here there was a deliberate, and quite long-term investment in 'high-forest'. As the bodgers were squeezed out of business, the Chiltern selection system broke down and a lot of second- and third-rate wood was left to over-mature and degenerate, leaving a legacy of management problems that was apparent by the 1920s. Under the closed canopy of high beech, seedlings failed to regenerate and the ground flora became much more limited than in the traditional woods.

The history of these woodland changes can be read in the trees themselves. A great swathe of mature beechwood was clear-felled at Hailey Wood as the M40 motorway sliced through the Chiltern escarpment at Lewknor. George Peterken of the Nature Conservancy studied the age and ring-growth of the felled beeches.[33] What appeared even-aged in fact ranged over 100 years from 1760-1876 in date. The older trees had narrow growth rings up to about 1851, then spurted and later slowed in pace. For these and other details, Peterken suggests that before 1851 the wood had been repeatedly lightly thinned on the selection system, with regeneration in the gaps. A major thinning in 1851 led to a period of rapid growth, which ceased in about 1876 as the canopy closed and further seedlings failed to survive.

In the 1920s and 1930s the Cambridge ecologist A. S. Watt made a series of classic studies of the Chiltern beechwoods.[34] On the plateau he examined a whole group of woods around Hampden, and found that the approximate age of the high beech forming the canopy was 105-140 years, dating the bulk to 1794-1830. This was true both for the ancient woods named in the Hampden Wood Books like Hampden Coppice and Oaken Grove, and for the 'newer' woods such as Hillock's Wood, enclosed from scrubby 'hill-work' in the early 19th century. This evidence fits with our picture of the decay of fuel-wood coppicing, and woods like Hillocks must have been allowed to grow rapidly to high forest, though multiple leaders suggest some coppicing in the early years. Watt puzzled over whether this plateau beech could be regarded as the natural 'climax community', the natural and stable end of the process of ecological succession. On the thin, chalky soils of the escarpment edge this seemed possible, but he was dubious about the woods on clay-with-flints. There was too little oak, and high beech eventually degenerates the soil: 'the ultimate fate of the beechwoods would be retrogression to heath'. There was, however, no evidence of the latter happening. It is hard, therefore, on ecological grounds to see plateau high beech as 'natural', but the ecological evidence fits very well with the economic and social history of the woodlands.

Chapter Eleven

The 19th-Century Chilterns

Parliamentary Enclosure

If we could have stood on the top of Coombe Hill near Wendover around the year 1800, we would have seen a landscape in transformation. The great canal from London to Birmingham had just been constructed across Tring summit, a branch to Wendover was being built, and the

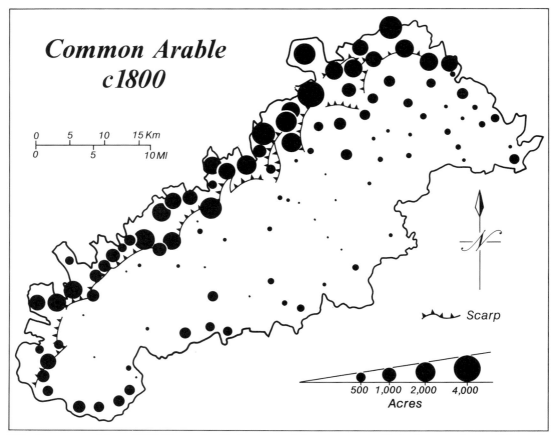

125. Common arable, *c*. 1800. The contrast between surviving common arable in the scarp-foot parishes and along parts of the Thames stands out clearly against the interior of the Hills where most common fields had disappeared much earlier. [Based on Roden, 1965. Note that Roden does not include south-east Buckinghamshire in his Chiltern region.]

land would still have seemed torn and scarred. In the Vale a process of enclosure by Parliamentary Acts was well under way, replacing the open-fields with a new planned landscape of enclosed and hedged fields. The fields of Wendover itself had been enclosed by Act in 1795. The very long-standing contrast of 'champion' and 'woodland' was to be softened by these changes as the new hedges began to green the bare browns of the Vale.

Across the plains and vales of midland England, piecemeal enclosure had made less headway than in the Hills. Enclosure of the big open-field systems had to be root-and-branch or nothing, and getting unanimous agreement of the landowners was virtually impossible. The solution was the process of Parliamentary Enclosure. This involved groups of landowners applying for an Act authorising enclosure, setting up Enclosure Commissioners to look into the details, adjudicate all the claims and make an Award.[1] The shared costs of the process could be high, and many a smallholder found himself with a tiny allocation of land and a bill to pay. Because the Acts were comprehensive they enclosed commons as well as common-fields, and the loss of such rights allegedly finished off many smaller farmers and cottagers. From 1740 onwards a wave of such Acts began to enclose midland England.

By the 1770s such Acts were lapping around the edges of the Chiltern Hills: Aylesbury in 1772 (the date of the Award), Waddesdon (1775), Wendover (1795), Tring (1804). Enclosure was slowest where a substantial group of prosperous landowners and smallholders shared in the open-fields. Getting sufficient support for an Act was difficult. Many of the Chiltern-foot parishes were of just this type, especially along the Icknield Belt all the way from Luton to South Stoke by the Thames. Enclosure came to the Kimbles and Ellesborough in 1805, Saunderton (1807), Marsworth (1811), Bledlow (1812), Aston Clinton (1816), Princes Risborough (1823), Ivinghoe (1825) and Monks Risborough (1839). In Oxfordshire, Watlington's fields were awarded in 1815, as were those of Lewknor. A similar process was also occurring on the other side of the Hills in south-east Buckinghamshire, with enclosure of the remaining open-fields at Iver (1804), Wooburn (1804), Upton (1819) and Farnham Royal (1831).

These Acts and their Awards redrew the landscape, with rectangular fields and new farms away from the village centres, what Oliver Rackham calls 'Planned Countryside'. At Lewknor today we can still see many of the hedged fields that were made (though some of the fields have since been re-amalgamated). The Award here allocated 1,800 acres, 1,550 former arable and meadow. Nine landholders received allocations, varying from 45 acres to over 400 for the lord of the manor and for All Souls College. As well as Church Farm, the College now held the new Field Farm (119 acres) on the Shirburn Road, and Hill Farm (also known as Linky Downs) on 260 acres of old sheep-walk and hill-land.[2] Parliamentary enclosure did not completely erase all signs of the previous system. From the escarpment slopes above Hill Farm one can look down on this 'new' rectangular layout of fields, and within it one can still trace survivals of the old open-fields. There is no neat ridge-and-furrow, for this was never very pronounced at Lewknor. Arthur Young wrote in 1813: 'In Aston and Lewknor fields ... the ridges broad, and very little arched; some nearly flat'.[3] But some old furlongs survive. Off the Weston road, just past the moated Moor Court, is a public footpath on the left. It is the old Lower Icknield Way, marked on the 1598 map, which takes you down to the Shirburn boundary. It is a dead-end, for beyond the boundary the old right of way has been extinguished, and this path will surely lapse in time. At the very end, to one's left, is a field running up the boundary to Field Farm and the B4009: this is the old 'Preste Furlonge' of alternating glebe and manor strips coloured on Langdon's map.

Some of the Chiltern-foot open-fields took an unconscionable time to die. They lingered on past the canal age and well into the railway age, and some are amongst the last Acts in the whole country. The Great Western Railway had cut through South Stoke village more than

126. Map of Stokenchurch and Lewknor, 1797. This extract from Richard Davis' very detailed map of Oxfordshire brings out the striking difference between the wooded and enclosed Chiltern country above the scarp, and the open, hedgeless Vale below. This contrast, probably at its most marked when Davis surveyed, was about to disappear. Lewknor was enclosed within 20 years in 1815. The accuracy of the Davis map is remarkable, but his hedged enclosures are somewhat 'conventional' in shape, and the reality was much less rectangular. Note also the commons and the turnpike milestones. [Bodleian: C.17:49.al.]

ten years before the 1,750 acres of open-fields, still made up of very scattered strips, were enclosed by an Award of 1853. At Crowell the little Watlington branch railway ran through the small open-fields there for 10 years before enclosure in 1882. In the north large open-fields lasted at Pitstone, Cheddington and Edlesborough into the 1850s and '60s, and at Totternhoe 1,717 acres were awarded as late as 1891. There the essentially medieval system is only a century away from us.

In one or two cases disputes and opposition to enclosure allow us to get a glimpse of the issues involved. In both Princes Risborough and Monks Risborough there were disputes that are well documented.[4] At Monks Risborough the Earl of Buckinghamshire (of Great Hampden House) was the leading landowner, and he applied for an Act of enclosure in 1830. The common waste on the Chiltern hillside proved the source of dispute—300 acres used for grazing and for fuel by the poor. A counter-petition came from four smallholders and another from the poor of the village. His lordship's agent argued that opposition was being led by those who abused their common rights, cutting wood not just for themselves, but to sell to commoners who lived too distant to collect their own. The Act was eventually passed, but with a unique clause appointing a special commissioner for the poor. The Earl was informed: 'Sir John Dashwood King is appointed Commissioner for the poor, it is a matter of no consequence he is a blundering blockhead and in fact will not trouble himself about the matter'. Sir John was, however, more active than anticipated, and it took until 1839 to get final agreement.[5]

In these Chiltern-and-Vale strip-parishes, such as Monks Risborough, the enclosure of open-fields affected lands at the scarp-foot in the Vale. The commons, wastes, and 'hill-works' allocated in the various Awards lay on the Chiltern scarp sides and summit. After the Awards some of these commons were enclosed and converted into farms and fields. Hill Farm in Lewknor is one example, and in Princes Risborough parts of Risborough Hillock near Lacey Green were enclosed into fields. Some land on the plateau top was fenced and converted to high forest, as at Hillock Wood in Monks Risborough. Some of the steepest or least desirable slopes were left open and somewhat neglected, to be reclaimed by scrub, juniper and expanding woodland. Reduced grazing pressure later in the century added to this last category, and parts of the scarp line put on a more wooded overcoat.

The parliamentary enclosure waves also ran over the residual open-fields that had hung on within the Chilterns themselves. In 1802, 500 acres in Kings Walden were awarded. The largest was at Amersham in 1816, affecting over 900 acres, but most were much smaller scale, such as the 61 acres at Chalfont St Peter in 1847 that comprised Latchmore Field. At Little Gaddesden in 1836 it was the last 52 acres which were enclosed. The 19th-century tithe maps also revealed tiny blocks of common strips that had survived like dinosaurs of some former age, and which were extinguished by private agreement during the century. Within the Hills there was, however, an important category of late Parliamentary Enclosure. This was the commons and heaths, which deserve their own discussion.

The Chiltern Commons and Heaths

The piecemeal enclosure within the Hills after 1550 had not destroyed the major heaths and commons. They had been nibbled at and eroded in places, mostly small-scale but ranging up to the 300 acres taken from Berkhamsted Frith in 1616. Late 18th-century maps, like Davis' of Oxfordshire, demonstrate the sharp contrast of open Vale and enclosed Chiltern, but they also show the large areas of common surviving within the Hills (Plate 126). They included Wycombe and Holmer Heath, Naphill Common, Prestwood Common, Stokenchurch and Chequers Commons. In the Hertfordshire Chilterns there were commons at Berkhamsted, Wigginton and Cholesbury; in Oxfordshire there were heaths at Goring, Checkendon, Chazey and Ipsden, and such lists could be extended.

It is worth casting back in time to look at the role of these commons and heaths in the life and economy of the Chilterns. Many were on patches of the least fertile soils, such as outliers of Reading Beds and Plateau Gravels, with mixtures of sands, gravels and clays. Some had their own perched water tables. These commons provided rough grazing and fuel. Some were wooded, but others, especially in the north, had been so heavily used that they had very few trees or bushes left. Kalm described the furze only four inches high on Ivinghoe Common being cut by boys with scythes and bound into bundles for fuel. They also provided a safety-valve, a place where those without landholding could sometimes find a perch and scrape a livelihood. Here also industries like brick-making and tile and pottery kilns were located, making use of the local clays and sands, and wood fuel. Nettlebed Common provided quite

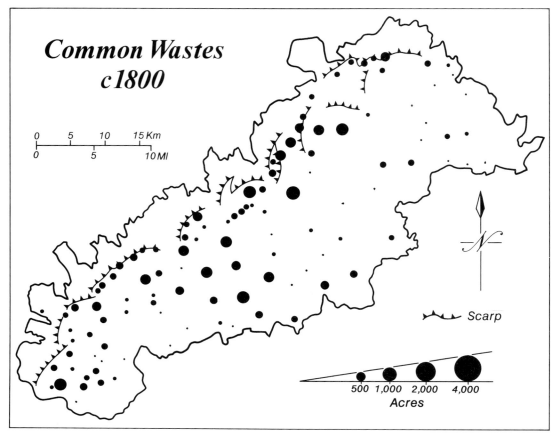

Common Wastes c1800

0   5   10   15 Km

0   5   10 MI

Scarp

500 1,000 2,000 4,000

Acres

127. Common wastes, *c*.1800. Many commons and heaths survived within the Chilterns at this date, and waited until Parliamentary Acts enclosed them after 1845. Many have survived to this day. [Based on Roden, 1965.]

an industrial scene over many centuries, with claypits, waterpools, brickyards and tilekilns. In 1851 William Thompson of Nettlebed, brickmaker and potter, employed 30 men and 25 boys, and Thomas Hobbs employed 10 men and two boys there.[6] The last kilns closed in 1927, but tramways, pools, pits and a kiln can still be seen in Nettlebed (Plate 128). Russell's Water takes its present name from the Russell family of brick-makers, and Russell's kiln occurs in a Stonor rent account for 1695. The pool of the brick-works and an old kiln house of brick remain there today.

The edges of such commons attracted cottages and 'encroachments'. Some individuals had legitimate rights, others squatted. Some were locals, others migrated from parishes where such havens did not exist at all. It may be an illusion produced by our random discovery of references, but cottage encroachments seem most active in the early 17th and 19th centuries, and the Chilterns may have attracted migrants from the less hospitable Vale country. Such encroachments were usually fined, but often allowed to remain, and later 'quit rents' sometimes have their origin in such fines. The early 17th-century court rolls for Cholesbury contain several such entries, and several houses facing the Common today have their origin in these encroachments (Plate 129).[7]

By Queen Victoria's reign these commons were seen as targets by improving and profit-minded landowners. They were quick to catalogue abuses. In Hughenden in 1846 John Cartwright of Piggott's Farm was reporting to Edward Grubb, a London-based land entrepreneur: William Smith was 'cutting stone on Denner Hill Common'; Amos Tree was 'not filling all his stone holes up in Sprion Coppis'; and Cartwright asked, 'whether I should summon Morris Hearn son and daughter for cutting two beech trees in Sprion Coppis'.[8] In February 1852 the Rector of Radnage, a George Phillimore, was writing to the lord of the manor (in this case the Dean and Chapter of St George's, Windsor):

> Radnage common consists of 100 acres and upon this constant encroachments are made, frequently by parties who have no right of common whatever, who after a time, if not interfered with, have a legal right to the property to Inclose ... The same remark applies to other waste lands by the roadside, where houses have been built by parties not connected with this parish.[9]

128. The kiln at Nettlebed. This relic of 19th-century tile and pottery making in Nettlebed towers above a small cul-de-sac of modern housing.

The result was enclosure of many of the commons by the General Acts of 1845 onwards. Over 2,000 acres of Penn, Wycombe and Holmer Heath was awarded in 1855; 700 acres at Stokenchurch Common in 1861; 259 acres at Wigginton in 1854. Radnage and Andridge Commons were awarded in 1862, and Denner Hill (as part of Hughenden) in 1855. Some of this land was parcelled up and divided into fields, giving us patches of geometric field boundaries in the midst of the older Chiltern enclosures. Perhaps the two best examples are at Holmer Green, north of High Wycombe, and south of Wigginton. They stand out beautifully on the larger scale 2½ inch Ordnance Survey maps showing field boundaries, and at Wigginton a post-enclosure road across the former common runs in a straight line for two miles past the Champneys Health Resort. Not all the common land was actually enclosed. The ancient commons were often on poor soils, and even in the 19th century they were not worth farming. In several cases only the edges were fenced off and divided. At Naphill Common in Hughenden parish, sections on the north-east side were taken away, but most was left to revert to scrub and wood as grazing ceased, so that today we can discover pollards from the old common hidden amongst the later tall trees. Others found their fate as poor quality land available for later housing developments. The outline of modern, urban Prestwood fits almost perfectly into the old form of the common. Similarly the houses and estates of Hazlemere, Widmer End, Holmer Green and Great Kingshill follow closely the outlines of the 19th-century heath.

129. A 17th-century cottage on Cholesbury Common. This is one of the cottages mentioned in the 17th-century Court Rolls containing entries about building and encroachments on the common.

Many pieces of heath and common—even if not legally 'common'—have come down to us today.[10] That at Wheeler End, west of Wycombe and between the M40 and A40, is a good example of the sort of small common most Chiltern villages used to have. Larger pieces, like Naphill, have become overgrown, returning to scrub and woodland or to bracken and furze. Some were only preserved after dispute or public action. At Berkhamsted there were nearly 1,200 acres of common to the north of the town. In 1865 Lord Brownlow bought out the rights of many tenants and enclosed part of the area by five-foot iron railings. But he reckoned without Augustus Smith of Ashlyns, who had not sold his rights to the common: Smith brought in 120 men from London to pull down the three miles of railings, and eventually defeated Brownlow in the courts.[11] At Burnham Beeches in the south-east Chilterns the Corporation of the City of London bought the land in 1880 to preserve the old grazed common with its fine pollards as a public space.

Cottage industries: lace-making and straw-plaiting

Before mechanisation and the necessities of industrial discipline drove production into urban factories, much manufacturing was based in the countryside as rural crafts and cottage industries. Some, like the blacksmith and the carpenter, were found in almost every village as full-time occupations. Some were localised because they were tied to particular resources—like the brick and tile-making and the wood-bodging industries of the Chilterns. Others also grew up in a strongly regional pattern, but without the tie to natural resources. The agricultural historian Joan Thirsk has suggested that there was a strong association between wood-pasture regions and rural industries such as cloth-making.[12] Pastoral farming left men with time to take on secondary jobs such as weaving, whereas arable farming was more demanding the whole year round. As we have seen, the Chilterns were very much an arable rather than pastoral region, and they did not develop such cottage industries, although some writers have instinctively placed the woody Chilterns with such wood-pasture regions as the Weald and the Forest of Arden.

Yet the Chiltern counties did become centres for two cottage industries: lace-making and straw-plaiting. Starting slowly in the 17th century, they created a quiet revolution in employment, very different from the usual clatter of industry, and rose to a zenith in the 19th century when they employed tens of thousands across the counties and dominated many local communities. The employees were mostly women and children, many the wives and families of agricultural workers who were earning meagre incomes. In the Hills, at places like Stokenchurch, they were wives of chair-makers (Plate 130). It was rural poverty which the lace-making and straw-plaiting areas held in common: this transcended other boundaries of Chiltern and Vale, enclosures and open fields, arable and pasture.

To understand this rural employment, it is worth stepping back from the 19th century to examine their origins and growth. Both lace-making and straw-plaiting gave families the opportunity to supplement earnings. The opportunity arose from the extravagant tastes which had sprung from the Renaissance, and became popular in Elizabethan and 17th-century England.

130. Extract from the 1871 Census Enumerator's Return for Stokenchurch. These entries for houses on the village green show families of chair-makers and lace-makers, such as the Deans: James (46) and his son George (15) are chair-makers, whilst his wife Sarah (43) and daughter Clara (9) are lace-makers. [PRO: RG/10/14606/4lb, 4.]

Contemporary fashions, most of which emanated from Italy, meant that lace edgings and later straw hats and bonnets were *de rigueur* and the women and children who made them were perhaps to give new meaning to the term 'slaves to fashion'. Rising incomes and population expanded the demand for such goods, and when both industries were at their height the women and children could earn much more than they would in either of the viable alternatives of agricultural work or domestic service. It also gained the women greater independence than was usual at that time. We see several instances of wives and families supporting unemployed husbands. The two industries had much in common, both in their geography and their organisation with cottage out-workers and 'schools', but each also had its own distinctive history.

Lace-making

English lace-making seems to have begun in the late 16th century, around the time when (in 1590) Sir Francis Bacon commented: 'Our English dames are much given to wearing costly laces', with most coming from Flanders, Italy and France. The location of English lace-making is traditionally ascribed to refugee Flemings and Huguenots settling in our region. This may have played a part, but there is little real evidence, and the early localities are quite scattered.[13] The earliest reference is for Eaton Socon (in north-east Bedfordshire) in 1596, when the authorities agreed to pay 'the woman that teacheth the pore chilren to worck bone lace ...'. The lace-making region came to span four local counties: Bedfordshire, Buckinghamshire, Oxfordshire and Northamptonshire. In Buckinghamshire centres became established at Olney, Aylesbury and High Wycombe where lace-makers are recorded to be in distress in 1623. In Marlow in 1625 Sir Henry Borlase established a school for 24 boys and 24 girls where the girls were taught lace-making. The industry expanded over the border into Oxfordshire, where it became particularly important around Chinnor, Stokenchurch and Henley.

The early references to 'Bone lace' were so called because it was first made using bone bobbins. It later became known as pillow lace because the lace-maker used a large stuffed cushion on her knees to support her work. She attached her pattern (pricked out on parchment) to the cushion, using pins through the small holes. The threads were looped around the pins with a bobbin on each end and the pattern was worked diagonally by twisting and crossing the threads using the bobbins in groups and adding new pins as each line grew. It was a skilled and laborious process not easily learnt or transferred. This helps to explain why it became so localised, and why lace-villages could co-exist with neighbouring communities where the skills were unknown.

The driving force in lace fashions was the tastes of the royal court and the wealthy. Changing and extravagant fashions in lace continued. The reigns of Charles II through to William and Mary showed lace cravats at the height of fashion, and the petticoats of the ladies of King Charles's court were noticed and recorded by Samuel Pepys, who writes in 1663 of a visit to White Hall Gardens: 'And in the privy garden saw the finest smocks and linnen petticoats of my Lady Castlemaine's, laced with rich lace at the bottom, that I ever saw; and it did me good to look at them'.[14] Fanciful lace fashions remained popular with the rich. The *Spectator* was soon deploring 'Childish Gewgaws, Ribbands and Bone Lace' and thought a woman wearing the latest lace gowns and high head-dresses with lace frills and flounces resembled 'a Friesland hen'. More important for the growth of the lace industry was the spread of lace-wearing to a much wider social range as part of the emergence of a consumer goods market. Daniel Defoe's Country Grocer's wife (1727) bought 'her Lace and Edgings from Stony Stratford the first and Great Marlow the last'.[15] The growing market was not, however, a very stable one, for the lace-maker had to keep up with the vagaries of fashion, constantly competing with continental designs. She also had to contend with very uncertain national policies on protection against foreign imports.

Just how many were employed at this time is difficult to assess; we only get reliable information much later with the 1851 Census. All we can say for certain is that the numbers were large and the impact on local communities quite substantial. Because women and children were the main workers, records tend to neglect the industry, and comments are sometimes patronising or slighting. Langley in his *History of the Hundred of Desborough* (1797) says, 'The lace manufactory, for which this county has long been celebrated, employs a great number of females. But from the general appearance of the peasantry, the trade does not induce the habits of neatness and industry which appear highly necessary to render an occupation beneficial to a county.'[16] Such stuffy and largely derisory remarks by middle- and upper-class gentlemen colour much of the literature and must be swallowed with the customary dose of salt!

Our best information records not the female and child lace-makers, but the lace-dealers and wholesalers who were normally men.[17] William Statham of Great Missenden died in 1685, leaving his household goods to his wife, 'excepting and other than my stock of lace silk thread and other things belonging to and concerning my trade and calling of lacebuyer'. One prominent local lace merchant was Ferdinando Shrimpton of Penn, who kept several hundred workers constantly employed, and was eight times Mayor of Chepping (High) Wycombe. He was one of many dealers and wholesalers who travelled to the London markets at Aldersgate, and was instrumental in gaining wholesaling status for the lace merchants so that they were not deemed hawkers or pedlars. The 1717 petition states that, 'The wholesalemen travel weekly to London, where they sell their lace and buy thread and silk which they bring home and deliver to their workwomen who by their directions work or weave it into several sorts of lace, as their respective masters direct, which when done, the workwomen deliver to their respective masters who can pay them what they earn'.

The lace-makers were wholly reliant on the buyers for their threads (which had to be imported from Holland and were expensive) and more importantly for their patterns. It was in this way that the merchants controlled their monopoly: all lace worked on a pattern supplied by a buyer must be sold back to him. The relationship allowed considerable exploitation of the workers, both in the selling of the threads and the prices paid for the finished lace. Translating designs into working patterns was the most difficult task and fashions for lace were constantly changing. From the late 1770s point ground lace with patterns copied from Lille or Mechlin was the staple pillow lace usually used for edgings, and large quantities were exported to the United States until the start of the American Civil War. The softer and lighter fabrics which were being worn in place of the stiff, heavy silks required simpler and less intricately woven lace and the local designs showed a light meshed background (the point) scattered with small sprigs. In the early 19th century Regency point lace was in vogue, and the frills and flounces of the wider skirts were trimmed in blond or black lace. Buckinghamshire black lace was renowned and highly esteemed. Local laces were displayed at the Great Exhibition in 1851, and this gave the industry a welcome boost by introducing Maltese guipure lace made of thread and silk. This style became very popular and it seriously undermined the older forms of Buckinghamshire lace.

Lace-makers tended to start learning their craft at a very tender age (five or six years old was quite normal) and to work for extremely long hours. The early apprenticeship was generally in a 'school' where they would work under the watchful eye of a formidable matron for anything up to 11 hours a day, and the children paid 2d. or 3d. to attend each week. Lace-making required considerable skill and instruction with the children bent over the bulky pillow

131. The lace-maker. An elderly lace-maker sitting at her cottage doorway in Princes Risborough, working on her lace with the parchment-pattern fixed to her lace pillow.

for hours on end. Incentives came at the end of a big stick and special rhymes and tales were recited to reduce the tedium.[18]

Lace employment in the Chiltern counties probably peaked during the French wars, but there are no reliable figures before the 1851 Census. This records 17,991 for Bedfordshire, Buckinghamshire and Oxfordshire. The industry was threatened by machine-made lace, and prices and incomes fell. It proved difficult to maintain quality through the out-worker system. Lace-dealing was becoming concentrated in fewer hands and Thomas Gilbert of High Wycombe claimed to employ 3,000 in 1862, but this meant less frequent contact and supervision of pattern and quality. Old, worn patterns were used, innovation was less, and there was much 'pirating', with lace being sold by poor workers in short 'cut-offs' to meet immediate bills.

A few lace merchants tried to fight the decline. James Millward of Olney advocated copyright patents for designs, and Thomas Lester of Bedford argued that it was the lack of a school of designs which was effecting the decline of the industry. Lester successfully made the transition to Maltese lace, and his new designs helped to keep the Bedfordshire lace-workers employed for longer than otherwise.[19] Even he could not reverse the tide of machine production, and he only delayed the death of the cottage industry. By the 1870s even Maltese guipures were being produced by machine, and a commentator at the Chicago Exhibition in 1893 noted that the 'Coarser pillow laces from Buckinghamshire ... can never compete with the machine made lace, the resemblance being so close in all points except price'.

The problems in the industry were reflected in the Census: in 1881 only 9,520 lace-makers were recorded in the three counties. By 1891 it had dropped to a mere 2,672 and almost all of those were middle-aged or older. Long after the eleventh hour the government sent A. S. Cole to visit the region with a view to salvaging practical lace-making by concentrating on design. However, his conclusion was that 'Commercial influence is insufficient to foster the higher possibilities of lace making'.[20] He noted that in the appropriately named Chiltern village of Lacey Green, there were several very old, perfect and superior patterns in the hands of the village dealer, a Mrs. Forrester, which had never been worked because the purchasers 'will not wait to get a length' and the lace-makers were making quicker and simpler designs. It was left to the local nobility, distressed at the effect the decline was having on the poor in their neighbourhoods, to set up Lace Associations to collect and sell lace at a better price than they would get from the dealers. They collected patterns and revived interest in point ground lace but their efforts were to little avail and the industry shrank to almost nothing. However, a little vestige remained dormant until the 1950s, when an entirely new generation, with time to spare and the will to learn, started an enthusiastic craft pursuit. Today residential courses are held in Missenden Abbey, a far cry from the lace-makers of whom Cowper wrote:

> Yon cottager, who weaves at her own door,
> Pillow and bobbins all her little store;
> Content though mean, and cheerful if not gay,
> Shuffling her threads about the livelong day:
> Just earns a scanty pittance, and at night
> Lies down secure, her heart and pocket light.

Straw-plaiting

In the 17th and 18th centuries hats and bonnets were as essential a part of fashionable dress as lace-edged collars, cuffs and handkerchiefs. Straw-plaiting was already an industry around Dunstable in 1689 when a group of villages (including Edlesborough, Studham, Great Gaddesden and Flamstead) joined Dunstable and Luton to protest against proposed laws to enforce the wearing of woollen hats, claiming 'near a thousand families' depended on the straw-hat trade.[21] One of the reasons for the establishment of the straw-plaiting industry in this region may have been connected to the availability of a wheat straw that was 'best adapted in colour and texture'. It needed to be soft and pliable and the thin Chilterns' soils produced these easily worked straws in abundance. The fashion for straw-hats almost certainly spread from Italy where the Leghorn (Livorno) district produced very fine pale straw which was plaited and made into hats that were exported to England in ever increasing numbers. The numbers give an impression of the expanding consumer market: 17,117 imported in 1721, but 477,024 in 1760.

The straw-plaiting and lace-making regions overlapped, but the two were not coincident; by the early 19th century straw-plaiting extended further eastwards into Hertfordshire and Essex and did not drift northwards beyond the Ouse. The centre of the industry was first in Dunstable but later moved to Luton. It was very extensive with centres like those at Ivinghoe, Amersham and Tring and deep into traditional lace-making country at High Wycombe and Aylesbury where women switched crafts when demands for lace decreased and more money could be earned by plaiting straw and sewing bonnets. Gibbs in his *History of Aylesbury* (1885) confirms that: 'The fashion of wearing Dunstable straw hats had established itself, and many persons abandoned the working of pillow lace ... and betook themselves to straw plaiting, finishing and bleaching as a more profitable employment.'[22]

Straw-plaiting had a real boost while the French wars were being fought (1793-1815) and foreign plaits were not being imported. The quality of British manufacture was improved dramatically when a little device for splitting straws became widely available sometime around 1815, enabling much finer straw plait to be made. Numbers employed reached their peak in the 1871 Census when 45,179 female plaiters were counted. These Census figures are under-estimates because of part-time workers not declaring their occupations to the enumerators. The Children's Employment Commission of 1862 suggests higher numbers, varying between 50,000 and 100,000 depending on whether trade was good or bad. These figures exclude all those that were given employment besides those who plait and make hats and bonnets: 'bleachers, cutters, dyers, flatters, stringers, drawers etc', according to Gibbs. We do know that the craft all-pervaded some of the communities involved. Laszlo Grof has made a marvellously detailed

132. Hitchin plait market in the late 19th century, showing a hive of activity as women buy straw and sell finished plait.

study of Edlesborough, where over half the female population was employed in straw-plaiting in 1851: 459 out of 824.[23] At nearby Ivinghoe, the proportion was similar (275 out of 456 in 1871), and Pamela Horn has noted that these proportions are comparable to the figures for cotton employment in the industrial towns of Lancashire. Places like Ivinghoe were miniature 'industrial communities'.[24] James Greenwood in *On the Tramp* (1883) describes the scene in Hitchin (Plate 132) which was one of the larger plaiting centres and typical: 'Dozens and dozens of them, little girls, big girls, buxom matrons and dames bent and grey ... They moved among the men and lads laughing and larking, but never for a moment staying the movement of their nimble fingers'.[25]

How much they earned depended on how fast they could work and how complicated the pattern was. Like lace-making, there were a great many variations with each village having three or four patterns to which it became accustomed. We get a measure of the wealth of variety in the Stock Book of Henry Horn, a local dealer who carried 137 different kinds of plait in stock in the mid-1880s. His book, now in Luton Museum, shows how seasonal the work was, with the numbers of outworkers lowest after the harvest in August to October and then building up for the spring, when the ladies purchased their new Easter bonnets.[26] The adult plaiters in the 1870s could earn as much as 12s. a week doing 20 yards a day (though this was well above the average) and a child could add a further 6d. a day. Unlike the lace-makers,

133. Gray and Horn's stall on Luton plait market. This shows the variety of types of plait that were made.

whose mobility was restricted by their bulky pillow, the plaiters could work on the hoof almost continously, tucking their cut straw lengths under one arm, their semi-finished plait looped over it, and completing their one-woman band with a few split straws in their mouth being softened ready to work. The wages compared well with those of the average agricultural labourer who brought home around 13s. to 14s. a week.

There were inevitable consequences that stemmed from the long hours that women and children worked and also from the unusual degree of independence that straw-plaiting created in these starchy Victorian times. The bounds of respectability were stretched to breaking point and the women were reputed to be slovenly housewives, 'utterly ignorant of such common things as keeping their houses clean, minding their children's clothes and cooking their husband's dinners'. Worse still were the insinuations about their loose moral standards, some of which were said to be invited by their predilection for pretty clothes. The evidence does not substantiate what David Thorburn refers to as their 'supposed want of chastity and lascivious escapades' and he suggests that most were exaggerated stories.[27] Similarly Laszlo Grof fails to discover the untold numbers of unwed women and illegitimate children in Edlesborough that the diatribes of the Vicar of Toddington would have us believe were harboured in the straw-plaiting villages.[28] But observations as to the literacy, or lack of it, that the Vicar and others made about the women and children in these areas are borne out in parish registers, where few brides could sign their names and female literacy here lagged behind the rest of the country.

This was a consequence of the straw-plaiting schools, where children learned the craft but not their ABC. The plait schools were like those for lace, but often larger and in cramped conditions. We learn a great deal about these establishments from the evidence given to the Children's Employment Commission in 1864. Mrs. Wimbush's Straw-Plait School in Northchurch was typical—a room just over ten feet square with a low ceiling in which were squashed between forty and sixty children between the ages of four and fourteen. There was no fire in winter because it was essential to keep the work clean, so children brought their 'chaddy pots' filled with hot embers to keep their hands warm enough to plait, making the air close, heavy and smelly. At Mrs. Wimbush's, the Commission recorded: 'Sarah Wellin, age eight. Have been here since five years old. Did three score (yards) yesterday, 2½ of them at home after work at school. Do not know how much mother gets for my plait. Do not know A or B; go to Sunday school'.[29] Sixty yards is a huge amount for a little girl, and one suspects some exaggeration or miscounting here. The 1867 Workshops Regulation Act tried to ban all child labour under eight years, and only allowed 'half-time' for 8-13 year olds, whilst the 1870 Education Act was the first step in a long battle to ensure that children attended elementary school for at least 10 hours a week. Plait and lace children tended to become reluctant 'half-timers', but their attendance was often appalling and reflected their split loyalties. The Rev. A. Birch summed up the parents' dilemma: 'Plait means bread ... dearer than knowledge'. Improvements resulted less from the implementation of the Act than the collapse of the cottage industries in the last decades of the century.

The decline of straw-plaiting came quickly in the period after 1870. Change was largely brought about by cheap foreign competition from new and distant sources. The new Chinese plait sold at 7d. for 120 yards, compared with English plait which sold at 6¾d. for only 20 yards. Even the superior Italian plait was cheaper at 8d. for 50 yards. The result was that although the plait halls of Luton remained the 'Emporium for the World', by 1893 less than five per cent of the plait sold was English. The introduction of the sewing machine in 1874 meant that women could earn more by machining foreign plaits, their English equivalents being too short to machine. The price paid to the plaiters fell drastically, leaving the women 'plaiting eternally

134. Hat boxes at Luton station. These boxes are all filled with hats awaiting shipment by rail to the London market. The picture gives some idea of the scale of the hat industry in the early part of this century, and the industry is the source of the nickname for Luton Town football club, 'The Hatters'.

from morn till night, for a wage of about 1s 3d a week'. The manufacturers maintained that, just as with the lace industry: ' If the English plaiters would invent new designs and imitate new patterns for which there is a demand they could obtain good earnings'. But they could not or would not, and as a consequence many were forced to give up. The lucky ones who lived in the chair-making regions changed to chair-caning and some learned tambour beading. These remain within living memory: reminiscences in *A Pattern of Hundreds* include those of a resident of Stokenchurch who remembers women sitting at their front doors with a bundle of canes hanging from a nail, caning chairs for which they were paid 2d. a chair. In Lacey Green Mrs. Adams can remember sitting up all night with three others beading a dress for the theatre.[30]

    Some workers found jobs in the factories in Luton where hat-making became an industrial occupation rather than a rural craft, and machinery replaced the hand craftsmanship of the home-worker. Other straw-plaiters returned to a pittance in the fields, or more often joined their families in the drift to the cities for new lives and new occupations. The era of the rural craft industry was waning and old ladies who could remember their patterns were all that remained of skills that had involved long hours for no great reward, but had brushed increased prosperity into so many households, before being swept away in the name of progress.

High Farming and Depression

The two decades after 1850 marked the high tide for traditional Chilterns arable farming. Corn was profitable, and farmers and landlords were doing well, even if their labourers remained badly paid. Most farmers followed the traditional four-course rotation, either by choice or because of restrictions on their leases. High output required much labour: farms in Watlington parish such as Lower Greenfield, Watcombe Manor and Dame Alice, all between 275 and 350 acres, employed 11 to 18 farmhands each.[31] There was investment in improving efficiency, and much chalk was dug out of pits in the fields to fertilise the clay topsoil. Many of the hollows or 'dell-holes' in Chiltern fields date from these years. Hedges were grubbed up to create larger fields, and in some Chiltern valleys more hedgerow destruction can be dated to these Victorians than to modern wheat-barons. Peter Casselden's detailed study of the Pednor district shows the loss of over 16,000 yards of hedgerow between 1843 and 1873, representing over 21 per cent of all the internal field-hedges.[32]

Water supply remained a persistent problem in many parts of the Hills, and these years saw many attempts at digging wells to provide upland farms and villages with a reliable and clean supply. For many homes the only sources were the local pond, and rainwater collected from the tiled roof into a tank. Stokenchurch was one village in this category. It suffered from persistent water-shortages in the summer months, when water had to be brought by horse-drawn wagons up Aston Hill from Lewknor. In 1870 the two leading landowners financed the digging of a well for the village. The water-table was not reached until a depth of 360 feet (110 metres).[33] Such depths were common on the Chiltern plateau: the Maharajah's Well at Stoke Row (Plate 135) reached water at 365 feet.

Many new houses and farm buildings date from this period, and the prosperity and confidence is marked by the many church 'restorations' such as Ellesborough, Great Kimble and Turville. Some old medieval chapels were abandoned and rebuilt. The isolated St James in Bix (Plate 156) was replaced by a new church in the village, and the St Mary le More chapel at Moor End was rebuilt at Cadmore End.[34] At The Lee a Victorian church hides a tiny medieval chapel that still sits within the churchyard.

The year 1879 probably saw the largest extent of ploughed arable land in the Hills at any date in history.[35] The following years saw the tide of rural prosperity turn and ebb. A succession of bad harvests hit yields, but the real damage was caused by foreign grain imports from new, cheaper sources in Europe and North America. English farmers found it hard to compete, and farming went into a depression that really lasted until 1940. Prices and incomes fell. Rents had to be reduced to keep tenant farmers, and the West Wycombe estate rentals fell by 19 per cent between 1876 and 1888. Fewer labourers were employed and, in Hugh Prince's phrase, 'the polish went out of cultivation'.[36]

The Chilterns suffered less than many areas, but the depression altered the face of much of the Chiltern landscape. Some marginal land was abandoned, and much went to weed and thistle. In the regular cropping cycle the temporary grasses or leys were extended from the usual one or two years to four or five years and many eventually became permanent pasture. Sheep had been kept mainly to fold on the arable, and their numbers were reduced as the arable contracted. This was to have major effects on the downlands along the scarp as scrub and bushes began to colonise. The number of cattle rose—'down corn, up horn' as the traditional expression has it—both as a by-product of the expansion of grass and to take advantage of new markets. The move towards dairy cattle was strongest in the south Chilterns, never the best arable land in the region. These areas were close enough to the GWR line to catch the milk-train or the 'Milky Way' as it was known, or to serve the Huntley & Palmer biscuit factory at Reading.[37] The improvements in well-digging and water-supply also helped the growth of dairying. Milk cows can drink 10 gallons or more of water each day and water shortage had been a major restriction on pastoral farming in the Hills. Full release from this constraint had to await piped water in the 1930s. This change to dairying can still be seen in the surviving farm buildings and equipment: large traditional barns from earlier centuries, together with late Victorian cow-stalls and feeding troughs. Richard, a farmworker at Newnham Hill near Stoke Row, was interviewed in his eighties in 1937 and recalled his youth: 'Then most of it was ploughed to grow corn and roots; now scores of acres have "fallen down" to grass, or grow nothing but weeds'.[38]

J. T. Coppock has traced the changes across the Chilterns, and we can use his figures for Great Missenden as an example of a 'middling parish' where change was marked but by no means extreme.[39] In the 1870s arable land made up 80 per cent of the farming area, but this fell to 70 per cent in 1900 and 50 per cent by 1915. Tillage (the land actually ploughed in any one year, so excluding temporary grass) dropped from 67 per cent to 50 per cent to 40 per cent, a significant 'greening' of the Chiltern scene. As well as growth in permanent pasture, there were other changes. Some former ploughland on hillsides was turned to woodland, and such plantations are often marked by

135. The Maharajah's Well, Stoke Row. A gift from the Maharajah of Benares in 1864-65. Edward Reade, a member of a prominent Ipsden family, was a District Commissioner in India. Hearing about the water-problems of this Chiltern hamlet, the Maharajah financed this well. It was dug to 365 ft. through the chalk before water was struck.

their straight boundaries and their names, such as Jubilee Plantations (at both Fawley Bottom and at Luxters). These woods, often of larch, are the beginning of conifer plantations in the Hills. Some areas closer to railway stations or to London turned to fruit-growing, such as the Holmer Green orchards. Parts of the Chilterns had a long tradition of cherry growing. William Ellis had lamented government interference in the trade (they were used in liquors and gins) as long ago as 1730.[40] Around Stoke Row, Checkendon and Highmoor cherry orchards became important, and parties of cherry-pickers came out from Reading, and later from London, at harvest-time (Plate 136).

The north-east Chilterns saw fewer changes in their farming traditions. The rolling loams had always given better wheat yields, and arable remained more profitable. The overall effect of the depression was to make the contrast between Chiltern and Vale more muted, and some of the unified character of the Chiltern scene began to be lost in these years.[41] As the Chiltern-

136. The cherry orchards at Checkendon. The southern Chilterns, especially the area around Stoke Row, was renowned for its cherry orchards. This photograph was taken in the 1920s before many had been removed.

Vale contrast lessened, so differences between the north-east and south-west Chilterns emerged more strongly. These internal differences were not to find full expression until more recently, but the divergence began in the 1880s.

This farming depression was part of a wider rural decline with crafts like lace, straw and wood-bodging also declining. Rural incomes fell, there was little investment, and people were migrating from the land. Many Chiltern parishes saw their populations fall in these years. Bledlow and Bledlow Ridge dropped from 1,070 in 1881 to 854 in 1901, and Radnage from 476 to 385. But population growth in the commuter towns and settlements along the railway lines offset much of the rural losses in the Chilterns themselves, and the region suffered nothing like the declines experienced in northern Buckinghamshire. The Chilterns' accessibility to London also continued to make them attractive as a location for a country home for the wealthy, like the London solicitor Sir Frank Crisp who built Friar Park outside Henley in 1889-90. The biggest impact of 'outside money' was felt around Tring and Aston Clinton, where the Rothschild family had a whole network of country houses. They spent a lot of money in these depression years rebuilding farmhouses and entire villages, all in the

137. Dancers End Waterworks. The Rothschilds built everything in their distinctive style, including this waterworks originally built to provide water to their estate villages.

distinctive Rothschild gothic-cum-Swiss style with tall, twisting chimneys. Everything was built to match, even the posh waterworks (at The Crong) to serve their estate (Plate 137).

The end of the century does indeed mark an important transition for the Chilterns. The traditional rural scene was in decay, setting in train changes in the landscape of woods and downs that only had their full impact over many decades. At the same time the area was becoming a dormitory region for London, a role that was to increase dramatically after the turn of the century. It was a new balance that had to be achieved between town and country.

Chapter Twelve

Metro-land

Metro-land is not strictly a place. It is an evocative name that christened an image: the metropolis on the move down shiny railway tracks with puffing steam trains pulling laden carriages of 'peaky' citizens out of the grime and into the countryside. The word 'Metro-land' was part of a very successful marketing ploy to promote the Metropolitan railway and it first appeared in 1915 as the title of their annual guide produced under their new commercial and publicity manager John Wardle.[1] The guide (which appeared each year from 1915 to 1932) claimed to be a 'comprehensive description of the country districts served by the Metropolitan railway' and was part of a growing mound of literature romanticising the countryside. The new *Metro-land* booklet (Plate 152), thanks to improved printing techniques, was enhanced by colour photographs, many of the more idyllic sun-dappled corners of the Chilterns and beyond. It marketed the villages and landscapes served by the line leading through Harrow-on-the-Hill to the Chalfonts, Chesham, Amersham and on to Missenden and Wendover. The descriptions of this 'rural arcadia', in varying hues of purple, painted their own scenes of the countryside— 'Each lover of Metro-land may well have his favourite beech wood and coppice—all tremulous green loveliness in Spring and russet and gold in late October'. It also described the small towns and villages—'neat, prim little towns which keep their old-world aspect, like Amersham and Missenden and Wendover'.[2] Nostalgia was interrupted by tempting historical tit-bits and interspersed with allusions to the improved levels of personal well-being that were to be found in this milk and honey landscape: 'The good air of the Chilterns invites to health by day and to sleep by night'.

'The beautiful unknown country' was being laid open to a very wide market with the express intention of making it much less unknown. The inter-war period, despite the depression, saw a new attitude develop towards leisure and the railway companies were quick to catch on to its commercial possibilities. They encouraged a new wave of walkers and ramblers, many of them working-class Londoners who were exercising their fatter paypackets and longer weekends in the countryside.The Chilterns were a popular destination as visitors could step off the train and walk into the immediate surrounds through a series of public footpaths that weave in and out of valleys and hills, woods and fields. There were fewer problems of access and trespass than in many parts of England as so much ancient common and trackway had always maintained rights of passage in the Chilterns.[3] As early as 1905 the Metropolitan had started their *Country Walks* booklets, giving suggested walks along with little sketch maps enticing participants into the 'most charming and intimate rural recesses of Middlesex, Herts and Bucks'. This led some (including the poet Rupert Brooke) to explore the Hills before 1914, but the great enthusiasm for rambling came after the First World War. The Metropolitan advertised with slogans such as 'Go for a Ramble', and offered 'Cheap tickets to Metro-land' at about the single fare for the double journey on Thursdays, Saturdays and Sundays. Other railways later followed suit. The GWR produced its *Rambles in the Chiltern Country*, mapping

138. Metropolitan steam. One of Charles Jones' H-class engines starting a pull up a Chiltern gradient in the 1920s, taking Metro-land commuters home for the weekend.

an area completely separate from the Metro's Chilterns, but reaching up to Princes Risborough and Watlington.[4] After London Transport absorbed the Metropolitan in 1933, the Metro-land theme was dropped but they continued to promote the Chilterns. A 1936 press campaign featured various animals telling people, 'Good spot, the Chilterns' (Plate 139), whilst a second campaign used woodcuts and dialogue with Chilterns locals. No wonder the day-trippers poured out of the railway stations with their picnics of fish-paste sandwiches and lemonade, along with the serious hikers, in walking boots and with the latest Ordnance Survey maps (Plate 151), who could get special tickets to arrive and return using different stations. Behind them trooped the 'Week-enders' and the campers and golfers, all swayed by the growing national conviction that the fresh air would do them good.

Attracting tourists was only one part of the Metro-land publicity campaign. Most of all it was the new wave of house-hunters that the Metropolitan Railway sought to woo. In the annual *Metro-land* booklets, after the colour plates and seductive rural prose came the 'House Seekers Section'. The company was unique among its rivals at the time in holding a controlling interest in a property company ('The Metropolitan Railway Country Estates Ltd.') which was set up to build on land it had purchased during the construction of the line and never sold.[5] They started building on the first two estates at Chalk Hill in Wembley and the Cedars Estate at Rickmansworth in the early 1920s. Further estates were to follow at Rayners Lane and then deep into the Chilterns at Amersham. Eventually nine estates were opened, mostly with ready-

— though I know the place is my home,' said the Donkey, 'and I love my own juicy hedgerow there. But, frankly, is there anywhere a view more glorious, more stirring, than from the top of Bacombe Hill and Coombe Hill on a clear Spring day? Is there?'

'Good spot, the Chilterns –

OBACCO

Bacombe Hill begins near Wendover Station, on the Metropolitan Line, and rises gradually until it reaches Coombe Hill, the headland which, at 852 feet, is the highest point in the Chilterns. Cheap return tickets to the Chiltern country are issued, daily, from all stations on the Metropolitan and East London Lines. On Sundays and Bank Holidays by all trains. Mondays to Fridays between 10 and 4. Saturdays by all trains after 10. The return fare to Wendover Stn. is 4/3 from Baker Street (Metropolitan) or Marylebone (L.N.E.R.) Stations. AWAY BY METROPOLITAN

LONDON TRANSPORT

139. London Transport advertisement, 1936. This was one of a series of advertisements for the Chilterns which featured 'talking animals'.

built houses to buy, or as plots of land where purchasers could build individual architect-designed properties. The general manager of the Metropolitan line was intent on populating these estates with daily commuters (first class, please!) who could travel from the countryside to the city and back again. Sir John Betjeman captured it perfectly:

> And woodsmoke mingled
> with the sulphur fumes
> And people now could catch
> The early train
> To London and be home
> Just after tea.[6]

From 1910 the wealthier commuter could travel on one of two Pullman cars (the Mayflower and the Galatea) which marshalled individually in the centre of some express trains (Plate 140). For a sixpenny supplement over and above the first-class fare, these Pullmans offered spacious comfort, with armchairs, carpets and a bar where the weary traveller could refresh himself with a 'gin and splash'.

The Suburban Dream

The Metro-land Estates were the tip of a larger iceberg. The first encouragement of rail commuting goes back much further—as early as the 1850s the London and North Western Company were offering a free first-class season ticket to those building houses of an annual rented value of £50 or more at places as far out as King's Langley, Boxmoor and Tring. From late Victorian times well-appointed villas were being built around all the new stations on the Chilterns lines, especially the new Marylebone line out to High Wycombe and the Metropolitan line to Chesham and Amersham. The same was occurring on the main line routes of the GWR and LNWR at towns like Berkhamsted. However, it was after 1918 that the real

140. The Pullman Car. This is one of the Pullman carriages which enabled first-class passengers to travel home on the Metropolitan Line in the lap of luxury.

urban explosion took place. The period between the wars saw the urban area of England increase by 26 per cent, with housing as the largest single component: over four million dwellings were constructed in two decades as the suburban dream became a reality. Of course, in these years Metropolitan Country Estates only built the tiniest fraction of the new houses in the region, even in Metro-land villages. But *Metro-land* encapsulated and articulated a widespread suburban aspiration, and reflected the mood of the times. The Metro-land experience was contagious and it was caught by a broader society than the bank managers and company directors who lived in elegant Voysey-designed houses on the spacious Cedars Estate, or in Amersham and Chesham Bois.

There was a new breed of middle-class Londoners who, in Alan Jackson's words, 'Aiming at a new house in the suburbs were seeking to renew contact with the rural environment which their ancestors had deserted in the hope of attaining higher living standards in the metropolis'.[8] It was for this group that semi-detached suburbia marched into the Chilterns at places close to the railway line like Amersham, Chesham, Beaconsfield and Gerrards Cross, forming the first dormitory towns in the region. Jackson suggests that the semi-detached house was a popular and affordable compromise between the urban terrace with its lack of privacy, and the detached homes that were too greedy of land to come within the price range of the white-collars and artisans. Semi-detached homes were built at a density of ten or twelve per acre, allowing fair-sized gardens and an illusion of privacy with private access to back doors. Although the layouts were roughly similar, a measure of individuality was maintained by varying the style of the exterior elevations and the internal finishing. Many harked back to

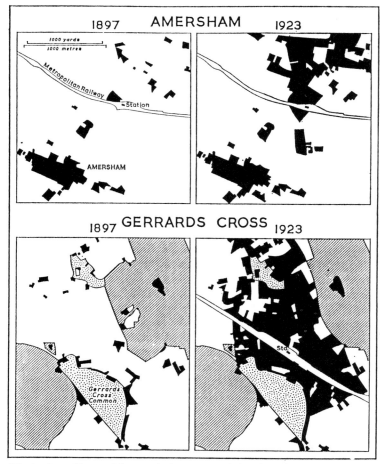

<figure>1897 AMERSHAM 1923

1000 yards
1000 metres

Metropolitan Railway
Station
AMERSHAM

1897 GERRARDS CROSS 1923

Gerrards
Cross
Common

Std.
</figure>

141. The growth of Amersham and Gerrards Cross. This map, from Coppock and Prince (1964), shows the growth of Metro-land commuter estates astride the railway.

'Tudor' styling with mock beams and leaded lights in the front door. The houses on some estates were matched by parades of shops, banks, public houses and even petrol stations, all with similar mock façades.

The influence of the railway on these early Metro-land estates in the Chilterns is unmistakable, because the railway line in many cases by-passed the old town, leaving the station on the outskirts. This created the opportunity for an entirely new dormitory town to spring up, near to the station and without interfering with the old town centre. Such was the case in Amersham with the new town situated on the hill, while the old broad High Street remained in the valley half a mile away. Prior to the opening of the station Amersham's population was falling, but it then grew rapidly as the suburban villa community of Amersham-on-the-Hill expanded. By 1931, when the Metropolitan acquired and developed the Weller estate there, the population had reached 29,000. Advertisements at the time showed, 'A few semi-detached and detached houses with built-in garages' available at £875 to £1,225 Freehold. A new straight row of mock-Tudor shops completed the scene, in sharp contrast to the old High Street with its broken skyline and pleasing cocktail of oddly-sized old buildings. In rather stark contrast to both mock-Tudor and genuine traditional styles, several concrete modernist houses, white with flat-roofs, were built on Amersham Hill (Plate 142).

142. Modernist architecture at
Amersham-on-the-Hill. These
were *avant garde* houses
following Le Corbusier's ideas.

Beaconsfield, which had been something of a backwater between the end of the coaching
era and the new railway station in 1906, was to grow in much the same way, with two distinct
parts, although they now run into each other. The unmistakable dormitory complete with a
heavily beamed Lloyds Bank sits astride the railway line (Plate 143). The building land was
offered for auction by Verney and Sons, and the plans show the plots close to the railway at

143. Metro-land in Beaconsfield. These buildings typify the style of the period (*c.*1906-10), with mock-
Tudor frontages on the road to the station. The bank is still there, now a Lloyds branch.

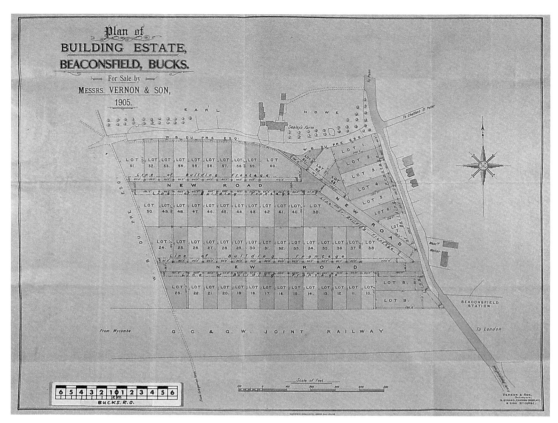

144. Plan of building plots offered for sale in Beaconsfield in 1905 by Vernon & Sons: 63 sites for 'villas and country cottage homes'. The location is immediately north of the railway line, and the 'new roads' are now Baring and Reynolds Roads. Lots 1-9 became shops, and a hotel built just north of the station has been pulled down to make way for the modern Waitrose supermarket.

low densities by today's standards (Plate 144). The development at Gerrards Cross, on the same line, went a stage further, transforming a tiny loose-knit hamlet scattered around the common into an entirely new dormitory that grew from a population of 552 to 2,942 in 30 years. The railway from Marylebone through High Wycombe opened in 1906, and along with it the rush for new houses. Farms and parkland were dug up to become the streets and gardens of over 400 houses, although the common remained intact. Neither Beaconsfield nor Gerrards Cross lies on the Metropolitan Line, but they display the quintessence of 'Metro-land' just as much as the Chalfonts or New Amersham. These leafy suburbs achieved much more of the Metro-land dream than did those closer to Baker Street. Pinner, Rayner's Lane and Harrow-on-the-Hill lost their rural context as development intensified, but here, further out in Chiltern country, more has survived and Metro-land seems less a case of advertising hyperbole.

Further west the town of High Wycombe was expanding, both from local jobs and commuting. Estates began to spring up on the hillsides north-east of the station. One of these was at Totteridge Farm, owned by a Charles Pettit. Together with Gilbert Lean, his architect and surveyor, he put together his own sales brochure in Metro-land fashion.[9] Called *High on the Chiltern Hills* and complete with photographs of local views, it asks:

The Question of Today

How can I find a real country home, in a healthy, elevated position, with unspoilt rural sur-
roundings, and yet accessible by good main rail service to London?

The Answer

Take a contoured map of the country adjoining a main line, and, for choice, the newest (the
G.W. and G.C. Railways joint line) as more likely to pass through unspoilt country. Ignoring
suburbs and low-lying places, find a station within 30 miles where the ground rises to 500 feet
above sea level within about a mile; and, if there is any choice, a station serving a large town.
Select a spur on the station side of town, sloping southwards, and away from a main road. Go
there, and you will discover the unique spot described in this booklet.

Another estate nearby was built on the fields of Bowerdean Farm. Here the transformation was captured by the local photographer Edward Sweetland, who photographed the rural
scene in 1905 and again (with perfect repositioning) in 1938 when the houses were complete
(Plate 146).

While it is not difficult to describe the growth associated with the inter-war period, it is
perhaps more difficult to explain.[10] The changes that were taking place must be set against a
background of a huge re-distribution of land holdings, with many of the big private estates
being broken up and sold to farmers in much smaller units. The costs of running a big estate
and especially the increases in duties and taxation meant that only very wealthy landowners
could maintain the status quo. Added to this was the agricultural depression, with falling prices
and contraction of the arable acreage especially in marginal areas. The last vestiges of rural
craft were extinguished over this period leaving rural areas with a disintegrating economy. The
opportunity to sell some of their land for development must have been a godsend to these new
farming owner-occupiers who were struggling to make ends meet. And they were satisfying

145. Air photograph of Gerrards Cross. This tiny hamlet, built around the common, grew to become a sizeable town on either side of the railway. The common now remains as an island in the midst of a suburban sea.

146. Bowerdean Farm in High Wycombe, before and after development. This pair of photographs was taken by the local High Wycombe photographer, Edward Sweetland. Bowerdean Farm was on the hillside to the east of the railway station and old centre of High Wycombe.

a need; for although the population as a whole was not increasing, the south saw the migration tide of the previous century turn and people were moving away from the industrial heartlands of the north and the midlands and heading towards the Home counties. There was a new outlook among those seeking homes which sought to get away from the lack of space and privacy of urban housing, and the literature of the period created the image of the new estate as the place to live.

The improved life-style was not restricted to those who could purchase. There was an enormous increase in council rented accommodation and this was not confined to areas near to railway lines. It is hard to find a village or a town anywhere that does not have its rows of inter-war council houses fringing the older centres. The *Metro-land* issue for 1932 specifically mentions local councils who had built a number of estates in Chorley Wood and Chenies; in Chesham the 'Local Council have erected 150 houses and cottages, 50 more in course of construction, 200 more contemplated. Extensive private building is taking place on Lowndes Avenue, Shepherd's Farm, Charteridge lane and Chiltern Hills Estates'. The story was repeated over and again in almost every town and village in the region, with councils keen to replace former dilapidated farm dwellings (read 'picturesque cottage') and to house newcomers.

Preservation of the countryside

By the mid-1920s the threat to the countryside from unplanned mushroom growth was becoming increasingly apparent. It was not just the eruption of huge estates on the edges of existing towns, or the ribbon development creeping along the roads, but the fact that even the remotest spots were all succumbing to 'pepperpot development', where building was seen to be shaken at random and dabbed occasionally over the land. This growth could now be seen in a new perspective through the increased use of air photography and it was not going to be allowed to proceed totally unimpeded, or without protest. A growing body of people was moved to shout very loudly at what they saw as the wanton destruction of the countryside. It was apparent that the pace of housing development was way beyond the capacity of any statutory planning body to control or channel. Like a rash, building was breaking out all over the place, and no-one could forecast where it might appear next. The government produced a first effort at regulation in the Town and Country Bill in 1932, but it was not until after 1945 that planning gained really effective control.

It fell to the lot of voluntary bodies and individuals to protest about and protect the rural landscape. The National Trust had already demonstrated that Britain's heritage was not only its buildings, and G. M. Trevelyan had written forcefully on their behalf in a small book entitled *Must England's Beauty Perish?*[11] To Trevelyan, natural beauty was the highest common denominator of the spiritual life of contemporary Britain, and as a former Chilterns' resident he was particularly concerned about this region. So much so that he bought part of the Ashridge estate to prevent it falling under the auctioneer's hammer, and donated it to the Trust. Other preservation groups were set up during this period. The most influential among them was the CPRE (Council for the Preservation of Rural England), founded in 1926 under the enlightened eye of architect and planner Patrick Abercrombie. Beneath its umbrella, organisations and individuals concerned with rural preservation formed a crusade to reduce the scale of the 'personal and corporate thoughtlessness and selfishness of which the despoliation of the countryside was a symptom'. They attacked on a broad front and not necessarily with consensus: houses (especially bungalows), roads, petrol stations, electricity pylons and wirescapes, billboards and factories all came under fire.[12]

One of the most outspoken critics of the time was Clough Williams-Ellis who as a self-proclaimed angry young man published an impassioned plea against 'urban beastliness' in

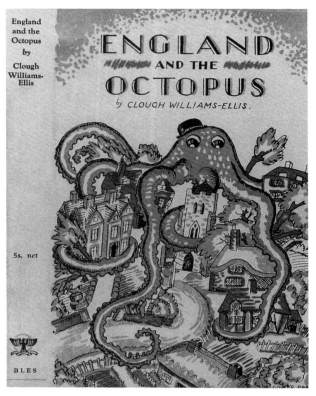

England
and the
Octopus
by
Clough
Williams-
Ellis

ENGLAND
AND THE
OCTOPUS
by CLOUGH WILLIAMS-ELLIS.

5s. net

BLES

147. Dust cover for *England and the Octopus*, by Clough
Williams-Ellis. This was the most outspoken of the many
protests about the 'Octopus' of urban sprawl spoiling the
English countryside.

1928 in his book *England and the Octopus* (Plate 147). This was followed in 1937 by a series of 26 essays which he edited in *Britain and the Beast*.[13] The CPRE represented a very middle- and upper-class viewpoint, lamenting so many of the changes that were overrunning the countryside now that the big country landlords were no longer its guardian. They sent a travelling exhibition called 'Save the Countryside' with Saint George for Rural England battling against a dragon whose scaled wings represented cigarettes, petrol, tyres and other billboard advertising slogans which so incensed the preservationists (Plate 148).[14] The Council were not all against building *per se*: the *Face of the Land* book, which reproduced many of the photographs from the exhibition, celebrated many new, urban 20th-century constructions such as bridges, roads and factories as improvements on their Victorian predecessors, and aesthetically pleasing.[15] But, as David Matless has argued, their vision of the countryside extolled the 18th century with its ordered estates and landscaped parks (but of course ignored the oppression). They saw some modernism in architecture and landscaping as following this tradition, and approved. What they could not stand was the chaos of popular individualism (whereas writers like J. B. Priestley applauded it), nor the 'sham history' of mock-Tudor.[16] H. J. Massingham, who did not like much new, caught this last viewpoint with his opinion of Latimer,

> is now an Ideal Homes Exhibition of bogus and beading. There is one pigmy house of half-timber and brick with gables, dormers, porch, casement windows and gently rolling russet roof which represents this voluptuous corner with a felicity just short of Birket Fosterish sweetness.[17]

It was the wholesale 'invasion' of the countryside with building at random that was to cause the verbal baring of teeth and gnashing of jaws so evident in the publications of the CPRE and Clough Williams-Ellis. The desire was to keep the urban and rural areas separate but the reality was that the towns, their buildings and their occupants were creeping outwards at an alarming rate. The Metro-land dormitory settlements that we have described were one major element in this, but at least their estates were generally 'contained' and restricted to the areas adjacent to the line and the stations. Just as significant, and even more dramatic in its impact, was the 'sudden triumph, in the interwar period, of the internal combustion engine over all its rivals'. Harold Perkin in *The Age of the Automobile* described it thus: 'In the automobile age, the flexibility of the bus, the car and the goods vehicle enabled the city and the suburbs to burst like a poppy head, scattering its seeds into every available space ...'.[18]

155. Bungalows and petrol station at Aston Rowant. This is the spot that so upset S. P. B. Mais. This photograph was taken in the early 1960s, but the garage and buildings have now gone.

and softened the scene. Three generations have grown up in Metro-land and beyond, enjoying the Chilterns landscape, and the sum of human happiness is undoubtedly greater for it.

Yet the Chilterns were badly hit and wounded, scarred by their share of ill-planned housing, ruined views, lost lanes and urban sprawl. For those who remembered the Hills before 1914, it must have been hard to take. Clough Williams-Ellis had been inspired to explore the Chilterns by reading R. L. Stevenson's essay on a Chiltern walk, and he later recalled Stevenson's description of Wendover:

> Wendover lay well down in the midst, with mountains of foliage about it. The great plain stretched away to northward, variegated near at hand with the quaint pattern of the fields, but growing ever more and more indistinct until it became a mere hurly-burly of trees and bright crescents of river, and snatches of slanting road, and finally melted away into the ambiguous cloud-land over the horizon.[27]

In 1933 he reflected despairingly: 'What, between them, have the Air Force and the civilian commuters left of Stevenson's picture?'[28]

Our answer, standing above Wendover today, must be, 'More than you allowed for, Mr. Williams-Ellis'. Time mellows disruption to the landscape, and even Joad (less of a fool than he sometimes appeared) admitted that people would learn to like the roads as he liked the railways. The Chilterns were spared wholesale devastation as much development could be absorbed and 'hidden' by the dissected wooded landscape, and some areas were still too remote at that time. Thousands of acres were spared because they remained in the hands of large private estates and were managed in the time-honoured fashion. Much of the region south of the A40 was spared, most notably the lovely Wormsley valley, owned by the Fane family.

156. The ruin of Bix church. The old medieval church at Bix Bottom, well outside the village, was subsequently replaced by a new church in Bix itself and the fittings removed. The ruined church is tucked in a beautiful secret valley.

157. The Stonor valley. The upper Stonor valley, remaining wholly unspoilt, is an example of the remoter parts of the Chilterns that were always in the hands of large estates.

158. Meadow flowers in the Chilterns. The variety of species in the BBONT reserve at Aston Clinton includes the Bee Orchid, the Fragrant Orchid, and the Pyramidal Orchid, as well as many other chalkland flowers.

159. Bungalow near Hughenden. This 1930s 'snap' was captioned 'Uncle Rheuben's bungalow', and was typical of the period.

With the benefit of hindsight the overall balance-sheet can be be drawn in the black. However, the period highlighted and left unresolved all the problems of countryside planning, housing growth and transport that the Chilterns have had to wrestle with since then.

Chapter Thirteen

The Changing Countryside

Farming Change

Chiltern farming in the last 70 years has seen both depression and boom, with conflicting impacts on the landscape. The agricultural depression which began in late Victorian times persisted until 1939 and the Second World War. There was a minor reversal towards the end of the 1914-18 War, when British food imports were threatened by German submarines. The government encouraged arable by the 1917 Corn Production Act, but the conversion only took effect in 1918, and the repeal of the Act in 1921 led to a collapse in grain prices. The tumbling down to grass therefore continued: in Great Missenden parish the lowest point was reached in 1937 with only 40 per cent of the farming acreage under arable, and tillages below 30 per cent.[1] These years saw a down-at-heel, unkempt Chiltern landscape, with weed-ridden fields and overgrown hedges.

This was all changed by the outbreak of war in 1939. There was none of the dilatory reaction seen in 1914-18. Very quickly a great plough-up campaign, backed up by orders and requisitions, turned large areas back to arable. Land-girls and prisoners-of-war helped till the land. In Missenden the arable expanded back to 65 per cent by 1943. Most of the new arable had been fields laid down to grass since 1875. Some, however, was on old downland or commons, land either never ploughed or not for a very long time. On the plateau top at Russell's Water, for instance, 139 acres of the Common were requisitioned and cultivated, and the same happened to 240 acres of Berkhamsted Common.[2] At Grangelands, above Great Kimble, scarp grazing land was taken under the plough. Some of the more marginal attempts only lasted a few years, but unlike the previous post-war experience there was no wholesale reversal back to pasture after 1945.

Instead of withdrawing arable support, the 1947 Agriculture Act instituted a system of guaranteed prices for the farmer. This was the basis for farming expansion and prosperity in Britain until it was replaced by the CAP or Common Agricultural Policy, with membership of the European Community in 1973. Both policies kept farmers' incomes high, and created incentives to greater and more efficient production. These last 40 years have seen the great mechanisation of farming. In 1939 tractors were not commonplace; after 1945 combine harvesters and other equipment became widespread. New hybrid varieties, chemical fertilisers and pesticides led to massive increases in yields. The intensity of the new 'agri-business' depended less on farm labour than on capital. These high years of farming, and especially the CAP system, led to grain surpluses, 'milk lakes' and 'beef mountains', and the last decade has seen a questioning of the costs and rationality of this type of farming. Now farmers are being encouraged to reduce the output they strove to increase, to 'set aside' land for non-production. These changes raise issues of the whole role of farming in the Chiltern countryside, and we shall look at them in our final chapter. Here we shall trace out three strands in the way these farming and rural changes have affected the Chiltern landscape and ecology, before turning to these present-day issues of conservation and planning.

160. Open downland on Ivinghoe Beacon. Sheep grazing on this famous landmark has kept bushes and scrub at bay, and gives us the downland turf which elsewhere has been disappearing.

161. Old flowering cherry tree. A magnificent and very old coppiced wild cherry marking part of an ancient hedgerow in Pednor valley.

162. Harvest time, between Little Missenden and Holmer Green. Modern farming with its weed-free fields and mechanised baling, but still with a Chilterns profile of hedged field and beech hanger.

163. Sheep in Aston Clinton ragpits. BBONT sheep flock on this reserve during midwinter.

Chalk Downlands and Neglected Commons

The long rural and arable decline from 1875 to 1940 destroyed the farming role of many Chiltern scarp-pastures and commons. The practice of grazing on the downland and folding on the Vale arable declined, and the landscape began to change in various ways. Where the grazing was simply reduced or ceased, then scrub began to colonise, followed by trees and woodland. Where the land was ploughed up, either for arable or to sow improved grasses for permanent grazing at a higher stocking-rate, the old chalk grassland was equally transformed.[3]

Either way, an ancient and fragile ecosystem was being lost. Traditional chalk downlands have an amazingly rich and colourful flora, which in turn attract and host a wide variety of insects and butterflies. The chalk soils are poor in nutrients, and the sheep nibble down and hold back the stronger, more competitive grasses, allowing the flowers to flourish. Take away the sheep, or 'improve' the grass with artificial fertiliser, and this fragile system is gone, and is extremely difficult to re-create. Amongst the chalk downland species are the many wild orchids, which flower in May to July. Some rarities like the military and monkey orchids are only found on a few sites, but fragrant, pyramidal and bee orchids are more widespread. Other delights are the gentians, the little vetches (such as the horseshoe vetch on which the caterpillar of the chalkhill blue butterfly feeds), and the rare but beautiful purple of the pasque-flower.[4] Of this Oliver Rackham comments: 'It is quite robust; it survives picnicking and lack of grazing; but it is instantly destroyed by ploughing and never returns'.[5] Across all the English chalklands, this traditional downland has been ravaged, and the Chilterns are no exception. The more northerly Chilterns have probably suffered most from ploughing and improvement, and here the only remaining old downland is left clinging to the steeper and less accessible sections of the scarp-edge. A number of fine sites survive at Knocking Hoe, Totternhoe Knolls and the Barton Hills in Bedfordshire, and at Pitstone and Ivinghoe Beacon. Even on Pitstone Hill, however, the economics of grazing have led to improvement of the grass on the summit. The rarer species, and the old anthills so indicative of traditional grassland, are now restricted to the steeper slopes.

South of the Tring Gap, downland has faced the same problems, but neglect, rather than 'improvement', has been more frequent. The scarp is higher and steeper, so improvement is less attractive. More land here has therefore been left to revert to scrub, and adjacency to the woods of the plateau has aided this colonisation. One needs the evidence of old photographs and postcards to recapture just how open and bald the Chiltern tops were at the turn of the century. All along—at Coombe Hill, Whiteleaf Cross, Bledlow and Beacon Hill, Lewknor— the wood and scrubs have crept forward on the summit and invaded the scarp sides. It has been a long process, and still continues. The rabbit population helped to keep it at bay, but myxomatosis after 1954 removed this check (at least until recently).

A. S. Watt studied this colonisation in the early 1930s, and identified two types of succession (though later ecologists would complicate this).[6] On the drier, shallower, steeper slopes, juniper scrub colonised. These bushes then gave shelter to the beech seedlings, which later grew into beech woodland. Where there was more shelter and slightly deeper soils, hawthorn bushes were the coloniser, followed by ash seedlings, ash wood and finally beech. Juniper bushes used to be a common sight on chalk downland, but farmers have burnt and ploughed them over much of the English chalk.[7] On these steep escarpment slopes they have often flourished, with excellent colonies at Beacon Hill. Unfortunately protecting the wood seedlings leads to their own demise, for they cannot survive in the shade. Dead juniper is, however, slow to decay and desiccated bushes can be found within these woods they fostered, as at Windsor Hill above Risborough.

164. The changes on Coombe Hill, Wendover, *c.*1913. The old postcard shows how open Coombe Hill was when it was still grazed downland. Since 1913 the scarp has changed dramatically, with scrub and trees enveloping the slopes. The second photograph, taken from Butlers Cross, shows the changes which have occurred all round the hill.

165. The Wormsley Valley. This valley, unpenetrated by public roads, remained in the Fane family until the 1980s, when they sold it to J. P. Getty II, who has not only renovated and extended the house, but also ensured the preservation of this secluded Chiltern valley. (See Hart-Davis, 1991.)

The Chiltern heaths and commons have faced similar colonisation by scrub and wood. Grazing and woodfuel-cutting declined, often earlier than on the chalk downlands. These open spaces were on the acidic soils of the clay-with-flints or patches of Reading Beds, with a different flora to the chalk. Here reduction of grazing soon leads to ling, heather or bracken colonising and growing. These are succeeded by scrub, oak and beech woods. These woods, like Naphill, are widely regarded as some of the most valuable ecologically, with their diverse structure and good ground flora. Yet the heaths are disappearing under this growth, and they have attracted less attention than their downland compatriots. The exception is the renowned

166. Hardings Wood. This Chiltern meadow and the ancient woodland (which belongs to local conservationist Richard Mabey) have just escaped the line of the new A41 bypass.

167. Stonor House, home to the Stonor family for 800 years. The house has a Tudor E-shape, but the windows were remodelled in the 18th century. The chapel and parts of the house are medieval.

Burnham Beeches, maintained by the City of London. Some of the commons in more built-up areas are kept reasonably open by mowing (as at Gerrards Cross), but many are vanishing, like Ipsden Heath, Chesham Bois Common and the fascinating extent of Turville Heath and Summer Heath, where old Samuel Rockall used to wood-bodge.

Farming Landscapes

The rundown Chiltern farms of the 1930s have long gone, and with them have gone long-standing features of the Chiltern landscape. The agri-business has demanded a new efficiency in the scale and management of farming. Farms have been amalgamated, with redundant buildings sold off for homes. Old barns, no longer needed for grain storage, have also been converted into houses and workshops. But the most visible changes have been in the fields themselves—their boundaries and their very colour.

Mechanisation of farming, especially the combine harvesters, made very small fields a real nuisance. The result was hedgerow destruction, most obvious on the more open, loamy North Chilterns where arable farming was most profitable. It also occurred in the extreme south-west on the 'Ipsden Prairies', as Lionel Brett called them.[8] Here late enclosure generated

168. Harvesting at Whiteleaf, Princes Risborough, in 1910. This traditional rural scene also shows the openness of the scarp around Whiteleaf Cross at that time.

large fields and fewer hedges in the first place. Tony Harman of Chesham recalls how he was one of the first to begin this in the War, arranging a demonstration of hedge removal for the Ministry of Agriculture in 1944.[9] The big field he created by bulldozing six little fields (and they were small) into one can be seen on the left as you drive from Ashley Green to Chesham via Lye Green. Most of the Chiltern hedgerows were not recent creations, but part of the ancient countryside, some relics of the woodland itself, and their antiquity cannot be remade. Many other hedgerows have died by neglect rather than deliberate murder. Without the farm labour to maintain them, they have become overgrown, hacked back rather than relaid, and inadvertently poisoned. Yet it is in only a few parts of the Hills that all this has gone the way of East Anglia. Although many miles of boundaries have gone, the majority remain and the Chiltern topography of slope and bottom places limits on what can be done.

Intensive farming has also altered the colour of the Chiltern landscape. There are new pressures for farmers to grow different crops in response to changes in consumer tastes and European Community policy. Currently there are subsidies to encourage the growing of a variety of oilseeds, and these are reflected in new colours. The brilliant-yellow oilseed rape has been visibly on the increase throughout the nation. More recently, since 1987, there has been an incentive scheme to grow flax, both for linseed and for fibre. More and more Chiltern fields can be seen shrouded in the pale-blue haze of this flax in full bloom. Fertilisers make the sown grassland a vivid green, contrasting with the more subdued hues of old chalk downland. Fields sown with a crop are simply that crop: a wheat-field is just wheat (or almost), a hay-crop is just sown grass. The plethora of other species that got in with the sown-seed or sowed themselves naturally are largely a thing of the past, eliminated by seed-selection and selective weed-killers. The former diversity of corn-flowers, poppies and other species was much reduced, as were the old unploughed banks around the field edges which sustained a mass of flowers. Like the hedgerow, such species hosted a varied insect and butterfly population. None of these things completely vanished, but it is difficult for children of the 1980s to know just how different the fields were in the early 1950s before the great industrialisation of farming took effect. Capital-intensive farming produces very simple, but highly efficient, ecosystems, and maintains them artificially. Traditional farming was part of a more diverse ecosystem, and the price of high yields has been the loss of that scenic and ecological diversity in the landscape.

The Chiltern Woodlands

The beechwoods of the Hills have had their own set of problems this century. The previous century had seen their conversion to high forest, and the decline of the bodger and therefore of the Chiltern Selection System meant that woods were over-maturing. Their composition was too even-aged, with a closed canopy preventing seedling regeneration and creating a rather bleak ground-cover. Only the best timber was being taken, and much second-rate wood was left rather than being cut early. Heavy demands in both World Wars for rifle butts and plywood for aircraft took their toll, witnessed first by the felling of the Rothschild beechwoods above Halton. The unhealthy state of many beechwoods was recognised in the 1920s, and brought out clearly in the early aerial surveys of Ray Bourne.[10]

In a purely biological sense, a tract of senile wood is not a problem. When the trees rot or are brought down by storms like those in 1987 and 1990, the natural process of succession would lead through bush and scrub to new trees and broad-leafed wood. It would be a very long-term process, and, with the sheer number of Chiltern mature beechwoods, would be unacceptable in either scenic or economic terms. Some form of management, such as produced the beechwoods, is necessary.

Chapter Notes

In these chapter notes manuscript sources are given in full: books and articles are given by author and date, which can then be located in the alphabetical list of References.

Manuscript Abbreviations:

BL	British Library (formerly British Museum)
Bodl	Bodleian Library, Oxford University
BRO	Buckinghamshire Record Office
ORO	Oxfordshire Record Office
PRO	Public Record Office

Chapter 1
1. Blythe (1986), 122
2. Esposito (1917). The original hoax is in *The Monthly Magazine* (1802) 13, 447-50
3. Smith, L. J. (1907), vol.2, 112
4. Mead (1954)
5. Elvey, G. R. (1977)
6. Oschinsky (1971), 323 [*Walter* c.49]
7. Petrie (1926)
8. Davies, A. M. (1951-52)
9. Stevenson (1907)
10. Roberts, C. (1934, 1935, 1936, 1938)
11. Thomas (1913), 154
12. Chenevix Trench (1973)
13. Home (1925), 21
14. Baines (1981a)
15. Young, A. [Arthur] (1804)
16. Betjeman (1960), 56

Chapter 2
1. Dyer (1978); Sampson (1978)
2. Wymer (1968)
3. Loveday (1962)
4. Peel (1950), 14
5. Ollier and Thomasson (1957)
6. Evans, J. G. (1975), 64
7. Farley (1978), 614
8. Stainton (1989)
9. Head (1955)
10. Head (1974)
11. Matthews (1964, 1976)
12. Dyer and Hales (1962)
13. Childe and Smith (1954)
14. Head (1955, 1974); Dyer (1959)
15. Bodl: Gough MS 47 [Delafield's *History of Stokenchurch*]
16. Evans, J. G. (1966, 1972); Evans and Valentine (1974)
17. Evans and Valentine (1974)
18. Cunliffe (1991)
19. Saunders (1971)

20. Richardson and Young (1951); Harding (1972)
21. Evans, J. G. (1966, 1972)
22. Hawkes (1940)
23. Dyer and Hales (1962)
24. Cotton and Frere (1968), 203
25. BL: Harley MS 3688, at end. Not printed in Jenkins (1938, 1955, 1962), but see Hughes (1931), 295
26. Crawford (1931); Dyer (1963); Bradley (1968); Davis, J. (1981)
27. Plot (1672), 324
28. Dyer (1961)
29. Davis and Evans (1984)

Chapter 3
1. Cunliffe (1991); Frere (1987); Millett (1990); Stead and Rigby (1989)
2. Stead (1967)
3. Wheeler and Wheeler (1936); see also Saunders (1982)
4. Hunn (1980)
5. Branigan (1985)
6. Case (1958)
7. Branigan (1985)
8. Neal, Wardle and Hunn (1990)
9. Branigan (1985), 105
10. Taylor (1983)
11. Bell (1983)
12. Wheeler and Wheeler (1936); Frere (1972, 1983, 1984)
13. Viatores (1964)
14. Branigan (1967, 1968, 1971a, 1973, 1985)
15. Neal (1976); St. Joseph (1965)
16. Branigan (1985), 105
17. Branigan (1967, 1971b)
18. Branigan (1985), 135
19. Orna (1976); also *Britannia* v (1974), 438; vi (1975), 257; vii (1976), 338-39
20. Thompson (1957)
21. Branigan (1971b)

22. Branigan (1971b)
23. Frere (1983), 24
24. Frere, personal communication, 28 February 1992
25. Esmonde Cleary (1989), 172
26. Wheeler and Wheeler (1936) 35
27. Buchan (1916)

Chapter 4
1. Gelling (1979), but see also Baines (1984a)
2. Farley (1976); Baines (1984a)
3. Matthews, Hawkes and others (1985)
4. Meaney (1964), 59
5. Matthews, Hawkes and others (1985)
6. Stenton (1975), 27; see also Sims-Williams (1983)
7. Hawkes (1986), 86
8. Gelling (1978); on -ham, see Cox (1972-73)
9. Cox (1975-76); Gelling (1976)
10. Frere (1966), 98
11. Davis, K. R. (1982)
12. Frere (1987), 369
13. Davies, W and Vierck, H. (1974); BL: Harley 3271 f6v
14. Baines (1981b, 1984a)
15. Bailey (1989), 111
16. Chenevix Trench (1973); Baines (1984a, 1984b)
17. Seebohm (1883)
18. Baines, in Branigan (1971a), 192; Baines (1984a), 126-27
19. Chenevix Trench (1973)
20. Collett (1926), 247; Beddoe (1885)
21. Stonor (1951), 8 and 358
22. Cole (1982, 1985, 1989, 1990); see also Gelling (1984)
23. Baines (1981a); Davies, A. M. (1949)
24. Gelling (1976); Blair (1989); Hooke (1985)

25. Sawyer (1983)
26. Blair (1988a, 1988b)
27. Cam (1944)
28. Sawyer (1968), no.217; BL: Cotton Tiberius A xiii f28v-29v and f195-196.
29. Hooke (1985)
30. Blair (1989), 98
31. Chenevix Trench (1973)
32. Rowley (1973), 5
33. Lobel (1964), 2
34. Davies, A. M. (1949)
35. Newnham Murren: Grundy (1933), 39-42; Sawyer (1868), no.738; BL: Harley 596 f17v-18v. Bensington: Sawyer (1968), no.887; BL: Cotton Claudius B vi, f98v-99v.
36. Baines (1981a); Gelling (1953-54)
37. Baines (1981b); Reed(1979)
38. Lennard (1959)

Chapter 5
1. Darby and Campbell (1962)
2. Sellar and Yeatman (1930)
3. Seebohm (1883); Gray (1915)
4. Fox (1981, 1984); Williamson (1988)
5. Fox (1981), 96-97; Fowler (1926), 252; BL: Harley MS 1885 f7-8
6. Williamson (1988)
7. Harvey (1965)
8. Roden (1965), 236-270; Roden (1966)
9. Beresford (1953), 6
10. For a useful comparision with Kentish downland (rather than Weald), see Everett (1986)
11. Gray (1915), 401
12. Roden (1965-1973)
13. Campbell (1990)
14. Roden (1970), 61
15. Chenevix Trench (1973); Davies, A. M. (1949); Baines (1981a)
16. Hale (1858); Roden (1965), 296-301
17. Talbot (1959)
18. Roden (1965), 128-131; Roden (1970), 60-63
19. Vollans (1959), Jenkins (1938, 1955, 1962)
20. Casselden (1986, 1987)
21. Jenkins (1938), 154-55; Vollans (1959); BL: Harley 3688 f45r
22. Kosminsky (1956); Ulyanov (1966, 1971, 1972)
23. Kosminsky (1956), 128 and 143 ('peculiar')
24. Fox (1984)
25. Chibnall (1966),
26. Power and Campbell (1992); Campbell, Galloway and Murphy (1992)
27. Dyer, C. C. (1989), 54
28. Roden (1965,), 174-175; Roden

(1969b), 234; BL: Stowe 849
29. Chenevix Trench (1978), 418; Jenkins (1955), no.311
30. Ulyanov (1966)
31. Lobel (1964), 225; Salter (1935), 408
32. Roden (1965), 159-205; Levett (1938); Slota (1984, 1988); BL: Stowe MS 849
33. Roden (1965), 236-70; Roden(1966)
34. Young, A. [Alison] (1964), 271
35. Holt, R. (1988); Bloch(1967)
36. Ault (1972), 61
37. Oschinsky (1971), 277 [Seneschausy, c.38]
38. Ault (1972), 91, 113-14, 173-74
39. Ault (1972), 91, 107
40. Fox (1986)
41. Dahlman (1980)
42. BL: MS Stowe 849, f91-91v and f104
43. Roden (1965), 141-145
44. Roden (1965), Appendices F and G, 391-419; Slota (1988)
45. Holt, R. (1988)
46. Jenkins (1935), 42
47. Langdon (1986),
48. Oschinsky (1971), 319 [Walter, c.36]
49. Oschinsky (1971), 319 [Walter, c.41]
50. Chibnall (1966); Cornwall (1975)
51. Campbell (1988); later quote at 198
52. Reed (1978), Postles (1987)
53. Farmer (1991), 336
54. Beresford (1967)
55. Power (1941), 113; Lloyd (1977), 56
56. Ashford (1960)
57. Keene (1989); Galloway and Murphy (1991); Campbell, Galloway and Murphy (1992)
58. Postles (1984), Farmer (1991)
59. Holt, N. R. (1964), 153 and 156; Farmer (1991), 368
60. Ashford (1960)
61. Davis, R. H. C. (1973)
62. Farmer (1991), 353
63. Gras (1915), 164-165; Farmer (1991), 371-72; Roden (1966)
64. Kingsford (1919)

Chapter 6
1. Campbell (1990)
2. Kershaw (1973)
3. Titow (1962, 1972)
4. Kershaw (1973); Roden (1965); BL: MS Stowe 849 f43v
5. Baker (1966, 1970)
6. Baker (1970), 15
7. Roden (1970); Ashford (1960)
8. Elvey E. M. (1961), 32
9. Roden (1970), 66
10. Roden (1970), 67; Register of

Edward the Black Prince, iv (1933), 342
11. Harvey (1991), 676
12. Elvey E. M. (1961), 33
13. Preece (1990c), 15
14. Anon (1981); Riley (1867-69), vol. 3
15. Beresford (1953, 1954)
16. Beresford (1954), 231
17. Glennie (1983), 25-51
18. Roden (1970), 68. Oxwik: Roden (1965), 181; BL: MS Stowe 849, f89-89v
19. Johnson and Fenley (1971-74); Hughes (1931)
20. Chambers (1973)
21. Lobel (1964), 210-33; Allison et al. (1965)
22. Elvey E. M. (1961), 37-39
23. Roden (1965), 329-30
24. Cornwall (1970, 1988)
25. Roberts, E. (1974)
26. Bond, Gosling and Rhodes (1980); Stebbing, Rhodes and Meller (1980)
27. Money and Smith (1973); Turner, H. L. (1972); Fletcher (1975)
28. Evans, R. W. (1987)
29. Johnson and Fenley (1974)

Chapter 7
1. Darby and Campbell (1962), 211; Rackham (1980), 111-27
2. Rackham (1980), 123
3. Riley (1867-69)
4. Fitzstephen (c.1180)
5. Calendar of Ancient Deeds vi (1915, PRO), 168 c5065; see also Roden (1968), 62
6. Roden (1965,1966)
7. Lobel (1964), 166
8. Roden (1968), 64
9. PRO: C 47/37/5; Preece (1987, 1987-88, 1990a)
10. Roden (1965), 259
11. Lobel (1964), 166
12. Jenkins (1938), 68-69; BL: Harley 3688 f24v-25r
13. Kingsford (1919), vol.2, 141, no.307
14. Calendar of Ancient Deeds vi (1915, PRO), 245, c5623
15. Fowler (1926); BL: Harley 1885 f76v
16. Rackham (1990), 145
17. Jenkins (1938), 122-23; BL: Harley 3688 f37v
18. Hanley (1987)
19. Lobel (1964), 106
20. PRO: C 133/95
21. Hassall (1951)
22. Preece(1987, 1987-88, 1990a)
23. Prince (1954, 1959)
24. Lobel (1964), 230; PRO: E 36/157, 14-15
25. Kingsford (1919), vol.2, 19, no.176

26. Pavry and Knocker (1957-58), 170
27. Peterken (1981)
28. Mansfield (1952)
29. La Sueur (1955)
30. Bowen (1977, 1980); Harding and Rose (1986)
31. Roden (1965), 306-235
32. *Register of Edward the Black Prince*, iv (1933)
33. Rackham (1980), 325-26

Chapter 8
1. Cornwall (1959), 265
2. Hartley, D. (1931), 178-82
3. Roden (1965), 51060; Roden (1969a), 119
4. BRO: D/MH/28/2; see Roden (1965), 69-75; Roden (1973); Owen (1984)
5. Munby (1977), 168-69
6. Lobel (1964), 105
7. Gibson (1989); Havinden (1961a)
8. Dils (1987); Gras(1915)
9. PRO: SP 12/198, item 27
10. Blome (1673); see Dils (1987)
11. Kussmaul (1990)
12. Bodl: Gough MS 47 [Delafield's *History of Stokenchurch*], f173
13. Blith (1652)
14. Havinden (1961a); Glennie (1983, 1988a, 1988b)
15. Glennie (1983, 1988b)
16. Glennie (1988b), 150
17. Havinden (1961a), 255
18. Young, A. [Arthur] (1813), 119
19. Havinden (1965); Lobel (1964), 31
20. Ellis (1733), preface, ii
21. Ellis (1733), quotes at 2, 19 and 3
22. Bodl: Gough MS 47 [Delafield's *History of Stokenchurch*], f174
23. Ellis (1733), 26
24. Quoted in Bell (1956), 107
25. Ellis (1733), 20 and 4
26. Lucas (1892); Mead (1962)
27. Lucas (1892), quotes at 178, 255, 281-82, 327, 232, 187
28. Dils (1987)
29. Ashford (1960), 203
30. Elliman (1987)
31. Ashford (1960), 215
32. Prince (1954, 1959)
33. Kemp (1967)
34. Stroud (1975); Prince (1959)
35. Stroud (1962); Prince (1959)
36. Repton (1803), 61

Chapter 9
1. Baker (1932)
2. Lambert (1953)
3. quoted in Starey and Viccars (1992), 76
4. Pawson (1977)

5. Pawson (1977), 246, quoting *Journal of House of Commons*
6. Lobel (1964), 16
7. Bodl: MS Ad A262 [William Bayzard, 'Coaching In and Out of Oxford from 1820 to 1840 by A Chip off the old Block, with Anecdotes and Reminiscences in his 75 years'], 35-36
8. Quoted in Briers (1939)
9. Chibnall (1963)
10. Godber (1969), 316-17
11. Roberts, C. (1936), 44
12. Homer (1767), 6
13. Lambert (1953), 225
14. ORO: CH/S/II/i/1 [Stokenchurch to Woodstock Trust Minute Book 1740-93]
15. Hart (1975)
16. Faulkner (1972, 1975)
17. Richardson, A. (1969); Ware (1989)
18. Priest (1810), 338
19. Lambert (1953), 267-68
20. Faulkner (1975)
21. Evans, J. (1955)
22. Boyle (1848), 20
23. Simmons (1961), 7
24. quoted in Page, W. (1908), 104
25. Simmons (1961), 6
26. Scott (1907)
27. Cockman (1972, 1974); Coles (1980); Oppitz (1991)
28. Kirkland (1956); Christiansen (1981)
29. Coles (1980)
30. Bagwell (1974), 109
31. Disraeli (1845)
32. Whetham (1964-65)

Chapter 10
1. Rackham (1980), 167
2. *Calendar of Patent Rolls*, 16 August 1559
3. Prior (1981)
4. Bodl: MS Top Oxon d.46; Dils (1987); Mansfield (1952), 129
5. Defoe (1724-27)
6. Plot (1672), 267
7. BRO: D/D/14/55 and D/D/14/56 [Dashwood Deeds]
8. BRO: D/MH/30 [Hampden Wood Books; 30/4 is 1695-99]
9. Bodl: MS Top Oxon c404 172-75
10. Bodl: MS Top Oxon c206 107-16
11. Mansfield (1952), 22-42
12. Lobel (1964), 166, quoting Stonor Muniments
13. Bodl: MS Top Oxon c446, 11: MS Top Oxon c206, 184
14. Commissioners of Land Revenue (1792)
15. Ellis (1733), 93
16. Langley (1797), 1
17. Young, A. [Arthur] (1813), 221
18. BRO: D/MH/30; Mansfield

(1952), 123
19. Commissioners of Land Revenue (1792), 70
20. James and Malcolm (1794), 41
21. Collins (1989)
22. Mansfield (1952), 146
23. James and Malcolm (1794); Langley (1797), 9; Priest (1810), 225
24. McCreath (1986); Beckett (1985)
25. Mayes (1960); Sparkes (1989)
26. North (1882)
27. Sheahan (1862), 920
28. McCreath (1986)
29. Stokenchurch: quoted by Mansfield (1952), 131
30. Massingham (1940); for Stoke Row, see Baker (1959)
31. Peterken (1981)
32. Preece (1987, 1990b)
33. Peterken (1981), 74-76
34. Watt (1934)

Chapter 11
1. Tate (1978); Turner, M. E. (1980); for Bucks., see Turner, M. E. (1973)
2. Lobel (1964), 105-6; ORO: Lewknor Inclosure Award
3. Young, A. [Arthur] (1813), 103
4. Turner, M. E. (1973), 197-208; BRO: Princes Risborough and Monks Risborough Enclosure Papers
5. BRO: IR/M/1/7
6. Bond, Gosling and Rhodes (1980); Stebbing, Rhodes and Meller (1980)
7. Hay and Hay (1971), 120-21
8. Owen (1984), quoting BRO: D42/c28/1
9. Jackson, C. C. (1977)
10. Hoskins and Stamp (1963)
11. Whybrow (1934)
12. Thirsk (1961)
13. Palliser (1864); Spenceley (1973)
14. Pepys Diary, May 21 1663: Palliser (1864), 314
15. Defoe (1727), 332
16. Langley (1797)
17. Buck (1978)
18. Horn (1974, 1991)
19. Buck (1981)
20. Cole, A. S. (1892)
21. Gróf (1988), 14-19
22. Gibbs (1885)
23. Gróf (1988)
24. Horn and Horn (1983)
25. Greenwood (1883), 28
26. Gróf (1988)
27. Thorburn (1989)
28. Gróf (1988), 84
29. Children's Employment Commission (1864), 201
30. Buckinghamshire Federation of Women's Institutes (1975), 20-21

31. Lobel (1964), 231
32. Casselden (1987)
33. Starey and Viccars (1992), 153-57
34. Greening Lamborn (1936);
    Baines (1981a)
35. Coppock (1960a, 1961)
36. Prince (1981), 20
37. Coppock (1961), Whetham
    (1964-65)
38. Baker (1937), 182
39. Coppock (1957, 1961)
40. Ellis (1738), 65-70
41. Coppock (1961, 16)

Chapter 12
1. See Edwards and Pigram (1977,
   1979, 1983); Jackson, A.A. (1986)
2. *Metro-land* (1987 reprint), 37
   and 38
3. Lowerson (1980)
4. Page, H. E. (1937)
5. Jackson A. A. (1973, 1976)
6. Betjeman (1978), 231
7. Coppock (1964)
8. Jackson A. A. (1973)
9. Lean and Pettit (n.d.)
10. Sheail (1981)
11. Trevelyan (1929)
12. Jeans (1990)
13. Williams-Ellis (1928; 1937)
14. Matless (1990b)
15. Peach and Carrington (1930)
16. Matless (1990a)
17. Massingham (1940), 106
18. Perkin (1976), 135 and 147

19. *Motor Owner* (1920)
20. In Williams-Ellis (1937), 72-73;
    Jeans (1991)
21. Massingham (1940), 73
22. King (1984)
23. In Williams-Ellis (1937), 213
24. Harman (1986)
25. Hardy and Wood (1984), 184
26. Williams-Ellis, in Peach and
    Carrington (1930)
27. Stevenson (1907), 140
28. Williams-Ellis, in CPRE [Penn
    Branch] (1933), 105

Chapter 13
1. Coppock (1957)
2. Hoskins and Stamp (1963)
3. Smith C. J. (1980)
4. Smith C. J. (1980)
5. Rackham (1986), 342; Wells
   (1968); Wells and Barling (1971)
6. Watt (1923, 1934)
7. Ward (1973)
8. Brett (1965)
9. Harman (1986)
10. Bourne (1931); Robbins (1931)
11. Forestry Commission (1961)
12. Chilterns Standing Conference
    (1971)
13. Sheail (1976, 1987)
14. Tansley (1939)
15. Salisbury (1918)
16. Sheail (1976), 153
17. Ratcliffe (1978); Peterken
    (1981)

Chapter 14
1. Abercrombie (1945)
2. Hall (1989), 36
3. Hall (1989)
4. Hall (1963)
5. Chilterns Standing Conference
   (1971)
6. Mabey (1980), 111; Mabey
   (1990)
7. Cobbett (1830)
8. Chilterns Standing Conference
   (1971)
9. Chilterns Standing Conference
   (1991, 1992)
10. Chilterns Standing Conference
    (1971), 73-74
11. Chilterns Standing Conference
    (1988, 1991, 1992, 1993, 1994);
    Countryside Commission (1992)
12. Smart and Anderson (1990);
    Heynes in Chilterns Standing
    Conference (1992)
13. Chilterns Standing Conference
    (1971), 9
14. Chilterns Standing Conference
    (1991), 3
15. Chilterns Standing Conference
    (1993, 1994)
16. Chilterns Standing Conference
    (1988); see also Hornby (1987)
17. The 1725 map is displayed in
    Stonor House: the details are
    given in Ulyanov (1972)
18. Hoskins (1955)

References

Abercrombie, P. 1945 *Greater London Plan 1944*. London: HMSO.

Allen, R.C. 1992 *Enclosure and the Yeoman*. Oxford: Clarendon Press.

Allison, K.J., Beresford, M.W. and Hurst, J.G. 1965 *The Deserted Villages of Oxfordshire*. Leicester: Leicester University Department of English Local History, Occasional Paper 17.

Anon (ed.) 1981 *The Peasant's Revolt in Hertfordshire: The Rising and its Background*. Hertford: Hertfordshire Publications (Hertfordshire Library Service)

Ashford, L.J. 1960 *The History of the Borough of High Wycombe, from its origins to 1880*. London: Routledge and Kegan Paul.

Ault, W.O. 1972 *Open-Field Farming in Medieval England. A Study in Village By-Laws*. London: George Allen and Unwin.

Avery, B.W. 1964 *The Soils and Land Use of the District around Aylesbury and Hemel Hempstead. Memoirs of the Soil Survey of Great Britain*. London: HMSO.

Bagwell, P.S. 1974 *The Transport Revolution from 1770*. London: B.T.Batsford.

Bailey, K. 1989 'The Middle Saxons', in Bassett, S. (ed), *The Origins of Anglo-Saxon Kingdoms*, 108-22. Leicester: Leicester University Press.

Baines, A.H.J. 1981a 'Turville, Radenore and the Chiltern Feld', *Records of Buckinghamshire* 23, 4-22.

Baines, A.H.J. 1981b 'The boundaries of Monk's Risborough', *Records of Buckinghamshire* 23, 76-101.

Baines, A.H.J. 1983 'The Lady Elgiva, St.Aethwold and the Linslade charter of 966', *Records of Buckinghamshire* 25, 110-38.

Baines, A.H.J. 1984a 'Anglo-Saxon Buckinghamshire: the evolution of a duality in the cultural landscape'. Unpublished Ph.D. thesis, The Open University.

Baines, A.H.J. 1984b 'Cholesbury-cum-St.Leonards: a modern perambulation of ancient boundaries', *Records of Buckinghamshire* 26, 131-34.

Baker, A.R.H. 1966 'Evidence in the Nonarum Inquisitiones of contracting arable lands in England during the early fourteenth century', *Economic History Review*, series 2, 19, 518-32.

Baker, A.R.H. 1970 'Contracting arable lands in 1341', *Bedfordshire Historical Record Society* 39, 7-18.

Baker, J.H. 1932 *The Story of the Chiltern Heathlands*. Reading: Jas Golder.

Baker, J.H. 1937 *Land of the Gap*. Oxford: Basil Blackwell.

Baker, J.H. 1959 *The Ipsden Country*. Reading: William Smith.

Beckett, I.F.W. (ed) 1985 *The Buckinghamshire Posse Comitatus of 1798*. Aylesbury: Buckinghamshire Record Society, 22.

Beddoe, J. 1885 *The Races of Britain*. Bristol: J.W. Arrowsmith.

Bell, M. 1983 'Valley sediments as evidence of prehistoric land-use on the South Downs', *Proceedings of the Prehistoric Society*, 49, 119-50.

Bell, V. 1956 *To Meet Mr.Ellis. Little Gaddesden in the Eighteenth Century*. London: Faber.

Beresford, M.W. 1953 'Glebe terriers and open-field Buckinghamshire. Part II', *Records of Buckinghamshire* 16, 5-28.

Beresford, M.W. 1954 *The Lost Villages of England*. London: Lutterworth Press.

Beresford, M.W. 1967 *New Towns of the Middle Ages*. London: Lutterworth Press.

Betjeman, J. 1960 *Summoned by Bells*. London: John Murray.

Betjeman, J. 1978 *The Best of Betjeman*, selected by J.Guest. London: Penguin.

Blair, J. (ed) 1988a *Minsters and Parish Churches: The Local Church in Transition 950-1200*. Oxford: Oxford Committee for Archaeology.

Blair, J. 1988b 'Minster churches in the landscape', in Hooke, D. (ed) *Anglo-Saxon Settlements*, 35-58. Oxford: Basil Blackwell.

Blair, J. 1989 'Frithuwold's kingdom and the origins of Surrey', in Bassett, S. (ed) *The Origins of Anglo-Saxon Kingdoms*, 97-107. Leicester: Leicester University Press.

Blith, W. 1652 *The English Improver Improved*. London: John Wright.

Bloch, M. 1967 'The advent and triumph of the watermill', in *Land and work in Medieval Europe: Selected Papers*, 136-68. London: Routledge & Kegan Paul.

Blome, R. 1673 *Britannia*. London: Thomas Roycroft for R.Blome.

Blythe, R. 1986 *Divine Landscapes*. Harmondsworth: Viking.

Bond, J., Gosling, S. and Rhodes J. 1980 *Oxfordshire Brickmakers*. Woodstock, Oxford: Oxford Museums Service Publication 14.

Bourne, R. 1931 *Regional Survey, and its relation to stocktaking of the agricultural and forest resources of the British Empire*. Oxford: Clarendon Press.

Bowen, H.J.M. 1977 'Indicators of old forest', *Reading Naturalist* 29, 2-8.

Bowen, H.J.M. 1980 'A lichen flora of Berkshire, Buckinghamshire and Oxfordshire', *Lichenologist* 12, 199-237.

Boyle, T. 1848 *Hope for the Canals, Showing the evil of Amalgamations with Railways to Public and Private Interest*. London.

Bradley, R. 1968 'The South Oxfordshire Grim's Ditch and its significance', *Oxoniensia* 33, 1-12.

Branigan, K. 1967 'The distribution and development of Romano-British occupation in the Chess Valley', *Records of Buckinghamshire* 18, 136-49.

Branigan, K. 1968 'Romano-British rural settlement in the western Chilterns', *Archaeological Journal* 124, 129-59.

Branigan, K. 1969 'The Romano-British villa at Saunderton reconsidered', *Records of Buckinghamshire* 18, 261-76.

Branigan, K. 1971a *Latimer: Belgic, Roman and Dark Age and early modern farms*. Chesham: Chess Valley Archaeological and Historical Society.

Branigan, K 1971b 'Pavements and poverty in the Chiltern villas', *Britannia* 2, 109-16.

Branigan, K. 1973 *Town and Country: Verulamium and the Roman Chilterns*. Bourne End: Spur Books.

Branigan, K. 1985 *The Catuvellauni*. Gloucester: Alan Sutton.

Brett, L. 1965 *Landscape in Distress*. London: The Architectural Press.

Briers, P.M. 1939 *History of Nuffield*. Oxford: privately published (Lord Nuffield)

Buck, A. 1978 'Middlemen in the Bedfordshire Lace industry', *Bedfordshire Historical Record Society* 57, 31-58.

Buck, A. 1981 *Thomas Lester, his Lace and the East Midlands Industry 1820-1905*. Carlton, Bedford: Ruth Bean.

Buchan, J. 1916 *The Power House*. Edinburgh & London: W. Blackwood & sons.

Buckinghamshire Federation of Women's Institutes 1975 *A Pattern of Hundreds*. Chalfont St Giles: Richard Sadler Ltd.

Burn, J.S. 1861 *A History of Henley-on-Thames*. London: Longman.

Cam, H. 1944 *Liberties and Communities in Medieval England*. Cambridge: Cambridge University Press.

Campbell, B.M.S. 1988 'The diffusion of vetches in medieval England', *Economic History Review*, 2nd series, 41, 193-208.

Campbell, B.M.S. 1990 'People and land in the Middle Ages, 1066-1500', in Dodgshon, R.A. and Butlin, R.A. (eds), *An Historical Geography of England and Wales* (2nd Edition), 69-121. London: Academic Press.

Campbell, B.M.S., Galloway, J.A. and Murphy, M. 1992 'Rural land-use in the metropolitan hinterland, 1270-1339: the evidence of the Inquisitions Post Mortem', *Agricultural History Review* 40, 1-22.

Case, H. 1958 'A late Belgic burial at Watlington', *Oxoniensia* 23, 139-41.

Casselden, P 1986 'Chartridge and Pednor hedgerows: a landscape study. Part 1', *Records of Buckinghamshire* 28, 182-210.

Casselden, P. 1987 'Chartridge and Pednor hedgerows: a landscape study. Part 2', *Records of Buckinghamshire* 29, 133-59.

Chambers, R.A. 1973 'A deserted medieval farmstead at Sadler's Wood, Lewknor', *Oxoniensia* 38, 146-67.

Chenevix Trench, J. 1973 'Coleshill and the settlement of the Chilterns', *Records of Buckinghamshire* 19, 241-58.

Chenevix Trench, J. 1978 'Fields and farms in a hilltop village', *Records of Buckinghamshire* 20, 410-30.

Chenevix Trench, J. 1983 'The houses of Coleshill: the social anatomy of a seventeenth century village', *Records of Buckinghamshire* 25, 61-109.

Chibnall, A.C (ed) 1966 *Early Taxation Returns*. Buckinghamshire Record Society 14. Welwyn Garden City: Broadwater Press.

Chibnall, J. 1963 'The roads of Buckinghamshire with special reference to turnpike roads'. Unpublished M.Sc. thesis, University of London.

Childe, V.G. and Smith, I.F. 1954 'The excavation of a Neolithic barrow on Whiteleaf Hill, Bucks', *Proceedings of the Prehistoric Society* 20, 212-30.

Children's Employment Commission. 1864 *Second Report of the Children's Employment Commission*. Parliamentary Papers, 1864, vol. 22.

Chilterns Standing Conference 1971 *A Plan for the Chilterns*. Aylesbury: Chilterns Standing Conference.

Chilterns Standing Conference 1988 *A Plan for the Chilterns: Woodland Policy*. Aylesbury: Chilterns Standing Conference.

Chilterns Standing Conference 1991 *The Chilterns Area of Outstanding Natural Beauty. A Statement of Intent*. Aylesbury: Chilterns Standing Conference.

Chilterns Standing Conference 1992 *The Chilterns...What Future?* Proceedings of a Seminar, 1 July 1992.

Chilterns Standing Conference 1993 *The Chilterns AONB Draft Management Plan*. Bedford: Chilterns Standing Conference.

Chilterns Standing Conference 1994 *The Chilterns AONB Management Plan*. Bedford: Chilterns Standing Conference.

Christiansen, R. 1981 *Thames and Severn: A Regional History of the Railways of Great Britain*, volume 13. Newton Abbot: David and Charles.

Cobbett, W. 1830 *Rural Rides*. London.

Cockman, F.G. 1972 'The railway era in Buckinghamshire', *Records of Buckinghamshire* 19 (2), 156-168.

Cockman, F.G. 1974 *The Railway Age in Bedfordshire*. Bedford: Bedford Historical Record Society, 53.

Cole, A. 1982 'Topography, hydrology, and place-names in the chalklands of southern England: cumb and denu', *Nomina* 6, 73-87.

Cole, A. 1985 'Topography, hydrology, and place-names in the chalklands of southern England: *funta, -ewiell and -ewielm*', *Nomina* 9, 3-19.

Cole, A. 1989 'The meaning of the OE place-name element ora', *Journal of the English Place-Name Society* 21, 15-22.

Cole, A. 1990 'The origin, distribution and use of the place-name element ora and its relationship to the element ofer', *Journal of the English Place-Name Society* 22, 27-41.

Cole, A.S. 1892 *Report on Northampton, Bucks. and Beds. Lace-Making, 1891*. London: Department of Science and Art.

Coles, C.R.L. 1980 *Railways through the Chilterns*. London: Ian Allan.

Collett, A. 1926 *The Changing Face of England*. London: Nisbet & Co.

Collins, E.J.T. 1989 'The coppice and underwood trades', in Mingay, G.E. (ed), *The Agrarian History of England and Wales, volume VI 1750-1850*, 485-501. Cambridge: Cambridge University Press.

Commissioners of Land Revenue 1792 *The Eleventh Report of the Commissioners appointed to enquire into the State and Condition of the Woods, Forests, and Land Revenue of the Crown*. London: House of Commons Paper 4322.

Coppock, J.T. 1957 'The changing arable in the Chilterns 1875-1951', *Geography* 42, 217-29.

Coppock, J.T. 1959 'The Chilterns as an Area of Outstanding Natural Beauty', *Journal of the Town Planning Institute* 45, 137-41.

Coppock, J.T. 1960a 'The agricultural geography of the Chilterns, 1870-1951'. Unpublished Ph.D. thesis, University of London.

Coppock, J.T. 1960b 'Farms and fields in the Chilterns', *Erdkunde* 14, 134-46.

Coppock, J.T. 1961 'Agricultural changes in the Chilterns, 1875-1900,' *Agricultural History Review* 9, 1-16.

Coppock, J.T. 1964 'Dormitory settlements around London', in Coppock, J.T. and Prince, H.C. (eds), *Greater London*, 265-91. London: Faber & Faber.

Coppock, J.T. 1968. *The Chilterns*. Sheffield: The Geographical Association (Landscapes through Maps, 4).

Cornwall, J. 1959 'An Elizabethan census', *Records of Buckinghamshire* 16 (4), 258-73.

Cornwall, J. 1970 'English population in the early sixteenth century', *Economic History Review,* 2nd series, 33, 32-44.

Cornwall, J. 1975. 'Medieval peasant farmers', *Records of Buckinghamshire* 20, 57-75.

Cornwall, J.C.K. 1988 *Wealth and Society in Early Sixteenth Century England*. London: Routledge & Kegan Paul.

Cotton, M.A. and Frere, S.S. 1968 'Ivinghoe Beacon excavations 1963-1965', *Records of Buckinghamshire* 18, 187-260.

Countryside Commission 1992 *The Chilterns Landscape*. CCP 392. Cheltenham: Countryside Commission.

Cox, B. 1972-73 'The significance of the distribution of English place-names in -ham in the midlands and East Anglia', *Journal of the English Place-Name Society* 5, 15-73.

Cox, B. 1975-76 'The place-names of the earliest English records', *Journal of the English Place-Name Society* 8, 12-66.

CPRE (Council for the Preservation of Rural England) 1929 *The Thames Valley from Cricklade to Staines*. London: University of London Press.

CPRE (Penn Branch) 1933 *'The Penn Country of Buckinghamshire,* London: Council for the Preservation of Rural England.

Crawford, O.G.S. 1931 'The Chiltern Grim's Ditches', *Antiquity* 5, 161-71, 291-314, 370.

Cunliffe, B. 1991 (3rd edn) *Iron Age Communities in Britain*. London: Routledge.

Dahlman, C.J. 1980 *The Open Field System and Beyond*. Cambridge: Cambridge University Press.

Darby, H.C. and Campbell, E.M.J. (eds) 1962 *The Domesday Geography of South-East England*. Cambridge: Cambridge University Press.

Davies, A.M. 1949. 'Abefeld and Ackhamstead: two lost places', *Records of Buckinghamshire* 15, 166-77.

Davies, A.M. 1951-52 'The hundreds of Buckinghamshire and Oxfordshire', *Records of Buckinghamshire* 16, 231-49.

Davies, A.M. and Baines, A.H.J. 1953 'A preliminary study of the sarsen and pudding-stone blocks of the Chilterns', *Proceedings of the Geologists' Association of London* 64, 1-9.

Davies, W. and Vierck, H. 1974 'The contexts of the Tribal Hidage: social aggregates and settlement patterns', *Fruhmittelalterliche Studien* 8, 223-93.

Davis, J. 1981 'Grim's Ditch in Buckinghamshire and Hertfordshire', *Records of Buckinghamshire* 23, 23-31.

Davis, J. and Evans, J.G. 1984 'Grim's Ditch, Ivinghoe', *Records of Buckinghamshire* 26, 1-10.

Davis, K Rutherford, 1982 *Britons and Saxons. The Chiltern Region 400-700*. Chichester: Phillimore.

Davis, R. 1794 *A General View of the Agriculture of the County of Oxford*. London: Board of Agriculture.

Davis, R.H.C. 1973 'The ford, the river and the city', *Oxoniensia* 38, 258-67.

Defoe, D. 1724-27 *A Tour thro' the Whole Island of Great Britain, divided into circuits or journeys*. 3 vols. London: G.Strahan. [Everyman edition, 1962, by Dent, London]

Defoe, D. 1726-27 *The Compleat English Tradesman*. 2 vols. London: Charles Rivington.

Dils, J.A. 1987 'Henley and the river trade in the pre-industrial period', *Oxfordshire Local History* 2(6), 182-92.

Disraeli, B. 1845 *Sybil; or, The Two Nations*. London: Henry Colburn.

Dyer, C.C. 1989 'The retreat from marginal land': the growth and decline of medieval rural settlements, in Aston, M., Austin, D., and Dyer, C. (eds), *The Rural Settlements of Medieval England*, 45-57. Oxford: Basil Blackwell.

Dyer, J.F. 1959 'Barrows of the Chilterns', *Archaeological Journal* 116, 1-24.

Dyer, J.F. 1961 'Dray's ditches, Bedfordshire, and early Iron Age territorial boundaries in the eastern Chilterns', *Antiquaries Journal* 41, 32-43.

Dyer, J.F. 1963 'The Chiltern Grim's Ditch', *Antiquity* 37, 46-49.

Dyer, J. 1978 'Worthington George Smith', in *Worthington George Smith and Other Studies, presented to Joyce Godber*, 141-79. Bedford: Bedfordshire Historical Record Society, 57.

Dyer, J.F. and Hales, A.J. 1962 'Pitstone Hill—a study on field archaeology', *Records of Buckinghamshire* 17, 49-54.

Edwards, D. and Pigram, R. 1977 *Metro Memories.* (1988 edition) London: Bloomsbury Books.
Edwards, D. and Pigram, R. 1979 *The Romance of Metro-land.* (1988 edition) London: Bloomsbury Books.
Edwards, D. and Pigram, R. 1983 *The Golden Years of the Metropolitan Railway.* (1988 ed.)London: Bloomsbury
Eland, G. 1911 *The Chilterns and the Vale.* London: Longmans, Green & Co.
Elliman, P.D. 1987 'Glassmaking in Henley-on-Thames in the 17th century', *Henley Archaeological and Historical Group Journal,* 5, 2-15.
Ellis, W. 1733 *Chiltern and Vale Farming Explained.* London.
Ellis, W. 1738 *The Timber-Tree Improved.* London.
Elvey, E.M. 1961 'The Abbot of Missenden's estates at Chalfont St Giles', *Records of Buckinghamshire* 17, 20-40.
Elvey, G.R. 1977 'Walter of Henley reconsidered', *Records of Buckinghamshire* 20 (3), 470-77.
Emery, F.V. 1974 *The Oxfordshire Landscape.* London: Hodder and Stoughton.
Esmonde Cleary, A.S. 1989 *The Ending of Roman Britain.* London: B.T.Batsford.
Esposito, M. 1917 'The letters of Brunetto Latino. A nineteenth-century literary hoax', *Modern Languages Review* 12, 59-63.
Evans, J. 1955 *The Endless Web. John Dickinson & Co. Ltd 1804-1954.* London: Jonathan Cape.
Evans, J.G. 1966 'Late-glacial and post-glacial subaerial deposits at Pitstone, Buckinghamshire', *Proceedings of the Geological Association,* 77, 347-64.
Evans, J.G. 1972 *Land Snails in Archaeology.* London: Academic Press.
Evans, J.G. 1975 *The Environment of Early Man in the British Isles.* London: Paul Elek.
Evans, J.G. and Valentine, K.W.G. 1974 'Ecological changes induced by prehistoric man at Pitstone, Buckinghamshire', *Journal of Archaeological Science* 1, 343-351.
Evans, R.W. 1987 'A gazetteer of cruck buildings in Buckinghamshire', *Records of Buckinghamshire* 29, 205-10.
Everitt, A. 1986 *Continuity and Colonization. The Evolution of Kentish Settlement.* Leicester: Leicester University Press.
Farley, M. 1976 'Saxon and Medieval Walton, Aylesbury: excavations 1973-4', *Records of Buckinghamshire* 20, 153-290.
Farley, M. 1978 'Excavations at Low Farm, Fulmer, Bucks. 1: The Mesolithic occupation', *Records of Buckinghamshire* 20 (4), 601-16.
Farley, M. 1979 'A bell-pit or chalk well at Lane End', *Records of Buckinghamshire* 21, 135-40.
Farmer, D.L. 1991 'Marketing the produce of the countryside, 1200-1500', in Miller, E. (ed), *The Agrarian History of England and Wales,* vol.III 1348-1500, 324-429. Cambridge: Cambridge University Press.
Faulkner, A.H. 1972 *The Grand Junction Canal.* Newton Abbot: David & Charles.
Faulkner, A.H. 1987 *The Grand Union Canal in Hertfordshire.* Stevenage: Hertfordshire Publications.
Fenwick, C.C. 1983 'The English poll taxes of 1377, 1379 and 1381. A critical examination of the returns'. Unpublished Ph.D. thesis, London School of Economics, University of London.
Fitzstephen, W. (*c.*1180) *Vita Sancti Thomae Cantuariensis Archiepiscopi,* edited by J. Sparke (1723). London: Bowyn.
Fletcher, J. 1975 'The medieval hall at Lewknor', *Oxoniensia* 40, 247-53.
Forestry Commission 1961 *Forestry and Mature Beech. Chilterns: Queen Wood.* London: Forestry Commission.
Fowler, G.H.(ed) 1926 *A Digest of the Charters Preserved in the Cartulary of the Priory of Dunstable.* Apsley Guise: Bedfordshire Historical Record Society, 10.
Fox, H.S.A. 1981 'Approaches to the adoption of the Midland system', in Rowley, T. (ed), *The Origins of Open-field Agriculture,* 64-111. London: Croom Helm.
Fox, H.S.A. 1984 'Some ecological dimensions of medieval field systems', in Biddick, K. (ed), *Archaeological Approaches to Medieval Europe,* 119-58. Kalamazoo, Michigan: Western Michigan University (Studies in Medieval Culture 18, Medieval Institute Publications).
Fox, H.S.A. 1986 'The alleged transformation from two-field to three-field systems in medieval England', *Economic History Review,* 2nd series, 39, 526-48.
Frere, S.S. 1966 'The end of towns in Roman Britain', in Wacher, J.S. (ed), *The Civitas Capitals of Roman Britain,* 87-100. Leicester: Leicester University Press.
Frere, S.S. 1972 *Verulamium Excavations, 1.* London: Report of the Research Committee, Society of Antiquaries of London, 28.
Frere, S.S. 1983 *Verulamium Excavations, 2.* London: Report of the Research Committee, Society of Antiquaries of London, 41.
Frere, S.S. 1984 *Verulamium Excavations, 3.* Oxford: Oxford University University Committee for Archaeology, 1.
Frere, S.S. 1987 (3rd edn) *Britannia. A History of Roman Britain.* London: Routledge & Kegan Paul.
Galloway, J.A. and Murphy, M. 1991 'Feeding the city: medieval London and its agrarian hinterland', *The London Journal* 16, 3-14.
Gelling, M. 1953-54 *The Place-Names of Oxfordshire.* 2 vols. Cambridge: Cambridge University Press.
Gelling, M. 1976 *The Place-Names of Berkshire,* volume 3. Nottingham: English Place-Name Society.
Gelling, M. 1979 *Early Charters of the Thames Valley.* Leicester: Leicester University Press.
Gelling, M. 1978 *Signposts to the Past.* London: Dent.
Gelling, M. 1984 *Place-Names in the Landscape.* London: Dent
Gibbs, R. 1885 *A History of Aylesbury.* Aylesbury: R.Gibbs
Gibson, R. 1985 'A farm in the Chilterns', *Oxfordshire Local History* 2(3), 94-98.
Gibson, R.E. 1989 'Continuity and change in a Chiltern Parish: Harpsden 1586-1879'. Unpublished dissertation for joint degree in Archaeology and History, University of Reading.
Glennie, P.D. 1983 'A commercialising agrarian region: late medieval and early modern Hertfordshire'. Unpublished Ph.D.

thesis, University of Cambridge.

Glennie, P.D. 1988a 'Continuity and change in Hertfordshire agriculture, 1550-1700: I - patterns of agricultural production', *Agricultural History Review* 36, 55-75.

Glennie, P.D. 1988b 'Continuity and change in Hertfordshire agriculture, 1550-1700: II - trends in crop yields and their determinants', *Agricultural History Review* 36, 145-61.

Godber, J. 1969 *History of Bedfordshire 1066-1888*. Bedford: Bedfordshire County Council.

Gras, N.S.B. 1915 *The Evolution of the English Corn Market*. Cambridge, Massachussetts: Harvard University Press.

Gray, H.L. 1915 *English Field Systems*. Cambridge, Massachussetts: Harvard University Press.

Greening Lamborn, E.A. 1936 'The churches of Bix', *Oxoniensia*, 1, 129-39.

Greenwood, J. 1883 *On the tramp*. London: Diprose and Bateman.

Gróf, L.L. 1988 *Children of Straw. The Story of a Vanished Craft and Industry in Bucks, Herts, Beds and Essex*. Buckingham: Barracuda Books.

Grundy, G.B. 1933 *Saxon Oxfordshire. Charters and Ancient Highways*. Oxford: Oxfordshire Record Society, volume 15.

Hale, W. (ed) 1858 *The Domesday of St.Paul's of the Year M.CC.XXII*. London: Camden Society Publications, 69.

Hall, P. 1963 *London 2000*. London: Faber and Faber.

Hall, P. 1989 *London 2001*. London: Unwin Hyman.

Hanley, H.A. 1975 'Population and mobility in Buckinghamshire, 1578-1583', *Local Population Studies* 15, 33-39.

Hanley, H.A. 1987 'The inclosure of Pitstone Common Wood in 1612', *Records of Buckinghamshire* 29, 175-204.

Harding, D.W. 1972 *The Iron Age in the Upper Thames Basin*. Oxford: Clarendon Press.

Harding, P.T. and Rose, F. 1986 *Pasture-woodlands in lowland Britain. Monks Wood,* Huntingdon: Institute of Terrestrial Ecology, NERC.

Hardy, D. and Ward, C. 1984 *Arcadia for all. The legacy of a makeshift landscape*. London and New York: Mansell.

Harman, T. 1986 *Seventy Summers*. London: BBC Publications.

Hart, H.W. 1975 'Henley-on-Thames: pre-railway road services', *Journal of the Railway and Canal History Society*, 21, 50-54.

Hart-Davis, D. 1991 'Waking the white ghost', *Country Life*, April 4, 82-85.

Hartley, D. (ed) 1931 *Thomas Tusser. His Good Points of Husbandry*. London: Country Life.

Hartley, F.D. 1953 'The agricultural geography of the Chilterns c1840', unpublished M.A. thesis, University of London.

Harvey, P.D.A. 1965 *A Medieval Oxfordshire Village: Cuxham 1240-1400*. Oxford: Oxford University Press.

Harvey, P.D.A. 1991 'The Home Counties', in Miller, E. (ed) *The Agrarian History of England and Wales*: volume III 1348-1500, 106-19 and 254-68 and 662-79. Cambridge: Cambridge University Press.

Hassall, W.O. 1951 'Hillwork', *Oxoniensia* 16, 89-90.

Havinden, M.A. 1961a 'The rural economy of Oxfordshire, 1580-1730', unpublished B.Litt thesis, University of Oxford.

Havinden, M.A. 1961b 'Agricultural progress in open-field Oxfordshire', *Agricultural History Review* 9, 73-83.

Havinden, M.A. 1965 'Review of Lobel, M.D. (ed), A History of the County of Oxford, volume 8', *Agricultural history Review* 13, 61-63.

Hawkes, C.F.C. 1940 'A site of the Late Bronze-Early Iron Age transition at Totternhoe, Beds', *The Antiquaries Journal* 20, 487-91.

Hawkes, S.C. 1986 'The early Saxon period', in Briggs, G., Cook, J. and Rowley,T. (eds), *The Archaeology of the Oxford Region*, 64-108. Oxford: Dept. of External Studies, University of Oxford.

Hay, D. and Hay J. 1971 *Hilltop Villages of the Chilterns*. London and Chichester: Phillimore.

Head, J.F. 1955 *Early Man in South Buckinghamshire*. Bristol: John Wright.

Head, J.F. 1974 'An important early valley route through the Chilterns', *Records of Buckinghamshire* 19, 422-28.

Hinton, D.A. and Rowley, T. (eds) 1973 'Excavations on the route of the M40', *Oxoniensia* 38, 1-183.

Holt, N.R. 1964 *The Pipe Roll of the Bishopric of Winchester 1210-1211*. Manchester: Manchester University Press.

Holt, R. 1988 *The Mills of Medieval England*. Oxford: Basil Blackwell.

Home, G. 1925 *Through the Chilterns to the Fens*. London: J.M.Dent.

Homer, H. 1767 *An Enquiry into the Means of Preserving and Improving the Public Roads of this Kingdom*. London.

Horn, C.A. and Horn, P. 1983 'The social structure of an "industrial" community: Ivinghoe in Buckinghamshire in 1871', *Local Population Studies* 31, 9-20.

Horn, P. 1971 'The Buckinghamshire straw plait trade in Victorian England', *Records of Buckinghamshire* 19, 42-54.

Horn, P. 1974 'Child workers in the pillow lace and straw plait trades of Victorian Buckinghamshire and Bedfordshire', *The Historical Journal* 17, 779-96.

Horn, P. 1991 *Victorian Countrywomen*. Oxford: Basil Blackwell.

Hornby, R. 1987 'Nature conservation in Chiltern woodlands—a Nature Conservancy Council view', *Quarterly Journal of Forestry* 81, 116-21.

Hoskins, W.G. 1955 *The Making of the English Landscape*. London: Hodder and Stoughton.

Hoskins, W.G. and Stamp, L.D. 1963 *The Common Lands of England and Wales* (New Naturalist series). London: Collins.

Hughes, M.W. 1931 'Grimsditch and Cuthwulf's expedition to the Chilterns in A.D.571', *Antiquity* 5, 291-314.

Hunn, J.R. 1980 'The earthworks at Prae Wood', *Britannia* 11, 21-30.

Hussey, T. 1987 'Hedgerow history', *The Local Historian* 17, 327-42.

Jackson, A.A. 1973 *Semi-detached London*. London: George Allen & Unwin.

Jackson, A.A. 1986 *London's Metropolitan Railway*. Newton Abbot: David & Charles.

Jackson, C.C. 1977 *Radnage*. Radnage: published by author.

James, W. and Malcolm, J. 1794 *A General View of the Agriculture of the County of Buckingham*. London: Board of Agriculture.

Jeans, D.N. 1990 'Planning and the myth of the English countryside, in the inter-war period', *Rural History* 1, 249-64.

Jenkins, J.G. 1935 *A History of the Parish of Penn in the county of Buckingham*. London: Saint Catherine's Press.

Jenkins, J.G. 1938 *The Cartulary of Missenden Abbey, Part I*. Publication No.2, Records Branch of Buckinghamshire Archaeological Society. Aylesbury & London: Buckinghamshire Archaeological Society.

Jenkins, J.G. 1955 *The Cartulary of Missenden Abbey, Part II*. Publication of Buckinghamshire Records Society 10 (for 1946). Twitchells Ends, Jordans: the author.

Jenkins, J.G. 1962 *The Cartulary of Missenden Abbey, Part III*. Publication no. 12, Buckinghamshire Record Society. London: Historical Manuscripts Commission.

Johnson, I and Fenley, P. 1974 'Grange Farm, Widmer End', *Records of Buckinghamshire* 19 (4), 449-56.

Keene, D. 1989 'Medieval London and its region', *London Journal* 14, 99-111.

Kemp, B. 1967 *Sir Francis Dashwood. An Eighteenth-Century Independent*. London: Macmillan.

Kershaw, I. 1973 'The Great Famine and agrarian crisis in England 1315-1322', *Past and Present* 59, 3-50.

King, A.D. 1984 *The Bungalow*. London: Routledge & Kegan Paul.

Kingsford, C.L. (ed.) 1919 *The Stonor Letters and Papers, 1290-1483*. 2 vols. London: Royal Historical Society (Camden series publications 29 and 30)

Kirkland, R.K. 1956 'The Watlington & Princes Risborough Railway', *Railway Magazine* 102, 355-61.

Kosminsky, E.A. 1956 *Studies in the Agrarian History of England in the Thirteenth Century*. Oxford: Basil Blackwell.

Kussmaul, A. 1990 *A General View of the Rural Economy of England 1538-1840*. Cambridge: Cambridge University Press.

Lambert, A.M. 1953 'Oxfordshire about 1800 AD: A study in human geography'. Unpublished Ph.D. thesis, University of London.

Langdon, J. 1986 *Horses, Oxen and Technological Innovation. The Use of Draught Animals in English Farming from 1066 to 1500*. Cambridge: Cambridge University Press.

Langley, T. 1797 *History and Antiquities of the Hundred of Desborough, and Deanery of Wycombe in Buckinghamshire*. London: R.Faulder.

La Sueur, A.D.C. 1955 *Burnham Beeches*. London: Corporation of the City of London.

Lean, G. and Pettit, C.E. no date (c.1928) *High on the Chiltern Hills [Totteridge]*. Totteridge, High Wycombe: the authors.

Lennard, R.V. 1959 *Rural England, 1086-1135: A study of social and agrarian conditions*. Oxford: Oxford University Press.

Levett, A.E. 1938 *Studies in Manorial History*. Oxford: Clarendon Press.

Lloyd, T.H. 1977 *The English Wool Trade in the Middle Ages*. Cambridge: Cambridge University Press.

Lobel, M.D. (ed) 1964 *A History of the County of Oxford*, volume 8. London: Oxford University Press.

Loveday, J. 1962 'Plateau deposits of the southern Chiltern Hills', *Proceedings of the Geologists' Association of London* 73, 83-102.

Lowerson, J. 1980 'Battles for the countryside', in Gloversmith, F. (ed), *Class, Culture and Social Change*, 258-80. Brighton: Harvester Press.

Lucas, J. (translator) 1892 *Kalm's Account of his visit to England on his way to America in 1748*. London: Macmillan.

Mabey, R. 1980 *The Common Ground*. London: Hutchinson.

Mabey, R. 1990 *Home Country*. London: Random Century.

McCreath, N. 1986 'The impact of the industrial revolution on selected aspects of the furniture industry in High Wycombe borough, Buckinghamshire, 1750-1900', unpublished B.Sc.dissertation, Department of Geography, University of Bristol.

Mansfield, A.J. 1952 'The historical geography of the woodlands of the southern Chilterns, 1600-1947', unpublished M.Sc. thesis, University of London.

Marren, P. 1992 *The Wild Woods. A regional guide to Britain's ancient woodland*. Newton Abbot: David & Charles.

Massingham, H.J. 1940 *Chiltern Country*. London: B.T.Batsford.

Matless, D. 1990a 'Ages of English design: preservation, modernism and tales of their history, 1926-1939', *Journal of Design History* 3, 203-12.

Matless, D. 1990b 'Definitions of England 1928-1939', *Built Environment* 16, 179-91.

Matthews, C.L. 1964 *Ancient Dunstable*. Dunstable: Manshead Archaeological Society (Revised edition, 1989).

Matthews, C.L. 1976 *Occupation Sites on a Chiltern Ridge. Part 1: Neolithic, Bronze Age and Early Iron Age*. Oxford: British Archaeological Reports 29.

Matthews, C.L., Hawkes, S.C. and others 1985 'Early Saxon settlements and burials on Puddlehill, near Dunstable, Bedfordshire', *Anglo-Saxon Studies in Archaeology and History* 4, 59-115.

Mawer, A. and Stenton, F.M. 1925 *The Place-Names of Buckinghamshire*. Cambridge: Cambridge University Press (English Place-Name Society 11).

Mayes, L.J. 1960 *The History of Chairmaking in High Wycombe*. London: Routledge and Kegan Paul.

Mead, W.R. 1954 'Ridge and furrow in Buckinghamshire', *Geographical Journal* 120, 34-42.

Mead, W.R. 1962 'Pehr Kalm in the Chilterns', *Acta Geographica* (Helsinki) 17 (1), 2-33.

Mead, W.R. 1966 'The study of field boundaries', *Geographische Zeitschrift* 54, 101-12.

Meaney, A. 1964 *A Gazetteer of Early Anglo-Saxon Burial Sites*. London: George Allen & Unwin.

Metro-land 1987 *Metro-land* (1932 edition). Reprinted, with introduction by O.Green. Harpenden: Oldcastle Books.

Miller, E. and Hatcher, J.1978 *Medieval England: Rural Society and Economic change 1086-1348*. London: Longman.

Millett, M. 1990 *The Romanization of Britain. An Essay in Archaeological Interpretation*. Cambridge: Cambridge University Press.

Money, M.C.J. and Smith, J.T. 1973 'The Great Barn', Lewknor: the architectural evidence, *Oxoniensia* 38, 339-45.

Motor Owner 1920 'Motor Owner visits Shirburn Castle', *Motor Owner*, June 1920, 33-36.

Munby, L. 1977 *The Hertfordshire Landscape*. London: Hodder and Stoughton.

Neal, D.S. 1976 'Northchurch, Boxmoor, and Hemel Hempstead Station: the excavation of three Roman buildings in the Bulbourne Valley', *Hertfordshire Archaeology* 4, 1-135.

Neal, D.S., Wardle, A., and Hunn, J. 1990 *Excavation of the Iron Age, Roman and medieval settlement at Gorhambury, St.Albans*. English Heritage: Archaeological Report 14. London: Historical Buildings & Monuments Commission for England.

North, B. (1882) *Autobiography of Benjamin North*. Aylesbury: Samuels.

North, J.D. 1976 *Richard of Wallingford*. 3 volumes. Oxford: Clarendon Press.

Oliver, J.L. 1966 *The development and structure of the furniture industry*. Oxford: Pergamon Press.

Ollier, C.D. and Thomasson, A.J. 1957 'Asymmetrical valleys of the Chiltern Hills', *Geographical Journal* 123, 71-80.

Oppitz, L. 1991 *Chiltern Railways Remembered*. Newbury: Countryside Books.

Orna, B. 1976 'A native town at Berkhamsted', *Current Archaeology* 5, 139.

Oschinsky, D. 1971 *Walter of Henley and other treatises on estate management and accounting*. Oxford: Clarendon Press.

Owen, J. 1984 'Hill and Vale: a comparison of the effects of enclosure in Buckinghamshire, 1550 to 1865', unpublished B.A. thesis, Department of Geography, University of Cambridge.

Page, H.E. 1937 *Rambles in the Chiltern Country*. Paddington, London: Great Western Railway.

Page, W. (ed) 1908 *Victoria County History of Buckinghamshire, volume 2*. London: Archibald Constable.

Palliser, F.B. 1864 *History of Lace*. London: Sampson Low, Son & Marston.

Pavry, F.H. and Knocker, G.M. 1957-58 'The Mount, Princes Risborough, Buckinghamshire', *Records of Buckinghamshire* 16, (3), 141-78.

Pawson, E. 1977 *Transport and Economy: the Turnpike Roads of Eighteeenth Century Britain*. London: Academic Press.

Peach, H.H. and Carrington, N.L. 1930 *The Face of the Land*. London: George Allen and Unwin.

Peel, J.H.B. 1950 *The Chilterns*. London: Paul Elek.

Perkin, H. 1976 *The Age of the Automobile*. London: Quartet.

Peterken, G.F. 1981 *Woodland Conservation and Management*. London: Chapman and Hall.

Petrie, F. 1926 *The Hill Figures of England*. London: Royal Anthropological Institute.

Plot, R. 1672 *The Natural history of Oxfordshire*. Oxford: The Theatre.

Postles, D. 1984 'Customary carrying services', *The Journal of Transport History*, 3rd series, 5, 1-15.

Postles, D. 1987 'Markets for rural produce in Oxfordshire, 1086-1350', *Midland History* 12, 14-26.

Power, E. 1941 *The Wool Trade in English Medieval History*. Oxford: Oxford University Press.

Power, J.P. and Campbell, B.M.S. 1992 'Cluster analysis and the classification of medieval demesne-farming systems', *Transactions of the Institute of British Geographers* (New Series) 17, 227-45.

Preece, P.G. 1987 'Firewood from the Oxfordshire Chilterns', *Arboricultural Journal* 11, 227-35.

Preece, P.G. 1987-88 'Woodmen of the Oxfordshire Chilterns 1300-1800', *Folk Life* 26, 70-77.

Preece, P.G. 1990a 'Medieval woods in the Oxfordshire Chilterns', *Oxoniensia* 55, 55-72.

Preece, P.G. 1990b 'Wood products from the Oxfordshire Chilterns before 1830', *The Local Historian* 20 (2), 73-79.

Preece, P.G. 1990c 'The Black Death in Woodcote?' *South Oxfordshire Archaeological Group Bulletin* 45, 15-16.

Priest, St.John 1810 *General View of the Agriculture of the County of Buckingham*. London: Board of Agriculture.

Prince, H.C. 1954 'Landscape Gardens in the Chilterns'. Unpublished M.A. thesis, University of London.

Prince, H.C. 1959 'Parkland in the Chilterns', *Geographical Review* 49, 18-31.

Prior, M. 1981 'The accounts of Thomas West of Wallingford, a 16th-century trader on the Thames', *Oxoniensia* 46, 73-93.

Prior, M. 1982 *Fisher Row. Fishermen, Bargemen and Canal Boatmen in Oxford, 1500-1800*. Oxford: Oxford University Press.

Rackham, O. 1980 *Ancient Woodland*. London: Edward Arnold.

Rackham, O. 1986 *The History of the Countryside*. London: Dent.

Rackham, O. 1988 (2nd edn) *Trees and Woodlands in the British Landscape*. London: Dent.

Ratcliffe, D. (ed) 1977 *A Nature Conservation Review*. 2 vols. Cambridge: Cambridge University Press.

Reed, M. 1978 'Markets and fairs in medieval Buckinghamshire', *Records of Buckinghamshire* 20, 563-85.

Reed, M. 1979a 'Buckinghamshire Anglo-Saxon estate boundaries', in Gelling, M., *The Early Charters of the Thames Valley*, 168-87. Leicester: Leicester University Press.

Reed, M. 1979b *The Buckinghamshire Landscape*. London: Hodder and Stoughton.

Repton, H. 1803 *Observations on the Theory and Practice of Landscape Gardening etc*. London: J.Taylor.

Richardson, A. 1969 'Water supplies to Tring Summit', *Journal of the Railway and Canal Society* 15, April, 21-27 and 54-62.

Richardson, K.M. and Young, A. 1951 'An Iron Age site on the Chilterns', *Antiquaries Journal* 31, 132-48.

Riley, H.T. (ed) 1867-69 *Gesta Abbatum Monasteri Sancti Albani, by Thomas Walsingham.* 3 vols. London: Longman, Green.

Robbins, C.R. 1931 'An economic aspect of regional survey', *Journal of Ecology* 19, 25-33.

Roberts, C. 1934 *Gone Rustic.* London: Hodder & Stoughton.

Roberts, C. 1935 *Gone Rambling.* London: Hodder & Stoughton.

Roberts, C. 1936 *Gone Afield.* London: Hodder & Stoughton.

Roberts, C. 1938 *The Pilgrim Cottage Omnibus.* London: Hodder & Stoughton.

Roberts, E. 1974 'Totternhoe stone and flint in Hertfordshire churches', *Medieval Archaeology* 18, 66-89.

Robinson, M. and Wilson R. 1987 'A survey of environmental archaeology in the South Midlands', in Keeley, H.C.M. (ed.) *Environmental Archaeology. A Regional Review,* 16-100. London: Historic Buildings and Monuments Commission for England (English Heritage Occasional Paper 1).

Roden, D. 1965 'Studies in Chiltern field systems'. Unpublished Ph.D. thesis, University of London.

Roden, D. 1966 'Field systems in Ibstone, a township of the south-west Chilterns, during the later middle ages', *Records of Buckinghamshire* 18, 43-58.

Roden, D. 1967 'Inheritance customs and succession to land in the Chiltern Hills in the thirteenth and early fourteenth centuries', *Journal of British Studies* 7, 1-11.

Roden, D. 1968 'Woodland and its management in the medieval Chilterns', *Forestry* 41, 59-71.

Roden, D. 1969a 'Enclosure in the Chiltern Hills', *Geografiska Annaler* 52B, 115-26.

Roden, D. 1969b 'Fragmentation of farms and fields in the Chiltern Hills thirteenth century and later', *Medieval Studies* 31, 225-38.

Roden, D. 1969c 'Demesne farming in the Chiltern Hills', *Agricultural History* Review 17, 9-23.

Roden, D. 1970 'Changing settlement in the Chiltern Hills before 1850', *Folk Life* 8, 57-71.

Roden, D. 1973 'Field systems of the Chiltern Hills and their environs', in Baker, A.R.H. and Butlin, R.A. (eds), *Studies of Field Systems in the British Isles,* 325-76. Cambridge: Cambridge University Press.

Rotuli Hundredorum 1818 *Rotuli Hundredorum temp. Hen. III & Edw. I in Turr' Lond'.* London: House of Commons.

Rowley, R.T. 1973. 'The archaeology of the M40', *Oxoniensia* 38, 1-5.

St Joseph, J.K. 1965 'Air reconnaissance in Britain 1961-1964', *Journal of Roman Studies* 55, 485-501.

Salisbury, E.J. 1918 'The ecology of scrub in Hertfordshire: a study of colonisation', *Transactions of the Hertfordshire Naturalists' Field Club* 17, 53-64.

Salter, H.E. (ed) 1935 *Cartulary of Oseney Abbey,* volume 4. Oxford: Oxford Historical Society, volume 47.

Sampson, C.G. 1978 *Paleoecology and Archaeology of an Acheulian Site at Caddington, England.* Dallas: Department of Anthropology, Southern Methodist University.

Saunders, C. 1971 'The Pre-Belgic Iron Age in the central and western Chilterns', *Archaeological Journal* 128, 1-30.

Saunders, C. 1982 'Some thoughts on the oppida at Wheathampstead and Verulamium', *Hertfordshire Archaeology* 8, 31-39.

Sawyer, P.H. 1968 *Anglo-Saxon Charters: An Annotated List and Bibliography.* London: Royal Historical Society.

Sawyer, P.H. 1983 'The royal tun in pre-Conquest England', in Wormald, P. (ed) *Ideal and Reality in Frankish and Anglo-Saxon Society,* 273-99. Cambridge: Cambridge University Press.

Scott, W.J. 1907 'How the West Midland railway tried to come to London', *Railway Magazine* 21, 314-16.

Seebohm, F. 1883 *The English Village Community.* London: Longman, Green & Co.

Sellar, W.J. and Yeatman, R.J. 1930 *1066 and All That.* London: Methuen.

Sheahan, J.J. 1862 *History and Topography of Buckinghamshire.* London: Longman.

Sheail, J. 1976 *Nature in Trust. The History of Nature Conservation in Britain.* Glasgow: Blackie.

Sheail, J. 1981 *Rural Conservation in Inter-war Britain.* Oxford: Clarendon Press.

Sheail, J. 1987 *Seventy-five Years in Ecology: the British Ecological Society.* Oxford: Blackwell Scientific Publications.

Simmons, J. 1961 *The Railways of Britain.* London: Routledge & Kegan Paul.

Sims-Williams, P. 1983 'The settlement of England in Bede and the Chronicle', *Anglo-Saxon England* 12, 1-41.

Slota, L.A. 1984 'The land market on the St.Albans manors of Park and Codicote 1237-1399', unpublished Ph.D. thesis, University of Michigan.

Slota, L.A. 1988 'Law, land transfer, and lordship on the estates of St.Albans Abbey in the thirteenth and fourteenth centuries', *Law and History Review* 6, 119-38.

Smart, G. and Anderson, M. 1990 *Planning and management of areas of outstanding natural beauty.* Cheltenham: Countryside Commission, Paper 295.

Smith, C.J. 1980 *Ecology of the English Chalk.* London: Academic Press.

Smith, L.T. (ed) 1907 *The Itinerary of John Leland in or about the years 1535-1543.* Parts I-V. (5 vols) London: George Bell & Sons.

Sparkes, I.G. 1989 *Wycombe Chairmakers in Camera.* Buckingham: Quotes.

Spenceley, G.F.R. 1973 'The origins of the English pillow lace industry', *Agricultural History Review* 21, 81-93.

Stainton, B. 1989 'Excavation of an early prehistoric site at Stratford's Yard, Chesham', *Records of Buckinghamshire* 31, 49-74.

Starey, C.J.H. and Viccars, P.G. (eds) 1992 *Stokenchurch in Perspective.* Horsleys Green, High Wycombe: STARVIC.

Stead, I.M. 1967 'A La Tene III burial at Welwyn Garden City', *Archaeologia* 101, 1-62.

Stead, I.M. and Rigby, V. 1989 *Verulamium: the King Harry Lane site.* London: Archaeological Report 12, English Heritage.

Stebbing, N., Rhodes, J. and Meller, M. 1980 *Oxfordshire Potters. Woodstock,* Oxford: Oxford Museums Service Publication13.

Stevenson, R.L. 1907 'An autumn effect', in *The Works of Robert Louis Stevenson*, volume XX, 129-150. London: Cassell.

Stonor, R.J. 1951 *Stonor: A Catholic Sanctuary in the Chilterns from the Fifth Century till Today.* Newport: R.H.Johns.

Stroud, D. 1962 *Humphry Repton.* London: Country Life.

Stroud, D. 1975 *Capability Brown.* London: Faber & Faber.

Talbot, C.H. (ed.) 1959 *The Life of Christina of Markyate; a twelfth-century recluse.* Oxford: Clarendon Press.

Tansley, A.G. 1939 *The British Islands and their Vegetation.* Cambridge: Cambridge University Press.

Tate, W.E. 1978 *A Domesday of English enclosure acts and awards.* Edited with an introduction by M.E.Turner. Reading: The University Library.

Taylor, C.C. 1983 *Village and Farmstead. A history of rural settlement in England.* London: George Philip.

Thirsk, J. 1961 'Industries in the countryside', in Fisher, F.J. (ed), *Essays in the Economic and Social History of Tudor and Stuart England,* 70-88. Cambridge: Cambridge University Press.

Thomas, E. 1913 *The Icknield Way.* London: Constable.

Thompson, R.D. 1957 'The Roman villa site at Little Kimble', unpublished report; copy in Buckinghamshire County Museum.

Thorburn, D. 1989 'Gender, work and schooling in the plaiting villages', *The Local Historian* 19, 107-13.

Titow, J.Z. 1962 'Land and population on the bishop of Winchester's estates, 1209-1350', unpublished Ph.D. thesis, University of Cambridge.

Titow, J.Z. 1969 *English Rural Society 1200-1350.* London: George Allen and Unwin.

Titow, J.Z. 1972 *Winchester Yields. A Study in Medieval Agricultural Productivity.* Cambridge: Cambridge University Press.

Trevelyan, G.M. 1929 *Must England's beauty perish?* London:Faber & Gwyer

Turner, H.L. 1972 '"The Great Barn", Lewknor: the documentary evidence', *Oxoniensia* 37, 187-91.

Turner, M.E. 1973 'Some social and economic considerations of parliamentary enclosure in Buckinghamshire, 1738-1865'. Unpublished Ph.D. thesis, University of Sheffield.

Turner, M.E. 1980 *English Parliamentary Enclosure.* Folkestone: Wm Dawson.

Ulyanov, Y.R. 1966 'Oksfordshirskii manor Uotlington v 1086-1300 gg [Watlington Manor, Oxfordshire, 1086-1300]' *Srednie Veka* 29, 28-69.

Ulyanov, Y.R. 1971 and 1972 'Obrazovanie i evolyutsiya strukturi manora Stonor v xiv-xv vv [The genesis and structural evolution of the Stonor Manor in the 14th and 15th centuries]' *Srednie Veka* 34, 117-44 and 35, 154-73.

Viatores, The 1964 *Roman Roads in the South-East Midlands.* London: Victor Gollancz.

Vollans, E.C. 1959 'The evolution of farmlands in the central Chilterns in the twelfth and thirteenth centuries', *Transactions and Papers of the Institute of British Geographers* 26, 197-214.

Ward, L.K. 1973 'The conservation of juniper. I. Present status of juniper in southern England', *Journal of Applied Ecology* 10, 165-88.

Ware, M.E. 1989 *Britain's Lost Waterways.* Ashbourne, Derbyshire: Moorland Publishing.

Watt, A.S. 1923 'On the ecology of British beechwoods, with special reference to their regeneration', *Journal of Ecology* 11, 1-48.

Watt, A.S. 1934 'The vegetation of the Chiltern Hills, with special reference to the beechwoods and their seral relationships', *Journal of Ecology* 22, 230-70 and 445-507.

Wells, T.C.E. 1968 'Land use changes affecting *Pulsatilla vulgaris* in England', *Biological Conservation* 1, 37-44.

Wells, T.C.E. and Barling, D.M. 1971. 'Biological flora of the British Isles: *Pulsatilla vulgaris*', *Journal of Ecology* 59, 275-92.

Wheeler, R.E.M. and Wheeler, T.V. 1936 *Verulamium: a Belgic and two Roman cities.* London: Report of the Research Committee of the Society of Antiquaries of London, 11.

Whetham, E.H. 1964-65 'The London milk trade', *Economic History Review* (2nd series) 17, 369-80.

Whitehand, J.W.R. 1967 'Traditional building materials in the Chilterns', *Oxoniensia* 32, 1-9.

Whybrow, C.H. 1934 *The History of Berkhamsted Common.* London: Commons, Open Spaces and Footpath Preservation Society.

Williams-Ellis, C. 1928 *England and the Octopus.* London: Geoffrey Bles.

Williams-Ellis, C. (ed) 1937 *Britain and the Beast.* London: J.M.Dent.

Williamson, T.M. 1988 'Explaining regional landscapes: woodland and champion in southern and eastern England', *Landscape History,* 10, 5-13.

Wordie, J.R. 1984 'The South: Oxfordshire, Buckinghamshire, Berkshire, Wiltshire, and Hampshire', in Thirsk, J. (ed), *The Agrarian History of England and Wales,* volume V 1640-1750: I Regional Farming Systems, 317-57. Cambridge: Cambridge University Press.

Wymer, J.J. 1968 *Lower Palaeolithic Archaeology in Britain, as represented by the Thames Valley.* London: John Baker.

Young A. [Alison] 1964 'Bledlow: I Land tenures and the three-field system', *Records of Buckinghamshire* 17 (4), 266-85.

Young, A. [Arthur] 1804 *General View of the Agriculture of Hertfordshire.* London: Board of Agriculture.

Young, A. [Arthur] 1813 *General View of the Agriculture of Oxfordshire.* London: Board of Agriculture.

General Index

Index of Place Names

Note: county names (Bedfordshire, Buckinghamshire, Hertfordshire, Oxfordshire) are not indexed, nor are there entries for the cities of London and Oxford.

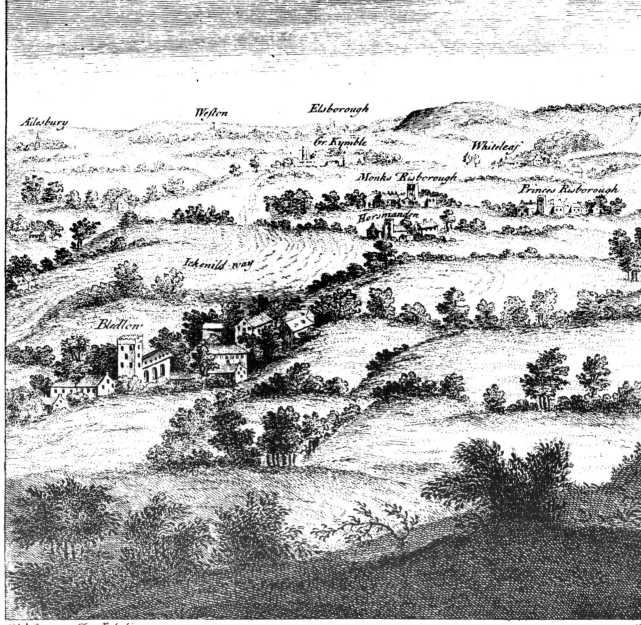

CRVX

Ailesbury
Weston
Elsborough
Gr. Kymble
Whiteleaf
Monks Risborough
Princes Risborough
Horsmanden
Ickenild way
Blatton

W. Greene Jun.ʳ delin.

Viro amicissimo BROWNE
Ad instaurandum Buckinghamiæ
Tabula